Contextualizing Security

STUDIES IN SECURITY AND INTERNATIONAL AFFAIRS

Contextualizing Security

A READER

EDITED BY
TOBIAS T. GIBSON
KURT W. JEFFERSON

THE UNIVERSITY OF GEORGIA PRESS
Athens

Set in 10/12.5 Minion Pro Regular by Kaelin Chappell Broaddus

Most University of Georgia Press titles are
available from popular e-book vendors.

Printed digitally

Library of Congress Cataloging-in-Publication Data

Names: Gibson, Tobias T., 1972– editor. | Jefferson, Kurt W., 1966– editor.
Title: Contextualizing security : a reader / edited by Tobias T. Gibson, Kurt W.
    Jefferson.
Description: Athens : The University of Georgia Press, [2022] | Series: Studies in
    Security and International Affairs | Includes bibliographical references and index.
Identifiers: LCCN 2021058272 | ISBN 9780820361871 (Hardback) | ISBN 9780820361888
    (Paperback) | ISBN 9780820361864 (eBook)
Subjects: LCSH: Security, International—Study and teaching (Higher)
Classification: LCC JZ5588 .C676 2022 | DDC 355/.033—dc23/eng/20220304
LC record available at https://lccn.loc.gov/2021058272

TTG: For Scout, Jakob, and Q. I couldn't do this without you, your support, and your understanding.

KWJ: To Lori, Kelly, Andrew, Everly, Megan, and Nicole. You are my source of inspiration.

CONTENTS

Contextualizing Security

Contextualizing the Study of Security

Kurt W. Jefferson, Spalding University
Tobias T. Gibson, Westminster College

The concept for this book was born in early 2015, as we worked together to plan a two-day symposium on our (then) shared campus. The organizing topic was "Security versus Liberty: Balancing the Scales of Freedom." Contemporary national security issues included a rather recent leak of documents from National Security Administration (NSA) contractor turned whistleblower and hero/traitor Edward Snowden; the Obama administration's oblique attempts to define uses and limits of a still-in-its-infancy drone program; the U.S. government's attempt to address the fallout of the Arab Spring and the rising forces of the Islamic State of Iraq and Syria (ISIS) in the MENA (Middle East and North Africa) region—including the forced migration of hundreds of thousands of refugees; and various other items that, while important, do not continue to resonate in ways that the above do.

As the director of the annual symposium at Westminster College, Dr. Jefferson served to guide the composition of the speakers selected to offer their insight over the course of this event. Dr. Gibson was selected, based on his research and Security Studies Program design, to head the committee charged to select specific speakers for the event. By the time the on-campus symposium ran, the list of speakers included U.S. secretary of homeland security Jeh Johnson, best-selling author and journalist Jeremy Scahill, former CIA attorney John Rizzo, and the chair of Georgetown Law School's National Security Law Program professor Laura Donohue, U.S. senator Roy D. Blunt (R-Mo.), and several other key professionals. In short, it was a stellar opportunity to secure knowledge in a singular place—in a book, as well as on a small campus in rural Missouri.

Despite the unique place that Westminster plays in the history of American foreign policy and, by extension, post–World War II security policy, a program dedicated expressly to security had not been part of the curriculum at the college. It wasn't until the Spring 2013 semester that the Westminster College faculty approved a new minor in Security Studies. The minor had only a few courses unique to Security Studies, including an introductory course and an upper-level course on "Terrorism." Every other class in the minor was housed in a more developed, traditional discipline like history or political science. Of the two unique classes, the introductory class served to help the students taking the classes—and the professors teaching them—to develop an understanding of the discipline of Security Studies. Terrorism, in retrospect at least, was a direct nod to the single most influential act that led to the development of Security Studies, and the related areas of Homeland Security, Homeland Defense, and perhaps even Emergency Management—the coordinated attacks on the United States on September 11, 2001.[1]

Yet, even a seemingly basic security issue like terrorism has seen expansion in the way it is studied and, importantly, the way it is interpreted and countered. The terrorism class was originally conceived as a manner of teaching undergraduate students about threats to national security—in particular the security of the United States. This was the popular view, the way that the media, politicians, and even many scholars thought about terrorism. One need only look at one of the most enduring images and rhetorical moments in the nearly immediate aftermath of 9/11 to see this (overly) simple imperative: President George W. Bush standing at "ground zero," in the ruins of the felled World Trade Center on September 14, 2001, telling the rescue workers through his bullhorn "I can hear you! The rest of the world hears you! And the people— and the people who knocked these buildings down will hear all of us soon." Predictably, given the angst in New York and throughout the country, the response of the gathered crown was a prolonged, emphatic, and heartfelt chant of "USA! USA!" It was a moment felt by citizens across the country—and served as a link between the threat of terrorism and the security of what once seemed like an impenetrable border.[2]

However, terrorism since its ancient inception has been about more than impacting security of enemy nations. One of the most important aspects of terrorism, and one that seemingly was lost on President Bush and his administration's efforts to irradicate terrorism in the Global War on Terror (GWOT), is that terrorism is a tactic, not an enemy with a political ideology or religious belief system. Terrorism is a methodology, a rational decision, to be utilized when pushing an agenda, a movement, or an idea.[3] Because terrorism is a tactic, it cannot be defeated.

Beyond the realization that terrorism can never be fully eradicated, however, in an effort to minimize the use of terrorism, cursory studies of terrorism delve into its religious causes and impacts. Rich studies of terrorism consider the economics, including its financial impact, its funding, and the rationality of the act.[4] Psychology and biology study why individuals become radicalized and join terrorist groups or become "lone wolf" terrorists—and why and how extremists can become deradicalized.[5] Scholars and policymakers have examined terrorist group organizational makeup and design. Doctors, hospitals, and scientists have worked diligently to learn and develop best practices if a terrorist activity does occur.[6] Distinguishing between a terrorist and a simple criminal is more than a philosophical issue; it is a legal one.[7] Indeed, defining terrorism is an issue all by itself, as even the U.S. government has various definitions. Beyond understanding the terrorist, much headway has been made in understanding the impact on victims and their families too.

The discussion of terrorism only sets the stage for the incredible complexity of Security Studies. As scholars and teachers, we take Winston Churchill's "Sinews of Peace" speech, delivered at Westminster College on March 5, 1946, as a lesson and a blueprint for the study and policymaking of security. Churchill described the "Iron Curtain descending" across Europe and in some ways ushered in the Cold War.[8] To that end, Churchill's speech is often understood simply as a nod to traditional national security. And, to be sure, it was a warning about the encroachment of the Soviet Union into Eastern Europe. However, that is an oversimplified look at a complex oration. Indeed, the titular "sinews" are the soft tissues holding peace together—often lost in the subsequent telling of the impact of the Iron Curtain dropping across the European landscape.

As Gibson argues, Churchill moved well beyond the commonly held limits of national security and recognized the needs of the people were beyond mere sustenance; security necessitated more than simply basic rights. Churchill declared in no uncertain terms, "All this means that the people of any country have the right, and should have the power by constitutional action, by free unfettered elections, with secret ballot, to choose or change the character or form of government under which they dwell; that freedom of speech and thought should reign; that courts of justice, independent of the executive, unbiased by any party, should administer laws which have received the broad assent of large majorities or are consecrated by time and custom. . . . Churchill's speech was as much a description of security as justice, human rights and rule of law as it was a blueprint for the security of nations."[9]

This book is an effort toward melding the traditional views founded in international relations theory, of national security being paramount to understanding security politically and academically.[10] Increasingly, however, the wisdom of Churchill's unbounded view of securing citizens and rights must also be a focus in security studies.[11] Furthermore, national security is also limiting. It may prevent answers to international issues such as climate change, which continues to impact nations across the globe: the United States, the Caribbean island nations, Australia, the Maldives, and the polar ice caps. Increasingly, populist movements based in racial animus long thought past threaten democratic norms, the rule of law, and racial, gender, religious, and ideological minorities. And a global pandemic rages, impacting the political, economic, physical, and psychological health of nations and persons globally.

In short, we and the authors of these chapters offer contextual positions based on a wide range of issues related to security. Collectively, this book moves well beyond understanding security through a national or nationalistic lens.[12] That is, this collection marks a realization that national security matters, but the sinews—of peace, of security, of democracy, of the rule of law, of technological development, of ethical considerations in policymaking—matter too.[13]

To that end, we offer a set of chapters that individually dive into some of the most pressing issues in the study and application of security and, on occasion, some of the most overlooked themes and topics of our present era. This book is something of a collage, a set of disparate views that, when combined, form a larger picture.

Organization of the Book

The book is organized in general themes. The first theme focuses on "Law, Ethics, Security, and Liberty" and includes contributions from Tobias T. Gibson and Kurt W. Jefferson; President Barack Obama's secretary of homeland security Jeh C. Johnson; James McRae, professor of philosophy at Westminster College; U.S. senator Bernie Sanders (I-Vt.); Mark Boulton and Tobias T. Gibson from Westminster College; Obama-era deputy director of the National Security Agency Richard Ledgett; and former military judge James E. Baker.

The second theme centers on "Technology: Securing Liberty and the Nation." Chapters in this section come from Robert E. Burnett, dean of faculty and academics at the National Defense University; Anna Holyan, an independent scholar, and Tobias T. Gibson of Westminster College; U.S. senator Roy D. Blunt (R-Mo.); and Kristan Stoddart of the University of Swansea.

The third theme we offer is "International Security and Components of Liberty." Authors in this section include Jeremy B. Straughn of The Ohio State University, Lisa C. Fein from the University of Michigan, and Amelia Ayers; Kali Wright-Smith, Westminster College; Naji Bsisu (Maryville College), Laila Farooq (Institute of Business Administration Karachi), and Amanda Murdie (University of Georgia); Daniel Egbe, of Philander Smith College, and Kurt W. Jefferson; journalist Jeremy Scahill; Kurt W. Jefferson and JR Swanegan, University of Missouri College of Law; and Gibson, Jefferson, and entrepreneur David L. McDermott.

The first chapter in this collection, "Foundations and Evolutions of Security Studies," is another Gibson and Jefferson offering. We offer a historical overview of security studies, but more importantly provide a distinct view into its future. While Westphalian and Just War Theory traditions inform institutions and norms implicitly and explicitly in security studies, current issues including the global COVID-19 pandemic and domestic protests for racial rights must also be included in a modern security construct.

Johnson's chapter is based on his John Findley Green Lecture, delivered at Westminster College on September 16, 2015, titled "Achieving Our Homeland Security while Preserving Our Values and Our Liberty." Secretary Johnson, a lawyer by training, discusses the importance of America maintaining its strong support for civil liberties and civil rights in the face of increased calls for restrictions on both areas in an era of war and global terrorism. He refers to President Truman's 1954 Green Lecture, "Witch Hunting and Hysteria," which discussed the Salem Witch Trials as similar in context to McCarthyism, which called for analogous restrictions.

McRae's "Liberty and Security: Reformulating the Classic Debate" reminds the reader of the importance of Machiavelli and Hobbes in discerning and establishing the security of the state, and Mill and Rousseau in building the foundations for modern liberties. He continues, however, by describing and defining the positive and negative foundations of security—and concludes that security not merely is the absence of fear but rather requires a state to "liberate and empower [citizens] to lead flourishing lives."

Sanders's speech, "A Renewal of American Purpose," was presented at Westminster College exactly because Sanders recognized the impact of delivering a defining foreign policy speech in the shadow of Churchill's legacy. Sanders outlines a modern, progressive foreign policy. His key focus is a meaningful return to the ideals explicit in the Constitution and the founding era, including explicit adherence to protecting religious beliefs—and protecting both people and government from the burgeoning "alt-right" movement that threatens authoritarian, populist retrenchment of American idealism and the "moral imperative." There is a short contextual chapter, from Cold War historian Mark Boulton and Gibson that places the importance of the Sanders offering in the early stages of the Trump administration and its accompanying domestic upheaval and purposeful withdrawal from the world stage.

Ledgett also uses Churchill as a springboard for his speech, presented April 4, 2016. The United States faced many issues at the time, such as a forthcoming presidential election, questions surrounding the proper roles of the member agencies of the intelligence community in surveilling Americans, heightened fears of terrorism, the rise of China and its commitment to challenge U.S. supremacy in the Pacific, and a nuclear North Korea and its increased belligerence—concerns that continue to resonate within American political and security questions today. One issue that Ledgett raises is the "pernicious" use of the Internet by the Islamic State of Iraq and the Levant (ISIL) to recruit fighters from across the world—then a major issue. Though this use by Islamist extremists predates the rise, or at least the recognition of the Russian use of the

Internet to sow discord into American elections and society, the chapter notes that several "big tech" companies played a role in minimizing ISIL's voice across their platforms. While most Americans likely appreciated the efforts, similar attempts to stop domestic extremists have led to outcries from some Americans about the role of these companies in supporting free speech.

Baker's chapter, "Deeds of Freedom: Lessons from the Cold War in a Time of Turmoil," is one of the keystones of this book. Understanding law in a national, homeland, or human security sense has become one of the most important additions to academic and policy spaces in the post-9/11 American experience. The creation of the USA PATRIOT Act, the construction of a detention center in Guantánamo Bay, Cuba, and the CIA's role in "enhanced interrogation"—and the very public debates about the wisdom, morality, and legality of these and many other programs—led to the rise of public consumption of law and security in unprecedented ways.

Noted blogsites including *Lawfare* and *Just Security* were created and offer articles consumable by the public on the nexus of law and security issues. This can also be seen in the creation of (national) security law centers at schools across the country, including Baker's Syracuse, NYU, Harvard, Duke, and Texas. Law schools including Oklahoma City, University of Missouri–Kansas City, and Cooley (in Michigan) also offer programs or classes in national and homeland security. And due to the demand from law schools, national security textbooks are now offered, further driving the area of study.[14] Moving well beyond the laws of armed conflict and statutes such as the USA PATRIOT Act, Judge Baker, however, includes the recognition of and respect for the rule of law as a national security imperative. Central to his chapter, Baker "worr[ies] that we are losing our unity even about law along with an understanding that law is our essential virtue as a country."

Burnett offers a chapter titled "A Survey of Humans and Autonomy in Three Areas: Surveillance, Economics, and Lethality in Combat Operations." Burnett delves into the theoretical and applied dimensions of science and technology policy building in his research related to an investigation into autonomous systems (artificial intelligence) in surveillance, labor economics (economic security), and lethal combat. He discusses how artificial intelligence, autonomy, and related technologies impact human agency and liberty. The chapter is based on a speech at the Australian Department of Defence's Defence Science Institute Meeting on Emerging Military Technology at the University of New South Wales in July 2015.

In "Under Fire: Targeted Killing, UAVs, and Three American Presidents," Holyan and Gibson take aim at one of the most discussed policy spaces of the U.S. War on Terror and continued counterterrorism efforts across the globe: the use of unmanned aerial vehicles, or drones, in targeted killing. They offer a brief history of drone development and their early use in the George W. Bush administration as an extension of his controversial preemptive strike doctrine. The heart of the chapter is devoted to several legal issues that arose under the expanded use of drones—geography, frequency, and reasoning—under the Obama administration. The administration faced several issues, including the high-profile killing of American citizens, a stalled and poorly developed drone "playbook" to establish norms for use by future presidents (and other nations), and policy that often seemed at odds with presidential statements. The chapter concludes with a discussion of the Trump administration's drone use and woes, including the administration's increased reliance on drone strikes, President Trump's expressed willingness to kill a suspected terrorist and his family, and a lack of continuity in administration officials' reasoning about why and when drone use is appropriate.

Blunt, in "The United States and Cybersecurity," outlines the challenges facing the United States in the realm of cybersecurity. He critiques the Obama administration's policies and then turns his attention to what the U.S. Senate is doing in terms of oversight and where foreign, defense, and security policies are moving in this ever-evolving arena. The chapter is based on his speech at Westminster College on September 14, 2015 (as part of the Hancock Symposium on Security versus Liberty).

Stoddart's chapter, "Edward Snowden and PRISM: Negotiating the Post-9/11 'Surveillance State,'" remains an exceptionally important and timely work. First, Stoddart offers an international eye to the importance of the Snowden revelations of the NSA's mass collection of electronic communications. Stoddart also discusses the ongoing impact of the debate, which intensified in the wake of Snowden's leaks, regarding the tools allowed for the protection of national security and their impact, most importantly surveillance and collection, on privacy rights and civil liberties. Stoddart also offers a suggestion on the balance of security and civil liberties in this increasingly connected world in which electronic communications and mass data flows are a part of daily life. This debate is especially important in light of President Trump's willingness to pardon Snowden.[15]

Straughn, Fein, and Ayers are the authors of "Divided Memory and the 'New Cold War' Thesis: The Rise and Decline of a Double-Edged Analogy," reprinted with permission of the University of Florida Press. Renewed tensions between Russia and the West have inspired attempts to conceptualize the current state of international relations in terms of historical analogies, with many commentators arguing that a "new Cold War" (NCW) could be on the horizon or even that such a condition has already materialized. Straughn, Fein, and Ayers note that although the NCW thesis is not new, the Ukraine crisis in 2014, and to a lesser extent the Russo-Georgian War of 2008, triggered the largest bursts of interest in the NCW analogy. The authors argue that NCW is an example of how historical narratives and memories based on complex events help to conceptualize, simplify, and misunderstand current events.

Wright-Smith's chapter demonstrates that although powerful states like the United States have damaged the use of the torture norm through noncompliance, they have not directly denied the jus cogens character of the norm. According to Emilie M. Hafner-Burton, limitations in international law create demands for actors who are willing to defend or advocate for human rights, including "steward states" who "can give perpetrators of abuse a reason to act differently even when legal procedures do not have much influence on their reasoning." The norm may likely grow weaker if states attempt to redefine its scope and boundaries in the name of security.

"Human Security and Migration," authored by Bsisu, Farooq, and Murdie, is an explicit move away from national security concerns and instead focuses on the security needs of individuals. In particular, the authors illustrate the importance of understanding forced migration and how man-made events including war and natural disasters such as floods, fires, and storms can impact previously habitable areas. They also present serious discussions about institutions—including governmental, legal, and economic—impact decisions to migrate and decisions about welcoming migrants into new homes, whether temporary or permanent. This chapter, too, is illustrative of issues facing people and governments across the globe—whether the American West and South due to environmental changes leading to increasing numbers of fires and destructive weather events, respectively; continued U.S. efforts to keep migrants, including those seeking asylum, from entering the United States; continued issues of the forced migration from Syria and the former ISIL-held Levant; border issues stemming from continued disputes facing the European Union as the United Kingdom moves toward Brexit, expanding terrorism issues in the African continent, and dozens of other issues. Regardless of cause, the authors suggest that "advocates of immigrant rights believe that most immigrants are individuals and families looking to make better lives, not criminals violating laws to harm the state. Refugees and asylum seekers especially come from a low human rights environment to an uncertain one." As such, international organizations like the United Nations and international laws and conventions play major roles in protecting the rights of migrants.

Egbe and Jefferson offer a chapter on American foreign policy toward Africa in light of the security challenges linked to Boko Haram in western Africa, al-Shabaab in eastern Africa, and al-Qaeda in the Islamic Maghreb of northern Africa. Egbe and Jefferson explore recent foreign policy under Obama and Trump and analyze the role that American foreign policy, terrorism, and other variables play in African political and economic development.

In "The U.S. Sees al Qaeda as Terrorism, and We Consider the Drones Terrorism," an excerpt from Scahill's *Dirty Wars: The World Is a Battlefield* (2014), he discusses the U.S. fight against various terrorist groups in Yemen and comes to the conclusion that the ill-fated, Bush-led Global War on Terror (GWOT) was expanding under President Obama and would continue to expand past his presidency after 2017. Importantly, the "Obama administration's Yemen policy had enraged many tribal leaders," an issue across the glove as the misguided GWOT has continued. This chapter was the foundation of Scahill's presentation at the Hancock Symposium on "Security versus Liberty: Balancing the Scales of Freedom" at Westminster College on "Dirty Wars" on September 15, 2015.

Jefferson and Swanegan provide a chapter called "Study Abroad as American National and Human Security Necessity." They focus on the historical nature of study abroad as a key component of building bridges between nations, people, and cultures and increasing Americans' and others' knowledge of other countries and peoples; they utilize Joseph Nye's concept of "soft power" as a way of providing human security as a national security and defense priority. They also look at security concerns related to study abroad and present case studies of the Stetson University College of Law's relationship with a university in Granada, Spain, and Westminster College's internationally recognized Take-A-Friend-Home program. These examples highlight the benefits of study abroad for countries and academe in terms of human security.

The final chapter, "Coming Challenges: China's Technology, Climate Change, Terrorism, and Disease," by Gibson, Jefferson, and McDermott, offers our final thoughts on the current state of affairs that the United States and other actors must be aware of moving forward. As the title suggests, the authors compare China's current technological advances to those in the United States and then focus on three still burgeoning issues that nations and global citizens face. And though many are very clearly tired of hearing about climate change, terrorism, and COVID-19, we aver that addressing these issues is key to seeking stability and security in the coming decades.

This collection of original essays, empirical studies, primary-source speeches, and secondary-source essays and empirical research in the fields of security studies, political science, international and transnational studies, sociology, journalism, national security law, and philosophy provides an excellent introduction to the field of security studies and the current debates in the academic, foreign, and domestic policy arenas and the transnational contexts related to the tension between freedom (political, legal, and existential) and security (political, national, international, and human). This collection advances knowledge and application and can assist undergraduate, graduate, and professional students in domestic and global-security-related fields in conceptualizing and contextualizing many of the cutting-edge debates in security studies, intelligence, American foreign policy, international relations, government, and history. The themes, concepts, and ideas utilize a broad interdisciplinary approach while connecting interesting examples and contexts for students, faculty, and scholars. This volume also is a good source of information for scholars and researchers trying to find more material on areas under scholarly investigation such as cybersecurity, national security, human security, legal aspects of security, intelligence, and broader epistemological discussions related to understanding security studies as a discipline and its relationship to the security communities both domestically and globally.

Notes

1. David H. McIntyre, *How to Think about Homeland Security*, vol. 2: *Risk, Threats, and the New Normal* (Lanham, Md.: Rowman & Littlefield, 2020).

2. Kenneth T. Walsh, "George W. Bush's 'Bullhorn' Moment," *U.S. News & World Report*, https://www.usnews.com/news/blogs/ken-walshs-washington/2013/04/25/george-w-bushs-bullhorn-moment.

3. Robert A. Pape, "The Strategic Logic of Suicide Terrorism," *American Political Science Review* 97, no. 3 (2003): 343–61.

4. Timothy Mathews and Shane Sanders, "Strategic and Experimental Analyses of Conflict and Terrorism," *Public Choice* 179, nos. 3–4 (2018): 169–74, https://doi.org/10.1007/s11127-018-0624-3.

5. John Horgon, *The Psychology of Terrorism*, 2nd ed. (New York: Routledge, 2014).

6. Peter Katona, John P. Sullivan, and Michael D. Intriligator, eds., *Global Biosecurity: Threat and Responses* (New York: Routledge, 2010).

7. Shannon French, "The Warrior Code Today: Are Terrorists Warriors?," in *The Code of the Warrior: Exploring Warrior Values Past and Present* (Lanham, Md.: Rowman & Littlefield, 2003), 231–44; Arthur H. Garrison, "Defining Terrorism: Philosophy of the Bomb, Propaganda by Deed and Change through Fear and Violence," *Criminal Justice Studies* 17, no. 3 (2004): 259–79, https://doi.org/10.1080/1478601042000281105.

8. Prime Minister Winston Churchill, "Sinews of Peace" (Iron Curtain Speech), John Findley Green Lecture, March 5, 1946, Westminster College, Fulton, Mo., https://www.nationalchurchillmuseum.org/sinews-of-peace-iron-curtain-speech.html.

9. Tobias T. Gibson, "70 Years Later, Churchill's Speech Still a Blueprint for National Security," *The Hill*, March 5, 2016, http://thehill.com/blogs/pundits-blog/defense/271901-70-years-later-churchills-speech-still-a-blueprint-for-national.

10. David H. McIntyre, *How to Think about Homeland Security*, vol. 1: *The Imperfect Intersection of National Security and Public Safety* (Lanham, Md.: Rowman & Littlefield, 2020).

11. Laura K. Donohue, *The Future of Intelligence: Privacy and Surveillance in a Digital Age* (New York: Oxford University Press, 2016).

12. Mark B. Salter and Can E. Mutlu, *Research Methods in Critical Security Studies: An Introduction* (New York: Routledge, 2013).

13. Linda Weiss, *America Inc.? Innovation and Enterprise in the National Security State* (Ithaca, N.Y.: Cornell University Press, 2014); Larry May, ed., *War: Essays in Political Philosophy* (New York: Cambridge University Press, 2008).

14. Geoffrey Corn, Jimmy Gurulé, Eric Talbot Jensen, and Peter Margulies, *National Security Law: Principles and Policy*, 2nd ed. (New York: Wolters Kluwer, 2019).

15. Raphael Satter, "Trump Says He Is Considering Pardon for Leaker Edward Snowden," Thomson Reuters, August 15, 2020, https://www.reuters.com/article/us-usa-politics-snowden/trump-says-he-is-considering-pardon-for-leaker-edward-snowden-idUSKCN25B10Z.

Law, Ethics, Security, and Liberty

Foundations and Evolutions of Security Studies

Tobias T. Gibson, Westminster College
Kurt W. Jefferson, Spalding University

From ancients to moderns, the field of security studies is important in understanding conflict and war on a global scale. As security studies developed and became more de rigueur, a realization, from the 1960s on, that it is not just a subdiscipline of multiple disciplines—including international relations, history, and political science—also evolved. This new discipline, many came to see, was an "interdisciplinary discipline." Despite this realization, scholars continued training in established fields and remained dependent on traditional tenure norms, leading Marshall Beier and Samantha L. Arnold to argue that security studies scholars were too busy talking to each other within their specialties and not across disciplines and that a "supradisciplinary" approach was needed. This approach is one where scholars talk across disciplines and not necessarily create an interdisciplinary discipline or an entirely new field; rather, they would end the silos and walls to enrich each other's fields with cross-disciplinary theories and conceptualizations. As Beier and Arnold state: "We must strive to become undisciplined. Above all else, a supradisciplinary study of security must in every instance treat disciplinarity as ubiquitous, as a practice in sundry incarnations that is everywhere shaping the production of knowledge even as the echoes of its past interventions can be heard in what we already know."[1]

Although this debate about the interdisciplinary versus cross-disciplinary approach to security studies will continue, the discussion of how security studies has evolved, the importance of ideas in security studies, and the need for continued theoretical and applied research in the field will remain and expand. Indeed, some scholars argue that subdisciplines of security studies now exist, including, for example, international security and homeland security.

This chapter focuses on the currents in the field of security studies, ideas that have developed the field, and how the study of security relates to other academic and applied fields of inquiry and practice. We offer thoughts about the future of security studies as a discipline with emerging subdisciplines of its own given the new challenges that social, political, technological, health, and cultural currents are providing in an era of political fragmentation, economic vicissitudes, and increasing threats to global public health.

Defining Security within a Discipline

Defining security is not easy, and the ways in which the concept is defined say much about the field and area of inquiry. Paul D. Williams and Matt McDonald define security as "the alleviation of threats to cherished values, especially those which, left unchecked, threaten the survival of a particular referent object in the near future."[2] Security can be nested within frameworks related to theorical constructs such as the historical foundations of realism and liberalism. Importantly, as the discipline progresses, theories evolve as well. Some of this advancement is refining positions within realism and liberalism, to include "rise and fall" realism and "neoliberal" liberalism.

From well beyond these theoretical foundations, the study of how, why, and whom security will benefit has expanded. Beyond realism and liberalism, both of which are founded in the security of the nation-state, scholars have begun to theorize and analyze questions of security with varied starting points. For example, some newer theories, such as critical theory, also assume the state as the starting point but take the position that the state is a means of securing rather than the end to be secured. Some feminist lenses in security focus on women's insecurity.

The concept of human security continues to grow in the academic study of security studies, especially as threats to human security continue to dominate news cycles and policy discussion. The recent Black Lives Matter protests in the United States and beyond are examples of the linkage of domestic and global human security concerns that then connect to the importance of various political, economic, and social variables that are fundamental to the study of security. Thus, security as a field of study is important for both academic and conceptual reasons as well as for applied reasons. The field takes disciplines such as political science, international relations, and history—and increasingly disparate disciplines such as psychology, economics, law, sciences, mathematics, and health care—beyond the debates regarding world order, power, and ideology and brings those frameworks toward important interfaces with applied outcomes in the field related to security that impact security architecture, military structures and processes, civil society development, political and economic development, and the broader evolution of public and private spaces that are affected by security-related activities and dialogue.

Contextualizing Security Types and Concepts

Security can be studied, first and foremost, in and of itself as a framework for understanding how security actors and contexts evolve and develop over time. Second, security can be understood through economic means. Scholars such as Williams and McDonald—but importantly also governments (e.g., DHS) and nongovernmental organizations—note the importance of economic resources and access to them. Third, political security is important and allows scholars and practitioners to understand now nation-states work together and clash over various policies and actions in the international organizations that promote and attempt to achieve global stability and peace. Fourth, military security is understood in the ways in which the extragovernmental variable of a country's military handles its offensive and defensive strategies and tactics in the security realm. Fifth, human security focuses on establishing and maintaining the basic necessities of life for citizens of various nation-states with the security of the state regarding other types of security. It is through this framework that we look at the role and importance of global health and the various coronaviruses that have seen at least five devastating outbreaks since 2003, including the COVID-19 virus that began spreading in China in fall 2019 and ended up in the West by early 2020. Sixth, "societal security" is "the sustainability and evolution of traditional patterns of language culture, and religious and national identity and custom."[3] This type of security is analogous to the concept of "political culture" found in the study of comparative politics. Political culture can be defined as "the attitudes, values, and orientations of individuals toward their government."[4]

Of course, the nexus of nationalism and territorial sovereignty links to the predecessor to political culture: "national character." Like societal security, the concept of "nation" and its development includes territory, economic ties, a common language, culture, and religion.[5]

To provide but one example, the application of societal security can be seen in the historical Slovaks, a Slavic people who coalesced into a nation in the late nineteenth century and eventually gained independence from the Czech-dominated state in 1938 due to the invidious Munich Agreement between Nazi Germany, France, fascist Italy, and Britain. The Slovaks would be reintegrated into communist Czechoslovakia after 1948 and then free to form an independent state in 1993 after the Velvet Divorce. The Slovaks, five million people, have been a historically Roman Catholic people, agrarian in economic development, and known for the development of a language separate from that of the dominant Czechs. The ability of the Slovak state to join NATO and the European Union in 2004 assisted the state in bolstering its claim to sovereignty and autonomy in spite of nationalistic tendencies (found in part of its culture and political culture not unlike many Slavic nations, such as Poland, Serbia, and Croatia, in the post-1989 era) in the political culture after the fall of the Berlin Wall. Last, environmental security may be an important component of global security arrangements in an era when climate change is a top agenda item for many nation-states and international governing organizations such as the UN and its many organs.[6]

The idea of security, ipso facto, as a framework is important. The philosophical and heuristic importance of examining the epistemological foundations of security as a field of study helps with conceptualizing and analyzing both theory and practice in the security realm. The development and ideation of new concepts in the field continues and will assist in not only growing the discipline but also assisting scholars and practitioners in understanding the limits and expansion of the field into new and fruitful areas of inquiry. One area of inquiry in security studies is decision making. Time-honored studies that connect the field to foreign policy and international relations such as Graham Allison and Phillip Zelikow's *Essence of Decision Making: Explaining the Cuban Missile Crisis* and Robert Jervis's *Perception and Misperception in International Politics* help us understand the importance of decision making, rational choice theory, and perception and misperception in international security and politics.[7]

Even though these works are nearly half a century old, Jervis's book can be linked metaphorically to new three-dimensional learning tools like Google Earth as decisions about security by nation-states and individual policy actors may be similar to a prism, akin to today's 3D Google Earth visual, and allowing the user to see the problem from multiple vantage points, with light shed on problems depending on the vantage point of the decision maker. In the study and application of security for the sake of security, decisions are therefore strategic, multifaceted, complex, and oftentimes unique. The literature in public policy and management in the 1960s and 1970s was dealing with this issue then and continues to do so today. In his classic *The Effective Executive*, Peter F. Drucker stated: "By far the most common mistake is to treat a generic situation as if it were a series of unique events; that is, to be pragmatic when one lacks the generic understanding and principle. This inevitably leads to frustration and futility." Furthermore, he argued that treating a new episode or "event" as a recurrence of a previous problem is an issue.[8] Thus, it would be problematic for President Obama or President Trump to compare policies intended to counter the economic downturns of 2008 and 2020 to President Franklin Delano Roosevelt's policies and institutional (re)designs during the Great Depression due to the increasingly complex policies and subsequent shortcomings of the twenty-first-century global economy.

The economic costs of decision making affect security as well. Economist

Thomas Sowell stated that the conflict of interests found in the government decision making related to the economy led to "differentials in the cost of information, differentials in transactions costs, and inherent conflicts of interest built into political decision-making processes." He argued that individuals would be acting irrationally to put their time, money, and effort into the lobbying and political grandstanding of special interests.[9] Thus, even in the field of applied security studies, decision making is important and has large economic trade-offs for organizations (both private and public) and private citizens as well. It should be no surprise then, that although bureaucracies become increasingly complex, bureaucrats and individual bureaucratic agencies become increasingly focused, in an attempt to cut transaction costs from expert to policymaker.

That the diffusion of knowledge and information connects security and economics to decision making and new networks of information and security is well established. Donald A. Schön wrote, "The extent that we experience a real impetus in the direction of learning systems, the priorities will be increasingly on what might be called network roles. These roles are essential to the design, creation, negotiation and management of ad hoc and continuing networks."[10] Nearly five decades later, Anne-Marie Slaughter argued that the future will continue to require the study of network theory and application and that moving from broad-scale foreign policy strategy to equally important specific network building requires great theory building in networks and networking similar to Thomas Schelling's work in game theory. "Different networks have different structures and properties for different purposes."[11] Again, reflecting on security in and of itself, its decision-making capacities, and its epistemological bases helps the student of security understand the field and its possibilities and pitfalls.

Security and economics are linked in numerous ways. A recent way of approaching the overlay of economics is through the concept of "securitization." The Copenhagen Peace Research Institute was at the vanguard of research in developing research in the area of securitization in the 1990s.[12] An example of securitizing national economic assets was the 2005 attempted takeover of Union Oil Company of California (Unocal), an American energy company, by the China National Off-shore Oil Company (CNOOC), a semiprivate entity. Both Unocal and politicians sounded the alarm bells of a takeover of a large energy company on American soil by a Chinese company. The bid was called a "threat to U.S. interests, and to U.S. national economic and energy security." Eventually, CNOOC revoked its bid to purchase Unocal, and Congress enacted an amendment to the 2005 Energy Policy Act targeting foreign companies and other nations attempting to take control of domestic American energy companies.[13] Although securitization may not always be about the economics of security, this case clearly evinces the linkage between security and state energy interests that leads to heightened tensions in geopolitical and domestic political spheres.

The intermixture of private business concerns with state security is important in the field of security studies. Perhaps no example is clearer than the role of social media giants like Facebook and Twitter. Since 2015, these platforms have increasingly come under scrutiny for their roles in the increasing threat of the "alt-right" movement of neo-Nazis and other racist organizations and individuals; for allowing Russian interference in the 2016 presidential election; and, more recently, for their negative impact on competition and ingenuity, undercutting historically entrenched economic ideals.

The May 30, 2020, launch of the SpaceX Falcon rocket carrying two NASA astronauts was the first manned launch into outer space in a decade and the first by a private company in the history of manned spacecraft. Prior to the historic event and since the end of NASA's Space Shuttle program in 2011, the United States had relied on Russia to take its astronauts to the International Space Station. Leaving from Cape Canaveral, from the same spot as Apollo 11, which sent the first space crew to the moon, astronauts Bob Behnken and Doug Hurley spent nineteen hours in orbit prior to landing at the Space Station. SpaceX, founded in 2002 by South African–born American entrepreneur Elon Musk, was created to take humans to Mars.[14] A Falcon 9 rocket costs $62 million, with the boosters composing around 60 percent, at $37 million. Musk claimed that Falcon 9 rockets could be used for "100 flights." However, the SpaceX chief operating officer suggested that a Falcon 9 rocket would need to be launched only ten times.[15] Musk started SpaceX to demonstrate how a private corporation could compete for government defense and aerospace dollars and develop efficient and time-saving products in the space business. However, years prior to the historical launch of the Falcon rocket in 2020, Musk was confronted with an industry that was the epitome of statist thinking in terms of political economy, as the former U.S. senator from Alabama Richard Shelby defended the United Launch Alliance (ULA; a partnership between Boeing and Lockheed Martin) with some of its operations in his state. He championed ULA's sixty-eight launches and questioned Musk on the efficacy of his company. When probed about the closing of the market to one company (the ULA), Shelby said, "Typically competition results in better quality and lower-priced contracts—but the launch market is not typical. . . . Its limited demand framed by government-industrial policies." Musk did not give up. Along with Boeing, SpaceX was eventually awarded $2.6 billion to get astronauts to the ISS (three years off target, with the launch originally set for 2017). Boeing received $4.2 billion from NASA.[16] The economics of security had overt political overtones, such as in the securitization of energy in the case of Unocal and CNOOC, but in the case of Musk and SpaceX, his patience, his focus on quality and efficiency, and his goal of delivering humans into outer space via his private rockets paid off. The long-term security issues of putting private companies and their products into space will have security and political ramifications.

SpaceX, the increasing reliance on communication and other artificial satellites, the determination of the United States and other countries to explore the moon and Mars for mining and possible settlement, recent announcements by the Pentagon about the existence of UFOs, and the advent of Space Force (the newest branch of the U.S. military, not the Netflix original program) illustrate the importance of reimagining the role of the United States as well as allied and competitor nations in the cosmos. Indeed, it is clear that the United States and China have been thinking about how to use, and arguably abuse, space for their comparative advantage. Similarly, some policymakers, scholars, and (I)NGOs have been forward thinking in advancing policy positions, such as human rights, property and sovereignty, gender and access, and economic security, related to the seemingly inevitable force projection to space.

Political security and military security can go hand in hand. The North Atlantic Treaty Organization (NATO), founded just after the start of the Cold War in 1949, consists of thirty member states in an international alliance. The importance of the NATO alliance came to the fore in the 1950s as the Anglo-American-dominated bloc confronted the Soviet-led bloc and its concomitant Warsaw Pact, the communist East's security apparatus. Both were set in place to check the ambitions of the other as both Russians and Americans and other Western states acquired thermonuclear weapons, which in the 1950s and 1960s took the world to the brink of nuclear conflict. President John F. Kennedy achieved success at the negotiating table in 1963 with a limited nuclear test ban treaty. Soviet-American relations improved during the 1960s, and in late 1970 the Soviets and Americans achieved some success with the Strategic Arms Limitation Talks (SALT) that saw the Russians promise not to place "offensive weapons in the Western Hemisphere or establish bases there." During the next year, when Americans under President Richard M. Nixon reached a diplomatic opening to the East in the People's Republic of China, the Soviets and Americans signed several agreements leading to détente.[17] Soviets and Americans debated the reduction in NATO and Warsaw Pact forces, and the NATO "alliance suffered its share of internal stresses and strains."[18]

Indeed, NATO held together, guided by its key principle of keeping Soviet and Eastern bloc forces from spreading to noncommunist areas. However, this changed on November 9, 1989, when the Berlin Wall fell and on December 25, 1991, when the Soviet Union dissolved. NATO was now seen as an international security organization without a mission. It drifted, looking for a raison d'être in the inchoate stages of the post–Cold War era. John S. Duffield states, "Rather than go out of business, NATO has, at least in some ways, thrived since 1990. It has added 17 new members, more than doubling in size. Forces under NATO command have engaged in extensive combat operations in places such as Bosnia, Kosovo, Afghanistan and Libya. Indeed, the core operational element of the treaty, Article V, which obliges members to provide assistance should one or more of them be the object of an armed attack, was invoked for the first time, following the terrorist attacks on the United States of 11 September 2001."[19] Thus, the politics and military lenses may be used to study, analyze, and understand security and its far-reaching implications for global stability and world order.

Human security can include concepts we have already discussed, including securitization and economic, social, and political security—and may extend to themes like codependency. Robin Alison Remington states: "In psychology, codependency enables and reinforces unhealthy behaviors among individuals or groups. Expanding this concept to the political arena, negative examples of codependency may appear as an attempt to escape from economic insecurity or fear, or . . . when internal authoritarianism is projected into external aggression. It may become reactive ethnic nationalism in response to collapse of the ideologically defined bipolar cold war security or rejection of regional integration in Europe. Or it may explode as ethnic, communal violence set off by growing North-South inequalities—the ever-widening gap between winners and losers of global interactions."[20] Colonial and regional dependency and violence have been part of the long-standing history of the Celtic areas of Britain and Ireland. Codependency was spawned in the sixteenth century by the Tudors in Wales and in the seventeenth century in Ireland as Queen Elizabeth I sent landed elites to the north of Ireland to settle the area and to establish both economic and political control that followed on the Norman conquest of the island to Britain's west one hundred years after the great conquest of England in 1066. Much like the Celtic areas, Kosovo, the tiny Albanian Muslim enclave in Serbia, had a codependent relationship with the Serb-led Yugoslav state under Tito and later during the Yugoslav wars of succession in the 1990s.[21] The security studies subfield of human security starts with the primary level of analysis on individuals, not the state, and the economic, psychological, social, cultural, and political predicaments they face. The promotion of democracy and markets, the standard of American foreign policy and the State Department since 1945, is part of the broader diplomatic output to improve civil society development abroad and democratization as well. The previously mentioned examples of negative codependency in Britain, Ireland, and the areas of the former Yugoslavia led to focusing more sharply on human security as a lens for understanding unique states, cultures, and regions and their security challenges via the nonmilitary realm, but more in the social, economic, and securitized realms of security studies.

Environmental security, a fairly recent area of inquiry, has grown in recent years, and viewing security through an environmental lens has become part of a broader approach to security. Ecological parties have been around since the early 1970s in Switzerland and England, and the most powerful example is Die Grünen (Greens) or the Green Party of Germany, which emerged on the political scene in 1980. Since that time, environmental issues have continued to grow in importance in polities throughout the world. As a part of the security landscape, the environment has continued to gain momentum and has been a continued part of global agendas in international organization such as the United Nations with its important United Nations Environmental Program (UNEP) and its climate change legislation, including various UN Security Council resolutions related to the environment.

In the United States, public opinion about environmental security traditionally ranges from disinterest to disregard for the threat. In recent years though, the U.S. military has begun to recognize and address environmental change and its impact on the military, its equipment needs, areas of global contention, and causes of global contention. Beyond the traditional "hard power" of this and other nations' military might, the United States and other nations around the world have begun to adopt diplomatic "soft power" to the environmental security issues threatening the globe. This has led to a nexus of traditional national security concerns coupled with emerging international relations theories such as feminism and concerns about human security, food security, and global health and security. We must note, however, that continued progress in the area is not guaranteed. For example, the Trump administration (2017–21) withdrew the United States from the Paris Climate Accord, in part because President Trump believed that the accord "disadvantage[d] the United States to the exclusive benefit of other countries," though this position remains demonstrably false.

According to Simon Dalby, humans are "pushing a number of crucial ecological systems beyond what seem to be safe boundaries; straining the systems in ways that may lead to dangerous disruptions to how the system has operated through most of the Holocene," that is, the immediate past. Dalby recognizes the ebbing of various planetary boundaries: (1) biodiversity loss, (2) atmospheric aerosol loading, (3) changes in land use, (4) chemical pollution, (5) global freshwater use, (6) climate change, (7) biogeochemical flow boundaries—the phosphorous cycle and the nitrogen cycle, (8) oceanic acidification, and (9) ozone depletion of the stratosphere. All are being damaged in various and serious ways.[22] Dalby recognizes various types of environmental security approaches that may assist in attempting to correct human-caused damage to the environment, including "ecological security" focused on maintaining nature's natural habitats; "climate security," keeping the earth's temperature at operative and optimal levels; "national security," focused on identifying threats and "mitigating" environmental threats in the use of energy in military operations; "global security," which focuses on avoiding conflicts and preventing "nuclear wars"; "cooperative security," finding common approaches among states and militaries to develop solutions to global environmental and other problems; "human security," studying and finding solutions to assist "vulnerable" populations in developing "infrastructure" and providing security that assists people in getting "essential needs" to survive; and "environmental security," which attempts to solve issues centered on pollution and conservation that links problems to conflict in various parts of the world.[23]

State and Post-state World Order

Security studies can be understood through the study of world order. In the 1950s and 1960s, as the Cold War matured (i.e., the bipolar world order began to develop and coalesce into the communist East versus the capitalist-democratic West), the study of world order centered on geopolitics and ideological constructs related to liberalism, communism, and realism. Liberalism was a classic American and British ideology rooted in time-honored approaches to politics and economy found in the writings of John Locke and others who believed in the primacy of the individual over the state and the capitalist state whereby individuals would produce and acquire goods and services based on their individual capacity to do so and their intellectual ingenuity. Writing in the late seventeenth century, Locke believed that humans were inherently good and that although individuals were not equal based on intelligence, work ethic, and so on, it was society's job to allow individuals to alienate their labor for financial gain and that individuals, not kings, queens, or states, were owed the fruits of that labor in order to survive and grow their own enterprises. It was understood economically that not everyone in society would be able to survive in a competitive economic environment and that private individuals would have to assist in helping the downtrodden and the less fortunate survive via a private welfare state.

About a hundred years after Locke had written his seminal thoughts on liberalism, those ideas would become the basis for Thomas Jefferson's championing of an individual's right to "life, liberty, and the pursuit of happiness" during the American Revolution in 1776. The Westphalian nation-state system had evolved after 1648, just prior to Locke's revolutionary ideas. According to Henry Kissinger, this system "represented the first attempt to institutionalize an international order on the basis of agreed rules and limits and to base it on a multiplicity of powers rather than the dominance of a single country." At this time the idea of "national interest" became important as states began to vie for power and status in the newly evolving multilateral system of political and economic development.[24] The Concert of Europe (1815–1914) saw a hundred years of relative calm in global affairs due to the diplomacy of the great powers (Austria, Britain, France, Prussia, and Russia). The incredible act of foresight and goodwill in the great powers welcoming France back into the fold after Napoleon I (Bonaparte) had nearly destroyed the continent from 1800 to 1815 in a decade and a half of warfare was vital in that it laid to rest, at least temporarily, the idea of security focused on vengeance and Carthaginian solutions; rather, it moved toward a more comprehensive idea of creating a more multilateral security, even if based on mainly bilateral treaties within a very conservative grouping of states and kingdoms that were not interested in the democratization of nations or the diplomatic process itself. However, according to Kissinger, the "concert mechanism functioned like a precursor of the United Nations Security Council. Its conferences acted on a series of crises, attempting to distill a common course: the revolutions in Naples in 1820 and in Spain in 1820–23 (quelled by the Holy Alliance and France, respectively) and the Greek revolution and war of independence of 1821–32 (ultimately supported by Britain, France, and Russia). The Concert of Powers did not guarantee a unanimity of outlook, yet in each case a potentially explosive crisis was resolved without a major-power war."[25] Incrementalism was the order of the day in this era.

The Cold War period was not radically different. Although President Woodrow Wilson had hoped for a new approach to diplomacy and world order with his Fourteen Points and "open covenants, openly arrived at," the failure of the United States to ratify the Treaty of Versailles in 1919 doomed a new era when, it was hoped, diplomacy would be more open and small and large nation-states alike would sit at the negotiating table and solve the world's problems. Thus, the march toward a continuation of World War I (1914–18) was inevitable by the early 1930s given fascist states' invasions across the globe, beginning in East Asia with Japan's 1931 invasion of Manchuria, which presaged further bloodshed. Italy's invasion of Ethiopia in 1935 and Nazi Germany's move into the Rhineland in 1936, annexation of Austria in 1938, and invasion of Czechoslovakia the same year put the world and its broken world order on the brink of war once again.

After the Allied nations forced fascist retraction and largely restored prewar borders, a standoff with the last two great powers ensued. The Cold War came as Sir Winston Churchill announced that "from Stettin in the Baltic to Trieste in the Adriatic, an Iron Curtain has descended across the Continent."[26]

According to political scientist Herbert K. Tillema, during the Cold War period, September 1945 to December 1988, 269 armed conflicts occurred in various places around the world.[27] The Cold War era saw fewer global conflicts; but by the early 1950s the potential for widespread security meltdowns and broad-scale wars, partly due to moving from the nuclear fission bombs of Hiroshima and Nagasaki, which killed a hundred thousand Japanese in August 1945, to nuclear fusion bombs with greater capacity for destruction, was real. The Cold War saw a number of interesting developments, as mentioned earlier in this chapter, regarding Soviet-American détente by the early 1970s.

President Ronald Reagan (1981–89) ushered in a mixture of realism and idealism in battling the Soviets both at the negotiating table and in the court of public opinion both in Russia and in the United States. As Kissinger states, "Without Reagan's idealism—bordering sometimes on a repudiation of history—the end of the Soviet challenge could not have occurred amidst such a global affirmation of democratic future."[28] It was Reagan's successor, President George H. W. Bush, who actually presided over the collapse of Soviet authority in Russia, its expansive former Soviet empire, and the Central European communist states. Watching the fall of the Berlin Wall on November 9, 1989, he and Secretary of State James A. Baker III were stunned. Yet post–Cold War security structures, including UN peacekeeping forces and NATO troops, would slowly emerge in the vacuum that came with the new post–Cold War world order and even post-state-centric world order.

The post-state-centric world order began to emerge after the end of the Cold War. Philip Bobbitt focused on the fluidity of ideas related to sovereignty and legitimacy as states begin to pool sovereignty in international organizations like the European Union. Anne-Marie Slaughter argued that the world was "collapsing" into greater world order, meaning that networks were forming that allowed for greater decentralization and functional linking of local and regional governments and business interests below the nation-state levels. Another type of functionalism—the concept that David Mitrany and Ernst B. Hass elucidated in the 1960s and 1970s focused on technical and economic areas of development and specialization that brought people and nations together, thereby facilitating closer international and political cooperation—has been "multilevel governance," which, when applied to the European Union, demonstrates that multiple levels of decision making are found within states that are subject not to the sovereign nation-state but to international organizations.

Scotland is an example of this type of pooled sovereignty, whereby it had representation at Brussels as part of the United Kingdom, and yet it still has its own representation at Brussels as a region and semisovereign nation, and its economic interests have political representation as well.[29] "European Celts now have multiple political, economic, and legal jurisdictions under international and European Union (EU) law. These overlapping jurisdictions in turn necessitate different responses from Brussels. Scotland, Wales, and Northern Ireland are governed by Common Law promulgated from London, and Scotland is also influenced by Scots Law issued from Edinburgh. This multilayered context muddies the waters of political power in the United Kingdom and Europe and the political contexts within which these polities operate." Security is thus affected in the post-state-centric global order as overlapping jurisdictions affect the development of security apparatuses and outcomes, as seen in the case of the Stability Pact for Southeastern Europe. This particular stabilization treaty was created in 1999 and reconstituted as the Regional Cooperation Council (RCC) in 2008. The RCC includes forty-six member states and works in the areas of regional security, justice and home affairs, energy issues, social and economic development, and interparliamentary affairs. Located in Sarajevo, this body serves much the same role as that of West European Union (WEU) and other international security organizations did in Brussels until the end of the cold war. Thereby, the general understanding is that the RCC will be folded into the newly evolving EU common foreign and defense policy structure of the twenty-first century.[30]

Cybersecurity and Advanced Technology

Into the third decade of the twenty-first century, cybersecurity continues to bedevil the globe as a threat to global order and security regimes and systems themselves. From Serbs attacking NATO's computer systems in the 1999 Kosovo War to the Stuxnet worm, nation-states have engaged in cyberwar for many years. As former U.S. special assistant for national security affairs H. R. McMaster says, China has constructed "an unprecedented [domestic] surveillance state" whereby a "system of personal 'social credit scores' is based on tracking people's online and other activity to determine their friendliness to Chinese government priorities. People's scores determine eligibility for loans, government employment, housing, transportation benefits, and more." McMaster further states that the military research units, working with universities, are promoting and growing civil-military linkages that grow the ability of state-owned and private firms to "acquire companies with advanced technologies, or strong minority stake in those companies, so that the technologies can be applied for not only economic but military and intelligence advantage. It fast-tracks stolen technologies to the army in such areas as space, cyberspace, biology, artificial intelligence, and energy." Moreover, McMaster asserts that the "Chinese Ministry of State Security used a hacking squad known as APT10 to target U.S. companies in the finance, telecommunications, consumer-electronics, and medical industries as well as NASA and Department of Defense research laboratories, extracting intellectual property and sensitive data. For example, the hackers obtained personal information, including Social Security numbers, for more than 100,000 naval personnel."[31]

The Stuxnet worm was a "malicious cyber worm" created to attack industrial technological "control systems." It was a kind of "weaponized" malware. A joint American-Israeli creation, it was identified in 2010 and was found to have ravaged Iran's nuclear system throughout fifteen of Iran's nuclear stations. The cyberattacks were piecemeal in nature and were actuated by humans who were unaware of the malware. The malware kicked in when normal "readings" of the computer and other actions took place by humans, and it caused the "nuclear centrifuges to spin out of control" as positive readings were taking place.[32] In 2011, the Cyber War Bureau, an advisory organ of the prime minister of Israel, was created to develop computerized defenses for the nation-state.[33] In 2013, during the Syrian civil war, it was divulged that an elite cybersecurity unit of the Israeli Defense Forces (IDF, Israel's army), named "Unit 8200," had formed. This group of Israeli soldiers work to "hack into just about any military network in the world. It is rumored that Unit 8200 can tap into electronic systems of enemies far and near, turn off power plants, radar stations and the electronic capabilities of enemies and allies alike."[34] Unit 8200 is the loose equivalent to the U.S. National Security Agency. The elite arm of the IDF whose graduates head this army unit are from Talpiot ("tower" in Hebrew). Talpiot is a unique unit where brains meet brawn. Young people join the unit for nine-year stints rather than the traditional and compulsory three-year military hitch in Israel. When selected into the elite unit, eighteen-year-olds begin university studies as soldiers and embark on accelerated studies in mathematics, hard sciences, psychology, engineering, business, computer science, and other disciplines. It is a mixture of having an MIT engineering and physics education with entrepreneurship, cyberintelligence, and military leadership and U.S. Army Ranger and paratrooper training. The education sets the soldier up for a leading role in the cultivation of broad swaths of research and development in the innovation culture of Israeli and global business upon graduation.[35] Of course, by 2007 the United States was giving three to four billion dollars in foreign aid and military support to Israel—representing around 2 percent of Israel's GDP and one-sixth of the U.S. foreign aid budget.[36] U.S. aid held steady at $3.8 billion by 2019.[37] Given that a substantial number of jobs are found in the Israeli defense industry, Talpiot graduates end up straddling the worlds of business, military, and government after they leave the military and have developed one of the largest Internet, communications, and technology sectors in the context of entrepreneurship via defense research and development in the world. "Today Israel, with just eight million people, captures about 10 per cent of the global cyber security market." For an economy that did six billion dollars in cybersecurity exports in 2014, the securitization of Israeli society does concern some, as 20 percent of the society (the fraction who are Arab) are virtually excluded from the cyberforce that has been developed in the country.[38]

Cybersecurity must continue to look forward, and those in security studies and positions related to cybersecurity must continue to review the ethical, moral, and political elements of cybersecurity. As Microsoft chief executive officer Satya Nadella, who replaced Microsoft founder Bill Gates, has said, there are at least six ways that trust can be built by "lawmakers" with people. First, a "more efficient system" for access to electronic data by authorities in "law enforcement" is required. Second, we need "stronger privacy protections so that the security of user data is not eroded in the name of efficiency." Third, we need a new system for gathering digital evidence across international boundaries as we understand the transnational nature of digital space and "information technology." Fourth, more transparency is needed in the information technology sector. Fifth, we need to "modernize laws" to come alongside the digital times that we live in. Finally, "we must promote trust through security."[39]

Cybersecurity concerns are increasingly relevant in an era of expanded connectivity. Our era has seen the fallout of Russian hackers and trolls on public opinion, and it has seen concerns about the security of elections, banking, and even apps allowing curbside pickup in the midst of a pandemic. Yet there are burgeoning technologies that, like cybertechnologies, have the power to alter conceptions of war—among them, the speed of war, who and what are fighting, and what constitutes the battle space (see the discussion of outer space above).

The building of new ethical, legal, and business frameworks to define and manage the future of cyberspace and emerging technologies will continue to be a double-edged sword for those confronted with the expansion of digital spaces in politics, society, and economics. The ethical, legal, and moral frameworks, as Nadella suggests, must continue to evolve in both the private and the public spheres. Security studies is but one area that will have to continue to develop its own literature, conceptual frameworks, and understandings of these fuzzy areas as they evolve.

Contextualizing Security within a Changing Global Landscape

In June 2020, massive protests broke out in Minneapolis, Minnesota, when a forty-six-year-old Black man, George Floyd, was killed after police officer Derek Chauvin knelt on Floyd's neck to restrain him. Chauvin was convicted of murder in April 2021. Previously, in March 2020, after issuing a "no-knock" warrant, the Louisville, Kentucky, police fired into the bedroom of an apartment belonging to Breonna Taylor. When her boyfriend Kenneth Walker, thinking the police were intruders, fired back, officers fired again, killing the twenty-six-year-old emergency medical technician Taylor. These two events moved millions around the world to march in support of civil rights, defunding police departments, and social justice in general. These events sparked outrage and fierce racial protests, burning of inner cities, and looting that had not been seen since the 1960s. Hundreds of millions of dollars in damage occurred in multiple U.S. cities. One of the underlying themes of these events was the changing nature of protest and the challenges that civil rights and liberties pose to security and the tender balance of security versus liberty—the theme of this collection of readings.

What is interesting about the public response to the killings of George Floyd and Breonna Taylor (and earlier Michael Brown in Ferguson, Missouri, in 2014) is that protests and the ways in which security officials and police were held accountable were changing. During the 2011 Arab Spring, mass rallies and protests were held in Tunisia and Egypt based on the ability of cyberactivists to organize via Facebook protests. Today, as Jeremy Heimans and Henry Timms, Australian social entrepreneurs and activists, argued in their compelling book, *New Power* (2018), crowdsourcing and social media are used not only as tools for challenging the status quo but also as ends in themselves in bringing about social change. These concepts, tools, and approaches present an interesting challenge to "old power" values. According to Heimans and Timms, "new power values" are juxtaposed against "old power values." The newer values include (1) "informal—networked—governance," "opt-in decision-making," and "self-organization"; (2) "collaboration, crowd wisdom, sharing, open-sourcing"; (3) "radical transparency"; (4) maker culture, "do-it ourselves ethic"; and (5) "short-term condition affiliation" and "more overall participation." The old power values include (1) "formal—representative—governance, managerialism, institutionalism"; (2) "competition, exclusivity, resource consolidation"; (3) "confidentiality, discretion, separation between private and public spheres"; (4) "expertise, professionalism, specialization"; and (5) "long-term affiliation and loyalty less overall participation."[40] The new era that Heimans and Timms describe was captured well in the protests over race in the United States and the West in June 2020. Although long-term structural and institutional changes did not happen immediately, as many supporters of the Black Lives Matter movement hoped for, the protests were examples of the new power phenomenon that Heimans and Timms described. What's more, security studies provides the context to study these protests not only from ideological and political reference points but from other angles including securitization, the environment, and geopolitics. Heimans and Timms recognize the importance of "new power" and warn that new power for socially just ends in crowdsourcing via social media can also be used by the enemies of the United States and the West: "New means of participation—and the heightened sense of agency that has come with them—are a key ingredient in some of the most impactful models of our time: big businesses like Airbnb and Uber, China's WeChat or Facebook; protest movements like Black Lives Matter; open software systems like GitHub; and terrorist networks like ISIS. They are all channeling new power."[41] Not only did new power play out empirically in the United States and the West in June 2020, but a steady march of new power protests and increased angst led to continued security challenges and changes in the recent past (for example, the Mouvement des gilets jaunes or "yellow vests movement" in late 2018 in France, which attempted to challenge the high costs of living and rising gas prices and was driven by postings on social media). All of this was important as the George Floyd and Breonna Taylor protests occurred in the middle of the COVID-19 pandemic.

The coronavirus began to take hold in the United States in March 2020, infecting several hundred thousand and taking the lives of thousands. Having been found to have started in bats in Wuhan, China, in fall 2019, the virus was the fifth coronavirus to infect the globe since 2003. Placing responsibility on the Chinese for COVID-19 may be questionable, as multiple organizations and news outlets have questioned this contention. Despite having been warned previously by the World Health Organization and the Centers for Disease Control and Prevention and other public health agencies, the nations of the world were caught off-guard at the virulence of COVID-19. For the first time since the Spanish Flu pandemic of 1918–19, which claimed the lives of thirty-three million globally, citizens took to wearing masks, using antibacterial soap, and engaging in "social distancing" to avoid spreading the virus via germs and coughing. The dean of the Graduate School of Public Health at the University of Pittsburgh, Donald S. Burke, argued that the severe acute respiratory syndrome (SARS) emerged in China in 2002. He claimed in 1997 that coronaviruses could have "intrinsic evolvability"—they could "mutate" with "the potential to emerge into and to cause pandemics in human populations."[42] By late April 2021, the coronavirus had infected 32.1 million and killed over 571,000 people in the United States;[43] globally, the virus had infected 147.5 million people and killed more than 3 million.[44] The ominous nature of COVID-19 and its sweep across the globe add another layer to human and environmental security challenges that are connected to the political security challenges of racial protests and political unrest in the United States and the West. Thus, the need for continued study of security, including its conceptual frameworks, history, and contexts, was apparent, and in spite of the frailty of humanity in the third decade of the twenty-first century, new threats and opportunities exist for the field to continue to assist students and scholars and practitioners of security to learn from and improve the field in moving forward in real time and space, as well as in the physical world, in the digital world, in technological fields, and in cyberspace.

Conclusion

This chapter has offered initial thoughts and considerations on the foundations of national security and security studies. We have discussed the historical and theoretical bases, but also some of the evolutionary and future considerations in light of these structures. However, we also explicitly and implicitly have suggested that some of the long-established norms and expectations must also be reconsidered as rights are expanded and as daily life and security are bound by security considerations and issues related to outer space. Questions arise, answers are offered, but rethinking and updating must occur. We can no longer simply apply historical frameworks, like Just War Theory or historical frameworks like a Westphalian assumption in international and interplanetary activities.

Notes

1. J. Marshall Beier and Samantha L. Arnold, "Becoming Undisciplined: Toward the Supradisciplinary Study of Security," *International Studies Review* 7 (2005): 41–61.

2. Paul D. Williams and Matt McDonald, eds., *Security Studies: An Introduction* (London: Routledge, 2018), 6.

3. Ibid., 4.

4. Kurt W. Jefferson, *Celtic Politics: Politics in Scotland, Ireland, and Wales* (Lanham, Md.: University Press of America, 2011), 246.

5. John G. Stoessinger, *The Might of Nations: World Politics in Our Time*, 10th ed. (New York: McGraw-Hill, 1993), 10–12.

6. Williams and McDonald, *Security Studies*, 4.

7. See Graham Allison and Phillip Zelikow, *Essence of Decision Making: Explaining the Cuban Missile Crisis*, 2nd ed. (1971; New York: Pearson, 1999) and Robert Jervis, *Perception and Misperception in International Politics* (1976; Princeton, N.J.: Princeton University Press, 2017).

8. Peter F. Drucker, *The Effective Executive* (New York: HarperCollins, 2002), 125.

9. Thomas Sowell, *Knowledge and Decisions* (New York: Basic Books, 1996), 38.

10. Donald A. Schön, *Beyond the Stable State* (New York: Norton, 1971), 197.

11. Anne-Marie Slaughter, *The Chessboard and the Web: Strategies of Connection in a Networked World* (Princeton, N.J.: Princeton University Press, 2017), 13.

12. Jonna Nyman, " Securitization," in Williams and McDonald, *Security Studies*, 101.

13. Ibid., 105.

14. Jacob Bogagae and Christian Davenport, "Dragon Capsule Achieves Orbit, Heads towards Space Station: SpaceX Became the First Private Corporation to Launch People into Orbit," *Washington Post*, May 30, 2020,.

15. Michael Sheetz, "Elon Musk Touts Low Cost to Insure SpaceX Rockets as Edge over Competitors," CNBC.com, April 16, 2020, www.cnbc.com/amp/2020/04/16/elon-musk-spacex-falcon-9-rocket-over-a-million-dollars-less-to-insure.html.

16. Ashlee Vance, *Elon Musk: Tesla, SpaceX, and the Quest for a Fantastic Future* (New York: HarperCollins, 2015), 252–53.

17. Stoessinger, *Might of Nations*, 61–62.

18. John S. Duffield, "Alliances," in Williams and McDonald, *Security Studies*, 276.

19. Ibid., 277.

20. Robin Alison Remington, "Introduction," in *Globalization and Regime Change: Lessons from the New Russia and the New Europe*, ed. Robin Alison Remington and Robert K. Evanson (Lanham, Md.: Rowman & Littlefield, 2019), 9.

21. Kurt W. Jefferson, "Transitions in Europe: The Celtic Polities and Kosovo," in Remington and Evanson, *Globalization and Regime Change*, 265–66.

22. Simon Dalby, "Environmental Change," in Williams and McDonald, *Security Studies*, 528–29.

23. Ibid., 531.

24. Henry Kissinger, *World Order* (New York: Penguin, 2014), 30.

25. Ibid., 65.

26. Patrick Wright, *Iron Curtain: From Stage to Cold War* (Oxford: Oxford University Press, 2007), 43.

27. Herbert K. Tillema, *International Armed Conflict since 1945: A Bibliographic Handbook* (Boulder, Colo.: Westview, 1991), 7–9.

28. Kissinger, *World Order*, 314.

29. See Philip J. Bobbitt, *The Sword of Achilles: War, Peace, and the Course of History* (New York: Anchor, 2002); Ernst B. Haas, *Beyond the Nation-State: Functionalism and International Organization* (Stanford, Calif.: Stanford University Press, 1964); Kurt W. Jefferson, *Christianity's Impact on World Politics: Not by Might, Nor by Power* (New York: Peter Lang, 2002); Gary Marks and Lisbet Hooghe, *Multi-level Governance and European Integration* (Boulder, Colo.: Rowman & Littlefield, 2001); David Mitrany, *The Functional Theory of Politics* (New York: St. Martin's, 1976); Anne-Marie Slaughter, *New World Order* (Princeton, N.J.: Princeton University Press, 2004).

30. Jefferson, "Transitions in Europe," 249–58.

31. H. R. McMaster, "How China Sees the World: And How We Should See China," *Atlantic*, April 17, 2020, https://outline.com/JyMnhc.

32. Rhea Siers, "Cybersecurity," in Williams and McDonald, *Security Studies*, 560.

33. Jason Gewirtz, *Israel's Edge: The Story of the IDF's Most Elite Unit—Talpiot* (Jerusalem: Green, 2016), 222.

34. Ibid., 85–86.

35. Ibid., 56–76.

36. John J. Mearsheimer and Stephen M. Walt, *The Israeli Lobby and U.S. Foreign Policy* (New York: Farrar, Straus and Giroux, 2007), 26–27.

37. James Kirchick, "Quit Harping on U.S. Aid to Israel: American Commitments to Asian and European Allies Require More Risk and Sacrifice," *Atlantic*, March 29, 2019, https:// theatlantic.com/amp/article/585988/.

38. John Reed, "Unit 8200: Israel's Cyber Spy Agency: Former Insiders and Whistle-Blowers Provide a View of the Formidable Military Intelligence Outfit," *Financial Times*, July 10, 2015, https://www.ft.com/content/69f150dg-25b8-11e5-bd83 -71cb60e8f08c.

39. Satya Nadella (with Greg Shaw and Jill Tracie Nichols), *Hit Refresh: The Quest to Rediscover Microsoft's Soul and Imagine a Better Future for Everyone* (New York: HarperCollins, 2017), 190–93.

40. Jeremy Heimans and Henry Timms, *New Power: How Power Works in Our Hyperconnected World—and How to Make It Work for You* (New York: Doubleday, 2018), 18.

41. Ibid., 8.

42. See, for example, "Frontline, China's Covid Secrets," PBS, February 2, 2021, https://www.pbs.org/wgbh/frontline/film/chinas-covid-secrets/; Peter Sullivan, "Overnight Health Care: U.S. Joins 13 Countries in Raising 'Concerns' with Data in WHO Team's Virus Report," *The Hill*, March 30, 2021, https:// thehill.com/policy/healthcare /overnight/545640-overnight-health-care-us-joins-13-countries-in-raising-concerns %3famp; and David Quammen, *Spillover: Animal Infections and the Next Human Pandemic* (New York: Norton, 2012), 512.

43. "Coronavirus in the U.S.: Latest Map and Case Count," *New York Times*, April 26, 2021, https://www.nytimes.com/interactive/2021/us/covid-cases.html.

44. Johns Hopkins University Center for System Science and Engineering, "Coronavirus Resource Center," April 26, 2021, https://www.arcgis.com/apps/opsdashboard/index.html#/85320e2ea5424dfaaa75ge62e5c06e61.

Achieving Our Homeland Security while Preserving Our Values and Our Liberty

Former U.S. Secretary of Homeland Security
Jeh C. Johnson

It is an honor to speak at this school. I am impressed that, here in the heartland of America, lays the most diverse small liberal arts college of the entire nation, consisting of students from twenty-eight states and seventy-six countries. Thank you also for bestowing on me an honorary degree. Most of all, it is an honor for me to give the Fifty-Sixth Green Foundation Lecture at Westminster, preceded in this lecture series by a truly extraordinary collection of presidents, prime ministers, philosophers, rock stars, and others who came here to Fulton, Missouri. . . . I enjoyed preparing this speech. I am an avid student of history, and there's a lot of history associated with the Green Lecture series. I believe that the decision making of public officials should be informed by history. I also believe what has been said many times before—that those who don't learn the mistakes of history are bound to repeat them.

Of course, the most famous Green Lecture [the seventh lecture in the series] was delivered by Winston Churchill on this campus on March 5, 1946—his Iron Curtain speech.[1] By March 1946, when Churchill gave that speech, he had been voted out of office as prime minister, just a few months after leading the British people to victory in the Second World War. In 1945 a British newspaper actually suggested that Churchill retire from politics while he was at the top of his game, rather than stand in the forthcoming elections. Churchill responded with a quote that I bet the students here will love. I certainly do. "Mr. Editor, I leave when the pub closes."[2] For Churchill, the pub did close in that election, and he was forced to leave office as prime minister.

It was a crushing defeat for Churchill. But, ironically, that loss may have been the reason he found time to come here to Fulton, Missouri. Once here, Churchill had actual little power. He was at that point the leader of the opposition party in the British Parliament. But he delivered one of the most powerful speeches of the twentieth century. One that Churchill himself considered his oratorical high-water mark. Winston Churchill and I have something in common: we were both terrible students in school. . . . So, as I accept this honorary degree, I feel as Churchill did when he said: "no one has ever passed so few examinations and received so many degrees."

The man who introduced Winston Churchill to the audience that day was President Harry Truman. Like many others, I am a fan of Harry Truman. He was no intellectual or aristocrat; he was not God-like like his predecessor in the eyes of the people. Not long before Truman became president upon Roosevelt's death, few people would have deliberately picked him to succeed the great Roosevelt as the leader of the nation during a time of world war. In the eyes of many, Harry Truman was just a high-school-educated haberdasher.

But today Harry Truman is considered one of our great presidents. He rose to the occasion. He had the strength of his convictions, clarity of thought, and a bright compass to lead the country through a dangerous and transformational time.

Five years after Churchill came here, Harry Truman returned to Westminster to deliver the Fourteenth Green Lecture. And it is that speech by former president Harry Truman, entitled "What Hysteria Does to Us," that is the inspiration for my remarks here today. Harry Truman delivered that speech in April 1954. It was during the period of the Red Scare, McCarthyism—the rise and fear of communism in the postwar, Cold War era. In his usual plain and blunt language, Truman rebuked the specter of McCarthyism with the words, the "descendants of the ancient order of witch-hunters have learned nothing from history." He went on to say "[t]he cause of freedom both at home and abroad is damaged when a great country yields to hysteria."[3]

[M]y grandfather was a college president. Dr. Charles S. Johnson was a writer, a sociologist, and president of Fisk University in Nashville, Tennessee, from 1947 to 1956. At the time, Fisk was the preeminent liberal arts college for Black people in this country.

At the same time in April 1954 that Harry Truman delivered his Green Lecture here, about "what hysteria does to us," Dr. Johnson was defending himself and his school for hiring a professor named Lee Lorch.[4] Lee Lorch was a PhD, a gifted mathematician, and a white man who could not find continued employment at any white college or university. Lorch was also suspected of being a member of the Communist Party. In 1950, Fisk was an all-Black school that needed a good mathematician of any race, so Johnson hired Lorch.

For years Johnson refused to surrender to the Red Scare.

In 1949, he testified before the House Un-American Activities Committee to refute allegations of communist infiltration into Black colleges.

In 1948, Johnson, a man with honorary degrees from Harvard and Columbia, was required to testify before a California State Senate version of the Un-American Activities Committee—the so-called Tenney Committee—about his own membership in the National Sharecroppers Fund, a suspected communist front. In terms similar to Truman's, Johnson testified to his view that the committee's inquiries amounted to a "witch-hunt," and "much more un-American than the un-American activities being pursued."[5] Sadly, after years of defending him, in 1955 Johnson had to set aside his principles and terminate Lorch, to protect Fisk University, its standing and its reputation. For Johnson, it was an agonizing decision that, according to one good friend, contributed to his sudden death from a massive heart attack a year later in 1956, at the age of sixty-three.[6] Johnson never saw the results of the civil rights movement that he helped harvest. And, it would have been beyond his comprehension that in the year 2013 his own grandson would become the secretary of homeland security. What Harry Truman said here in 1954 is consistent with the views he had been expressing for years. In 1950, Truman asserted in a statement to Congress: "Everyone in public life has a responsibility to conduct himself so as to reinforce and not undermine our internal security and our basic freedoms. Our press and radio have the same responsibility. . . . We must all act soberly and carefully, in keeping with our great traditions."[7] This assertion is timeless, and I agree with every word. All of us in public office, those who aspire to public office, and who command a microphone, owe the public calm, responsible dialogue and decision-making; not overheated, oversimplistic rhetoric and proposals of superficial appeal. In a democracy, the former leads to smart and sustainable policy, the latter can lead to fear, hate, suspicion, prejudice, and government overreach.

This is particularly true in matters of homeland security. Today's Department of Homeland Security is the third largest department of our government, with twenty-two components, 225,000 people, and a total spending authority of about sixty billion dollars a year. Our responsibilities include counterterrorism, border security, port security, aviation security, maritime security, cybersecurity, the administration and enforcement of our immigration laws, the detection of nuclear, chemical and biological threats to our homeland, the protection of our critical infrastructure, the protection of our national leaders, and the response to natural disasters such as floods, tornadoes, hurricanes, and earthquakes.

DHS includes within it: U.S. Customs and Border Protection; U.S. Immigration and Customs Enforcement; U.S. Citizenship and Immigration Services; TSA; FEMA; the Federal Protective Service; the Secret Service; the Federal Law Enforcement Training Centers; and the U.S. Coast Guard. DHS is also the agency of the U.S. government with which the American public interacts the most. Given all this, there are a lot of ways in which DHS can potentially assert itself into the daily lives of the American public, in the name of homeland security.

But, as secretary of this large department with all its resources, I know we must guard against the dangers of overreaction in the name of homeland security. It's not simply a matter of imposing on the public as much security as our resources will permit. Rather, both national security and homeland security involve striking a balance between basic, physical security and the law, the liberties and the values we cherish as Americans.

I understand that the theme of this year's Hancock Symposium, of which this lecture is a part, is "security versus liberty." National security officials must be the guardians of one as much as the other. This is why the FBI Director Jim Comey requires his agents to visit the Holocaust Museum in Washington, and keeps in his desk the document from 1963 by which the then-FBI director and the attorney general authorized government wiretapping of Martin Luther King at his home in Atlanta. This is why today's Department of Homeland Security has an Office of Privacy and an Office of Civil Rights and Civil Liberties that report directly to me, and review all our most sensitive security measures before we enact them.

We must recognize that our first impulse in reaction to a threat to the American people is often not the best one. This is as true today as it was in Harry Truman's time. Today the global terrorist threat to our homeland is evolving. It is no longer limited to terrorist threats that are recruited, trained, equipped, and directed overseas and then exported to the homeland. We now also live in a world that includes the potential homegrown threat—the so-called "lone wolf"—that may strike with little or no notice, and is terrorist-inspired by something he sees or reads in social media or the Internet.

In this environment, the first impulse may be to suspect all Muslims living among us in this country as potential terrorists. The reality is the self-proclaimed Islamic State does not represent the Islamic faith, and we must not confuse the two. Spend any time with Muslim leaders in this country and you will quickly learn of their own hatred for groups such as ISIL and al-Qaeda. Muslims are the principal victims of ISIL and al-Qaeda. To Muslim leaders across this country, ISIL is trying to "hijack my religion." Islam is about peace and brotherhood, not violence on others. The standard Muslim greeting *as salamu alaykum* means "peace be upon you."

On a different issue: Recall also the anxiety a year ago in this country associated with the outbreak of the Ebola virus in West Africa. The outbreak of a lethal virus always raises the potential for public anxiety, because of the great unknown at the initial stages of just how far or fast the virus will ultimately spread. For a period last fall almost every air traveler to the United States, from any part of the world, who got sick on an airplane came to the personal attention of the secretary of homeland security.

In the face of the spreading Ebola virus, I will admit that my first reaction was to limit the issuance of travel visas from West Africa to the United States. The second, better reaction, informed by the views of others on the National Security Council, was that this would be a mistake, because of the United States' leadership position in the world.

Had we suspended travel from West Africa at the height of the Ebola crisis, other nations would have followed our lead. This would have had the effect of isolating these small African countries from the rest of the world at a time when they needed us the most. Instead, we funneled all air travel into the United States from Liberia, Sierra Leone, and Guinea to one of five airports here, and thousands of members of the military and the health care profession in this country went to West Africa and helped defeat the spread of the Ebola virus. The United States led, and acted in a manner that should make all Americans proud.

The lesson is this:

- I can build you a perfectly safe city, but it will amount to a prison.
- I can guarantee you a commercial air flight perfectly free from the risk of terrorist attack, but all the passengers will be forced to wear nothing but hospital-like paper smocks, and not be allowed any luggage, food, or the ability to get up from their seats.
- I can do the same thing on buses and subways, but a twenty-minute commute to work would turn into a daily, invasive, two-hour ordeal. You'd rather quit your job and stay home.
- I can guarantee you an email system perfectly free from the risk of cyberattack, but it will be an isolated, walled-off system of about ten people, with no link to the larger, interconnected world of the Internet.
- I can profile people in this country based on their religion, but that would be unlawful and un-American.
- We can erect more walls, install more screening devices, and make everybody suspicious of each other, but we should not do so at the cost of who we are as a nation of people who cherish our privacy, our religions, our freedom to speak, travel and associate, and who celebrate our diversity and our immigrant heritage.

In the final analysis, these are the things that constitute our greatest strengths as a nation.

The last thing I want to say is directed to the students here.

Please consider a career in public service. We need smart, talented, and energetic young people to serve their country, their state, or their community. I have spent most of my thirty-three-year career since law school as a corporate lawyer. But, I will tell you that my time in public office has been the most satisfying and rewarding, though I make a small fraction of what I earned in private

U.S. Secretary of Homeland Security Jeh Johnson delivers the Fifty-Sixth John Findley Green Foundation Lecture in concert with the Hancock Symposium at Westminster College in Fulton, Missouri, on September 16, 2015. Photo credit: Jetta Disco, DHS.

law practice. The one last Churchill quote I will share with you is the one I repeat most often: "We make a living by what we get, but we make a life by what we give."

Gratification in life comes from making a difference, and service to others. As college students and young people, many of you have this impulse and this dream. I'm here to tell you that that dream need not fade as you grow older. You can really stay until the pub closes.

Thank you very much.

Notes

Jeh C. Johnson delivered this speech as the Fifty-Sixth Green Foundation Lecture, on September 16, 2015, at Westminster College, in Fulton, Missouri.

1. Prime Minister Winston Churchill, "Sinews of Peace" (Iron Curtain Speech), John Findley Green Lecture, March 5, 1946, Westminster College, Fulton, Mo., https://www .nationalchurchillmuseum.org/sinews-of-peace-iron-curtain-speech.html.

2. Anthony Lewis, "Churchill Is Dead at 90; The World Mourns Him; State Funeral Saturday," *New York Times*, January 24, 1965, http://www.nytimes.com/learning/general /onthisday/big/0124.html.

3. President Harry S. Truman, "Witch-hunting and Hysteria," Sixteenth John Findley Green Lecture, April 12, 1954, http://www.trumanlibrary.org/hstpaper/sound recording2.htm.

4. See Patrick Gilpin and Marybeth Gasman, *Charles S. Johnson: Leadership Beyond the Veil in the Civil Rights Era* (New York: New York University Press, 2003), 237–48.

5. Ibid., 239–40.

6. Ibid., 247.

7. President Harry S. Truman, "Special Message to the Congress on the Internal Security of the United States," August 8, 1950, http://trumanlibrary.org/publicpapers /viewpapers.php?pid=836.

Liberty and Security

REFORMULATING THE CLASSIC DEBATE

James McRae, Westminster College

Political theory is often characterized as the resolution of the tension between two goods: liberty and security. The purpose of this chapter is to examine the philosophical foundations of this tension, critique the limitations of this approach, and offer a reformulation of liberty and security that is more useful for solving practical political problems. The second section offers a summary of the classic tension between liberty and security, which is best formulated by John Stuart Mill in his treatise *On Liberty*. The third section expands on this view by articulating negative and positive conceptions of liberty and security, then uses semiotic squares to illustrate how the tension between these more robust notions can be reconciled. Liberty and security exist in a dynamic, creative tension that transcends the negative conceptions of freedom from interference and safety from threats to include positive notions that promote both self-actualization and peace.

The Classic Tension between Liberty and Security

Since the Enlightenment, political philosophy has often been conceptualized as the reconciliation of two competing values: liberty and security. Figure 1 illustrates the classic tension between these two values.

According to this classic conception, any political system is a balance between liberty, where citizens are free from government interference, and security, in which citizens are protected from threats. Every law or policy must fall somewhere between these two extremes, and justice is served when there is an appropriate balance between the two. A social contract that promotes total liberty at the expense of security is actually not a social contract at all; it is a state of anarchy (what Hobbes calls the "State of Nature").[1] A political system that promotes total security at the expense of liberty is a tyranny akin to

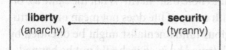

Figure 1. The classic tension between liberty and security.

what George Orwell depicts in his novel *1984*: in order for Big Brother to take care of you and protect you from danger, he has to regulate every aspect of your life.[2] Most modern philosophers advocate political systems that are somewhere in the mean between these two extremes, though all argue that we should err toward one side or the other. For example, Niccolò Machiavelli and Thomas Hobbes advocate governments in which an absolute monarch has the power to do anything that he deems appropriate to maintain a secure state.[3] In contrast, John Locke, Jean-Jacques Rousseau, and John Stuart Mill support social contracts that emphasize the freedom of their citizens.[4]

Mill offers the most famous treatment of this tension in *On Liberty*. He is the first to formally articulate the idea that politics is a struggle between liberty (maximizing personal freedom) and authority (maximizing safety). Mill argues that although security is important, we must err on the side of liberty:

> The object of this Essay is to assert one very simple principle, as entitled to govern absolutely the dealings of society with the individual in the way of compulsion and control, whether the means used be physical force in the form of legal penalties, or the moral coercion of public opinion. That principle is, that the sole end for which mankind are warranted, individually or collectively, in interfering with the liberty of action of any of their number, is self-protection. That the only purpose for which power can be rightfully exercised over any member of a civilized community, against his will, is to prevent harm to others. His own good, either physical or moral, is not a sufficient warrant. He cannot rightfully be compelled to do or forbear because it will be better for him to do so, because it will make him happier, because, in the opinions of others, to do so would be wise, or even right.[5]

This idea has come to be known as the "harm principle." Liberty to pursue one's own happiness is a fundamental good for all human beings because it allows us the possibility of actualizing higher pleasures for the goal of personal development. Thus, the government should infringe upon liberty only insofar as the exercise of a citizen's liberty harms (or threatens to harm) other persons. For example, it is wrong for the government to ban the consumption of alcoholic beverages, which might harm an individual's health, but it is permissible to prohibit drunken driving, which is likely to harm other people.[6] It is not permissible to prohibit free speech, but it is permissible to ban slander/libel or direct threats. While we might wish to counsel misguided individuals who are hurting themselves, we cannot reasonably ban these activities (e.g., I might try to talk a friend into quitting smoking, but the government should not make cigarettes illegal). It is also important to note that "harm" is not the same as "offense"; just because one disagrees with a way of life does not mean one is actually hurt by it.[7] For example, a religious fundamentalist might be offended by gay marriage, but he is not actually harmed by it, so it should not be banned.

Mill's harm principle stands in opposition to *paternalism*, which is the view that the state is justified in interfering with citizens' liberty for their *own* good. Possible examples of paternalism include prohibitions against sexual conduct between consenting adults, antidrug laws (where the drugs might hurt the user but do not lead to antisocial conduct), motorcycle helmet laws, requiring lifeguards for swimming, and criminalizing suicide (to name but a few). Mill condemns paternalism for two reasons. First, politicians are likely to abuse their power to restrict the liberty of citizens to promote their own interests and values. Second, well-intentioned leaders might misidentify the good of citizens who are more capable of determining their own good than the politicians are. The only paternalistic activity that Mill permits is an outright ban on individuals' ability to sell themselves into slavery. This is justified because it enhances autonomy rather than restricting it.[8] There are only a few cases in which paternalism is appropriate: the harm principle does not apply to legally incompetent individuals such as children or people with mental problems because they cannot give voluntary informed consent.

Mill endorses three types of liberty: (1) liberties of conscience and expression (e.g., freedom of religion and speech), (2) liberties of tastes, pursuits, and life plans (e.g., free choice of career, hobbies, or spouse), and (3) liberties of association (e.g., membership in political groups). For Mill, these liberties are essential for deliberating about one's ideals and forming a plan of action to promote them. Interfering with these liberties restricts one's ability to become the kind of person one wants to be.[9] The only time the government is justified in limiting these liberties is when one threatens to harm another person. Take the example of free speech. People's opinions are either good or bad. If they are good and we censor them, we will not benefit from their wisdom; if they are bad and we censor them, we will not get them out in the open where they can be clearly refuted. Many ideas that we take for granted these days—like liberal democracy or evolution—were considered crazy when they were first presented but have stood up to extended intellectual scrutiny. Other ideas such as racism and misogyny are dying a slow death because they are grounded in fallacious reasoning. Thus, it is in the long-term interest of society to promote free speech because it facilitates our intellectual and political progress.

Mill believes politics is the reconciliation of the tension between liberty and security. The harm principle allows us to adjudicate disputes between these two values and encourages us to err on the side of liberty so that we can avoid the pitfalls of a government that would exert paternalistic control over our lives.

Negative and Positive Liberty and Security

While Mill's harm principle is useful for reconciling the tension between liberty and security, the definitions of the terms "liberty" and "security" have come under close scrutiny since the mid-twentieth century. Some scholars argue that the classical conception of these values leads to problems when it comes to sacrificing liberty for enhanced security. For example, in the wake of the September 11 terrorist attacks on the United States, legislation such as the USA PATRIOT Act was passed that limits civil liberties with the goal of enhancing the government's ability to fight terrorism and thereby promote security.[10] David Luban criticizes this line of thinking:

> How much liberty should be sacrificed for security? I began by saying that this is the wrong question, because it rests on mistaken assumptions. Once we take care *not* to suppose that it is somebody else's liberty that will be sacrificed, nor to suppose that only the rights of the guilty and the terrorists are in jeopardy, nor that pro-security is the tough-minded, pragmatic answer, nor that these are military issues best left to the executive, nor that they are merely short-term emergency measures, the question takes a different form. It becomes something like this: *How much of your own protection against bureaucratic errors or malice by the government—errors or malice that could land you in jail—are you willing to sacrifice in return for minute increments in security?* This, it seems to me, is not an easy question to answer, but the most plausible answer is "not much"; and "none" seems like a reasonable place to start.[11]

Luban argues that this false dichotomy between liberty and security is not useful for dealing with practical issues such as our response to the threat of terrorism. The more we sacrifice civil liberties to ostensibly promote security, the more we degrade the quality of our existence and the legitimacy of our social contract.

Jeremy Waldron refers to the so-called tension between liberty and security as the "balance problem":

> A common suggestion invites us to think about this in terms of the idea of *balance*. According to this suggestion, it is *always* necessary—even in normal circumstances—to balance liberty against security. We always have to strike a balance between the individual's liberty to do as he pleases and society's need for protection against the harm that may accrue from some of the things it might please an individual to do. The former surely cannot be comprehensive even under the most favorable circumstances—nobody argues for anarchy—and the latter has to be given some weight in determining how much liberty people should have. So there is always a balance to be struck. And—the suggestion continues—that balance is

bound to change (and it is appropriate that it should change) as the threat to security becomes graver or more imminent.[12]

Waldron rejects the balancing approach to liberty and security for four reasons. First, it relies upon a purely consequentialist framework that is of limited use when discussing civil liberties. Second, it ignores the fact that the restriction of liberties might affect some people more than others. Third, it depends upon a purely *negative* conception of liberty and thus might have unintended consequences for the overall security of the state. Fourth, it often leads to measures that provide only symbolic enhancement of security without actually promoting security.[13]

Thus, while the classic tension between liberty and security is useful for analyzing some political issues, it is of limited value because it overlooks some of the key components of what it means to be both free and secure. As a result, some scholars have expanded the definitions of liberty and security in an attempt to circumvent these problems.

Negative and Positive Liberty

The classical conception of the tension between liberty and security is problematic because it hinges upon limited definitions of these terms. According to Isaiah Berlin, there is not one concept of freedom but two: negative liberty and positive liberty:

> The first of these political senses of freedom or liberty (I shall use both words to mean the same), which (following much precedent) I shall call the "negative" sense, is involved in the answer to the question "What is the area within which the subject—a person or group of persons—is or should be left to do or be what he is able to do or be, without interference by other persons?" The second, which I shall call the "positive" sense, is involved in the answer to the question "What, or who, is the source of control or interference that can determine someone to do, or be, this rather than that?" The two questions are clearly different, even though the answers to them may overlap.[14]

Negative liberty is "freedom *from*" constraints imposed by other people, while positive liberty is the "freedom *to*" pursue one's goals and live life independently. The first conception is *negative* because it indicates the *absence* of something (interference), while the second is *positive* because it describes the *presence* of something (self-realization).[15] Negative liberty is typically associated with civil liberties, while positive liberty relates to the capacity for autonomy (self-rule).[16] It is not enough that I live life without interference; I must also be able to cultivate myself so that I can actualize my life plan.[17]

Berlin is concerned with the way that positive liberty has traditionally been employed by authoritarian governments to enforce particular ways of life.[18] For example, fascist or theocratic governments typically force their citizens to cultivate themselves according to specific ideologies not freely endorsed by all citizens. However, positive liberty is not necessarily oppressive; a just government "should aim actively to create the conditions necessary for individuals to be self-sufficient or to achieve self-realization."[19] Such personal growth is not directly promoted by negative liberty, which is merely the absence of constraints, so some level of positive liberty is necessary in a just society. Yet how can we have positive liberty without authoritarianism?

In his final essay, "The First and the Last," Berlin argues in favor of moral pluralism, which is opposed to the monistic values of authoritarian regimes:

> There is a plurality of ideals, as there is a plurality of cultures and of temperaments. I am not a relativist; I do not say "I like my coffee with milk and you like it without; I am in favor of kindness and you prefer concentration camps"—each of us with his own values, which cannot be overcome or integrated. This I believe to be false. But I do believe that there is a plurality of values which men can and do seek, and that these values differ. There is not an infinity of them: the number of human values, of values that I can pursue while maintaining my human semblance, my human character, is finite—let us say 74, or perhaps 122, or 26, but finite, whatever it may be. And the difference it makes is that if a man pursues one of these values, I, who do not, am able to understand why he pursues it or what it would be like, in his circumstances, for me to be induced to pursue it. Hence the possibility of human understanding.[20]

There are a finite number of objectively valid human values that constitute appropriate ways of thinking and acting. They are objective in the Aristotelian sense: they are a "part of what it is to be a human being . . . , part of the essence of humanity rather than arbitrary creations of men's subjective fancies,"[21] and the promotion of these values helps to make us human beings in the fullest sense. Those values that are not characteristic of human beings—such as those that support murder, rape, violating contracts, and perjury—can be condemned, and thus relativism is not valid. Imaginative people are capable of thinking outside of their own sets of values to appreciate the validity of other people's ways of thinking, but this does not mean that all other ways of thinking are correct.

The advantage of this type of pluralism over absolutism or relativism is that it allows us to engage is a productive ethical dialogue with other people or cultures. Monism demands that all approaches to ethics other than our own must be condemned as immoral and that we have a duty to reeducate the ignorant and convert them to our way of thinking. Relativism asserts that no dialogue is possible at all; no matter how offended I might be by your values, there is nothing meaningful that I can say to convince you that they are wrong. Pluralism allows for the possibility that there might be multiple right ways of thinking about ethics.

But on what basis are we to make this kind of decision? There must be a set of criteria that will allow us to confirm the validity of some moral philosophies while rejecting others. Eliot Deutsch argues that dialogue with another tradition is a process of trying to comprehend that tradition in its own terms.[22] He suggests criteria through which a dynamic pluralism might be founded through the elimination of invalid philosophies.[23] He argues that there are exclusionary principles that apply to morality such that we can exclude certain acts as fundamentally immoral. Deutsch draws a distinction between two kinds of exclusionary principles. The first are *foundational* exclusionary principles, which, when followed, wholly prevent an immoral way of thinking from engaging in ethical discourse. Any ethics that endorse acts "of exploitation, of oppression and senseless violence are ruled out of possessing intrinsic moral value" because they are incompatible with values such as personhood and freedom that are necessary foundations for any moral philosophy.[24] The second type of exclusionary principle is *operational*: these principles define what constitutes sound reasoning within a particular context. To be a member of a *particular* moral community, one must follow that community's rules for moral inquiry and practice, rules that are delineated by operational exclusionary principles.[25] For example, a Buddhist monk might completely abstain from alcohol and violence to be part of the *sangha* (monastic community), but non-Buddhists would have no obligation to follow suit.

Exclusionary principles lead to a dynamic pluralism in which fundamentally immoral ways of thinking are rejected, and yet multiple, morally appropriate philosophies can participate in a constructive dialogue with one another.[26] They allow us to explore a creative pluralism of virtues without the danger of sliding into relativism. The relativist assertion that a dynamic pluralism is impossible because all critiques are made on the basis of one's own culturally embedded concept of truth is refuted by the notion of generalizable exclusionary principles that can be used as a basis for constructive dialogue between traditions.[27] Exclusionary principles allow us to enter into discourse, but do not suggest that there is only *one* right way to approach a particular moral problem.

Both negative and positive liberty are important for human flourishing. Negative liberty promotes civil liberties, while positive liberty promotes personal growth. Pluralism is essential to prevent positive liberty from becoming oppressive. Each citizen must be free to pursue his or her own conception of the good life so long as he or she does not harm others, and the state should promote this cultivation. It is not enough for the state to simply prevent harm; it must facilitate a positive good as well.

Negative and Positive Security

While a great deal has been written about negative and positive liberty, academic literature about negative and positive conceptions of security has developed more recently with the advent of the field of security studies. Paul D. Williams defines "security" as "an alleviation of threats to cherished values."[28] Security is not synonymous with survival: "Whereas survival is an existential condition, security involves the ability to pursue cherished political and social ambitions."[29] There are two philosophies of security. The first views security as the "accumulation of power" whereby the amassing of political, economic, and military strength makes people more secure.[30] The second view is "based on emancipation, that is, a concern with justice and the provision of human rights."[31] Whereas the former philosophy considers security as a commodity, the latter views it as a relationship between agents. Thus, as with liberty, security can be either negative (the absence of threats) or positive (making things possible). Proponents of the negative view try to amass money, power, and weapons to gain dominance over others, while those who endorse the positive view try to cooperate to "achieve security without depriving others of it."[32]

Rhonda Powell argues that while there has been a great deal of debate about how to reconcile liberty and security, most scholars do not adequately define what is meant by security.[33] She defines security as a relational concept that includes the following questions: security *for whom*, security *of what*, security *against what*, and security *by whom*. Without knowing the agent, the values/ interests being secured, the specific threats/risks, and the provider of security, we cannot adequately address this issue.[34] Powell argues that security is a relational concept that is radically contextualized and includes both negative and positive notions of security.[35] Negative security is the idea that we are secure if something *does not* happen to us. We are secure insofar as we are protected from threats. Positive security goes beyond mere protection to include a concept of *provision*. It deals more with what we do than what we are and is thus more related to the verb "to secure" than to the adjective "secure." Positive security focuses on the type of world we need to create to secure our interests and values. This parallels the distinction between negative and positive liberty. Negative liberty deals with *freedom from* interference, while positive liberty deals with *freedom to* pursue one's goals.[36] The negative and positive aspects of security indicate that it is a social concept that cannot be divorced from our sense of community. Powell argues that "if one's political theory aims to increase the well-being of individuals rather than preserve the status quo, the policies of security will need to include duties of facilitation or provision."[37] Politics is a matter of helping citizens both to survive and to thrive.

The term "secure" actually has two sets of meanings. As an adjective, "secure" can mean "safe" ("not subject to threats of harm") or "confident" ("a vivid consciousness of one's own dignity and worth").[38] As a verb, "secure" can mean "to make safe" and "to protect against threats," or it can mean "to succeed in attaining something." The former uses are negative, while the latter is positive. Negative security is related to "power," while positive security is related to "empowerment." Williams describes the difference between advocates of negative and positive views of security: "In practice, the differences are often stark with advocates of the former philosophy prioritizing military strength while supporters of the latter emphasize the importance of promoting justice and human rights."[39] These two understandings of security are not necessarily incompatible, but they deal with different relevant aspects of the issue.

Positive security addresses a different set of concerns than its negative counterpart. Mikkel Vedby Rasmussen argues:

> Positive security was a means to achieve peace by overcoming vulnerabilities. Where negative security focused on preventing, positive security focused on planning in the belief that threats were ascertainable and defeatable if only one were able to mobilise the political and/or military resources necessary to defeat them. The consequence was that security came to signify a new range of threats. When security was constructed in terms of dangers, threats were constituted by military threats—either directly by means of an attack or indirectly by means of alliance formation—because only they represented an immediate danger. But as positive epistemology made it the *raison d'être* of politics to overcome social ills and such, the means of strategy became employed against embryonic threats. When the government believed in the possibility of overcoming threats, it was the government's duty to attempt to eliminate them as soon as possible.[40]

This positive conception of security is often associated with the peaceful prevention of violence. The central concern of peace studies is the resolution of violent conflict via peaceful means, which promotes the reduction and eventual elimination of warfare.[41] Enlightenment philosophers such as Rousseau and Kant argue that war is irrational because it inhibits human progress.[42] Building upon this tradition, Johan Galtung develops both positive and negative concepts of peace. Peace involves both the absence or reduction of violence (negative peace) and the "integration of human society" and "human fulfilment" (positive peace).[43] Peace is possible because human beings "display a capacity for mutual empathy and solidarity" and consider themselves to be members of groups "where a norm of reciprocity is valid and cooperation a dominant mode of interaction."[44] Galtung observes that in warfare humans rarely use every available tool of destruction to the fullest extent. War contains certain limitations and rules that resemble elements of a game.[45]

Thus, like liberty, security has both positive and negative formulations, both of which articulate important concepts for political theory. What is needed is a new way to reconcile the tension between these positive and negative conceptions of liberty and security.

Reconciling Negative and Positive Liberty and Security

The addition of positive conceptions of liberty and security to the discussion demands a new framework to resolve the tensions between these concepts and their negative counterparts. Algirdas Julien Greimas was a leading theorist in semiotics, a field that studies the use and interpretation of signs and symbols. He developed the semiotic square—which is often called the Greimas square in his honor—as a tool for analyzing the creative tension between the meanings of words. Greimas was inspired by Aristotle's square of opposition, so the semiotic square bears some resemblance to the tool used in logic to explain the relationship between A, E, I, and O sentences. The semiotic square acknowledges that there is an ambiguity between so-called opposites in language. A Greimas square is generated by first naming a term, S_1, and its opposite, S_2 (see figure 2).

S_1 and S_2 are complex contraries: both cannot be wholly true at the same time. Each of these terms generates a contradictory term in the opposite bottom corner, $\sim S_1$ and $\sim S_2$, which exist in a neutral contrary relationship with each other (something *can* be properly described by both at the same time). Each side of the square indicates a relationship of implication (which moves in the opposite direction from Aristotle's logical concept of implication): $\sim S_2$ implies S_1, while $\sim S_1$ implies S_2. The four sides of the square generate new meta-terms based upon the relationship between the terms in each corner. Though there are theoretical terms for the diagonal relationships, it is virtually impossible to generate words that correspond to these because they are contradictions.[46]

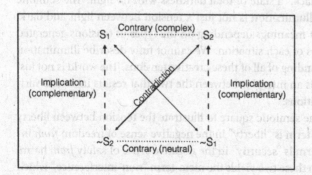

Figure 2. Greimas's semiotic square.

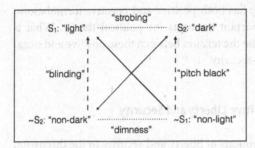

Figure 3. Semiotic square for illumination.

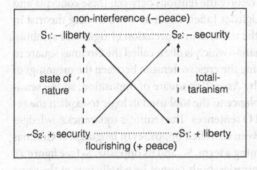

Figure 4. Semiotic square for liberty and security.

Figure 3 uses the semiotic square to illustrate the tension between "light" and "dark." "Light," the S_1 term, exists in a creative tension with "dark," the S_2 term. The opposite of light is "non-light" ($\sim S_1$), while the opposite of dark is "non-dark" ($\sim S_2$). The neutral term generated by the creative tension between "non-light" and "non-dark" is "dimness," a condition in which it is neither wholly light nor wholly dark. The complex term generated on the top of the square by the contrary relationship between "light" and "dark" is "strobing," a condition in which the ambient light is rapidly alternating between two opposites. On the left side of the square is the meta-term "blinding," a condition in which there is excessive light and no darkness. On the right side is the meta-term "pitch black," a state of total darkness with no light. The semiotic square shows that illumination is not just a tension between light and dark; it has a full range of meanings depending on the types of tensions generated by the particularities of each situation. We cannot fully describe illumination without an understanding of all of these creative tensions. The world is not just light or dark; there is an interplay between the two that results in a wide variety of lighting conditions.

Figure 4 uses the semiotic square to illustrate the tension between liberty and security. The S_1 term is "liberty" in the negative sense of freedom *from* interference. The S_2 term is "security" in the negative sense of safety *from* harm. The tension between these two yields the meta-term "non-interference," which relates to the concept of "negative peace" discussed above: violence is reduced via the limitation of liberty. The $\sim S_1$ term is "positive liberty," which refers to the freedom *to* actualize one's life plan.[47] The $\sim S_2$ term is "positive security," or the idea that one is safe *to* pursue one's interests and values. Together, $\sim S_1$ and $\sim S_2$ generate the meta-term "flourishing," which corresponds to Galtung's notion of positive peace as human fulfillment via the integration of human society. Positive liberty and positive security are neutral contraries: both can be true at the same time but not false at the same time. The promotion of positive liberty necessarily entails the promotion of positive security and vice versa. Two other meta-terms are generated on the left and right sides of the square. If we have positive security and negative liberty, we have what Enlightenment thinkers refer to as a "state of nature" in which there is no social contract: one is completely unrestricted and thus capable of doing whatever one likes to pursue one's own interests.[48] If we have negative security and positive liberty, we have the totalitarian state that Berlin criticizes: one might be safe from harm, but one is obligated to actualize only the life plan endorsed by the state.

Appropriate lawmaking observes the creative tension between the two types of liberty and security. Lawmakers who focus only on negative conceptions of liberty and security will emphasize non-interference while ignoring the importance of human flourishing. For example, the contentious issue of gun control tends to focus on the tension between negative liberty (freedom to own guns) and negative security (safety from violent criminals).[49] As a result, the gun control debate focuses on who should have access to firearms and what types of firearms should be legal to own. When there is a mass shooting, gun control activists ask for more restrictions on firearms, while gun rights activists resist attempts to limit citizens' access to weapons. Focusing on only this aspect of the debate causes us to overlook the more relevant issue: *why are people in American society inclined to use firearms to commit violent felonies?* The gun is just a delivery mechanism for the violence (as is a knife, club, or fist), so while reasonable firearms regulations might help to reduce gun violence to some extent, they will not eliminate all violence in society unless they are coupled with measures that address more fundamental concerns. One of the primary causes of violence is poverty, which leads to the absence of positive liberty and positive security.

Poverty is an important issue for security studies because "poverty and human insecurity are in many respects synonymous."[50] The poor suffer from a lack of positive security and positive liberty: without adequate food, water, housing, health care, education, employment, public safety, and political representation, one cannot actualize one's life plan.[51] Those who lack the opportunity to elevate themselves by legal means often turn to crime and violence.[52] This is exacerbated by American gun culture and the wide availability of firearms, but the root cause is poverty itself.[53] To put it in Rawlsian terms, the poor lack the "primary goods" necessary to lead a good life. A just society should give citizens equal access to basic liberties and provide the primary goods one needs to compete fairly in a free market.[54] Countries that have excellent social support networks for their citizens tend to have low incidences of violence regardless of their gun laws, while those that do not provide equal opportunity for their people tend to have a great deal of violence even though guns might be banned.[55] This is not an argument that we should or should not restrict the sale, ownership, or concealed carry of firearms. Rather, it is an argument that such restrictions often overlook a more fundamental issue that is a critical part of the debate.

Just as poverty promotes conflict, conflict can promote poverty in the following ways: depletion of a productive workforce, destruction of infrastructure (physical and social), destruction of agriculture, disruption of markets, diversion of children into the military, increased cultural acceptance of violence in urban areas, decline in economic growth and exports, rising government military expenditure, and a negative effect on national growth (which bleeds over into neighboring states). Poverty and violence are thus a kind of a feedback loop: poverty promotes violence, which in turn promotes poverty. A decrease in poverty leads to an increase in human security. Governments should view poverty and violence as fundamentally interrelated issues. Solving one helps to solve the other.[56] If we seek to promote positive liberty and security by empowering citizens to actualize their life plans, we can remove the environment of desperation that promotes violent conflict. The sensible regulation of firearms is an important part of this debate, but it deals with only the negative notions of liberty and security. The more fundamental question is one of equal opportunity, and thus we must also concern ourselves with positive conceptions of liberty and security.

Online privacy represents another arena of contemporary ethical and political debate in which there is tension between liberty and security.[57] Advances in technology have made it possible for governments and corporations to collect, store, and search massive quantities of information about individual citizens.[58] These "big data" can be used to exploit individuals in a variety of ways. Cookies are used to track online activity, often across multiple websites.[59] Social media sites collect personal information about their users and encourage them to exchange these data for the benefits of using the service. Big data are typically used for "surveillance capitalism," whereby corporations create user profiles for targeted advertising, but many of these data, such as religion, sexual preference, medical issues, financial information, political affiliation, or genetic/genomic data, include sensitive information that could be exploited either by the businesses themselves or by third parties.[60] Mobile devices contain microphones, cameras, and GPS (and, in the case of smartwatches, health data sensors) and can record and transmit sensitive data, often without the user's awareness or consent.[61] There are also increasing risks associated with e-government, including direct tampering with electronic ballots and misinformation campaigns using social media (like the ones that took place during the 2016 elections).[62] Law enforcement and intelligence services have increasingly used big data and electronic surveillance systems to monitor citizens.[63] All of these risks threaten both the liberty and the security of online users.

Political debate about big data issues tends to focus on the tension between negative and positive liberty whereby citizens are expected to sacrifice some degree of privacy in exchange for the conveniences provided by the Internet. This is a legitimate part of the debate because laws need to be in place to regulate activities like hacking, cyberbullying, election tampering, intellectual property violations, and blackmail. We need to be both free from interference and safe from harm, which is why many software and hardware designers now practice "value sensitive design" that respects ethical principles such as privacy.[64] However, negative approaches tend to be restrictive and reactive rather than empowering and proactive. There also needs to be an emphasis on positive liberty (the freedom to use information technology to promote one's own good and that of society and security) and positive security (being safe to attain one's goals). Privacy promotes positive liberty and security because (1) it facilitates interpersonal relationships with family, friends, and business associates, (2) it allows activists and workers to fight for justice without fear of reprisal, and (3) it helps journalists to investigate controversial stories and academics to perform cutting-edge research without interference. The unrestricted use of big data by corporations and governments threatens to undermine the privacy needed by citizens to actualize their life goals. A related issue has to do with the growing "digital divide" between the financially well-off, who have access to technology and proper training on how to use it, and the poor, who have neither. In the twenty-first century, it is increasingly difficult to actualize one's life plan without access to technology, so positive liberty and security demand that the digital divide be narrowed.

Conclusion

This chapter has explored a classic theme in political philosophy: the tension between liberty and security. This was a central issue for modern political philosophy, culminating in John Stuart Mill's classic text *On Liberty*. However, debate about this issue since the mid-twentieth century has raised some critical challenges for the classic conception by reframing the semantic structure on which it is grounded. Because there are both negative and positive notions of liberty and security, political debates cannot be resolved through an appeal to the classic tension that Mill articulates. Greimas's semiotic squares help to re-conceptualize liberty and security as positive, complementary notions that are not necessarily at odds with one another. Solutions to political debates need to take into account both negative and positive conceptions of liberty and security. It is not enough to simply keep citizens free from interference and safe from harm; we must also liberate and empower them to lead flourishing lives.

Notes

1. See especially chap. 13 of Thomas Hobbes, *Leviathan* (New York: Penguin, 1985). Other Enlightenment thinkers offer different conceptions of the state of nature (in which life is not quite as nasty, brutish, and short), but all share a common theme: total liberty is possible only when there is not government.

2. George Orwell, *Animal Farm* and *1984* (Orlando, Fla.: Harcourt, 2003).

3. Niccolò Machiavelli, *The Prince* and *Discourses*, in *Modern Political Thought: Readings from Machiavelli to Nietzsche*, ed. David Wootton (Indianapolis: Hackett, 2008), 9–88. In his *Discourses*, Machiavelli lauds the virtues of a democratic repub-lic, but such freedom is possible only once a secure state has been established. See also John Langton and Mary G. Dietz, "Machiavelli's Paradox: Trapping or Teaching the Prince," *American Political Science Review* 81, no. 4 (1987): 1277–88, doi:10.2307/1962589.

4. John Locke, *Second Treatise of Government*, in Wootton, *Modern Political Thought*, 285–353; Jean-Jacques Rousseau, *On the Social Contract*, in Wootton, *Modern Political Thought*, 427–87; John Stuart Mill, *On Liberty* (New York: Bantam Books, 1993).

5. Mill, *On Liberty*, 12.

6. Mill did not live to see the passage of the Eighteenth Amendment to the U.S. Constitution and its subsequent repeal via the Twenty-First Amendment after the trib-ulations of the Roaring Twenties.

7. Mill, *On Liberty*, 108–9. See also David Brink, "Mill's Moral and Political Philoso-phy," in *Stanford Encyclopedia of Philosophy*, August 21, 2018, §3.8, https://plato.stanford.edu/archives/win2018/entries/mill-moral-political/.

8. Mill, *On Liberty*, 133. See also Brink, "Mill's Moral and Political Philosophy," §3.6.

9. Brink, "Mill's Moral and Political Philosophy," §3.5.

10. Robert P. Abele, *A User's Guide to the USA Patriot Act and Beyond* (Lanham, Md.: University Press of America, 2005). See also Ronald Dworkin, "The Threat to Pa-triotism," *New York Review of Books*, February 28, 2002, www.nybooks.com/articles/2002/02/28/the-threat-to-patriotism/.

11. David Luban, "Eight Fallacies about Liberty and Security," in *Human Rights in the War on Terror*, ed. Richard Wilson (New York: Cambridge University Press, 2006), 242–57, 256.

12. Jeremy Waldron, "Security and Liberty: The Image of Balance," *Journal of Politi-cal Philosophy* 11, no. 2 (2003): 192.

13. Ibid., 194–95.

14. Isaiah Berlin, "Two Concepts of Liberty," in *Four Essays on Liberty* (New York: Oxford University Press, 1969), 2.

15. Ian Carter, "Positive and Negative Liberty," in *Stanford Encyclopedia of Philosophy*, Spring 2016 ed., ed. Edward N. Zalta, https://plato.stanford.edu/archives/win2019/entries/liberty-positive-negative/.

16. Berlin, "Two Concepts of Liberty," 2. See also Joshua Cherniss and Henry Hardy, "Isaiah Berlin," in *Stanford Encyclopedia of Philosophy*, Fall 2016 ed., https://plato.stanford.edu/archives/fall2016/entries/berlin/.

17. Berlin, "Two Concepts of Liberty," 2–8. See also Carter, "Positive and Negative Liberty."

18. Berlin, "Two Concepts of Liberty," 2–8, 16, 20, 31. See also Cherniss and Hardy, "Isaiah Berlin."

19. Carter, "Positive and Negative Liberty." See also Berlin, "Two Concepts of Liberty," 16.

20. Isaiah Berlin, "The First and the Last," *New York Review of Books* 45, no. 8 (February 2005): 52–60, http://www.cs.utexas.edu/users/vl/notes/berlin.html.

21. Berlin, "The First and the Last."

22. Eliot Deutsch, "Rationality and Traditions," in *The Empirical and the Transcendental: A Fusion of Horizons*, ed. Bina Gupta (Lanham, Md.: Rowman & Littlefield, 2000), 242–43.

23. Ibid., 245.

24. Eliot Deutsch, *Creative Being: The Crafting of Person and World* (Honolulu: University of Hawaii Press, 1992), 180.

25. Ibid., 182–89. Also see Deutsch, "Rationality and Traditions," 246–47.

26. Deutsch, "Rationality and Tradition," 248. Also see Deutsch, *Creative Being*, 181–82.

27. Deutsch, "Rationality and Tradition," 249.

28. Paul D. Williams, "Security Studies: An Introduction," in *Security Studies: An Introduction*, 2nd ed., ed. Paul D. Williams (New York: Routledge, 2013), 1, 6.

29. Ibid., 6.

30. Ibid., 6.

31. Ibid., 6.

32. Ibid., 6–7. Williams identifies these contrasting views with the distinction between "freedom from" and "freedom to" (though this is problematic because these concepts are related more to negative and positive conceptions of *liberty* than they are to security).

33. Rhonda Powell, "The Concept of Security," *Oxford Socio-Legal Review* 0, no. 1 (2012): 1–29.

34. Ibid., 5.

35. Ibid., 6.

36. Ibid., 20–23.

37. Ibid., 25.

38. This phrase is borrowed from Nitobe Inazō, who describes the virtue of honor as "a vivid consciousness of personal dignity and worth" in his book, *Bushido: The Soul of Japan* (Rutland, Vt.: Tuttle, 1969), 72.

39. Williams, "Security Studies," 7.

40. Mikkel Vedby Rasmussen, *The West, Civil Society and the Construction of Peace* (New York: Palgrave Macmillan, 2003), 120.

41. Peter Lawler, "Peace Studies," in Williams, *Security Studies*, 77–89.

42. Ibid., 81.

43. Ibid., 82–85, 88.

44. Ibid., 85–86.

45. Ibid., 86. Robert Wright makes a similar point in *Nonzero: The Logic of Human Destiny* (New York: Vintage, 2000). Human evolution has encouraged the formation of non-zero-sum relationships in which people cooperate for mutual benefit. War forces community members to unite against a common enemy and develop creative solutions to their predicament. See also James McRae, "From *Kyōsei* to *Kyōei*: Symbiotic Flourishing in Japanese Environmental Ethics," in *Japanese Environmental Philosophy*, ed. J. Baird Callicott and James McRae (New York: Oxford University Press, 2017), 47–63.

46. Algirdas Julien Greimas, *On Meaning: Selected Writings in Semiotic Theory* (Minneapolis: University of Minnesota Press, 1976). I am indebted to my colleague, Steve Bein, for educating me about the way that Greimas squares can be applied to resolving creative tensions in applied ethics. See Steve Bein, "Climate Change as Existentialist Threat: Watsuji, Greimas, and the Nature of Opposites," in Callicott and McRae, *Japanese Environmental Philosophy*, 105–20.

47. It might seem strange that positive liberty is the $\sim S_1$ term while negative liberty is the S_1 term. Keep in mind that in logic, the rule of double negation says that $\sim\sim P$ is logically equivalent to P. Thus, the negation of negative liberty is positive liberty.

48. It should be noted that Locke and Rousseau disagree with Hobbes about the state of nature. While Hobbes characterizes life in the state of nature as "solitary, poor, nasty, brutish, and short," Locke and Rousseau depict life without a social contract as a situation in which human beings are willing to cooperate for mutual benefit. When I use the term "state of nature" here, I am simply referring to a situation in which there is no government at all.

49. This paper does not attempt to resolve the issue of gun control or advocate a particular position on the issue. There is simply not room to do so within the confines of this chapter. The point here is that both sides of the debate tend to focus only on negative conceptions of liberty and security but should also consider positive liberty and security as important parts of the solution.

50. Caroline Thomas and Paul D. Williams, "Poverty," in Williams, *Security Studies*, 295–310.

51. Ibid., 295.

52. Ibid., 305.

53. Ibid., 299–302.

54. John Rawls, *A Theory of Justice* (Cambridge, Mass.: Harvard University Press, 1972). See also John Rawls, *Justice as Fairness: A Restatement* (Cambridge, Mass.: Harvard University Press, 2003).

55. John R. Lott, *More Guns, Less Crime: Understanding Crime and Gun-Control Laws* (Chicago: University of Chicago Press, 2010). See also Charles F. Wellford, John Pepper, and Carol Petrie, *Firearms and Violence: A Critical Review* (Washington, D.C.: National Academies Press, 2005). See also the Center for Disease Control's report "Ele-

vated Rates of Urban Firearm Violence and Opportunities for Prevention" (November 3, 2015), http://www.documentcloud.org/documents/ 2501613-cdc-delaware-final -report-110315.html.

56. Thomas and Williams, "Poverty," 300–307. See also James McRae, "Triple-Negation: Watsuji Tetsurō on the Sustainability of Ecosystems, Economies, and International Peace," in *Value and Values: Economics and Justice in an Age of Global Interdependence*, ed. Roger T. Ames and Peter Hershock (Honolulu: University of Hawaii Press, 2015), 68–81.

57. I am indebted to one of the reviewers of this volume for the suggestion to include ethical issues associated with big data in this chapter. There is not space here to give a thorough exposition of this topic, though I treat it briefly to show how the notions of positive liberty and security can shed some light on this important ethical and political issue.

58. Shoshana Zuboff, *The Age of Surveillance Capitalism: The Fight for the Future at the New Frontier of Power* (London: Profile Books, 2019).

59. Daniel E. Palmer, "Pop-Ups, Cookies, and Spam: Toward a Deeper Analysis of the Ethical Significance of Internet Marketing Practices," *Journal of Business Ethics* 58, nos. 1–3 (2005): 271–80.

60. Zuboff discusses this at length in *The Age of Surveillance Capitalism*. See also Linnet Taylor, Luciano Floridi, and Bart Van der Sloot, eds., *Group Privacy: New Challenges of Data Technologies* (New York: Springer, 2017).

61. Ovidiu Vermesan and Peter Friess, *Internet of Things: Converging Technologies for Smart Environments and Integrated Ecosystems* (Aalborg, Denmark: River, 2013), 67–69 and 207.

62. Jonathan Albright, "How Trump's Campaign Used the New Data-Industrial Complex to Win the Election," LSE USAPP American Politics and Policy Blog, https:// blogs.lse.ac.uk/usappblog/2016/11/26/how-trumps-campaign-used-the-new-data -industrial-complex-to-win-the-election/, cited in Jeroen van den Hoven, Martijn Blaauw, Wolter Pieters, and Martijn Warnier, "Privacy and Information Technology," in *The Stanford Encyclopedia of Philosophy*, Summer 2020 ed., ed. Edward N. Zalta, https://plato.stanford.edu/archives/sum2020/entries/it-privacy/.

63. Andrew G. Ferguson, *The Rise of Big Data Policing: Surveillance, Race, and the Future of Law Enforcement* (New York: New York University Press, 2020).

64. Batya Friedman and David G. Hendry, *Value Sensitive Design: Shaping Technology with Moral Imagination* (Cambridge, Mass.: MIT Press, 2019).

A Renewal of American Purpose

U.S. Senator **Bernie Sanders**

Let me begin by thanking Westminster College, which year after year invites political leaders to discuss the important issue of foreign policy and America's role in the world. I am honored to be here today, and I thank you very much for the invitation.

One of the reasons I accepted the invitation to speak here is that I strongly believe that not only do we need to begin a more vigorous debate about foreign policy, we also need to broaden our understanding of what foreign policy is.

Foreign Policy: Hard and Soft Power

So let me be clear: Foreign policy is directly related to military policy and has everything to do with almost seven thousand young Americans being killed in Iraq and Afghanistan, and tens of thousands coming home wounded in body and spirit from a war we should never have started. That's foreign policy. And foreign policy is about hundreds of thousands of people in Iraq and Afghanistan dying in that same war.

Foreign policy is about U.S. government budget priorities. At a time when we already spend more on defense than the next twelve nations combined, foreign policy is about authorizing a defense budget of some seven hundred billion dollars, including a fifty-billion-dollar increase passed just last week.

Meanwhile, at the exact same time as the president and many of my Republican colleagues want to substantially increase military spending, they want to throw thirty-two million Americans off of the health insurance they currently have because, supposedly, they are worried about the budget deficit. While greatly increasing military spending they also want to cut education, environmental protection, and the needs of children and seniors.

Foreign policy, therefore, is remembering what Dwight D. Eisenhower said as he left office: "In the councils of government, we must guard against the acquisition of unwarranted influence, whether sought or unsought, by the military-industrial complex. The potential for the disastrous rise of misplaced power exists and will persist." And he also reminded us that

> every gun that is made, every warship launched, every rocket fired signifies, in the final sense, a theft from those who hunger and are not fed, those who are cold and are not clothed. This world in arms is not spending money alone. It is spending the sweat of its laborers, the genius of its scientists, the hopes of its children. The cost of one modern heavy bomber is this: a modern brick school in more than thirty cities. It is two electric power plants, each serving a town of sixty thousand population. It is two fine, fully equipped hospitals. It is some fifty miles of concrete highway.

What Eisenhower said over fifty years ago is even more true today.

Foreign policy is about whether we continue to champion the values of freedom, democracy, and justice, values which have been a beacon of hope for people throughout the world, or whether we support undemocratic, repressive regimes, which torture, jail, and deny basic rights to their citizens.

What foreign policy also means is that if we are going to expound the virtues of democracy and justice abroad, and be taken seriously, we need to practice those values here at home. That means continuing the struggle to end racism, sexism, xenophobia, and homophobia here in the United States and making it clear that when people in America march on our streets as neo-Nazis or white supremacists, we have no ambiguity in condemning everything they stand for. There are no two sides on that issue.

Foreign policy is not just tied into military affairs, it is directly connected to economics. Foreign policy must take into account the outrageous income and wealth inequality that exists globally and in our own country. This planet will not be secure or peaceful when so few have so much, and so many have so little—and when we advance day after day into an oligarchic form of society where a small number of extraordinarily powerful special interests exert enormous influence over the economic and political life of the world.

There is no moral or economic justification for the six wealthiest people in the world having as much wealth as the bottom half of the world's population—3.7 billion people. There is no justification for the incredible power and dominance that Wall Street, giant multinational corporations, and international financial institutions have over the affairs of sovereign countries throughout the world.

At a time when climate change is causing devastating problems here in America and around the world, foreign policy is about whether we work with the international community—with China, Russia, India, and countries around the world—to transform our energy systems away from fossil fuel to energy efficiency and sustainable energy. Sensible foreign policy understands that climate change is a real threat to every country on earth, that it is not a hoax, and that no country alone can effectively combat it. It is an issue for the entire international community, and an issue that the United States should be leading in, not ignoring or denying.

My point is that we need to look at foreign policy as more than just the crisis of the day. That is important, but we need a more expansive view.

The World Has Changed since Churchill

Almost seventy years ago, former British prime minister Winston Churchill stood on this stage and gave an historic address, known as the Iron Curtain speech, in which he framed a conception of world affairs that endured through the twentieth century, until the collapse of the Soviet Union. In that speech, he defined his strategic concept as "nothing less than the safety and welfare, the freedom and progress, of all the homes and families of all the men and women in all the lands."

"To give security to these countless homes," he said, "they must be shielded from the two giant marauders, war and tyranny."

How do we meet that challenge today? How do we fight for the "freedom and progress" that Churchill talked about in the year 2017? At a time of exploding technology and wealth, how do we move away from a world of war, terrorism, and massive levels of poverty into a world of peace and economic security for all. How do we move toward a global community in which people have the decent jobs, food, clean water, education, health care, and housing they need? These are, admittedly, not easy issues to deal with, but they are questions we cannot afford to ignore.

At the outset, I think it is important to recognize that the world of today is very, very different from the world of Winston Churchill of 1946. Back then we faced a superpower adversary with a huge standing army, with an arsenal of nuclear weapons, with allies around the world, and with expansionist aims. Today the Soviet Union no longer exists.

Today we face threats of a different sort. We will never forget 9/11. We are cognizant of the terrible attacks that have taken place in capitals all over the world. We are more than aware of the brutality of ISIS, al-Qaeda, and similar groups.

We also face the threat of these groups obtaining weapons of mass destruction, and preventing that must be a priority.

In recent years, we are increasingly confronted by the isolated dictatorship of North Korea, which is making rapid progress in nuclear weaponry and intercontinental ballistic missiles.

Yes, we face real and very serious threats to our security, which I will discuss, but they are very different than what we have seen in the past and our response must be equally different.

But before I talk about some of these other threats, let me say a few words about a very insidious challenge that undermines our ability to meet these other crises, and indeed could undermine our very way of life.

A great concern that I have today is that many in our country are losing faith in our common future and in our democratic values.

For far too many of our people, here in the United States and people all over the world, the promises of self-government—of government by the people, for the people, and of the people—have not been kept. And people are losing faith.

In the United States and other countries, a majority of people are working longer hours for lower wages than they used to. They see big money buying elections, and they see a political and economic elite growing wealthier, even as their own children's future grows dimmer.

So when we talk about foreign policy, and our belief in democracy, at the very top of our list of concerns is the need to revitalize American democracy to ensure that governmental decisions reflect the interests of a majority of our people, and not just the few—whether that few is Wall Street, the military-industrial complex, or the fossil fuel industry. We cannot convincingly promote democracy abroad if we do not live it vigorously here at home.

Maybe it's because I come from the small state of Vermont, a state that prides itself on town meetings and grassroots democracy, that I strongly agree with Winston Churchill when he stated his belief that "democracy is the worst form of government, except for all those other forms."

In both Europe and the United States, the international order which the United States helped establish over the past seventy years, one which put great emphasis on democracy and human rights, and promoted greater trade and economic development, is under great strain. Many Europeans are questioning the value of the European Union. Many Americans are questioning the value of the United Nations, of the transatlantic alliance, and other multilateral organizations.

Threat of Right-Wing Extremism Undermining Democracy

We also see a rise in authoritarianism and right-wing extremism—both domestic and foreign—which further weakens this order by exploiting and amplifying resentments, stoking intolerance, and fanning ethnic and racial hatreds among those in our societies who are struggling.

We saw this antidemocratic effort take place in the 2016 election right here in the United States, where we now know that the Russian government was engaged in a massive effort to undermine one of our greatest strengths: the integrity of our elections, and our faith in our own democracy.

I found it incredible, by the way, that when the president of the United States spoke before the United Nations on Monday, he did not even mention that outrage.

Well, I will. Today I say to Mr. Putin: we will not allow you to undermine American democracy or democracies around the world. In fact, our goal is to not only strengthen American democracy, but to work in solidarity with supporters of democracy around the globe, including in Russia. In the struggle of democracy versus authoritarianism, we intend to win.

When we talk about foreign policy it is clear that there are some who believe that the United States would be best served by withdrawing from the global community. I disagree. As the wealthiest and most powerful nation on earth, we have got to help lead the struggle to defend and expand a rules-based international order in which law, not might, makes right.

We must offer people a vision that one day, maybe not in our lifetimes, but one day in the future human beings on this planet will live in a world where international conflicts will be resolved peacefully, not by mass murder.

How tragic it is that today, while hundreds of millions of people live in abysmal poverty, the arms merchants of the world grow increasingly rich as governments spend trillions of dollars on weapons of destruction.

I am not naïve or unmindful of history. Many of the conflicts that plague our world are long-standing and complex. But we must never lose our vision of a world in which, to quote the Prophet Isaiah, "they shall beat their swords into plowshares, and their spears into pruning hooks: nation shall not lift up sword against nation, neither shall they learn war anymore."

The Importance of International Institutions

One of the most important organizations for promoting a vision of a different world is the United Nations. Former First Lady Eleanor Roosevelt, who helped create the UN, called it "our greatest hope for future peace. Alone we cannot keep the peace of the world, but in cooperation with others we have to achieve this much longed-for security."

It has become fashionable to bash the UN. And yes, the UN needs to be reformed. It can be ineffective, bureaucratic, too slow or unwilling to act, even in the face of massive atrocities, as we are seeing in Syria right now. But to see only its weaknesses is to overlook the enormously important work the UN does in promoting global health, aiding refugees, monitoring elections, and doing international peacekeeping missions, among other things. All of these activities contribute to reduced conflict, to wars that don't have to be ended because they never start.

At the end of the day, it is obvious that it makes far more sense to have a forum in which countries can debate their concerns, work out compromises and agreements. Dialogue and debate are far preferable to bombs, poison gas, and war.

Dialogue however cannot only take place between foreign ministers or diplomats at the United Nations. It should be taking place between people throughout the world at the grassroots level.

I was mayor of the city of Burlington, Vermont, in the 1980s, when the Soviet Union was our enemy. We established a sister city program with the Russian city of Yaroslavl, a program which still exists today. I will never forget seeing Russian boys and girls visiting Vermont, getting to know American kids, and becoming good friends. Hatred and wars are often based on fear and ignorance. The way to defeat this ignorance and diminish this fear is through meeting with others and understanding the way they see the world. Good foreign policy means building people-to-people relationships.

We should welcome young people from all over the world and all walks of life to spend time with our kids in American classrooms, while our kids, from all income levels, do the same abroad.

Some in Washington continue to argue that "benevolent global hegemony" should be the goal of our foreign policy, that the United States, by virtue of its extraordinary military power, should stand astride the world and reshape it to its liking. I would argue that the events of the past two decades—particularly the disastrous Iraq war and the instability and destruction it has brought to the region—have utterly discredited that vision.

The goal is not for the United States to dominate the world. Nor, on the other hand, is our goal to withdraw from the international community and shirk our responsibilities under the banner of "America First." Our goal should be global engagement based on partnership, rather than dominance. This is better for our security, better for global stability, and better for facilitating the international cooperation necessary to meet shared challenges.

The History of U.S. Intervention

Here's a truth that you don't often hear about too often in the newspapers, on the television, or in the halls of Congress. But it's a truth we must face. Far too often, American intervention and the use of American military power has produced unintended consequences which have caused incalculable harm. Yes, it is reasonably easy to engineer the overthrow of a government. It is far harder, however, to know the long-term impact that that action will have. Let me give you some examples:

In 1953 the United States, on behalf of Western oil interests, supported the overthrow of Iran's elected prime minister Mohammad Mosaddegh, and the reinstallation of the shah of Iran, who led a corrupt, brutal, and unpopular government. In 1979, the shah was overthrown by revolutionaries led by Ayatollah Khomeini, and the Islamic Republic of Iran was created. What would Iran look like today if their democratic government had not been overthrown? What impact did that American-led coup have on the entire region? What consequences are we still living with today?

In 1973, the United States supported the coup against the democratically elected president of Chile, Salvador Allende, which was led by General Augusto Pinochet. The result was almost twenty years of authoritarian military rule and the disappearance and torture of thousands of Chileans—and the intensification of anti-Americanism in Latin America.

Elsewhere in Latin America, the logic of the Cold War led the United States to support murderous regimes in El Salvador and Guatemala, which resulted in brutal and long-lasting civil wars that killed hundreds of thousands of innocent men, women and children.

In Vietnam, based on a discredited "domino theory," the United States replaced the French in intervening in a civil war, which resulted in the deaths of millions of Vietnamese in support of a corrupt, repressive South Vietnamese government. We must never forget that over fifty-eight thousand Americans also died in that war.

More recently, in Iraq, based on a similarly mistaken analysis of the threat posed by Saddam Hussein's regime, the United States invaded and occupied a country in the heart of the Middle East. In doing so, we upended the regional order of the Middle East and unleashed forces across the region and the world that we'll be dealing with for decades to come.

These are just a few examples of American foreign policy and interventionism which proved to be counterproductive.

Now let me give you an example of an incredibly bold and ambitious American initiative which proved to be enormously successful in which not one bullet was fired—something that we must learn from.

Shortly after Churchill was right here in Westminster College, the United States developed an extremely radical foreign policy initiative called the Marshall Plan.

Think about it for a moment: historically, when countries won terrible wars, they exacted retribution on the vanquished. But in 1948, the United States government did something absolutely unprecedented.

After losing hundreds of thousands of soldiers in the most brutal war in history to defeat the barbarity of Nazi Germany and Japanese imperialism, the government of the United States decided not to punish and humiliate the losers. Rather, we helped rebuild their economies, spending the equivalent of $130 billion just to reconstruct Western Europe after World War II. We also provided them support to reconstruct democratic societies.

That program was an amazing success. Today Germany, the country of the Holocaust, the country of Hitler's dictatorship, is now a strong democracy and the economic engine of Europe. Despite centuries of hostility, there has not been a major European war since World War II. That is an extraordinary foreign policy success that we have every right to be very proud of.

Unfortunately, today we still have examples of the United States supporting policies that I believe will come back to haunt us. One is the ongoing Saudi war in Yemen.

While we rightly condemn Russian and Iranian support for Bashar al-Assad's slaughter in Syria, the United States continues to support Saudi Arabia's destructive intervention in Yemen, which has killed many thousands of civilians and created a humanitarian crisis in one of the region's poorest countries. Such policies dramatically undermine America's ability to advance a human rights agenda around the world, and empower authoritarian leaders who insist that our support for those rights and values is not serious.

Current and Future Global Security Challenges

Let me say a word about some of the shared global challenges that we face today.

First, I would mention climate change. Friends, it is time to get serious on this: climate change is real and must be addressed with the full weight of American power, attention, and resources.

The scientific community is virtually unanimous in telling us that climate change is real, climate change is caused by human activity, and climate change is already causing devastating harm throughout the world. Further, what the scientists tell us is that if we do not act boldly to address the climate crisis, this planet will see more drought, more floods—the recent devastation by Hurricanes Harvey and Irma are good examples—more extreme weather disturbances, more acidification of the ocean, more rising sea levels, and, as a result of mass migrations, there will be more threats to global stability and security.

President Trump's decision to withdraw from the Paris agreement was not only incredibly foolish and shortsighted, but it will also end up hurting the American economy.

The threat of climate change is a very clear example of where American leadership can make a difference. Europe can't do it alone, China can't do it alone, and the United States can't do it alone. This is a crisis that calls out for strong international cooperation if we are to leave our children and grandchildren a planet that is healthy and habitable. American leadership—the economic and scientific advantages and incentives that only America can offer—is hugely important for facilitating this cooperation.

Another challenge that we and the entire world face is growing wealth and income inequality, and the movement toward international oligarchy—a system in which a small number of billionaires and corporate interests have control over our economic life, our political life, and our media.

This movement toward oligarchy is not just an American issue. It is an international issue. Globally, the top 1 percent now owns more wealth than the bottom 99 percent of the world's population.

In other words, while the very, very rich become much richer, thousands of children die every week in poor countries around the world from easily prevented diseases, and hundreds of millions live in incredible squalor.

Inequality, corruption, oligarchy, and authoritarianism are inseparable. They must be understood as part of the same system, and fought in the same way. Around the world we have witnessed the rise of demagogues who once in power use their positions to loot the state of its resources. These kleptocrats, like Putin in Russia, use divisiveness and abuse as a tool for enriching themselves and those loyal to them.

But economic inequality is not the only form of inequality that we must face. As we seek to renew America's commitment to promote human rights and human dignity around the world we must be a living example here at home. We must reject the divisive attacks based on a person's religion, race, gender, sexual orientation or identity, country of origin, or class. And when we see demonstrations of neo-Nazism and white supremacism as we recently did in Charlottesville, Virginia, we must be unequivocal in our condemnation, as our president shamefully was not.

And as we saw here so clearly in St. Louis in the past week we need serious reforms in policing and the criminal justice system so that the life of every person is equally valued and protected. We cannot speak with the moral authority the world needs if we do not struggle to achieve the ideal we are holding out for others.

One of the places we have fallen short in upholding these ideas is in the war on terrorism. Here I want to be clear: terrorism is a very real threat, as we learned so tragically on September 11, 2001, and many other countries knew already too well.

Rethinking and Revitalizing American Foreign Policy

But, I also want to be clear about something else: as an organizing framework, the Global War on Terror has been a disaster for the American people and for American leadership. Orienting U.S. national security strategy around terrorism essentially allowed a few thousand violent extremists to dictate policy for the most powerful nation on earth. It responds to terrorists by giving them exactly what they want.

In addition to draining our resources and distorting our vision, the war on terror has caused us to undermine our own moral standards regarding torture, indefinite detention, and the use of force around the world, using drone strikes and other airstrikes that often result in high civilian casualties.

A heavy-handed military approach, with little transparency or accountability, doesn't enhance our security. It makes the problem worse.

We must rethink the old Washington mindset that judges "seriousness" according to the willingness to use force. One of the key misapprehensions of this mindset is the idea that military force is decisive in a way that diplomacy is not.

Yes, military force is sometimes necessary, but always—always—as the last resort. And blustery threats of force, while they might make a few columnists happy, can often signal weakness as much as strength, diminishing U.S. deterrence, credibility, and security in the process.

To illustrate this, I would contrast two recent U.S. foreign policy initiatives: the Iraq war and the Iran nuclear agreement. Today it is now broadly acknowledged that the war in Iraq, which I opposed, was a foreign policy blunder of enormous magnitude.

In addition to the many thousands killed, it created a cascade of instability around the region that we are still dealing with today in Syria and elsewhere, and will be for many years to come. Indeed, had it not been for the Iraq war, isis would almost certainly not exist.

The Iraq war, as I said before, had unintended consequences. It was intended as a demonstration of the extent of American power. It ended up demonstrating only its limits.

In contrast, the Iran nuclear deal advanced the security of the United States and its partners, and it did this at a cost of no blood and zero treasure.

For many years, leaders across the world had become increasingly concerned about the possibility of an Iranian nuclear weapon. What the Obama administration and our European allies were able to do was to get an agreement that froze and dismantled large parts of that nuclear program, put it under the most intensive inspections regime in history, and removed the prospect of an Iranian nuclear weapon from the list of global threats.

That is real leadership. That is real power.

Just yesterday, the top general of U.S. Strategic Command, General John Hyden, said, "The facts are that Iran is operating under the agreements that we signed up for." We now have a four-year record of Iran's compliance, going back to the 2013 interim deal.

I call on my colleagues in the Congress, and all Americans: We must protect this deal. President Trump has signaled his intention to walk away from it, as he did the Paris agreement, regardless of the evidence that it is working. That would be a mistake.

Not only would this potentially free Iran from the limits placed on its nuclear program, it would irreparably harm America's ability to negotiate future nonproliferation agreements. Why would any country in the world sign such an agreement with the United States if they knew that a reckless president and an irresponsible Congress might simply discard that agreement a few years later?

If we are genuinely concerned with Iran's behavior in the region, as I am, the worst possible thing we could do is break the nuclear deal. It would make all of these other problems harder.

Another problem it would make harder is that of North Korea.

Let's understand: North Korea is ruled by one of the worst regimes in the world. For many years, its leadership has sacrificed the well-being of its own people in order to develop nuclear weapons and missile programs in order to protect the Kim family's regime. Their continued development of nuclear weapons and missile capability is a growing threat to the United States and our allies. Despite past efforts they have repeatedly shown their determination to move forward with these programs in defiance of virtually unanimous international opposition and condemnation.

As we saw with the 2015 nuclear agreement with Iran, real U.S. leadership is shown by our ability to develop consensus around shared problems, and mobilize that consensus toward a solution. That is the model we should be pursuing with North Korea.

As we did with Iran, if North Korea continues to refuse to negotiate seriously, we should look for ways to tighten international sanctions. This will involve working closely with other countries, particularly China, on whom North Korea relies for some 80 percent of its trade. But we should also continue to make clear that this is a shared problem, not to be solved by any one country alone but by the international community working together.

An approach that really uses all the tools of our power—political, economic, civil society—to encourage other states to adopt more inclusive governance will ultimately make us safer.

Development aid is not charity, it advances our national security. It's worth noting that the U.S. military is a stalwart supporter of non-defense diplomacy and development aid. Starving diplomacy and aid now will result in greater defense needs later on.

U.S. foreign aid should be accompanied by stronger emphasis on helping people gain their political and civil rights to hold oppressive governments accountable to the people. Ultimately, governments that are accountable to the needs of their people will make more dependable partners.

Here is the bottom line: in my view, the United States must seek partnerships not just between governments, but between peoples. A sensible and effective foreign policy recognizes that our safety and welfare is bound up with the safety and welfare of others around the world, with "all the homes and families of all the men and women in all the lands," as Churchill said right here, seventy years ago.

In my view, every person on this planet shares a common humanity. We all want our children to grow up healthy, to have a good education, have decent jobs, drink clean water and breathe clean air, and to live in peace. That's what being human is about.

Our job is to build on that common humanity and do everything that we can to oppose all of the forces, whether unaccountable government power or unaccountable corporate power, who try to divide us up and set us against each other. As Eleanor Roosevelt reminded us, "The world of the future is in our making. Tomorrow is now."

My friends, let us go forward and build that tomorrow.

Note
Senator Bernie Sanders (I-Vt.) delivered this speech as the Fifty-Eighth John Finley Green Lecture at Westminster College on September 21, 2017.

Bernie Sanders's Progressive Vision for U.S. Foreign Policy and National Security

Mark Boulton, Westminster College
Tobias T. Gibson, Westminster College

On September 17, 2017, Vermont senator Bernie Sanders delivered an impassioned speech to a rapt audience on the campus of Westminster College in Fulton, Missouri. Despite an unsuccessful bid to become the Democratic candidate for the 2016 U.S. presidential election, Sanders had ignited a loyal support base. At the time of the speech, he was frequently listed as among the most popular politicians in the nation. As the longest-serving independent member of Congress, he appealed to a cross-section of voters with his agenda of expanding affordable housing and health care, increasing access to higher education, enacting gun reform, promoting environmental sustainability, and increasing workers' rights and through his commitment to racial and social justice. On this occasion, however, Sanders chose the visit to Westminster to focus on foreign policy in a speech titled "A Renewal of American Purpose." Winston Churchill's Iron Curtain speech was given at Westminster in 1946, and Westminster now has the legacy of being a destination for transformative speeches delivered by presidents, diplomats, and dignitaries. For Sanders, it represented an ideal location to present his vision. He duly offered a different approach to national security and global leadership than that which has dominated post–World War II foreign policy making. More importantly for the time at which he spoke, Sanders offered a profound corrective to the foreign affairs course on which President Donald Trump's administration seemed to be steering the nation.

Sanders's Progressive Foreign Policy

Few progressive politicians achieve the political prominence that Sanders enjoyed in 2017. Fewer still become genuine contenders for the presidency. As such, progressive politicians historically focus on domestic issues and seldom have need to venture into foreign affairs. Consequently, Sanders's Westminster speech stands as a rare articulation of what a progressive foreign policy might look like. While few politicians and thinkers have formulated a coherent progressive foreign policy, Van Jackson suggests that one would be based on the supposition that "the American interest is best served by having a more peaceful world, and that's only possible by pursuing greater justice and equity, and opposing tyranny wherever it arises."[1] These foundational positions are evident in Sanders's speech, and he raises important questions about what guiding principles ought to underpin foreign policymaking and what role the United States should play in global affairs.

For Sanders, long-term national security is best achieved by fully living up to the ideals of freedom and democracy that have been a cornerstone of the nation's identity since its inception. Further, he advocates robust engagement with the global community in order to create a more secure environment for Americans and so that all of humanity can be uplifted. While offering a fresh and idealistic perspective, his proposals built upon the historic role the United States played in world affairs over the last century.

Sanders used his Westminster speech as a foundation to further critique and express concern about the role of the United States under President Trump. To be sure, some of this was posturing for another presidential campaign that was to materialize in 2020—but his 2017 themes remained consistent. In 2018, Sanders leveled criticism at the administration for its continued reversion to an isolationist foreign policy—unless the foreign government receiving praise was authoritarian. For example, Sanders suggested that "we are seeing the rise of a new authoritarian axis . . . [that] share key attributes: hostility toward democratic norms, antagonism toward a free press, intolerance toward ethnic and religious minorities, and a belief that government should benefit their own selfish financial interests."[2]

The American Century and Beyond

For Sanders, these troubling trends undermined the role the United States had played in world affairs since the end of World War II. When *Time* magazine editor Henry Luce called for the advent of the American Century in February 1941, he castigated the nation's leaders for the global turmoil unleashed by their prewar indifference to global crises. His "cure" was for Americans "to accept wholeheartedly our duty and our opportunity as the most powerful and vital nation in the world . . . to exert upon the world the full impact of our influence."[3] Even before the Japanese attack on Pearl Harbor compelled the United States to join the ongoing fight against totalitarian aggression, Franklin Roosevelt had laid the foundations for Western democratic values to prevail in the aftermath of the conflict with his enunciation of the Four Freedoms and the Atlantic Charter. With the end of World War II ushering in the decline of the old imperial order and the advent of the Cold War, a bipartisan consensus emerged among U.S. policymakers that rejected the isolationism of the interwar years in favor of aggressive global engagement. FDR's successor, Harry S. Truman, ensured that the United States would play the leading role in bringing his vision to fruition both through the founding of the United Nations and through his commitment to halting the spread of communism. For the remainder of the Cold War and beyond, U.S. national security was predicated on an aggressive and multifaceted pursuit of a global order that was aligned with American ideological and political values while being conducive to the nation's economic interests.

In 1947, Truman's doctrine of containment committed the nation to a decades-long crusade to "support free peoples who are resisting attempted subjugation by armed minorities or by outside pressures." Thereafter, both Democrat and Republican leaders found different paths toward securing American global influence. These paths included massive military spending, covert operations to topple regimes deemed hostile to U.S. interests, sending supplies and military forces to support anticommunist regimes around the world, and building international organizations to enforce the liberal order. While generally opposing the Soviet Union and global communism, the United States often allied itself with authoritarian regimes across the globe, including in South Vietnam, Cuba, and Argentina. This alignment of U.S. anticommunist interests also forms a foundation of progressive concerns that the United States "should act abroad only with those who share our commitments and then, only in ways consistent with those commitments."[4]

With the end of the Cold War confirming the United States' geopolitical preeminence, the nation continued its commitment to maintaining the liberal order as the head of multinational military interventions both in the first Gulf War and in Kosovo, and through unilateral action in places like Haiti. The al-Qaeda terrorist attacks on September 11, 2001, prompted the nation to embark on a wide-ranging Global War on Terror. This included toppling the Taliban government in Afghanistan—which had supported al-Qaeda—and the overthrowing of Iraqi leader Saddam Hussein, whom the George W. Bush administration accused of supporting the terrorists, brutalizing the Iraqi people, and possessing weapons of mass destruction.

The presidency of Donald Trump threatened to upset the long-held notion that national security interests were best served by creating a world conducive to American values. Trump's vision centered around an "America First" foreign policy predicated on disengagement from global institutions and agreements unless they were of explicit benefit to the United States. In a May 2017 op-ed for the *Wall Street Journal*, Trump's national security advisor H. R. McMaster and

National Economic Council director Gary Cohn argued that the Trump administration would work with allies and international institutions only where "our interests align." They expressed little interest in creating a "global community" in which humanity strives to achieve common goals. Instead, they wrote of global politics as "an arena where nations, nongovernmental actors, and businesses engage and compete for advantage." Despite invoking echoes of the kind of social Darwinist environment that had unleashed many of the horrors of the twentieth century, the authors continue, "Rather than deny this elemental nature of international affairs, we embrace it."[5]

Sanders as a Balance to Trump's Foreign Policy

At the heart of this vision was the notion of sovereignty, a word Trump would use over twenty times in a speech to the United Nations shortly after Sanders spoke at Westminster. His concept of sovereignty contained two key tenets: first, that the power of any nation resides in its people; and second, that no external threats to that nation's sovereignty ought to be tolerated. Trump expected "all nations to uphold these two core sovereign duties: to respect the interests of their own people and the rights of every other sovereign nation." He pledged to "defend America's interest above all else" and implied that all national leaders should do the same for their own citizens. Advocating the preeminence of sovereignty for all nations risked creating a global environment in which any odious authoritarian regimes, repugnant ideologies, or hostile actions would remain unchecked unless they directly compromised U.S. security interests. Further, it signaled that the United States would not oppose and would even work with authoritarian regimes if doing so served their foreign policy goals. This approach portended an abdication of the nation's historical role in helping create the conditions necessary for the kind of global uplift engendered over the previous seventy-five years.

Responding to these concerns, Senator Sanders sought a reinvigoration of American leadership in ways that would allow the nation to live up to the idealism it had so long professed. Since the United States began expanding its territorial borders and global influence, nearly every president had sought to defend U.S. foreign policy under the rhetorical aegis of promoting freedom and democracy. For Sanders, however, the nation had too often failed to live up to those values both at home and abroad. He proposed several fundamental shifts in the approach to foreign policy that would—in his view—make these claims a reality while seeking a new pathway toward ensuring the nation's security.

Staying true to his progressive roots, Sanders began his speech with a call to reprioritize federal spending away from bloated military budgets. Echoing the words of Dwight Eisenhower, who warned of a "military-industrial complex" that took money away from building schools and hospitals, Sanders believed that prioritizing domestic programs would ensure greater economic security at home. Abroad, he repudiated the idea of aggressively promoting American interests at the expense of broader mutual uplift. He pointed to numerous historical examples of where U.S. intervention, both covert and overt, had disastrous effects on the supposed beneficiaries of the nation's largesse. In Sanders's view, the CIA-backed Cold War coups in places such as Iran, Guatemala, and Chile had thwarted the popular will by substituting left-leaning popular governments for repressive authoritarian regimes. During the Vietnam War, Sanders had identified as a conscientious objector, and he referenced that conflict as an example of the destructive costs of unwise military interventions. This trend had continued, he claimed, in the wars in Afghanistan and Iraq, which had devasted the lives both of the people of those nations and of the tens of thousands of American servicemen and women sent to fight them. Instead of trying to remake the world in America's image, Sanders viewed America's role as one of rebuilding through humanitarian aid, which would remove much of the suffering that produces fertile ground for dangerous ideologies to grow.

Sanders also wanted the nation to pay greater attention to human rights, both at home and abroad. Abroad, he bristled at the United States' cozying up to repressive regimes such as the Saudi government. He believed that the lack of condemnation for human rights abusers "empowers authoritarian leaders who insist that our support for those rights and values is not serious." Sanders insisted that Americans at home must practice what they preach by eliminating social and economic injustice. Citing the 2014 racial protests surrounding the police shooting of Michael Brown in Ferguson, Missouri, and the August 2017 "Unite the Right" rally, which brought neo-Nazi and other "alt-right" elements of American society out in the open, Sanders argued that Americans "must reject the divisive attacks based on a person's religion, race, gender, sexual orientation or identity, country of origin, or class." He also sought a change in tactics in the Global War on Terror, claiming that the nation's "moral standings" are undermined by "torture, indefinite detention, and the use of force around the world, using drone strikes and other airstrikes that often result in high civilian casualties." He hoped that by providing an unimpeachable example of a just society and a humane foreign policy the United States would become the beacon of hope it had always claimed.

Finally, Sanders called for robust leadership of a global community. McMaster and Cohn conceived the global order as one in which the United States competed with other nations for dominance. By contrast, Sanders called for vigorous engagement with other nations via transnational organizations. Sanders feared that many countries were turning away from cooperation toward a dangerous authoritarian nationalism that endangers global security. The

United Kingdom's decision to leave the European Union in 2016 and Donald Trump's questioning of the utility of both NATO and the UN, the Paris Climate Accords, and the Iran nuclear deal seemed to support this fear. While acknowledging the imperfections of such organizations and agreements, Sanders believed that they still represented the best hope of providing diplomatic resolutions to emerging crises. Unlike Trump, Sanders embraced the concept of a global community. Moreover, he called for the peoples of the world to circumvent diplomatic channels and reach out to each other to embrace a shared vision for humanity. Only by creating mutually beneficial partnerships, he argued, can the United States truly overcome such threats to its security as climate change and income inequality.

The Blueprint for the "Sanders Doctrine"

Senator Bernie Sanders's speech at Westminster College served two major purposes. First, and least important, it established the foundation for a series of speeches and essays that established a reputation for a foreign policy agenda, even if it may have fallen (slightly) short of establishing a "Sanders Doctrine."[6] This, in turn, laid the foundations for another presidential run in 2020, although he again fell short of the Democratic nomination. Second, and probably more significant for the American people and government, Sanders's speech provided the impetus for the formation of a progressive, not merely left-leaning, foreign policy paradigm.

Senator Sanders's view may be representative of an increasing number of Americans, particularly on the left. Fellow progressive legislator Alexandria Ocasio-Cortez argues vociferously that "corporate Democrats seem to find the cash to fund a $1.1 trillion fighter jet program" and are "re-fighting the Cold War with a new arms race that nobody can win." Moreover, "rank-and-file Democrats are more supportive than rank-and-file Republicans of decreasing America's military presence overseas and more skeptical of higher defense spending and of relying on military force to combat terrorism."[7]

While we write this essay, the United States is engaged in a series of social upheavals regarding what constitutes legitimate use of force, starting with the implications of centuries of racism in policy making and rethinking the institutions and monuments that America has taken for granted for decades or longer. As Sanders suggests in the speech, "when we talk about foreign policy, and our belief in democracy, at the very top of our list of concerns is the need to revitalize American democracy to ensure that governmental decisions reflect the interests of a majority of our people." If Richard Haass is correct that "foreign policy begins at home,"[8] then the formation of a viable progressive foreign policy—a renewal of American purpose—may truly have begun at Westminster College. Sanders's vision may yet light the path toward an enlightened approach to foreign policy for future presidential administrations to follow.

Notes

1. Van Jackson, "Wagering on a Progressive versus Liberal Theory of National Security," *Texas National Security Review*, January 14, 2019, https://tnsr.org/roundtable/wagering-on-a-progressive-versus-liberal-theory-of-national-security/#_ftnref22.

2. Bernie Sanders, "A New Authoritarian Axis Demands an International Progressive Front," *Guardian*, September 13, 2018, https://www.theguardian.com/commentisfree/ng-interactive/2018/sep/13/bernie-sanders-international-progressive-front.

3. Henry R. Luce, "The American Century," *Diplomatic History* 23, no. 2 (April 1999): 159–71, https://doi.org/10.1111/1467-7709.00161.

4. Michael Walzer, as quoted in Jackson, "Wagering on a Progressive versus Liberal Theory," n. 1.

5. David Frum, "The Death Knell for America's Global Leadership," *Atlantic*, May 31, 2017, https://www.theatlantic.com/international/archive/2017/05/mcmaster-cohn-trump/528609/.

6. Doyle McManus, "The World According to Bernie," *Los Angeles Times*, January 19, 2019, https://www.latimes.com/politics/story/2020-01-19/column-the-world-according-to-bernie.

7. Peter Beinart, "America Needs an Entirely New Foreign Policy for the Trump Age," *Atlantic*, September 16, 2018, https://www.theatlantic.com/ideas/archive/2018/09/shield-of-the-republic-a-democratic-foreign-policy-for-the-trump-age/570010/.

8. Richard N. Haass, *Foreign Policy Begins at Home: The Case for Putting America's House in Order* (New York: Basic Books, 2013).

America's National Security Agency in the Context of Churchill's "Iron Curtain" Speech

Former Deputy Director of the National Security Agency
Richard Ledgett

Winston Churchill was revered by many. He was a man of principle, distinct presence and multiple talents. A soldier, statesman, journalist, author, artist, sportsman, historian, orator, inventor, and stonemason. As an author he had more published words than Charles Dickens and Sir Walter Scott combined. As an orator in a time when most politicians turned to professional speechwriters to craft their messages, he wrote all his own material. He was a character who was larger than life in a time of momentous events. When John F. Kennedy granted Churchill honorary U.S. citizenship, he stated that Churchill "mobilized the English language and sent it into battle." Churchill's wartime addresses were carefully and thoughtfully crafted; his words inspired his nation to victory. He was a master of the English language, and it is said that no other author has ever been cited by more U.S. presidents.

On a personal level, I've been a fan of Churchill's for years, ever since reading *The Last Lion* [by William Manchester], and I've been known to quote him myself on occasion. I'm a fan of his wit as well—all of it, from his interactions with Lady Astor to his commentary on some of his contemporaries to his views on exercise. In fact, I'm a longtime follower of his fitness regime; whenever I get the urge to exercise, "I lie down until it goes away."

I truly would have enjoyed hearing him deliver his speech that day. And make no mistake, when Churchill stood in front of the crowd that had gathered in your gymnasium in 1946, he understood the significance of the speech he was about to give. His visit to Westminster College became a landmark event in the post–World War II era as the West refocused from fighting a multifront "hot" war to what became the Cold War. In his speech, Churchill acknowledged the United States had emerged as a new world power. At that time, Russia, which would become the other great power in a bipolar world, was already breaking promises it had made to the United States and other allies during the war. In Churchill's view it was just a matter of time before Russia would be asserting itself and its communist views outside the Soviet sphere delimited by the Iron Curtain. He based his assumptions on what he'd observed of the Russians during the war. He knew that the Western democracies would have to stand together to ensure their strength backed their principles and influenced the other nations of the world.

World War II, Cryptography, and the Special Relationship

In essence, his words foretold the Cold War, which began quietly in the two years after World War II, was in full force by 1947, and lasted more than forty-four years until the dissolution of the Soviet Union in 1991. Only then was the Iron Curtain finally lifted. The United States and Great Britain learned how to fight against an ideology that ran directly counter to our values, that relied on a prioritization of state interests over individual rights and intolerance of opposing ideals. It ruthlessly suppressed the freedoms we hold most dear and used fear and hatred as tools to control its people. Sadly, those lessons are applicable today in parts of the world. History must be our teacher. If not, we disadvantage our future. Churchill would likely agree, having once said "a nation that forgets its past has no future."

Coincidentally, this year [2016] also marks the seventy-fifth anniversary of another significant, historic Anglo-American interaction, the visit of the first American codebreakers to Bletchley Park, the epicenter of Great Britain's codebreaking efforts. The February 1941 visit was the outcome of discussions in London between the Americans and British about potential cooperation on codebreaking against the Axis powers. Neither side knew what the other had accomplished. The Americans had broken the Japanese PURPLE code used for diplomatic messages, and the British had broken the German ENIGMA code used for high level military messages. In approving the visit Churchill had prohibited any British discussion of their success against the ENIGMA. This decision reflected his recognition of the value of ENIGMA-derived intelligence, and his concern over keeping the British success a secret from the Germans. The Americans, two Army and two Navy officers, brought a copy of the device used to decrypt the PURPLE code. They gave the PURPLE device to the British and explained how to break the Japanese codes. This caused the British to reexamine their initial decision not to share the success against ENIGMA, and a couple of days later the sharing was approved—by none other than Winston Churchill himself.

This was the beginning of the "Special Relationship" Churchill referred to in his "Iron Curtain" speech. That sharing blossomed throughout the war and was the foundation of an intelligence relationship that helped shorten World War II by as much as two years. The exploitation of a few key flaws in the otherwise brilliant design of the commercial ENIGMA machine, along with clever math, early computing power, and some old-fashioned espionage, enabled Allied victory, and not only saved countless lives, but also brought the Holocaust to an early end. During the war both countries devoted significant efforts to jointly developing the science and art of cryptanalysis—codebreaking—and used the insights they gained from reading German and Japanese coded messages to build strategies and operational plans, and to avoid being surprised by enemy forces. In doing so they learned the value of partnership in this field and forged a trust relationship based on shared values and mutual respect for their technical skills. The relationship was codified in what became known as the United Kingdom–United States of America (UKUSA) agreement. An interesting fact—the UKUSA agreement was signed on March 5, 1946, the same day Churchill gave his famous speech here. In the aftermath of World War II, as the Soviet Union extended that Iron Curtain across Europe, the United States and United Kingdom built on their World War II experiences and worked to provide insights into Soviet and Warsaw Pact plans, intentions, capabilities, and activities. That common enemy helped strengthen the partnership even further.

Global War on Terror and Relationship Continues

After the curtain was lifted and the Soviet Union disintegrated, the partnership held up to the challenges of a unipolar world with a host of disparate national security threats. And the biggest tests came in 9/11 (2001) in the United States and 7/7 (2005) in the United Kingdom, the largest terrorist attacks on U.S. and British soil. In the aftermath, the partnership between NSA [National Security Agency] and GCHQ [Government Communications Headquarters] proved to be a match for the challenges we faced in providing insights to threats against our security, and to identifying those to be held accountable for their actions against us. The world today is very different from that of Churchill's in 1946. We are faced with a different set of threats and challenges, many of which are similarly motivated by the desires of some to force their views on others. It was only thirteen days ago [March 22, 2016] that terrorists detonated bombs in the airport and a metro station in Brussels, killing thirty-five and injuring nearly three hundred. These bombings were the work of the Islamic State of Iraq and the Levant, also known as ISIL. Victims of the attacks included Belgian citizens along with foreign nationals from at least eight different countries, among them the United States and United Kingdom. Like recent attacks in San Bernardino, Istanbul, Paris, Garland, and Chattanooga, this attack on innocent people going about their daily lives was a stark reminder that, for all our vigilance, the shadow of terrorism persists—both for Americans and for our allies. Sometimes, the attackers are homegrown, inspired by those overseas as in the San Bernardino case, the worst terrorist attack on the United States since 9/11. The terrorist threats we face today have evolved dramatically from the monolithic, centrally directed and controlled operations to a more decentralized model.

The Evolving Threat of Cybertechnology

Current threats are more wide-ranging—and less predictable. Where we once spoke of compartmented "networks" and "cells," today's threat is distributed across a broader, high-tech landscape. While we continue to see sophisticated and coordinated attacks, we have also entered a new period of opportunistic terror based on inspiration rather than direction. And what's more, these extremists are both on the ground AND online. Cyber threats led the list of topics that concerned the director of national intelligence at his annual threat assessment. That's because the one of the biggest threats to our national security these days is not from air, land, or sea—it comes from a computer with a simple Internet connection. More than any other nation, we are reliant on computer networks that underpin every aspect of our lives—transportation, power, communications, finance, water supply, and food supply. This makes us vulnerable to malicious cyber threats.

Foreign nation-state cyber actors already have the capability to take down critical infrastructure like the power grid, and they are stealing American defense technology and commercial intellectual property at alarming rates. But it's not just cyber threats. A nuclear-armed North Korea seems intent on developing intercontinental ballistic missiles with the express purpose of threatening the United States. Russia, currently the only existential threat to the United States, is executing a program to incite tensions in Russian ethnic minorities in the "Near Abroad," and has used those tensions as an excuse to annex part of the Ukraine via separatist proxies. China is raising tensions in the South China Sea by asserting its dominance over international waters and over competing claims from the Philippines, Vietnam, and Indonesia. The conflict in Syria is entering its sixth year, serving as a breeding ground for a host of terrorist groups including al-Qaeda, Al-Nusra Front, and ISIL. As foreign fighters numbering in the tens of thousands flock to Syria to wage jihad, they gain combat experience, make contact with core members of these groups, and learn how to conduct terrorist attacks. When they return to their home countries in Western Europe and the United States, they are a ready-made force able to conduct attacks like those we've seen in France, Turkey, and Belgium. And they are connected to their terrorist brethren.

Today's world is different because of the most complex system ever devised by man, the global telecommunications network. That network enables instantaneous communication between any points on the globe, and allows for real-time video to be streamed from personal mobile devices so that every significant event is shared right now, with the world. A key component of this network is the Internet, which links computers all over the Earth and provides an incredible array of useful—even essential—services from email to messaging to videoconferencing. The Internet brings the world's information to individuals, and allows them to interact with it and with others in real time and in ways Churchill's generation could never have imagined. It has been an undeniable force for good in the free flow of information to those who would never otherwise see it, and for calling immediate and wide attention to violence, abuse, and injustices.

A Digital Iron Curtain Has Descended

For those who live in nations that do not allow the free flow of information, the Internet has unfortunately become a barrier—a sort of digital Iron Curtain. Countries like Russia, Iran, and China support an Internet that would provide the means to censor political nonconformists and deny freedom of speech and thought. Fortunately, the development of protections—from Pretty Good Privacy to The Onion Router—has enabled many to freely communicate ideas without fear of reprisal.

The Internet has also been a boon to business, particularly American business, in two major ways. First, it increases productivity in all types of businesses. It provides a virtual storefront for businesses to interact with their customers, allows them to outsource key functions to lower costs and increase efficiencies, and (by analyzing customer data) allows them to immediately tailor offerings that are likely to meet customers' needs. Second, American businesses have been at the heart of the Internet since its inception, and have created a framework of information and communications services and products that comprise the infrastructure and many of the key features of the Internet, and are the envy of the world. Creativity, relentless innovation, and rapid product development have allowed companies like Microsoft, Google, Apple, Facebook, and Cisco to play the leading role in transforming the technology we use and sustaining economic vitality for the United States and innumerable partners who leverage and build upon this now irreplaceable global resource. It has been good for the world in terms of the capabilities they have created, and good for the country in terms of their impact on the U.S. economy.

Technology is neither inherently good nor evil, but it can be used for both. In the hands of a knowledgeable adversary, one computer connection can wreak havoc on an individual, a business, a city, or a nation. The ubiquity of the Internet, the ability to be anonymous, and the potential for security products to hide illicit activities make the Internet an attractive place to operate for those who would hide criminal activities. That is certainly going on today. The so-called "Dark Web" or "Hidden Web" is used to sell any drug you can imagine, from heroin to cocaine to counterfeit antibiotics. You can buy cyberattack tools and services, as well as information on vulnerabilities against which they can be used. Personally identifiable information is for sale at scale, to include financial information like bank accounts and credit card numbers. You can hire hit men and prostitutes. And you can find evidence of the sexual exploitation of children on a nearly unimaginable scale. The network connections are protected by encrypted tunnels, and the financial transactions are protected by online currencies like Bitcoin. It's a rich ground for criminals.

Online Radicalization by Terrorists

One especially pernicious misuser of Internet technology is ISIL, who has mastered the art of using social media to spread their message of hate and their poisonous ideology to every corner of the globe. ISIL is the principal counterterrorism threat to the United States; they are smart and adaptive, and have developed the ability to remotely radicalize and inspire attacks all around the world. They are unbelievably savage, executing hostages by sawing off their heads with knives or burning them alive; crucifying children in front of their parents; using rape and sexual bondage as tools of terror; and conducting genocidal acts against populations like the Yazidis and Coptic Christians. They are proud of their violent acts, posting videos of their savagery online. ISIL uses Facebook, YouTube, and Twitter, to name a few, and they do it at scale. According to the President's Homeland Security and Counterterrorism chief, Lisa Monaco, there are close to one hundred thousand Twitter accounts associated with or sympathetic to ISIL, some with as many as fifty thousand followers. Last year ISIL produced seven thousand pieces of slick, professional-looking propaganda that was disseminated by forty-three ISIL media offices. By comparison, the *New York Times* has about twenty-five branch offices. ISIL effectively uses the Internet to poison the minds of people far away from their Syrian stronghold, many of whom are middle-class and seemingly well-adjusted. The FBI has ISIL-related investigations in all fifty states. And this is not just an American or a Western problem—as we've seen in Copenhagen, Sydney, Paris, Turkey, and Brussels, this is a global problem.

Big Tech Reacts to Radicalization Efforts

Over the last year, the U.S. administration has been working with Silicon Valley on solutions for countering the ISIL threat. Companies like Google, Facebook, YouTube, and Instagram have all taken steps to mitigate the threat and attempt to deny ISIL safe haven by removing terrorist content that violates their terms of service. Twitter has suspended about 125,000 ISIL-linked accounts in the last six months. These and other companies are also throwing in with people from the tech, design, advertising, and media worlds to develop ways to identify and counter ISIL's messaging, and to amplify the voices that provide alternatives to ISIL's hateful worldview. The project is called "Madison Valleywood," after Madison Avenue, Silicon Valley, and Hollywood. These endeavors and others are important to our efforts to stop the spread of ISIL, and other terrorist groups like al-Qaeda and its affiliates. A key enabler of these efforts is providing enough "safe space" for them to take hold—by that I mean protecting our citizens and those of other countries against terrorist attacks, so those counter-ISIL messages have time to spread. Without that safe space, there is danger of a backlash of anti-Islamic sentiment, in response to successful attacks. That backlash supports those who would argue that there is a war between the West and Islam. There is not; but that sentiment feeds into the ISIL and al-Qaeda narrative and fuels their recruiting.

One challenging aspect of this campaign against terrorism is the use of strong encryption by ISIL and other terrorist groups, that use end-to-end encrypted applications over the Internet to secure their ability to interact with people they have or are in the process of radicalizing. Those applications are secure, and the service provider does not hold the keys to decrypt them—they are held only on the devices of the correspondents. This means when an organization like the FBI produces a lawfully executed warrant for the data, the provider cannot produce an unencrypted message. The lack of ability to see the content of the message means that we often don't have insight into the details of a planned terrorist attack that could be used to disrupt it—information like the target, the method, and the timing of the attack. When successful terrorist attacks do occur, they can inspire anti-Islamic violence as we've seen in France and Belgium. Again, these responses feed into the false narrative of "The West against Islam" that terrorist groups use as a tool for recruitment and radicalization.

This is not an argument against encryption. To be clear, NSA supports strong encryption. It's good for our nation and its citizens, and for people all over the world. Encryption protects us from criminal and cyber threats and helps safeguard our nation's intellectual property, critical communications, warfighters, and the future for our children. But as the president said last month at South by Southwest, we cannot take an absolutist view on this. We cannot choose between the two great goods of securing our information and securing our person.

Personal security and privacy rights are not things that need to be traded off against each other—it's both possible and essential that we do both simultaneously. We have two values, both of which are important. We need to secure our communications and our data, and use our lawful authorities to prevent activities that harm our safety. If you think of this as an old-fashioned sweep gauge, there are two ends—one is absolute security of data, the other is absolute security of person. In reality, neither is achievable. But if they were, I would argue against both of them. The right answer is somewhere in the middle. We have come to a place where we must make a choice about the kind of world in which we want to live. We are smart people; we can simultaneously hold two ideas in our head that are in conflict, and come to a decision on a reasonable course of action. And the answer can't be an Internet version of the Iron Curtain; it would be contradictory to the basic freedoms upon which this country is founded. This cannot be a unilateral decision by the government, and it cannot be a unilateral decision by a company or group of companies. It needs to be a thoughtful and reasoned discussion based on facts, without posturing and extremist arguments from either side of the issue. The discussion needs to include those from the tech sector, privacy advocates, academia, law enforcement, the intelligence community, domestic policy community, and Congress. And it needs to happen sooner rather than later, as the risk of a significant terrorist attack increases the longer we wait. If that happens, the backlash could cause the Congress to pass reactive legislation that would not have the right balance. And that's not good for any of us.

Once we understand how we want to proceed in the United States, we need to engage with our international partners. U.S. law will be an influencing factor on that of other countries, and we need to work with them to try to strike a good balance that works for them and for us. Churchill once said of the allied forces, "If we are together nothing is impossible, and if we are divided all will fail." This is true today, even in the face of the challenges brought on by twenty-first-century technology. One of our principal allies in this international discussion must continue to be the United Kingdom. Our set of shared values and traditions, our leadership roles in the free world, and our history of working hard problems together for the common good make this an easy decision. Together we can work to build an international consensus on how to simultaneously satisfy the need for both information and people to be secure. It's a challenge worthy of Winston Churchill himself, and one I'm sure he would relish.

Note

This chapter is taken from a speech delivered by Richard Ledgett, eighteenth deputy director of the National Security Agency (2014–17), at Westminster College, Fulton, Missouri, on April 4, 2016.

Deeds of Freedom

LESSONS FROM THE COLD WAR IN A TIME OF TURMOIL

James E. Baker, Syracuse University

There is a video of former secretary of defense [James] Mattis talking with Marines in the Middle East. In the video, Mattis tells the Marines to "Hold the Line." However, Mattis is not ordering the Marines to defend their position until relieved. "Our country right now, it's got problems," Mattis says, "You just hold the line until our country gets back to understanding and respecting each other and showing it." Mattis elaborates in his book, *Call Sign Chaos*: "What concerns me most as a military man is not our external adversaries; it is our internal divisiveness. We are dividing into hostile tribes cheering against each other, fueled by emotion and a mutual disdain that jeopardizes our future, instead of rediscovering our common ground and finding solutions."

This does seem a divisive time—less so in Syracuse, New York, or Fulton, Missouri, I suspect, than in Washington, D.C.—but divisive, nonetheless. Whatever one's perspective, many public officials do seem more committed to power and to party than to principle and to patriotism.

It is also a different time overseas. We all have read essays asking, "Is Democracy Dying?" The title of a recent issue of *Foreign Affairs*. An equal number of essays ask whether the liberal world order will survive, by which is meant the international governance structure President Truman and Prime Minister Churchill did so much to build. Like Dean Acheson, Churchill and Truman were present at the creation of the United Nations and NATO. These institutions—the liberal world order—were designed to address the two great themes of Churchill's speech—the prevention of war and defense against tyranny. If we are going to tear that order down, we ought to know what we are replacing it with.

Today, I would like to address these themes of division at home and turmoil abroad by drawing on the lessons of the Cold War. Many of these lessons are embedded in the speech Westminster College does so much to preserve.

One is the importance of law, by which I mean the principles embedded in the Constitution, not a particular statutory provision. The response to tyranny, Churchill reminds, is found in what he called the deeds of freedom, the Magna Carta and the Declaration of Independence and the principles they espouse. One of the things that united Americans during the Cold War, around which we found common ground, was our commitment to law as a bulwark against tyranny. May Day was countered with Law Day. Law was our strength; which is why the Soviet Union worked so hard to highlight instances, like Jim Crow law, when the United States fell short of its legal ideals. Law remains our strength today, which is why Russia (and others) work so hard to undermine the institutions that sustain the rule of law—our elections, our courts, and a free press.

I worry that we are losing our unity even about law along with an understanding that law is our essential virtue as a country. Therefore, after I identify three Cold War lessons, I will discuss the meaning of law and describe how we can do better to protect and celebrate our deeds of freedom.

I will close by telling you about my friend Jack Downey. His life illustrates some of the lessons of the Cold War. His life also exemplifies a different kind of deed of freedom, the daily acts some people take that define the difference between upholding and defending the law and treating it as a cynical tool to wield as a majority (or minority) might wish. Most importantly, Downey reminds me, as I hope he will remind you, to always look up with optimism, grace and hope, rather than down with anger, sadness, and dismay.

Personal Background and Perspective

Let me start with a bit of personal background so you understand the context in which I speak as well as my perspective.

I grew up in Cambridge, Massachusetts, in the late 1960s and early 1970s—think Berkeley, California. During the Vietnam War, I dressed up as a soldier on Halloween, in honor of the Minuteman tradition and the citizen-soldiers of World War II. This was not a common costume at that time and place; I was not always met at the door with smiles. When I turned eighteen, I joined the Marines and went to Officer Candidates School, seeking to fulfill my sense of civic duty as a citizen-soldier and to redeem my good fortune for having been born in the United States and to parents who valued education. It was a spur of the moment decision I had been preparing for all my life. My drill instructors called me a communist when they found out I was from Cambridge and Yale. My classmates called me a conservative when they found out I was in the Marines. I never spoke in class and rarely outside of class so it would have been impossible for anyone to have known what I was or wasn't. Do not judge the book by the cover, we are told, but we do it all the time.

I planned to stay in the Marines. It was the best school I ever attended. I liked that the Marines Corps was the most diverse and egalitarian organization I had ever been part of; it remains so to this day. I also liked how the mission and the diversity of the military meant you were invariably judged by the three Cs—character, commitment, and competence—not where you were from, who your parents were, or where you went to school, if you went at all. However, one day I received a phone call from Senator Daniel Patrick Moynihan, for whom I had interned one summer. He did not say hello or how are you. He simply said, "You are going to come work for me." I reminded the Senator that I was in the Marines and that one could not just leave. The Senator responded, "You start next week." "I have worked it out with the Commandant of the Marine Corps you will come work for me and if there is a war, I will send you back." After receiving a call from the commandant's office confirming these details, I did indeed start the next week. I resigned my commission and joined the Reserves. Welcome to Washington.

About one year later Moynihan called me into his office and said with some puzzlement, as if he had just discovered that I was an ameba, "You are apolitical; you have to go to law school." "I do not want to go to law school," I protested, "Who would want to be a lawyer?" Moynihan responded, "Oh. I don't want you to be a lawyer. You are going to work for the government all your life. And this way, if anyone ever asks you to do something immoral, unethical, or unlawful, you can tell them . . ." well I am not going to say what he said, but you get the point ". . . and you will have a profession to fall back on to provide for your family." Moynihan was right on both counts. I went on to serve as a career civil servant and I remain apolitical to this day.

As a result, when I was nominated to become a judge, I listed my political affiliation as "American." This drew a reprimand from the White House counsel who noted that "American" was not one of the choices. It ought to be. But to her credit, she did not care what I put down so long as I filled the form out correctly. We settled on "independent." My nomination was sent to the Senate where it languished. In Washington, it turns out, when you are not a member of a party you are rarely invited into the tent.

Why I am telling you all this. Three reasons.

First, like Churchill, Moynihan knew how to think big. No matter the immediate political context he never lost sight of his bottom line: a belief in constitutional government, a belief in America, and a relentless commitment to battle anything that would threaten either, which in his day meant communism. He also had that sense that Ronald Reagan had that America was a shining city on a hill and we ought always to act like it.

Second, knowing his bottom line—the principles that mattered most—he was able to work with the senators across the aisle who shared these same principles regardless of differences they might have about politics or individual policies; which is why he shared a quiet admiration for senators like Barry Goldwater, Bob Dole, John Chaffee, and Jeremiah Denton, the last of whom Moynihan likely shared few common views save the placement of country first. They were all politicians, but expedience was not part of their character.

Third, Moynihan loved being a senator, as he loved working in the White House for four presidents, two of either party. But he never valued his job more than he valued his integrity. You can always get another job, he knew, but you can never regain your self-respect once *you* give it away.

The Lessons of the Cold War

As I noted, Moynihan's worldview was shaped by the Cold War and the lessons of the Cold War, many of them found in Churchill's speech. Here are a few.

- Never lose sight of the big picture. Churchill like Moynihan could think big and stay big. With Churchill you always knew why you were holding the line—for freedom. Churchill's big message is vigilance against war and tyranny. If you shape the mission with clarity like that, you will never lose sight of why you come to work and what your purpose in life is, nor how you should order the priority of your policy work when principle confronts expedience.
- Churchill wasn't always right—by his day's standards or ours—I am thinking of the Gallipoli campaign, Ireland, and colonial imperialism. But just about everything in the Fulton speech was correct then. And, just about everything in the speech remains accurate today. The greatest threats to democracy are war and tyranny.
- What is more, Churchill like Truman and Moynihan, knew how to respond to these twin threats of war and tyranny, or as he described them—twin marauders.
  - First, with alliances. Churchill speaks of the special relationship between the United States and the British Commonwealth, a phrase he coined here; the fraternal association of the English-speaking peoples; and the Western democracies standing together, presaging the formation of NATO in 1949. And, oh by the way, here is Mattis today: "If we didn't have NATO today, we would have to create it in order to hold on to our Founding Fathers' vision of freedom and rights for all."
  - Second, with relentless attention to telling the truth. Truth builds trust at home, credibility abroad, and counters propaganda, in Churchill's day the lies promoted by the Soviet party paper cynically named *Pravda* (or "Truth"). Think here of Moynihan's statement,

"You are entitled to your own opinion, but not your own facts." He might also have been the one person whose favorite agency was the Bureau of Labor Statistics, which is charged by law with just providing objective statistics. It is no surprise either that Churchill was a historian and not just a politician.

- The third response to war and tyranny is law. Law is the bulwark against tyranny.

Law as a Foundation and Bulwark

1. If you work for the government, including serve in the military, you swear an oath to "uphold and defend the Constitution." Such an oath has been around since adoption of the Constitution in 1789 and the first Congress. In 1862, in the response to the Civil War, "defend" was added to the oath. While there is no exact understanding of what the oath means, for example, how the oath should guide when provisions of the Constitution are in seeming tension; we all know that it means one's loyalty in government is supposed to be to the country and the law, not to a person or a party. Contrast this oath with the Soviet oath, requiring soldiers to "unquestionably carry out the requirements of all military regulations and orders of commanders and superiors."

2. Point two. As eloquent as Churchill was about the Deeds of Freedom, law does not come from a document or the brick and mortar of courts. Law is an attitude. And, it is a culture of commitment to norms that bring law to life. "Elections and people on the street do not democracy make," Les Gelb said. "Democracy really is a series of institutions and attitudes; it's a free press, protection of minority rights, division of power. It's the confidence that if you lose an election, you're not going to lose your basic interests and values or your life. It's the rule of law. And those things take a long, long time to develop." The same is true of law.

3. In my field of practice, national security law, law serves three purposes. It provides the authority to act along with the left and right boundaries of that action. It provides essential process. And, it provides essential legal values, which in many cases are also national security values, like the humane treatment of prisoners, which both upholds Common Article III of the Geneva Conventions and may result in the collection of more information of value. Leon Fuerth captured this point well when he wrote, "the essential duty of a national security lawyer is to get to yes with honor, with the nation well taken care of and the Constitution intact." Yes is the authority part; honor is the values part.

4. That leads to point four. Law also depends on the moral integrity and courage of those who wield its power. That is because it is men and women who write law, interpret law, and apply law. But we tend to lose sight of the fact that one of the virtues of our constitutional design is that it is not supposed to be the same man or woman who does all three at once. There is also choice in which values we accent and how we deal with the twin pressures of expedience and personal preference.

Why am I telling you this?

Because I do not think we are doing a good job teaching law in this country, by which I mean what it means to live in a constitutional democracy and the constant commitment to legal values it takes if we are going to continue to do so. We seem to be missing the forest by focusing on the trees.

In my legal life, the central judicial debate has been about textualism, or its constitutional sister, originalism. Should one interpret law based exclusively on what is written in statute, or where the law is ambiguous or unclear should one look to legislative history or perhaps historical practice to inform interpretation. This is important stuff. And, whatever one's views, it has caused lawyers and judges to think about law in new and rigorous ways.

However, in considering the "Sinews of Peace," Churchill prompts me to see a larger issue about a different legal debate that is also occurring in silence about law and power. Is law just about authority, the first purpose of law I described, a spoil of politics to control and wield, or is law about values, the third purpose of law I described, a neutral body of principles to ensure we all play by agreed upon norms? Of course, law has always been a mix of both. But the big picture I see today is that there is pressure pushing the ship of state over to one side and I worry that the constitutional keel may yet lose the capacity to right the ship and return us and the Constitution to a place of equilibrium.

I have two solutions.

First, law is too important to leave to lawyers. We *all* have a duty to uphold and defend the Constitution. That starts with an understanding of the Constitution, its values and the history which informed those values. These values united Americans during the Cold War and served as a bulwark against tyranny. These values can and should unite us again today. Law is our common ground. That starts here, in the classroom, and a desire to think big about the greater whole. Whatever your affiliation, history teaches that power and law without values leads to trouble. It also shows what happens when you do not hold the line when given the chance to do so.

Second, law schools should spend as much time teaching professionalism as they do advocacy. Law schools still teach based on a turn-of-the-century model by which I mean the turn of the nineteenth to twentieth centuries. The same courses are taught, and those courses focus on the substance of the law and thinking like a lawyer, not the practice of law and acting like a professional. Law is a business and lawyers are advocates. But they are also professionals. And law is the profession most responsible for defining the culture of law in this country. They are guardians of democracy, officers of the court, or as the *Model Rules of Professional Conduct* state "officers of the legal system and public citizens having special responsibility for the quality of Justice." It is time to start acting this way and not just as advocates for our causes. Too much advocacy, and not enough professionalism, can result in a perception that law is just about viewpoints—a subtle version of law as cable television—not a core set of immutable values, attitudes, and a culture derived from our two great deeds of freedom the Declaration of Independence and the Constitution.

We have a choice to make. We can treat law solely as a tool—the authority to act and thus a spoil of power and a tool of power. Or, we can also treat it as the essential reservoir of values that makes a democracy a democracy. It is the difference between getting to yes and getting to yes with honor. History shows that if you do not tend to the garden of freedom it will wilt.

Judge Jack Downey and Humility

Let me close by telling you about one of my legal role models Jack Downey. I do so for two reasons. First, role models remind us of who we wish to be, aspire to be, and we hope we are. Second, Downey is a man who knew something of the costs of the Cold War as well as the virtues of law.

John "Jack" Downey was a juvenile court judge in New Haven, Connecticut, for thirty-five years. More precisely, he was a superior court judge, but he chose to serve in juvenile justice court for most of his career. You may not know this, but law is a very hierarchical profession and at times a snobby profession. People care where you went to law school and they care whether you are a federal judge in an Article III court versus an Article I court, versus a state court. In the hierarchy of state courts, the least prestigious of courts, in theory, are the family courts and juvenile justice courts. This, of course, is all complete nonsense, because state court is where most law in the United States is practiced and where law has the greatest impact on the most people. And, family court and juvenile justice court is where the impact is greatest, in my view, because these are the courts where young lives are made, saved, and broken.

Jack Downey chose to be a juvenile justice court judge for thirty-five years. He did it so well and with such grace that the state of Connecticut eventually named not just the courthouse after him but also the Juvenile Justice Detention Center. When I was in law school, I used to go watch Judge Downey in court and see with what grace, kindness, and care he treated the people who came before him, the young teenagers who had gotten in trouble. I marveled at how he could do this given his background, so when I became a judge, I called him up out of the blue. I said, "You don't know me, but I was wondering if I could buy you a beer because I think I have a lot to learn from you about being a judge as well as about living life with grace, civility, and kindness." When we met, I said, "You think hard when you sentence someone to detention, don't you?" He responded, "Oh yes, I know something about detention. I think about this with care." You will sense that there is a coming irony here.

You see, Judge Downey's career as a judge was his second career. His first career was as a CIA officer. He joined the CIA in 1951 out of Yale College because he had missed the Second World War and he felt that he had a duty to serve his country in some manner. Like many of his classmates at that time, before the CIA figured out that a great intelligence agency could not be comprised entirely of white men from Yale, he joined the CIA. Downey's first assignment was to send Chinese nationalist agents into Manchuria where they were supposed to create turmoil and trouble and create "a third way." The third way was neither the nationalist way nor the communist way but a third way that would cause China to change course away from communism. In addition, and importantly, the mission was intended to pull PLA [People's Liberation Army] units out of Korea where they were fighting American forces. They tried a third way approach in the Ukraine as well, dropping agents in by parachute. Not one of the agents was ever heard from again, not a single agent. Never. Not a word again. Nor was there a trace of them in the archives after the Cold War. It was equally successful in China.

There came a time when the cell that Jack Downey was running radioed out and said there was a high-level defector who wanted to come over to the American side. Such a high-level defector, it was determined, was too important and too secret to entrust to the Chinese nationals who ordinarily served as the crew of the clandestine flights into Manchuria. As a result, the base commander decided to send the two most junior case officers as air crew, Jack Downey who had been there for about a year and Richard Fecteau who had been there for all of about two weeks. They were given a moment of training then the two regular pilots of the CH-47 and Downey and Fecteau were off. Their job was to throw this swing set sort of a device out of the aircraft as they circled the rendezvous site at which point the defector would strap himself in and on the next pass, the aircraft would hook the harness and the two CIA officers would literally reel the defector in like a fish on a line. This required the plane to slow down at near stall speed so that they did not tear the person apart. They did not know if it would work, so they had asked for a volunteer at the base to try it out and it worked, so off they went on the mission.

They flew into Manchuria and approached the rendezvous point. The fires were lit, the call signs were given, and countersigns received. All correct. They dropped the swing set out and then came around again to hook the defector who is now in the harness in the swing set. But at this point, all heck breaks loose, machine guns start firing and it turns out that they have flown into an ambush. The cell, Downey's cell, has been turned by the Chinese and the PLA is there to shoot the aircraft down and capture anyone who survives. The two pilots are killed and Downey and Fecteau tumble about as the aircraft crashes. They survive and are immediately captured. Their families are told that they are both dead and that their bodies have not been recovered in a DoD aircraft crash in the Sea of Japan. Game over. Nothing is heard from them again.

What is actually happening is that they are being interrogated for two years. They do not see each other for two years, at which point the Chinese decide to put them on trial. They are put on trial and as they go in, they see each other for the first time. They are both wearing Mao suits, the ubiquitous Chinese pajamas, which prompts Fecteau to turn to Downey and say "nice suit Jack. Who's your tailor?" They both laugh and get hit with rifle butts. It turns out that a sense of humor is a very important thing in almost every context. They then meet their assigned lawyers. Downey asks his lawyer, "Don't you have any advice for me?" The lawyer says, "Good luck." That is the advice. The trial proceeds to the sentencing phase. There are all the members of the cell standing in a row with Fecteau and Downey and the end of the line. It turns out that if you were in the cell and cooperated you got five or ten years. If you did not cooperate you got death. So, they come down the line announcing the sentences—death, five years, death, death, ten years . . . Downey is at the end thinking and wondering how this is going to come out for him. They get to Fecteau, who the Chinese did not know. Because he was so new, he was unknown to the agents on the ground when they were captured. Fecteau gets twenty years. Then they get to Downey. He gets life. In Mao's China, life means life. They go off to confinement.

To make a really long and boring story shorter, as Jack Downey said to me while telling his story, into a shorter and boring story—Downey spent the next twenty-one years of his life in prison in China. At one point, he spent six straight years in solitary confinement. He did not learn Chinese because he did not want to emotionally commit to the fact that he might spend the rest of his life in China. Therefore, he learned Russian. His reading material at one point consisted of *The Collected Works of Joseph Stalin*. Then, when the Sino-Soviet split occurred, the guards came into his cell and tore it all up and accused him of being an imperialist dog, or words to that effect. He knew the Cultural Revolution was going on, although he did not know exactly what was occurring, because the camp commandant became the custodian and the custodian became the camp commandant.

Returning to the long and boring story, at the twenty-year mark Richard Fecteau was released. But not Downey. They used to drive the two men in a truck and tell them they were going home, and they would drive them around only to return them to their prison and to their cells. As part of Ping-Pong Diplomacy when Kissinger and Nixon opened relations with China there came a time when Kissinger called Zhou Enlai, the Chinese premier, and told him that Mrs. Downey was ill. He then asked if China would allow Jack Downey to come home. Zhou Enlai said yes on condition that President Nixon personally acknowledge in public that Jack Downey was a CIA officer. There is a press conference in which the president of the United States, Richard Nixon, is talking about the economy or whatever and there is a planted question in the audience. The reporter asks about Jack Downey totally out of context and the president responds that Downey is a CIA officer. Then he moves on to the next question. Thus, after twenty-one years the Chinese release Jack Downey. He is watching the national ping-pong championship at the time when the guards come to him and tell him to pack up his belongings. Thinking this is another game of drive around, Downey insists on watching the remainder of the ping-pong championship. But this time he is coming home. When he crosses the border into Hong Kong a U.K. police officer salutes him. He later describes the salute as the first act of human dignity he has seen in twenty-one years.

Downey comes home and what does he do? He could have been an angry man, a bitter man, a sad man, instead he goes to law school. He loves law school. It's his joke, not mine, he says, "I was the happiest guy in law school because I had twenty-one years of salary saved up. Law school was nothing but fun." Well, he earned his fun; Yale Law School would not admit him because at this point Yale and its professors had turned against the CIA and the public service it represents, notwithstanding that it was Yale that had let CIA recruit on campus for so many years. So, Downey went to Harvard Law School. Downey met his wife Audrey, a Chinese American woman, because she wrote him a letter when he came back and offered to buy him a cup of coffee to say welcome home. They fell in love and they had a son Jack Downey Jr. who they took to China at the invitation of the government of China many years later.

What's the point of all this?

Jack Downey started as a Cold Warrior. He also knew the cost of the Cold War. He reminds us that if you're going to take a national security action it ought to be worth it. Real people are impacted. Avoid mistakes where you can.

More importantly, Jack Downey reminds all of us, especially me daily, that it is never too late to make a difference. On one level, Jack Downey did not start his life and his career until he was forty-seven when he graduated from law school and what a wonderful life he led. He seemed to have no regrets. He said something like, "For thirty-five years I have done something important, the most important thing I could do which is helping the kids in New Haven, Connecticut, as a judge." (I might add that although I do not know Richard Fecteau, he too returned home to live and lead an exemplary life as an educator and role model as an assistant athletic director at Boston University.)

I also like to tell Downey's story because this is true as well, if you think you are having a bad day, or if I am feeling sorry for myself because I am engaged in some dry law task, I remind myself that Jack Downey's best days for twenty-one years were the days when there was pigeon in the soup, a pigeon soup day.

People become role models at different times in their lives. I didn't meet Downey until he was in his late seventies. I knew about him as a kid because I came from a New Haven family and a Yale family. We all knew about Jack Downey and we wished he would come home. But I did not get to meet him until he was an older man. He became one of the most important role models in my life and remains so. Never stop looking for examples to follow and never forget you may be the example someone else is following to help find a sense self-respect or the moral courage to do the right thing. Both ultimately must come from within, if you are in a prison cell for twenty-one years, or perhaps twenty-six years if your name is Nelson Mandela. Your courage must come from within and your own sense of identity.

Think about this as well. If Jack Downey could act with such grace, dignity, and kindness having experienced what he experienced. Can we not do the same as a nation and find our common ground again?

What does law look like in a functioning democracy? It looks like Jack Downey, a judge holding the line and not being pushed off his position by power, expedience, or ambition. For Jack Downey each day was an act, a small deed of freedom, reminding me of what Adlai Stevenson said about patriotism. "Patriotism is not short, frenzied outbursts of emotion, but a steady and tranquil dedication of a lifetime."

Thank you.

Note

This text is based on the prepared text of a speech given at Westminster College on October 17, 2019. The portion of the speech about Jack Downey was converted to text after the fact based on contemporaneous remarks delivered at Westminster College.

Technology

SECURING LIBERTY AND THE NATION

A Survey of Humans and Autonomy in Three Areas

SURVEILLANCE, ECONOMICS, AND LETHALITY IN COMBAT OPERATIONS

Robert E. Burnett, National Defense University

As we are here . . . as a group of scientists, engineers, social scientists, lawyers, and social designers of human and machine affairs, I'd like to conjure a thought on the intersection of science and the military from a British thinker and practitioner on the subject from years past. Sir Solly Zuckerman, a scientific advisor on bombing strategy to the allies and a fellow in the Royal Society, writing in *Scientists and War* in 1966, stated the following: "The distinction between pure basic research, as a step in the scientific process, and what is definable as applied research, is often blurred. . . . But none the less it is urgent that the existence of a difference be recognized if the world at large is to appreciate how much, or how little, choice it has in determining its future in this scientific and technological age of ours, and how fast its future is being both set and transformed." He goes on to say,

> I remember shortly after the end of the Second World War congratulating one of the top-level non-scientific directors of the Manhattan Project . . . on the success of his efforts. With the conversation flagging, I threw in a question about the widely advertised campaign then going on in the United States to raise funds in order to intensify and extend research into the cancer problem. "Do you think," I asked, "that if you personally were furnished with the same powers in administering a search for a cancer cure as you enjoyed in the Manhattan Project the problem would be solved?" "Yes," came the reply, "provided I could stop you scientists wasting time on the things which interest you." This answer epitomized once and for all the confusion which often exists in the minds of people who are not scientists about the nature of the scientific process."

Now, I, speaking many years later, should point out that this analogy should not be forgotten in that a few years later, President Nixon in 1971 declared the "War on Cancer" (an interesting militarization of human science and disease) and a war, I would like to point out, that was (to date) never won.

Was this a failure of science, or of military prowess? Zuckerman would suggest that it is largely a function of the scientific enterprise, as he says, "are spontaneously creative acts of particularly gifted individuals." But, then one must ask the question: How did we get so many spontaneous acts to combine with such focus and speed during the Manhattan Project? What do these historical ideas of science and politics portend for our work in automation and human affairs in the realm of defense?

The Promise and Pitfalls of Autonomous Weapons

First, let me extend my sincere thanks to you for having me here this evening. It is my distinct privilege to have your attendance and your attention to what I am about to say for some minutes here, and I honor that and thank you again for this opportunity. I am a social scientist and a philosopher, and one that studies the activities of scientists and engineers as sources of power in matters of defense and international political and economic affairs. It is this practice and perspective that I bring to my task here this evening.

A challenge that will continue before us is to communicate the reality, the benefit, and the continuing challenges of autonomous systems to the general public and, importantly, to the national decision makers in the years to come, and that also means to the politicians. While the benefits of what you have built are clear upon any general review of performance and accomplishment (for example, the fact that most of us take automated systems for granted in our daily lives is evidence of their success), a single failure that is paraded in the 24/7/365 media cycle can cause severe risk and potential damage to all sorts of engineering work. This is especially true of autonomous systems in the three areas that I wish to discuss here today: specifically, autonomy in the areas of surveillance, international economics and labor, and last, but certainly not least, lethality and human-machine symbiosis in combat.

As we have discussed, trust in autonomous decisions has a complicated meaning: on the one hand it denotes human confidence in objective machine actions with an extremely high probability of confidence in reliable actions within or between machines. On the other hand, it may denote more subtle subjective and fleeting understanding of risk and reliability between machines and humans. We note that often times failure in such systems is the result of human factors, both in the design phase of the system that can occur in hardware or software components. For our purposes, we must also note that failure can also occur as a result of another human factor, that of corruption in behavior, either after a design, or in spite of a design. The corruption can occur for several reasons, notably for known or unknown origins to include humans seeking advantage in a given system or game, permutations due to unforeseen combinations of human-machine interactions, or the seemingly random occurrences that stem from mental illness, that properly described in both biochemical and silicon-based information networks, can be either human or perhaps, as Arthur C. Clarke has suggested in fiction, machine-based disease. Trust in autonomy is pursued as a partial solution to many of these problems, in fact, and it has worked remarkably well, in large part, by taking human thinking away from such systems ever more so. But, the question, must be asked, will be asked; how are we to deal with such systems when the machines themselves begin to think more about themselves in these sorts of systems? This is a problematic question in all sorts of ways, and I will not solve it here today, but I intend to use some aspect of it to help us investigate how we might go forward in thinking about autonomy in the gray areas where human morality will have some very important political and social things to say about the evolution of machine systems. *So, let us center our thoughts on the centrality of our subject here today; what is it about humans, who are thinking about machines, that are evolving to be thinking about themselves, and their interactions with human systems, that is important for the decisions that we make about trusted autonomy in the days to come?*

Human decision making in governing social systems is at once both recondite and revealing to the observer—and we refer to the democratic style as both "sausage making" and "genius." And yet, those of us who live in advanced democracies can detect the irony in this statement (though most machines in their present states of artificial intelligence could not), yet we do not completely see the statement as an oxymoron, nor one of juxtaposition. As Winston Churchill once stated, "It has been stated that democracy is the worst form of government, except all those others that have been tried."

When we apply democratic decision making to what we consider to be another, i.e., higher, form of human thinking and decision-making process, such as science, we may become more offended and more concerned about potential damage that could result. Consider an example that I examine with my students in one of my seminars that is designed to investigate on the one hand the tremendous effect of scale upon human knowledge, and correspondingly, the limiting use of scope as a tool toward other ends—namely political power. Both effects, scale and scope, are impressive when seen in the following manner.

What you are about to see on the screen is a demonstration by a University of St Andrews and NASA team of the natural cosmological phenomenon known as gravitational lensing adapted by humans as a sort of astrophysical tool of observation (literally on an interstellar scale of both time and space) for the purpose of detecting a planet thousands of light years from our own location on

Earth. It is important for us as an audience tonight—interested in autonomy—to note that this technology too is built upon a particular form of automated computational observation.

The insight from this exercise is that knowledge beyond human scale, knowledge beyond our normal experience, but knowledge that once acquired, can be applied to human scale, to our everyday experience, and with profound effects. The takeaway from this exercise again is to consider the implications of the impact of democratic decision-making processes, particularly ones with highly contested poles of ideological power upon what would otherwise be considered to be evidence-based and logic-informed knowledge conditions and knowledge-based questions. The implications of this are profound for public and citizen decision making about societal science and technology programs in decentralized democracies. What are the implications of this for autonomy? What is the knowledge base of our decision makers and does this matter?

Allow me to borrow a short excerpt from a chapter that I wrote on remote control and autonomous systems from a book on these subjects and intelligent machines that has just been published this month in the United States.

How many of you would pay to board a civilian aircraft to make a flight to a domestic or international destination with the knowledge that the vehicle that you are boarding is in all practical manners and respects a human-laden "drone" with a flight plan that is a "remotely controlled" or autonomous operation from taxi/departure to taxi/arrival?

Let us examine this scenario in a bit more detail. The aircraft is very much the same sort of Boeing or Airbus that populates the skies today, however it will be modified in important ways to make it operationally different from current models. Human pilots will be replaced with software and hardware schemes allowing the aircraft to be remotely piloted from the ground, or in further future states, piloted from advanced autonomous systems both on-board and in tandem via telemetry-based control centers around the planet. Our fast progression in moving toward this kind of operational system is, in large measure, a logical progression of the powerful remotely piloted systems that are already in service in many aircraft today. There are also present in such a scenario, potent safety and risk logics at work indicating the likelihood of better flight risk profiles. This can come in the form of reducing human error (which have been empirically proven with current automatic pilot data sets). We are also seeing the creation of new kinds of risk reductions, including telemetry-controlled flight in a variety of "in-air" aircraft malfunction conditions where human pilots might be incapacitated. This latter example suggests at least one possible alternative outcome to Indonesian Flight MH-370. In other words, could a telemetry-controlled technology have continued the flight to a successful landing despite a variety of "on-board" scenarios?

In one sense, this scenario is the application of technology that we have been using for some time in the military realm of RPVs (remotely piloted vehicles) to contexts of civilian air transport. We have introduced some preliminary logic for why the industry might want to advance the utilization of such technology with regard to flight performance risk reduction. There is also the obvious logic for potential economic benefit to the airline industry in terms of labor savings—something that we understand well in terms of technological/innovation disruption to existing political, economic, and engineering systems. In fact, there are advancing schemes of implementing these kinds of drone delivery cargo aircraft in the business world today.

However, there is another important element to this remote-control event, one in which large numbers of human beings continue to achieve new states of symbiosis with mechanical systems. There is a compelling reason and logic for humans to do so from the perspective of the economist; it is rational for them to do so within a cost-benefit framework, and this holds true in both physical and psychological dimensions of human life. However, as is evidenced from the work of this and other analyses, it is also rational for humans to contemplate and analyze these kinds of behaviors (the increasing symbiosis with automated technologies), and we seek to do so here this evening.

Surveillance, Automation, and Autonomy

Let's apply this logic to the activity of surveillance as it is evolving in the modern security state. Surveillance as an automated activity is exploding in terms of demand and supply. But, for our purposes tonight, I would like to again focus upon the element of scale as it relates to the growing activity of surveillance as an automated phenomenon in modern democratic states. I am suggesting that there is a paradox in place that has resulted in a growing tension that has significant implications for the health of our societies and that as technologists and policy professionals, we have a responsibility to help resolve this dilemma. The paradox consists of two counterpositions that operate according to different logics. The first is the position of individual citizen political privacy that is codified in basic individual legal rights. These rights are constantly in tension with the needs of the state to perform some basic functions for the common good of the greater common citizenry. It is the function of the courts to interpret where these individual rights versus state needs reside at any given time depending upon the current political environment as read through the legal code or the rules of governance for a particular state. I should note that in an increasingly globalized polity, this becomes all the more complicated—though we have the record of norms of international law over time that have extended cooperative schemes across national borders.

The second position is that of technological systems that operated according to the efficient schemes of mathematics and economic cost-benefit schemes. For example, a primary component of surveillance technology is computational power and corresponding processing speed. In its current form, as silicon-based microcircuits, Moore's law is a powerful confirmation of such precision in terms of technological advancement, and this has implications for how technology has the ability to powerfully influence human evolution, in our case that of machines observing and recording the activities of human behavior over time without the concern for the human notions of where and or when or to what ends. True, these decisions of when and where are not machine decisions; yet, presently, they are still human decisions transferred to the automated process of collecting data, however, this may not always be the case and we may wish to review this prior to such a state of affairs.

Previously I mentioned the role of scale in this phenomenon, and I wish to introduce it here in the form of a short video of a powerful American technology developed for the surveillance of human activity at a scale much greater than previously capable. It could be suggested that the scale of this technology, its power of observation and collection, may be in part the reason that the U.S. government chose to declassify it and present it to the public for consideration, for contemplation, prior to its employment. But, interestingly, I have shown this to a few American audiences (you are the second Australian audience), and I am not surprised to note that anecdotally their (the Americans') total lack of knowledge of this technology. Americans are increasingly monitored by their own government, and this is not so different than what we contrasted ourselves against in the form of the Soviet Bloc countries during the Cold War. I am married to a Hungarian woman who remembers this all too well. Our allies, too, are increasingly monitored by American government technologies, and this is different than what they expected as compared to their realities and their perceptions during the Cold War. However, we must temper this point with the fact that European governments are not so far behind in their own surveillance technology activities too, as reluctant as they are to admit their existence.

A fundamental fact to the issue of automated surveillance is that it is not just governments that are doing the collecting or possessing or the analytics of the data. In democratic-capitalist states, it is the private sector that truly has astonishing power, and they challenge the abilities of governments in increasingly powerful ways. Here is where ideology has a role to play in terms of how this phenomenon will evolve. If we assert that the technology is politically agnostic (and this is at this point merely an assumption) then it is easier to see the technology evolving according to the previously stated logic of mathematics and economics. Analytics as modeling human behavior for predictive outcomes has been a tremendously profitable business model. And yet, we are seeing, that privacy, as a business model, also has some traction as evidenced by Apple Computer and others in its consortium, they who are challenging the U.S. DOJ with regard to encryption technologies in communication software and hardware. At least in this realm, we can say that there is a healthy tension, within a democratic tradition, of a "contest for power" between the needs of the state and the rights of the individual. At this time, as we see automation technology advance, powerfully so in the realm of surveillance, there remains a debate about how it should evolve, and in democratic governance logic, this is generally regarded as a positive development.

Automation and Economic Impacts

Automation is said to be causative to an increasing, but still unknowable degree, of human worker displacement in the overall labor force of the economies of many nations today. Many of you are likely to have been involved in the design or consulting activities for governments and/or corporations that seek to employ automation technologies for the purpose of increasing a variety of engineering, ergonomic, economic, and human safety outcomes. A side product of this, in fact economists refer to this as an externality, is the growing displacement of human workers in a variety of categories as we further advance automated technology deployment in manufacturing and service categories of the macroeconomy.

Hod Lipsom, a computer engineer at Cornell University, quoted in *MIT Technology Review* (June 16, 2015), says the following: "More and more computer-guided automation is creeping into everything from manufacturing to decision making." In the last two years alone, he says, the development of so-called deep learning has triggered a revolution in artificial intelligence, and 3-D printing has begun to change industrial production processes. "For a long time the common understanding was that technology was destroying jobs but also creating new and better ones," says Lipson. "Now the evidence is that technology is destroying jobs and indeed creating new and better ones but also fewer ones. It is something we as technologists need to start thinking about."

Let's apply this to our subject matter, defense: this impacts us too, and in some nontraditional ways that may be very troubling. First, soldiers are being displaced as labor. The classic example is pilots who are no longer needed in air forces, as in the example of the United States are producing more remote-control pilots for UAVs than they are for traditional aircraft. This will transition further as UAVs become more automated in the future where there will be a lower demand for pilots and operators. Let's look at how this impacts the human side of the equation in a bit more detail. Not only are numbers impacted (fewer UAV pilots), but a more qualitative element becomes problematic for defense forces, that of soldier morale. And, we can extend this logic down to the societal level to ponder what might happen to the relationship between soldiers and society in general. For example, how might a society view their combat heroes in the form of machines that hardware and software? In order to garner more human "buy-in" into these types of warriors, will we need to design more human traits, both physical and behavioral, into the automated platforms for the express purpose of developing a social relationship between weapons and citizens. This would be specific to buy political support for a nation's foreign policy. This is a curious proposition, yet an important one that stands in stark contrast to the familiarity of the flesh and blood soldier of history. How do you feel about engineering these types of systems? Do you find it to be patriotic, important, challenging, creepy, evolutionary? Importantly, let us go back to the thought experiment that we began with tonight: How should a diverse citizenry and its leadership—many of whom are technologically challenged—address this question with regard to a rational social outcome? Can we agree on beginning positions of what constitutes scientific knowledge, empirical reality, or objective knowledge for the purpose of making "best outcome" "societally-advantageous" decisions in these realms of technology such as automation, artificial intelligence, and machine-human interface?

Automation in Political Decision Making

Allow me to pose an awkward point; but one that may need to be investigated. I do so with great care, and I vow to do so within the full glaring light of constitutional authority and guidance in the tradition of my own nation's political traditions. But, here is the gist of what I seek to pose for your reflection now in summary of our second issue for examination tonight—that of automation and economics. Here I am extending the notion of economics as a behavioral activity of humans in the marketplace to that of public policy and that takes us into politics. But here too the discipline of economics has had much to say about human behavior and public policy for many decades.

There is no doubt that politics—as an activity that is a public forum and mechanism for debating and deciding about how the nation of America is to move forward into an uncertain future (risk) has evolved into a troublesome state of high disfunction. As many observers have stated, this has serious consequences both for our domestic health, but also for global fortunes. There are many excellent social scientific investigations, both theoretical and a substantial record of empirical research into this phenomenon that I do not have time to go into here, however, suffice to say, that many less than rigorous commentators have chalked up the phenomenon to failing politicians, or politicians who have lost their way. This could not be further from the truth. A proper social scientific analysis yields a view of politicians that are performing at the top of their game, perhaps at some of the highest levels of performance in history. The paradox, which is really not a paradox, comes from the fact that the social science helps us to understand the real forces that are at work upon the politicians, the real game that they are playing, the real economic structures within which they exist, and the real incentive and disincentive forces that are acting upon them. . . . And, this game is not aligned with the larger similar game of international statecraft. Politicians, their primary raison d'être, is winning the game of reelection, which due to technology and increasingly analytics is a 24/7/365 phenomenon. Raising funds and matching message to evolving groups of voters is their reality. Increasingly, matters of national and international importance, what we perhaps used to call "statesmanship" has receded and hard thinking, reflective thinking about hard problems has fallen by the wayside, or rather then have become enmeshed within the large game of reelection gaming and strategy. It is complicated. Congressional staff has had to pick up the slack, and even they are increasingly motivated by the reelection logic. This increasingly pits the legislative body against the executive (president) on matters of national and international importance.

What does this have to do with automation? Here is the awkward moment. If we are to move forward with reasoned resolve in such matters (national and international issues), is there, in part, a greater opportunity for analytics and automated policy analysis and guidance to enter into democratic societies decision-making systems? As we are beginning to enter into new stages of automated economic systems management, the so-called free-market asset management for individual portfolios, as well as institutional ones, can we increase such activity, that of automated management systems, for large swaths of public policy portfolios (transportation, defense, health care, etc.)? In a sense, this is what public policy is supposed to do anyway, to provide the expert social engineering advice toward more rational outcomes to the political democratic process—in other words to temper the extremes. But, to many, we are getting worse, not better. And this is in spite of us using the most automated machines to assist us in data management in our history.

Automation and the Future of Combat

In many ways the global public is already prepared for a much darker future with regard to machines of war. Hollywood has been preparing them for decades in the form of dystopias where humans have created and then lost control of technologies that then turn on humanity. If this were to happen, many of us would not be surprised. But, those of us who work in the industry, have a very different day job. We actually think about these things and work with a diverse and interdisciplinary community of engineers, scientists, social scientists, lawyers, and humanitarians who seek to continue to create defense forces that achieve several important social needs in simultaneous fashion. These also happen to include rules of war and how we value human life at the same time we seek to destroy it in the name of national security. It is a paradox no doubt, but again, a paradox that has a framework and rules.

In my seminar on science, technology, and war, I like to begin a Socratic dialogue with the following proposition: "Power is not merely a function of excellent philosophy. It is every bit as much a function of excellent physics. The rise of American power will be discussed in this manner." In this statement, I am suggesting for the students to consider that our traditional considerations of political power in regard to strategy (i.e., Clausewitz, Sun Tzu, Jominy, etc.) are inadequate to understand how modern nation-states conceptualize and innovate in terms of power and strategy. Mastering science and technology at the highest levels are fundamental to literally inventing new kinds of strategy for thinking about what power is and how to deploy it in future environments. Though, the early thinkers of this notion, people like Eugene Skolnikoff at MIT, were witnessing the impact of nuclear weapons as proof of this concept, today information technologies and automation and its associated technologies is part of this idea too.

Remotely piloted airborne systems have altered the public perception of combat. For our purposes, they have prepared the public for the specter of true automated combat and killing due to their perception of machines flying without human presence and delivering kinetic combat outcomes in virtually all times of the day in nearly all weather situations. This is not entirely true, however, perception matters. So what is the difference in terms of kind and meaning between remotely controlled human combat and automated combat? It seems to me that we could quickly look at three elements of this question for reflection tonight (technology, command, and control or C4I, and future outcomes—the so-called slippery slope). We can think about remotely piloted vehicles as might be applied to combat and/or surveillance scenarios for the purposes of thinking about future automation.

In our discussion I made the distinction between control of platform (which corresponds to the RPV) and command of the system (which corresponds to the battlespace in military terms) and some particular problems of risk to each of these dimensions. Here, in this slide, we are looking at the problem of control of platform and also here I am suggesting a spectrum of evolving kinds of control according to evolving states of technology. We can see that they range from what we are most familiar with in the example of human remote control of the RPV to what I refer to as "Automation 1" and that is what we have in operation today, RPVs that fly according to a range of increasingly intelligent software code instructions that interact with environment, but are still largely controlled by a human operator. Ultimately, I am describing a futuristic "Automation 2" that may not be an automated RPV flight event at all. Here, the RPV, operates on the basis of intelligent software that has evolved to a state where new forms of artificial intelligence exist and we could see what we refer to as synthetic and/or emergent pilot entities in the RPV/computational/ network combination of technology. In such an operation, we could expect to encounter novel flight events and outcomes; novel in that these events would be unique from any human input or control. Again, this is speculation for the purpose of thinking through technology in advance. At the Washington, D.C., meeting, I challenged the group of experts to consider how this contrasts to the way that we think about novel flight characteristics in civilian air transportation today, where a novel outcome in what is increasingly an automated system of global air traffic control is often referred to as an accident. This suggests that in the future, such AI systems may also force us to reconsider our nomenclature and the way that we think about such operations.

Let me add another consideration to this when we add in the technology of swarming RPV to this discussion. I am not sure that the public, nor even expert audiences such as ours here, truly have thought about the way that RPV technology may transform our environment. It is conceivable that evolution in swarm RPV technology could produce a tremendous number of artificial flying devices in our environment to interact with natural phenomena—animals, humans, and weather. We may have to expand our modeling capabilities to account for such machine behavior evolution for the purpose of planning and risk assessment. As noted at our meeting in Washington, D.C., we will also have to account for environmental impact as there will most certainly be life cycles and failure rates to the devices and clean-up will be necessary.

Let's get back to combat. In our present reality, what is the operational logic for automated killing machines? Again, the creation of a spectrum of uses can best inform how we might see development of such kinds of weapons. This also gives us the best ability to discuss the cost-benefit of such weapons in terms of mission and greater social wisdom. The evolution of combat automation comes from the remote-control platforms of the RPVs. Where human operators remotely pilot and launch weapons in the current protocols, these could easily give way to automated methods of RPVs in terms of flight and kinetic operations. But, is this desirable and optimal from a strategic, tactical, legal, and moral set of perspectives? As noted previously, we can understand that there is a technology push for these sorts of automated operations to evolve in this manner. We would realize greater efficiencies and greater mission outcomes as a result of greater ubiquity realized in terms of time on target and the resulting increased probabilities of finding target and destruction of target. Think about the power of ARGUS as a kinetic platform. However, one could argue that we essentially have this now even with human operators to a large degree. How can removing the final human element result in even greater mission success? In a cost-benefit calculation, it seems to many of us that the costs clearly outweigh the benefits, but this may reflect our particular social and cultural set of norms.

Let us sort of counter with the proposition that my colleague, Professor Phil Hall, makes: "When we build platforms where the human in the loop becomes the uncertain element, what sort of reliable system do we have?" We have wrestled with these conundrums before, during the Cold War in the forms of nuclear weapon triggering systems made up of human-machine symbiosis where we discovered human reliability problems in the psychological profile protocol studies of such systems. At the point of human action on the decision-making chain, what sorts of problems might arise that could result in individual human soldiers choosing to not "do their duty" and "turn the key" in the firing sequence of nuclear-tipped missiles? With the discovery of various outcomes where humans would not behave as desired in such systems, various fail-safe mechanisms were devised and some deployed in an attempt to further automate the system. This was done for two purposes, both important to nuclear weapon strategy. First was the logic of deterrence: we had to communicate to the enemy (the USSR) that we had a reliable system that would fire nuclear missiles in a reliable manner in certain situations for the express purpose of convincing them in their mindset that certain undesirable military outcomes had a high probability of occurrence that would modify their behavior to lower the threshold of such occurrence. Second was the logic that the system would indeed result in the firing of the missile as ordered by a constitutional authority, in the case of the failure of deterrence. In both situations, the solution was to evolve the system to one of more autonomy, greater reliability upon a machine or machine-like solution. How many of you in the audience, however, remain troubled by this solution and for what reasons? Is your position a reasoned and sound one, or is it counterintuitive? What lessons does this historical example have for advancing automation technologies in defense today? In my field of security studies, these examples of the so-called perversions of logic in nuclear weapon possession and strategy are still considered to be classic case studies. For example, in such a state of weapon standoff, the perversion of logic appears, the weapon loses it utility because of its sheer destructive power, yet its nonuse provides it constant utility to create the stalemate, a state of nonwar. Will there be similar technological evolutions in newer automated systems based upon advancing AI?

With regard to thinking about the future of automation, and humans too, we cannot truly see the future evolution of what we are working on due to the fact that we are primarily observing a nonlinear system. And, it is a futuristic example that I would like to close with tonight, for us to think about with regard to how automation might evolve in symbiosis with human beings. In my

Noetic Group exercise yesterday we discussed how automation examples may be ones in which we are building systems where humans adapt to automated machine systems for convenience now as opposed to more advanced systems where machines begin to adapt to human systems increasingly over time. I would like to suggest a third way, where humans and machines are physical hybrids in symbiosis and automation is a more complex thing. We have this now in some ways with smartphones and wearables, and we are beginning to advance more in the realm of implantable devices too for medical and more so for enhancement technologies.

This is a thought experiment, one that I put forth in an article in the IEEE Societies' *Technology and Society Magazine* in 2013 and presented to the National Intelligence Council's Science and Technology Committee in 2012. In it, I explored how the commingling of advanced computational engineering speed, ubiquitous networks with novel human-machine interfaces may result in what we refer to as "human information appliances." In a tactical intelligence event that I describe in the article, idealized for the purpose of exploring these advanced technologies, lies a version of autonomy that is at once both reminiscent of autonomous systems as they reside within human physiology and also troubling to the observer in that they may either (1) deny immediate human agency or (2) suggest a more complicated evolutionary outcome for democratic systems. Let me describe this scenario as follows:

Here we invoke the concept of the "battlespace" per Martin Libicki of the RAND Corporation as the operational environment for this kind of intelligence entity in the form of a "human information appliance" (HIA) schema for value-added outcomes in what we refer to the intelligence space. This is accomplished by borrowing conceptually from the Defense Advanced Research Projects Agency (DARPA) developed legacy and future digital systems such as artificial intelligence (AI) and future analog systems such as intelligence augmentation (IA, described below) as extrapolated in the HIA section of this discussion.

The merging of theoretical and empirical processes in the four areas of (1) exponential computational engineering (exaflop and greater speeds to produce deep event models); (2) cybernetic processes and applications (human-machine fusion and the legacy of DARPA's *AugCog*); (3) network cloud computing (netpliances); and (4) the continuing need for stealth, applied to the conduct of intelligence operations, is combined in this project. All presently defined stages of intelligence activities include, briefly, (1) collection of information, (2) analysis, (3) interpretation, (4) assignment of meaning, (5) assessment of error, (6) correction (aka learning), (7) communication with the cloud/HQ, and (8) production of intelligence and its utilization for immediate tactical decision making or long-term strategy may be substantially altered in terms of substance and time and dimension as a result of our work to engineer this kind of future intelligence space. Fundamentally, this project is about the design and effect of advancing technology (hence, the tendency to think signals intelligence [SIGINT]); however, it is primarily focused on a future variation of what we refer to as human intelligence (HUMINT) today.

Fully imagined and fully realized a squad of tactical combat soldiers can simultaneously be a tactical intelligence unit that, via the combined force-multiplying technologies that are the result of a human information appliance platoon, will be able to provide intelligence outcomes beyond Libicki's visions in 1996. To understand this tactical platoon as a sort of "human netpliance," let us break down the concepts and components that when combined make up a dynamic "tactical information cloud" that can perform all elements of the intelligence process as noted above, for example, in a combat environment in real time. Professionals who are already familiar with these steps in the intelligence process will already begin to understand the steps and technologies that we have already employed to compress time and reduce error in tactical environments to date. What we are describing here is an exponential growth in kind and capability that is a function of combining human activities with greater technological tools for data collection, analysis, and communication.

We can understand that advancements in these activities to date have chiefly come with the design and delivery of advanced electronic IAS (non-implanted) to augment human observation, analysis, decision making, and ultimately action/behavior. Such devices have provided the intelligence consumer with great advantages; however, they still take up space and interfere with stealth and they are not yet powerful enough nor have they truly achieved IA status (of talking to each other in constant and stealth manner). But, what if they could do so?

A particular kind of future national security critical infrastructure is explored next for the purpose of thinking about, in advance, evolving complexity and corresponding risk to this particular system for the purpose of learning about how to build in survivability and resilience for operational purposes and for societal outcomes as well.

Evolution of the Intelligence Cyborg

The intelligence cyborg will do what she/he has always done but in a more effective manner with the same level of seamless human/technical integration but via implantation of information technologies. This kind of human information appliance will be an unremarkable diminishable entity of tissue and hardware not so different in kind from her/his civilian cyborg counterpart.

We are suggesting that the evolution to these kinds of entities will move apace in both the military and civilian worlds as is already the case. In fact, this may help attenuate some of the potential ethical and moral problems that could arise from military activities to create cyborgs for strictly military purposes and outcomes. If they already exist as civilians (due to the evolution of the marketplace), the military can "assume" these capabilities for their purposes as they do with recruits now.

The human information appliance (HIA), in the form of an intelligence cyborg, will be monitoring the world, communicating with other like devices (e.g., platoon members), and enabling us to manage, store, and compare information quite effortlessly in the business of the collection of information and ultimately the production of intelligence. The appliance need not be overtly conscious of all tasks or even missions that are assigned to it/her/him in order to execute and complete them: remote persons/organizations will be able to task various automated systems "on-board" to acquire desired information even independently of the primary individual/person that serves as the *platform* for the IA. We can begin to realize the potential for this device. But, let's go deeper. As Libicki did in his *Orbis* article, we can imagine a greater power to be achieved and wielded in both the tactical environment and in a strategic one if this technology were to be realized.

We need to invoke a few more technological concepts to fully understand the plausibility and probability for the realization of such entities. An advanced HIA will be a cyborg that consists of implanted technologies that enhance the human senses; but, the real force multipliers will come in the form of the implantation and integration of IA hardware and software (code and algorithms) that speed up the process of analyzing environmental data that will be collected by the other enhanced sensory devices. CPUs, SSDs, memory cache, and power devices are the technologies necessary to realize these outcomes. Importantly, other technologies, especially medical and prophylactic in nature, are necessary in order to allow this to evolve so that the symbiosis can take place mitigated deleterious outcomes. Psychological and neurological research and development too is necessary as is R&D in the political, legal, and ethical dimensions of this kind of human evolution.

This kind of human information appliance, as a tactical intelligence/combat soldier, furthermore imbedded within a platoon of like HIAs that are a combined HIA cloud (that itself is networked to other HIA clouds and local, regional, and national command HQs to form an extended god-cloud) now allows us to posit the notion of extremely compressed time and space where tactical and strategic thought and operations begin to merge. Consider merely the tactical environment of a firefight for such a platoon for a moment. The platoon is an HIA cloud and the goal is to achieve superior situational awareness with a temporal advantage that can allow it to increase its probability of survival, according to present models, to a very significant degree. This cloud has the capability to collect an exponentially superior amount of environmental data about itself, and very importantly, about its enemy. As the data come in, the cloud in real time can, via the large array of parallel processing in its networked CPUs (again, networked to redundant systems in the larger god-cloud for reliability and redundant survivability), begin to immediately yield more robust probabilities for impending immediate decision events that correspond to present and/or future actions. In this sense, the HIA platoon cloud will have the ability to both see and model a past-present-future event for the purpose of more powerfully informing tactical decision-making needs. The unit has created a very small *time machine* that has the potential to see into the future a little bit faster than the enemy: this may be enough for immediate tactical advantage to win the day.

Intelligence at this level of evolution will become an effective multidimensional tool as the division of labor between the field and HQ blurs. We will begin to see a new information/intelligence model of rapid information acquisition and quantitative/qualitative analysis and delivery in which the foot soldier/HIA is connected via the IA cloud with other IAs who are working at the Pentagon, Langley, Bolling, Hoover, or Fort Meade. In a sense, we will have a single virtual analytical cloud with shared processing and data, and looking back down to the local platoon HIA cloud, we can imagine that it will become smarter on the fly as a result of its ability to learn and adapt via the temporal advantage mechanism.

Effect Arises from Exponential Computational Speed

How can exponential computational speed transform intelligence activity beyond the important task of NSA *archaeology* in the form of foreign document data mining? This project envisions the evolution and ultimate application of exponentially capable computational science and technologies—combined with advanced human information appliance (HIA) cybernetics to achieve situational awareness capabilities for intelligence functions in four-dimensional political and military intelligence spaces. The primary hardware-software-philosophy objective here is the development of schema that will allow human decision making (HDM) to accommodate the orders of magnitude of acceleration of data analysis and corresponding situational awareness for the purpose of superior HDM outcomes. Again, from Moreno, the reference to DARPA's *Aug-Cog* heuristic is a compelling one for us to apply to our own HIA intelligence scheme. Intelligence (i.e., the activity, the process, and various end positions) is our sole universe for this investigation and descriptive vision. As such, our utilization and description of information and cybernetic technologies in this chapter and our utilization of neuroscientific and even neuroethical heuristics (necessary to the cybernetic exploration) diverge from the usual discussions of applications to what are ultimately kinetic types of outcomes and events for combat/law enforcement purposes. We are interested here in ultimately a state of superior situational awareness of seeing, of knowing, of understanding, and this requires stealth. The goal here is to achieve not super soldiers or even super or expendable avatars; but rather enhanced-human intelligence producers that are, according to HIA parameters, absolutely human and unremarkable in most activities and appearances but extraordinary in outcomes as part of an overall intelligence cloud/netpliance.

Peter Singer in *Wired for War* cites Marc Galasco (of Human Rights Watch) as arguing for the fact that humans should retain ethical authority because of their "morality—an empathetic response—and an ability to make complex decisions." We seek to take the word/concept of "complexity" from Galasco's statement and add a great deal of more complexity to it due to the fact that the machine(s), in this example, are now cyborgs and the definitions are less clear. Consider this: How do we define machine and how do we define human for this kind of entity? Furthermore, how do we define *states of being* as they may inform the forensic process of decision making per the obligatory legal minds that will begin to apply their own analytical schemas to these entities and the processes and events within which they operate? One example comes to mind: will the addition of this kind of automation, rapid information processing, and big data analytical matrix actually influence the personalities and behaviors of the human cyborgs over time to where they start to exhibit different cultural traits?

An empirical example to inform this discussion (per another in-depth analytical paper) would be to consider and apply the phenomenon of the hearing-challenged (as opposed to the alternate label of deaf) community whose use of sign language has given rise to, for a particular subset of the population, a claim of a unique language and culture that results in an interesting juxtaposition of their legal status as "disabled" according to the Americans with Disabilities Act.

Does Enhancement Help Resolve or Confound Ethics?

Again, in the tradition of Libicki, we pause to conduct a reflection of such an achievement were it to come to pass. To do so efficiently, for the purposes of this chapter's goals, we will conduct the analysis for national security, homeland security, diplomacy, and intelligence spaces in simultaneous fashion. Like the *Orbis* article, this analysis compels us to consider the strategic and tactical implications of the application of such technologies to war, intelligence, security, and diplomacy. We will seek to do so in another paper, however, because our scenario is based upon the symbiosis of machine and humans that we choose to reflect now upon some of the ethical dimensions of this outcome and assert that this factors into a future security policy and diplomacy matrix. It would be deceptively easy to continue along the same analytical line or reasoning to complete this chapter by reflecting solely upon the strategic and tactical elements of these technologies. Yet, so much hinges on one very important construct that is elemental to what we have described thus far: the HIAs are undeniably, if realized, human and not just machine. Therefore, another proper analytical construct for this project is that of *human enhancement*.

I leave you here . . . with this question of where automation could take the relationship between humans and machines. It is time for reflection and consideration about the systems that we seek to build for the purposes of best outcomes for many important elements of human society. Security, economics, and democratic governance happen to be three of those areas that may be a good place to start. I thank you for this opportunity to explore the topic with you . . . and this opportunity to become acquainted with you and your work.[1]

Notes

This chapter is based on a paper given at the Australian Department of Defence Conference, University of New South Wales, July 16, 2015.

1. See James Bamford, "The NSA Is Building the Country's Biggest Spy Center (Watch What You Say)," *Wired*, March 15, 2012, http://www.wired.com/threatlevel/2012/03/ff-nsadatacenter/. Also see R. E. Burnett, "Brain Implants and Memory," *IEEE Technology and Society Magazine*, March 2017, 30–31; R. E. Burnett, "The Human Information Appliance in Combat, Intelligence, and Diplomacy," *IEEE Technology and Society Magazine*, Summer 2013; and Jonathan D. Moreno, *Mind Wars: Brain Science and the Military in the 21st Century*, repr. ed. (New York: Bellevue Literary Press, 2012).

Under Fire

TARGETED KILLING, UAVS, AND THREE AMERICAN PRESIDENTS

Anna Holyan

Tobias T. Gibson, Westminster College

Former President Donald Trump opened 2020 by ordering a UAV (unmanned aerial vehicle) strike on Iranian general Qasem Soleimani. This action indicates a willingness to increase hostilities with Iran and provides reason to question and critique the U.S. targeted killing program. It is well documented that the War on Terror under President George W. Bush began to use UAVs to kill suspected terrorists with minimal risk to U.S. troops and that the Barack Obama administration increased the targeted killing program and expanded the use of UAVs to new theaters of conflict.

Media and scholarly attention seemingly increased in concert with the dependence on UAVs as a means to fight terrorism abroad. However, during the Trump administration, though the use of UAVs has increased, the attention paid to the administration's use of drones has plummeted. As noted, Soleimani's death has provided fresh opportunity for further comment and consideration, which occurred in the short term, but as the news cycle turned, so did media attention away from the U.S. drone program.

Shortly following the terror attacks of September 11, 2001, the United States acquired surveillance video footage of Osama bin Laden in Kandahar, a remote city in southern Afghanistan. The United States had known of the al-Qaeda leader's whereabouts for some time, thanks to such footage, gathered by Predator drones equipped with sensors and cameras. With much of President George W. Bush's War on Terror being fought in remote areas of the Middle East (primarily Afghanistan and Pakistan), the first Predator drones served as a crucial surveillance tool.

The U.S. first began using drones (often referred to as unmanned aerial vehicles, remotely piloted vehicles, or unmanned aerial systems) in missions over Bosnia in the 1990s.[1] By 2001, the vehicles were still being used primarily as a surveillance tool, such that by the time the United States located Osama bin

Laden in 2001, an opportunity to kill him never arose. The usefulness and potential of the drone platform was obvious to the Bush administration: unable to reach remote areas with U.S. troops, it was the logical next step to weaponize the Predator. Early in the Global War on Terror, Predator drones, including the MQ-1, were mounted with Hellfire missiles, allowing the United States to track, engage, and terminate suspected terrorists.[2]

Presidents' reliance on drones as a keystone in fighting the War on Terror did not end with Bush. Since the beginning of the Obama administration, the United States not only remained reliant on drones but significantly increased the number of strikes on suspected terrorists. Though critics took note of the high number of civilians killed as a byproduct of early Bush-era strikes, much more has been written about the Obama-era drone program.[3] Among the major questions facing the Obama administration's drone program were the moral and legal weaknesses and implications of the program;[4] the high probability that drone strikes aided terrorist recruitment;[5] the global impact of the proliferation of drone usage;[6] the contradictory nature of Obama drone policy;[7] and finally the lack of transparency and oversight of the program.[8]

This chapter includes discussion of the drone programs under the Bush, Obama, and Trump presidencies. Despite a great deal of commentary regarding the Bush and Obama administrations' use of drones, President Trump's use has largely been ignored by scholars and critics. Despite Trump's continued reliance on drones, increased strikes,[9] and drone sales as a tool of American diplomatic policy for the first time,[10] it was not until his decision to kill General Soleimani that the press and scholars refocused on the global ramifications of U.S. drone dependence.[11]

Initially armed with congressional support in the passage of the Authorization of Use of Military Force passed following the 9/11 terrorist attacks, the Bush administration laid the groundwork for future reliance on drones as a tool of modern warfare. This chapter focuses primarily on the Obama administration, which cemented future presidents' abilities to carry out drone programs largely without oversight from Congress or the U.S. public. The inability of the Obama administration to codify checks on presidential power in his use of drones resulted in a Trump administration who inherited a program shrouded in secrecy and operating in the shadows.[12]

This chapter proceeds as follows: The next section serves as a brief introduction to the development of the Predator MQ-1 and its implementation and use during the Bush counterterrorism program. Following is a brief history of the rise of drones and the Obama administration's usage and reliance on them. The following section looks more closely at the Obama administration's program and calls into question much of the purported support and legal underpinnings justifying the program. The authors then offer an overview of the Trump administration's drone program and the ways in which the inherited program has changed or not. Next is a discussion of the global spread of drones, including the acquisition of such weapons by nations and subnational groups as well as a discussion of the implications of the Trump administration's foreign policy involving drones outside of counterterrorism uses. Then we examine in some detail the drone programs of four countries with questionable human rights records: China, Russia, Iran, and Pakistan. Finally, we offer concluding thoughts and concerns for the future of the drone program and what that means for the future of executive power.

Rise of the Drone

The first MQ-1 Predator drone was originally developed in the early 1990s by the Defense Advanced Research Projects Agency (DARPA) and remotely piloted by CIA squads in the desert of Nevada to monitor forces in Serbia.[13] At the time, Osama bin Laden was a long-known threat to the United States. The era of modern terror really began with the 1998 bombings of two U.S. embassies in the capitals of Kenya and Tanzania, in which 224 people were killed, including 12 Americans. In response President Clinton promised to "use all the means at our disposal to bring those responsible to justice, no matter what or how long it takes."[14]

It was a little over two years later, on September 27, 2000, when the Predator drone located bin Laden (the orchestrater of the attacks), in Kandahar, but was unable to do anything more than report information because the drone was not weaponized.[15] Just days later, al-Qaeda attacked the USS Cole, catalyzing the process of equipping Predator drones for both surveillance and elimination of known terrorists.[16] Initial weapons tests were unsuccessful, but the terrorist attacks of 9/11 renewed the fervor to weaponize Predator drones. By December 11, 2001, in a speech given at The Citadel military college in South Carolina, President Bush addressed the breadth and depth of the hunt for bin Laden and other al-Qaeda operatives. Hints at the future reliance on the capabilities of the Predator came up in the speech, the president stating,

> No cave is deep enough to escape the patient justice of the United States of America. . . . We are fighting shadowy, entrenched enemies, enemies using the tools of terror and guerrilla war. Yet we are finding new tactics and new weapons to attack and defeat them. This revolution in our military is only beginning, and it promises to change the face of battle. Afghanistan has been a proving ground for this new approach. These past two months have shown that an innovative doctrine in high-tech weaponry can shape and then dominate an unconventional conflict. The brave men and women of our military are rewriting the rules of war with new technologies and old values, like courage and honor. . . . The Predator is a good example. This

unmanned aerial vehicle is able to circle over enemy forces, gather intelligence, transmit information instantly back to commanders, then fire on targets with extreme accuracy. Before the war, the Predator had skeptics because it did not fit the old ways. Now it is clear: The military does not have enough unmanned vehicles.[17]

Among other uses of force, drones offered the ability for greater precision.

As a New York University professor constitutional law put it, "Drones are the most discriminating use of force that has ever been developed."[18] With ever-increasing technology came the ability to limit the civilian to combatant deaths. The 9/11 attacks hastened the increase in new technology and capabilities of drones. By Bush's Citadel speech, new orders were being placed for drones that could be flown at increasing distances all over the globe, from Creech Air Force Base in Nevada.[19] The U.S. drone arsenal went from 16 Predators and 82 total drones in 2001 to 8,000 drones—165 of which were Predators equipped with surveillance and Hellfire missile capabilities and 73 of which were Reaper drones—in 2010.[20]

The increasing availability of drones meant increased opportunities to use them. The first U.S. attack on a suspected terrorist occurred in Yemen in 2002. However, most U.S. drone-based counterterror efforts were focused in the Federally Administered Tribal Areas (an extremely remote and largely ungoverned area of Pakistan). Although President Bush has singled out the Predator and suggested its ability to "dominate an unconventional conflict," U.S. drone strikes in Pakistan occurred only ten times between 2004 and 2007. By 2008, that number had more than tripled for the Bush administration.[21]

While there was outcry because of the high percentage of civilian casualties, news coverage of enhanced interrogation techniques and prisoner treatment at Guantánamo Bay meant that the Bush administration would not particularly be tainted by or remembered for its drone usage. The Obama administration came to rely heavily on the Predator and attacked more in 2009 than the Bush administration had in total. That number more than doubled again in 2010.[22] It is little wonder that the critics increased under Obama.

Moral, Legal, and Pragmatic Issues from American Drones

In 2010, the Obama administration authorized 122 Predator strikes in Pakistan. That number dropped to 72 in 2011, and then dropped each subsequent year of his administration. However, Obama also authorized more strikes in Yemen and more strikes globally in Libya, Somalia, and elsewhere.[23] It should be noted that advances in technology increased the advantage of precision weaponry leading to fewer unintentional deaths, which led to a dramatic decrease in reported civilian casualties;[24] however, questions about how these strike decisions were being made lingered.

For example, according to *New York Times* reporter Scott Shane, the Obama administration was concerned about how a Romney administration might establish its "kill list." Shane reported that "national security officials insist that the process is meticulous and lawful, the president and top aides believe it should be institutionalized, a course of action that seemed particularly urgent when it appeared that Mitt Romney might win the presidency. 'There was concern that the levers might no longer be in our hands,' said one official, speaking on condition of anonymity."[25] President Obama was clearly concerned about the long-term ethics of his administration's program: "This new technology raises profound questions—about who is targeted, and why; about civilian casualties, and the risk of creating new enemies; about the legality of such strikes under U.S. and international law; about accountability and morality."[26]

One of the biggest questions surrounded the Obama administration's use of "signature strikes," defined by the administration as precise strikes of unknown individuals who meet certain behavioral patterns the administration associated with terrorism.[27] Signature strikes offer an imprecise use and justification for precise weaponry. Such strikes mean that the targets are not identified as specific and known threats; rather, the targets meet some threshold of behavioral qualities that are common to terrorists and are not themselves on the "kill list" that, according to its officials, the administration so diligently and carefully crafted.[28] Arguably, the administration targeted unknown persons—and carefully avoided, through the manipulation of its own definitions and descriptions, killing probable innocent civilians.[29]

In 2013, NBC News released a Department of Justice (DOJ) "white paper" about the parameters of the drone program. The DOJ's focus was on the administration's claim that it would prefer to capture rather than kill a suspected terrorist.

The administration argued it would target only individuals who were an "imminent threat" to the United States. The elimination of an individual required "near certainty" that the intended target was at the site that would be hit and a "near certainty" that innocent noncombatants would not become causalities.[30] This policy position led to several questions from critics. Among the questions were the meaning of "imminent" and the definition of "noncombatant," due to the administration's claims that "military age males" in some areas can be legitimate targets, and how a "signature strike" squares with any of the legal standards divined by the DOJ.[31]

To provide but one detailed example from the above issues, "traditionally, 'imminent' was understood to mean 'instant, overwhelming, and leaving no choice of means, and no moment for deliberation.'"[32] However, the Obama administration's definition was rather loose. According to the DOJ white paper, "Certain aspects of this legal framework require additional explication. First, the condition that an operational leader present an 'imminent' threat of violent attack against the United States does not require the United States to have clear evidence that a specific attack on U.S. persons will take place in the immediate future."[33] This leads to questions about "how the U.S. government determines the 'imminence' of unknown types of future attacks being planned by unknown individuals."[34]

What is remarkable is that the Obama administration did not have a formalized set of rules, at least by the end of his first term. According to Shane, even after the 2012 presidential election, the administration was still pushing to make the rules formal and resolve internal uncertainty and disagreement about exactly when lethal action is justified. Mr. Obama and his advisers were still debating whether remote-control killing should be a measure of last resort against imminent threats to the United States or a more flexible tool, available to help allied governments attack their enemies or to prevent militants from controlling territory.[35]

This is a remarkable proclamation, for at least three reasons. First, as noted above and in many other outlets, the Obama administration relied heavily on drone strikes as a cornerstone to its counterterrorism policy. Second, this reliance came without a clear blueprint and foundational legal reasoning about when drone use was appropriate and whom legally eligible targets would be. This indecision may have had a legal impact, including on American citizens accused of terrorism. According to an April 2015 report, Mohanad Mahmoud Al Farekh, who was arrested in 2013, "'stood before a federal judge in Brooklyn this month. . . . [His] court appearance also came as the Obama administration was struggling to fashion new guidelines for targeted killings.'"[36] Third, some members of the intelligence community reported conflict within the administration between the CIA and DOD—both of which wanted few restrictions—and the Department of Justice and the Department of State.[37]

There is concern that pervasive drone use minimizes the oversight of lethal force by the president. This may happen for two reasons. First, in the Obama administration, there were two drone programs. One, in the Department of Defense was relatively well known and subject to public oversight. The other, housed in the CIA, had much less oversight.[38] And even when Congress—or more accurately, the intelligence committees in both chambers—decide to exert more oversight over the CIA's drone program, reports suggest that it "continued to operate with near autonomy." Porter fears that "drones attract policymakers because they seem to make war easier."[39]

The Obama administration said on two occasions that it would make the drone "playbook" public, though it was slow to do so and came only after much public pressure. The first suggestion of its release came when it was faced with the possibility that Obama might be leaving the White House and that the drone program would be led by 2012 presidential hopeful Mitt Romney.[40] The second announcement was made on March 4, 2016, just as the presidential campaign ran headlong toward the parties' nominations. This announcement came in response to a judicially mandated release of the Presidential Policy Guidance (PPG) regarding the drone program. The eighteen-page redacted set of rules was declassified and released by the American Civil Liberties Union (ACLU) in August 2016.[41] It is not clear whether or not the government would have released the PPG without being required by the U.S. District Court judge Colleen MacMahon's order. What is clear is that the Obama administration—despite all of the criticism the president received—trusted no one else to run the drone program. As Obama himself stated, "I think creating a legal structure, processes, with oversight on how we use unmanned weapons is going to be a challenge for me and for my successors for some time to come."[42]

International Implications of Obama-Era Policy

The United States no longer monopolizes drone activity worldwide. Nearly one hundred states now have drones. While the vast majority of these are surveillance drones, there are at least six states that have weaponized drones.[43] Several states, the United States, the United Kingdom, Israel, Nigeria, and Pakistan, have used weaponized drones in combat.[44] As of 2014, at least twenty-three states had budding domestic programs to develop weaponized drones and at least sixty states had some domestic production capabilities.[45]

Whether the Obama administration took its self-professed doctrine regarding a preference to capture rather than kill seriously is a major question. Evidence seems to suggest otherwise. It has been widely argued that because of the ease (see the following paragraph) of using drones, the difficulty of accessing remote areas of Afghanistan and Pakistan, the safety of Americans, and the legal challenges to the U.S. detention and interrogation policy (Mazzetti quotes former CIA attorney John Rizzo as noting that "once the interrogation was gone, all that was left was the killing"), it may not be the case that capture is preferred in many instances.[46]

As the United States became more reliant on the use of drones and took the fight to several countries beyond the "hot battlefields" in Pakistan, Afghanistan, and Iraq, the acquisition of drones globally exploded. Twenty-nine states have now developed a domestic armed drone industry, an increase of more than 25 percent since 2015.[47]

And the example provided to the world by the Obama administration seems to be that drones are inexpensive alternatives (though, as the technology advances, this may be less true) under difficult circumstances.[48] However, the real lessons appear to be that the world's lone superpower projects its force into sovereign states with or without permission. There are some clear instances, like in the instance of failed governments in Somalia and Yemen, and other less clear instances. The United States reserves the right to use targeted killings in states that are "unwilling or unable" to mount effective counterterrorism operations.

Simultaneously, diplomatic issues arise when the United States strikes. Former U.S. ambassador to Pakistan Cameron Munter discovered that U.S. influence with the Pakistani government waned "with nearly every strike."[49] Mazzetti reports that "Munter wondered whether the pace of the drone war might be undercutting relations with an important ally for the quick fix of killing midlevel terrorists." But "in the Obama administration, when it came to questions about war and peace, it was what the CIA believed that really counted."[50] And the CIA believed by then that Pakistan was an enemy, not a partner.[51] The U.S. targeted killing program in the wake of 9/11 and the invasion of Afghanistan, and its extension to Pakistan, Yemen, Somalia, and elsewhere, was sure to raise some eyebrows. For example, the United States had recently rebuked Israel's targeted killing of senior members of Hamas, with the U.S. ambassador to Israel saying that the program amounted to "extrajudicial killings and we do not support this."[52]

The diplomatic difficulties extend well beyond Pakistan and include long-term allies in Europe. According to the Stimson Drone Task Force,

> In February 2014, for instance, the European Parliament voted 534–49 for a resolution condemning U.S. drone strikes, asserting that "thousands of civilians have reportedly been killed or seriously injured by drone strikes [but] these figures are difficult to estimate, owing to lack of transparency and obstacles to effective investigation." The resolution went on to call for EU member states to "oppose and ban the practice of extrajudicial targeted killings [and] ensure that the member states, in conformity with their legal obligations, do not perpetrate unlawful targeted killings or facilitate such killings by other states."[53]

While the legal and moral issues about U.S. culpability matter, perhaps the biggest question for future presidents is whether drone strikes have the desired long-term counterterrorism benefits. Some scholars, journalists, ethicists, and practitioners argue that "U.S. [drone] strikes and particularly those that kill civilians . . . are sowing the seeds of future generations of terrorists."[54] This is especially true when the U.S. government allows the "legal slippage" resulting in the use of signature strikes.[55] In sum, it is not the technology but the use of the technology that is the issue. Charli Carpenter, for one, argues that the United

States' misuse of the newly developed military assets in these shadow wars has cast a pall over those assets themselves as legitimate tools of war, properly understood:

> Remote-controlled weaponry is hardly inconsistent with the rules of war and drones were engineered as a precision weapon capable of reducing civilian casualties. Had they been used exclusively for this purpose in legitimate, occasional just wars . . . they would perhaps have been hailed as a humanitarian advance. Instead both the Bush and Obama administrations have used them as a tool of shadow "warfare" . . . to carry out a summary execution campaign that violates the U.N. Charter, human rights law and the law of armed conflict, and has exacted a grievous toll among civilians. Thus, far from being seen as humanitarian tools, drones now elicit widespread fear and condemnation among populations both at home and abroad in their own right.[56]

It is worth noting that some disagree with the claim that the drone program violates legal norms.[57] Stack states unequivocally that "there is now near-consensus that drone use in Afghanistan is consistent with [international humanitarian law]," based on the principles of necessity, distinction, and proportionality.[58] But Rosa Brooks suggests that there is more nuance to this issue. Due to the secrecy and often changing legal arguments presented by the Obama administration and its members, "it is impossible to say whether any given strike (or the totality of strikes) satisfies . . . legal . . . principles."[59] This is important because it suggests that different aspects of the drone program may have differing levels of legal support. For example, targeted killings of a particular, named, known suspected terrorist, in which there has been deliberation based on intelligence before placing a name on the "kill list," may meet legal standards that the more arbitrary "signature strikes" failed to meet.

When the United States alters its legal reasoning to allow the decidedly low bar resulting in "signature strikes," it is not difficult to imagine a government that has no need for legal pretense to take advantage of the signature strike justification and abuse the reasoning even further. William Hartung notes that U.S. sales of drones to other countries may present serious issues. In particular, he notes that "U.S. standards on the use of drones are themselves inadequate."[60] He argues that until the administration's policy is vetted, there is concern that U.S. drone program policy will become the global standard.

It appears that Hartung's cautioning was not for naught. Iraq announced in January 2016 that it accidentally killed nine members of a Shiite militia in an armed drone attack.[61] Both Pakistan and Nigeria have used drones against domestic armed insurgents.[62] The Pakistani government announced in September 2015 via Twitter that its first "ever use of Pak made Burraq Drone today hit a terrorist compound in Shawal Valley killing 3 high profile terrorists."[63]

Analysts suggest that although the Pakistani government may not use surgical strikes, the process by which targets are selected is unknown. Even more similarly to the United States, "the Israel Defense Forces frequently uses armed drones to target suspected militants in Syria, Gaza, and Sinai. As with the United States, however, Israel is not forthcoming with details because of the military sensitivity of the strikes and the political sensitivity of diplomatic relationships that facilitate those strikes, such as with the Egyptian government with respect to strikes in the Sinai."[64]

Among the states that either have weaponized drones or are seeking to develop them are adversarial states such as Russia, China, Iran, and Pakistan.[65] Several of these countries have their own programs. China, for example, has had missile-capable drones since at least 2012.[66] At least since 2010 Iran has had drones capable of firing missiles, which former President Ahmadinejad described as an "ambassador of death."[67] Both Iran and China have domestic drone production.

China's UAV program is especially well developed, and it has been producing armed drones since at least 2012. Due to U.S. reticence under the Obama administration to sell its wares on the global market, China filled that vacuum and became the world's primary exporter of drones. According to a representative of the Chinese Chengdu Aircraft Design and Research Institute, "The United States doesn't export many attack drones, so we're taking advantage of that hole in the market."[68] China has exported drones to Iraq, Saudi Arabia, UAE, Pakistan, and Nigeria.

"American practices . . . are . . . providing SANSA [state and nonstate actors] with clear justification for their programs. Without a transparent policy, SANSA are apt to mirror American precedents when creating their programs."[69] Indeed, the Stimson Drone Task Force opines strongly about the real dangerous precedent set by U.S. drone policy. In a hypothetical situation, the task force suggests:

U.S. practices also set a dangerous precedent that may be seized upon by other states—not all of which are likely to behave as scrupulously as U.S. officials. Imagine, for instance, if Russia began to use UAV strikes to kill individuals opposed to its annexation of Crimea and its growing influence in Eastern Ukraine. Even if the United States strongly believed those targeted by Russian were all nonviolent political activists lawfully expressing their opinions, Russia could easily take a page out of the United States' book and assert that the targeted individuals were members of anti-Russian terrorist groups with which Russia is in an armed conflict. Pressed for evidence, Russia could simply repeat the words used by U.S. officials defending U.S. targeted killings, asserting that it could not provide any evidence without disclosing sources and methods and creating a risk that terrorists would go underground. In such circumstances, *how could the United States credibly condemn Russian targeted killings?*[70]

Representative Adam Schiff, chairman of the House Permanent Select Committee on Intelligence, argued in 2014 that the United States is the only country with "a significant armed drone capability, but that distinction will not last forever. As other nations develop and deploy these technologies, we will be better positioned to urge their responsible and transparent use if we have set an example ourselves. We must hold ourselves to a high standard and do it in public, not behind closed doors."[71]

William C. Banks concurs, noting that "the significant shortcoming in the U.S. policy is its lack of transparency. . . . If the United States does nothing to remediate its domestic law rules and processes . . . , this international legal precedent will likely open the door for other states to pursue the use of drone strikes untethered by legal constraints."[72]

Transitioning from Obama to the Trump Era

Critics have long expressed concern that war waged by drone "may take the destructive power of war outside the boundaries of democratic legitimacy, because we are far more willing to delegate the power to use force without risk to the president than we are a power to commit the nation to the sacrifice of its citizens."[73] This is exceptionally problematic. President Obama said in 2012 that "one of the things we've got to do is put a legal architecture in place, and we need Congressional help in order to do that, to make sure that not only am I reined in but any president's reined in, in terms of some of the decisions that we're making."[74] We agree with the former president and have suggested since 2013 that "it has become apparent that Congress needs to reinsert itself in the nation's war-making."[75]

In addition to separation of power issues, concerns about the U.S. role in the world if drone strikes occurred without more consideration of internal and global politics were clearly understood as the Obama administration handed the reins to his successor, President Trump. Based on the public and international pushback regarding the U.S. drone program, we might expect the next president might work to restore global trust, including among key allies, and could have considered a transparent policy drafted with the aid of Congress. Instead, the fears that a future president might not act within the same confines that the Obama administration at least claimed to adhere to have proved to be, if anything, undersold.

There have been at least five events that have led the Trump administration's drone use to become part of the news cycle. First, like Obama before him, Trump dramatically increased the drone strikes from the level of his predecessor. It should be noted here, however, that at the end of his term Obama had curtailed his use of drone strikes.[76] While Trump's expansion included only eight strikes in Pakistan, he expanded the global reach of drone strikes to include Syria and Iran.

Second, President Trump made news when he seemed to question even the basic assumptions about the laws of armed conflict related to his drone strikes. In April 2018, after a strike in which the CIA waited until the target left his home, President Trump asked why the strike did not occur when the target's family could also have been killed. This is in line with then-candidate Trump's 2015 assertion that "when you get these terrorists, you have to take out their families. They care about their lives, don't kid yourself. But they say they don't care about their lives. You have to take out their families."[77]

Third, Trump administration foreign policy has utilized the sale of drones in ways that were prevented under the Obama administration. This can be seen as part of the consistent effort to limit Chinese economic heft globally and could undercut at least some of the Chinese international drone sales. However, the immediate benefit seems to be limited. Although the drone sales policy was loosened, several components within the government, including the State Department, Commerce Department, and the Air Force, were slow to initiate and finalize sales.[78] More recent news suggests that the administration may be making headway, as the United States and India have announced a drone sale to India for use in its military branches.[79]

Fourth, on March 6, 2019, President Trump issued Executive Order 13862, which overturned the Obama requirement to report drone strike casualties, an action taken in response to concerns discussed above.[80]

Most recently and most importantly, President Trump opened 2020 with the successful drone strike on Iranian general Qasem Soleimani, head of the Islamic Revolutionary Guards Corps Quds Force. Soleimani was inarguably responsible for several attacks on and fatalities of U.S. troops. Nevertheless, the strike caused an explosion of drone policy discussion from within the administration, from pundits and practitioners and, importantly, Congress.

Arguably, the administration did itself no favors with the inconsistent rhetoric surrounding the purpose and intention of the strike. In the wake of the strike, several administration officials, including the president, took to network news and social media to explain the importance of the strike. The Department of Defense, Secretary of State Mike Pompeo, and President Trump reported that Soleimani was plotting an imminent attack or attacks on the United States, with potential targets being military or embassy targets. Secretary Pompeo told Fox News: "There is no doubt that there were a series of imminent attacks being plotted by Qassem Soleimani. We don't know precisely when and we don't know precisely where, but it was real."[81]

However, President Trump, in a Twitter post, potentially undermined this already amorphous reasoning (see the discussion of "imminence" above) when he tweeted that "fake news media and their democrat partners are working hard to determine whether or not the future attack by terrorist Soleimani was 'imminent' or not," but continued by saying that "it doesn't really matter because of his horrible past!"[82] In other words, the president again seemed to suggest that he either does not know or does not care about the limitations of international law.

Separation of power issues are also key to the current discussion. As discussed above, the decision to allow a strike is that of the president alone. As Goldsmith argues, "The executive branch will have an easy time justifying the strike under extant opinions, because for many years it has staked out ever-broader theories of presidential uses of force under both domestic and international law. Both parties in Congress have gone along with this expansion of presidential war power, especially with regard to the complex Middle East wars." In short, our country has—through presidential aggrandizement accompanied by congressional authorization, delegation, and acquiescence—given one person, the president, a sprawling military and enormous discretion to use it in ways that can easily lead to a massive war.[83]

For the first time in a long time, the decision to kill Soleimani, and therefore to increase tensions with Iran, seems to have led Congress to act in a manner that may limit seemingly unlimited war-making powers of a sitting president—in this case, President Trump's ability to attack Iran, even if this limit is not a broad constraint. In a bipartisan act, both chambers of Congress agreed to place limits on President Trump's unilateral power to attack Iran. According to the Senate sponsor, Tim Kaine, "The resolution just says no war with Iran, unless you come and make that case to Congress. And if you make the case to Congress, in front of the American people, and we all have the discussion, ask the tough questions and conclude, sadly, it's in the national interest, that's one thing."[84] In the end, however, even this minimal fettering of presidential powers failed, as President Trump vetoed the bill.

Conclusion

Winston Churchill once noted that "want of foresight, unwillingness to act when action would be simple and effective, lack of clear thinking, confusion of counsel until the emergency comes, until self-preservation strikes its jarring gong—these are the features which constitute the endless repetition of history."[85] This is the weakness of President Obama's drone policy development. Said differently, "If we truly believe in . . . human rights . . . the lack of transparency and accountability characterizing U.S. drone strikes should chill us to the bone."[86] Brooks goes further, asserting that "when the U.S. asserts a unilateral right to use force in a secretive and unaccountable way, we must consider that we are essentially handing every repressive and unscrupulous regime a playbook for how to violate sovereignty and get away with murder."[87]

Many scholars and critics have suggested a variety of oversight mechanisms for the U.S. drone program, including "drone courts."[88] We disagree with this proposal and believe that a well-designed and -defined program, with effective and active congressional oversight, is the preferred institutional protection. We believe that a "drone court" would have the counterintuitive impact of limiting effective oversight for two reasons. First, it would further dissipate oversight and accountability away from the elected branches, especially the president. We contend that a president must take ultimate responsibility for targeted killings, no matter what the methods of the killing may be. Second, we fear that reassigning oversight to the judicial branch would limit the incentive of Congress to fulfil its constitutionally mandated roles regarding oversight of the executive branch.

In many ways, the failings of the Obama administration were laid bare in the midst of the Trump presidency. Through the Obama administration's failure to codify standards for drone warfare and Congress's failure to exert appropriate checks on presidential authority, the American public is left to wrestle with the reality of a president with little knowledge of or respect for law and precedent. The established lack of transparency inherited by the Trump administration means that there is no public expectation for oversight. The hubris of the Obama administration was that it assumed that future presidents would be similarly thoughtful (if their claim is to be believed) in their use of drones as a means of warfighting. The "presidential aggrandizement" Goldsmith wrote about can be met with oversight only if there is any hope to rein in future presidents.

Notes

1. Nicholas Grossman, *Drones and Terrorism: Asymmetric Warfare and the Threat to Global Security* (London: I.B. Tauris, 2018), 39.

2. Richard Whittle, *Predator: The Secret Origins of the Drone Revolution* (New York: Picador, 2015).

3. Grossman, *Drones and Terrorism*, 63–66.

4. Kenneth R. Himes, *Drones and the Ethics of Targeted Killing* (Lanham, Md.: Rowman & Littlefield, 2016). See also John Kaag and Sarah E. Kreps, *Drone Warfare* (Cambridge, Mass.: Polity, 2016); Sarah Kreps, "Ground the Drones?," *Foreign Affairs*, December 18, 2013, https://www.foreignaffairs.com/articles/2013-12-04/ground-drones. See also Kenneth Anderson, "Targeted Killing and Drone Warfare: How We Came to De-

bate Whether There Is a 'Legal Geography of War,'" SSRN, April 27, 2011, https://papers
.ssrn.com/sol3/papers.cfm?abstract_id=1824783.

5. Shuaib Almosawa, "Teenagers Are Droned, and a Family Cries Out," *Foreign Policy*, November 4, 2013, https://foreignpolicy.com/2013/11/04/teenagers-are-droned-and
-a-family-cries-out/.

6. Peter L. Bergen and Jennifer Rowland, "World of Drones," in *Drone Wars: Transforming Conflict, Law, and Policy*, ed. Peter L. Bergen and Daniel Rothenberg (Cambridge: Cambridge University Press, 2015), https://www.cambridge.org/core/books
/drone-wars/world-of-drones/847220C7D673E94EBECB2C70D58300DB. See also Ulrike Esther Franke, "The Global Diffusion of Unmanned Aerial Vehicles (UAVs), or 'Drones,'" in *Precision Strike Warfare and International Intervention: Strategic, Ethicolegal and Decisional Implications*, ed. Mike Aaronson, Wali Aslam, Tom Dyson, and Regina Rauxloh (London: Routledge, 2016). See also Elias Groll, "Iran Is Deploying Drones in Iraq. Wait, What? Iran Has Drones?," *Foreign Policy*, June 25, 2014, http://
foreignpolicy.com/2014/06/25/iran-is-deploying-drones-in-iraq-wait-what-iran-has
-drones/.

7. Mark Bowden, "The Killing Machines," *Atlantic*, September 2013, https://www
.theatlantic.com/magazine/archive/2013/09/the-killing-machines-how-to-think-about
-drones/309434/. See also Sarah Knuckey, "Human Rights Groups Release Investigation Reports into U.S. Targeted Killings: A Guide to the Issues," *Just Security*, November 14, 2013, https://www.justsecurity.org/2316/hrw-ai-targeted-killings-guide-pakistan
-yemen/.

8. Conor Friedersdorf, "What If Mitt Romney Inherits Obama's Killer Drone Fleet?," *Atlantic*, October 23, 2012, http://www.theatlantic.com/politics/archive/2012/10/what-if
-mitt-romney-inherits-obamas-killer-drone-fleet/263977/.

9. Gareth Porter, "America's Permanent-War Complex," *American Conservative*, November 15, 2018, https://www.theamericanconservative.com/articles/americas
-permanent-war-complex/.

10. Lara Seligman, "Trump's Push to Boost Lethal Drone Exports Reaps Few Rewards," *Foreign Policy*, December 6, 2018, https://foreignpolicy.com/2018/12/06/trump
-push-to-boost-lethal-drone-exports-reaps-few-rewards-uas-mtcr/.

11. Ryan Pickrell, "The Trump Administration Is Struggling to Explain Why the U.S. Killed Top Iranian General Soleimani—Here's All the Shifting Explanations," *Business Insider*, January 13, 2020, https://www.businessinsider.com/trump-administrations-
shifting-explanations-for-soleimani-killing-2020–1. See also Jack Goldsmith, "The Soleimani Strike: One Person Decides," *Lawfare*, January 8, 2020, https://www.lawfareblog
.com/soleimani-strike-one-person-decides.

12. Kelsey D. Atherton, "Trump Inherited the Drone War but Ditched Accountability," *Foreign Policy*, May 22, 2020, https://foreignpolicy.com/2020/05/22/obama-drones
-trump-killings-count/.

13. Ahmed S. Hashim and Grégoire Patte, "'What Is That Buzz?' The Rise of Drone Warfare," *Counter Terrorist Trends and Analyses* 4, no. 9 (2012): 8–13.

14. Andrea Mitchell and Haley Talbot, "Two Far-Away Bombings 20 Years Ago Set Off the Modern Era of Terror," *NBC News*, August 7, 2018, https://www.nbcnews.com
/news/world/two-far-away-bombings-20-years-ago-set-modern-era-n898196.

15. Whittle, *Predator*, 180–81. See also Andrew Cockburn, *Kill Chain: The Rise of the High-Tech Assassins* (New York: Picador, 2016), 70.

16. Cockburn, *Kill Chain*, 70.

17. George W. Bush, "Address to Citadel Cadets," Charleston, S.C., December 11, 2001, https://americanrhetoric.com/speeches/gwbushcitadelcadets.htm.

18. Mark Bowden, "How the Predator Drone Changed the Character of War" (Smithsonian Institution, November 1, 2013), https://www.smithsonianmag.com/history/how-the-predator-drone-changed-the-character-of-war-3794671/.

19. Whittle, *Predator*, 210–18.

20. Ibid., 210–18.

21. Grossman, *Drones and Terrorism*, 65.

22. Ibid., 65.

23. Ibid., 65.

24. Gregory McNeal, "Are Targeted Killings Unlawful? A Case Study in Empirical Claims without Empirical Evidence," in *Targeted Killings: Law and Morality in an Asymmetrical World*, ed. Claire Oakes et al. (New York: Oxford University Press, 2012), 326–46. See also Patrick Porter, *The Global Village Myth Distance, War, and the Limits of Power* (Washington, D.C.: Georgetown University Press, 2015), 206. However, Adam B. Schiff, "Let the Military Run Drone Warfare," *New York Times*, March 13, 2014, https://www.nytimes.com/2014/03/13/opinion/let-the-military-run-drone-warfare.html, and Knuckey, "Human Rights Groups," offer key nuances to this observation. Grossman, *Drones and Terrorism*, 65.

25. Scott Shane, "Election Spurred a Move to Codify U.S. Drone Policy," *New York Times*, November 24, 2012, https://www.nytimes.com/2012/11/25/world/white-house-presses-for-drone-rule-book.html.

26. Barack Obama, "Remarks by the President at the National Defense University" (National Archives and Records Administration, May 23, 2013), https://obamawhitehouse.archives.gov/the-press-office/2013/05/23/remarks-president-national-defense-university.

27. Himes, *Drones and the Ethics of Targeted Killing*, 125–28. See also Mark Mazzetti, *The Way of the Knife: The CIA, a Secret Army, and a War at the Ends of the Earth* (New York: Penguin, 2014), and Kreps, "Ground the Drones?"

28. Kaag and Kreps, *Drone Warfare*; Shane, "Election Spurred a Move to Codify U.S. Drone Policy"; Himes, *Drones and the Ethics of Targeted Killing*, 95–116.

29. Mazzetti, *Way of the Knife*, 4; Himes, *Drones and the Ethics of Targeted Killing*, 95–116.

30. Kaag and Kreps, *Drone Warfare*, 39. See also Andrew Blake, "Obama-Led Drone Strikes Kill Innocents 90% of the Time: Report," *Washington Times*, October 15, 2015, http://www.washingtontimes.com/news/2015/oct/15/90-of-people-killed-by-us-drone-strikes-in-afghani/.

31. Kaag and Kreps, *Drone Warfare*, 40. See also Tobias T. Gibson, "Obama, Drones, and the Matter of Definitions," *Duck of Minerva*, May 28, 2013, https://duckofminerva.com/2013/05/obama-drones-and-the-matter-of-definitions.html.

32. John P. Abizaid and Rosa Brooks, "Recommendations and Report of the Task Force on U.S. Drone Policy," 2nd ed. (Washington, D.C.: Stimson, 2015), 34, http://www

.stimson.org/sites/default/files/file-attachments/recommendations_and_report_of_the
_task_force_on_us_drone_policy_second_edition.pdf.

33. "Lawfulness of a Lethal Operation Directed Against a U.S. Citizen Who Is a Senior Operational Leader of Al-Qa'ida or an Associated Force" (Washington, D.C.: U.S. Department of Justice, November 8, 2011), 7, https://www.justice.gov/sites/default/files/oip/legacy/2014/07/23/dept-white-paper.pdf.

34. Abizaid and Brooks, "Recommendations and Report," 35.

35. Shane, "Election Spurred a Move to Codify U.S. Drone Policy."

36. Tobias T. Gibson, "Bring Back the Drone Debate, Sen. Paul," *The Hill*, April 21, 2015, http://thehill.com/blogs/pundits-blog/defense/239483-bring-back-the-drone-debate-sen-paul.

37. Kaag and Kreps, *Drone Warfare*, 37.

38. Schiff, "Let the Military Run Drone Warfare." See also Tobias T. Gibson, "The Oversight of Too Much Oversight," *Monkey Cage*, June 14, 2013, http://themonkeycage.org/2013/06/14/the-oversight-of-too-much-oversight/.

39. Megan Braun, "Predator Effect: A Phenomenon Unique to the War on Terror," in Bergen and Rothenberg, *Drone Wars*, 270.

40. Shane, "Election Spurred a Move to Codify U.S. Drone Policy."

41. Charlie Savage, "U.S. Releases Rules for Airstrike Killings of Terror Suspects," *New York Times*, August 6, 2016, https://www.nytimes.com/2016/08/07/us/politics/us-releases-rules-for-airstrike-killings-of-terror-suspects.html?_r=0.

42. Bowden, "How the Predator Drone Changed the Character of War."

43. Bergen and Rowland, "World of Drones."

44. Ibid. See also Michael C. Horowitz, Sarah E. Kreps, and Matthew Fuhrmann, "The Consequences of Drone Proliferation: Separating Fact from Fiction," SSRN, January 26, 2016, http://ssrn.com/abstract=2722311.

45. Michael Boyle, "The Race for Drones," *Foreign Policy Research Institute E-Notes*, January 2015, https://www.files.ethz.ch/isn/187861/boyle_on_drones.pdf.

46. Mazzetti, *Way of the Knife*, 219; Himes, *Drones and the Ethics of Targeted Killing*, 142–45.

47. "World of Drones" (New America, n.d.), https://www.newamerica.org/international-security/reports/world-drones/who-has-what-countries-developing-armed-drones.

48. Abizaid and Brooks, "Recommendations and Report," 22–23.

49. Bowden, "How the Predator Drone Changed the Character of War," 65.

50. Mazzetti, *Way of the Knife*, 263.

51. Ibid., 264.

52. Ibid., 98.

53. Abizaid and Brooks, "Recommendations and Report," 30.

54. Gregory Johnsen, as quoted in Bowden, "How the Predator Drone Changed the Character of War," 65.

55. Kreps, "Ground the Drones?"

56. Charli Carpenter, "Out of the Shadows: A New Paradigm for Countering Global Terrorism," *World Politics Review*, November 5, 2013, 2.

57. Jane Stack, "Not Whether Machines Think, but Whether Men Do," *UCLA Law*

Review 62 (2015): 760–93. See also Michael W. Lewis, "Drones and the Boundaries of the Battlefield," *Texas International Law* 47 (2012): 293–314.

58. Stack, "Not Whether Machines Think, but Whether Men Do," 769–77.

59. Rosa Brooks, "Drones and the International Rule of Law," *Journal of Ethics and International Affairs* 28 (2014): 83–104.

60. William D. Hartung, "A Lot Could Go Wrong Here," *U.S. News & World Report*, March 4, 2015, http://www.usnews.com/opinion/blogs/world-report/2015/03/04 /obamas-new-drone-export-policy-needs-careful-congressional-review.

61. Adam Rawnsley, "Meet China's Killer Drones," *Foreign Policy*, January 14, 2016, http://foreignpolicy.com/2016/01/14/meet-chinas-killer-drones/.

62. Horowitz, Kreps, and Fuhrmann, "Consequences of Drone Proliferation."

63. Usman Ansari, "Pakistan Surprises Many with First Use of Armed Drone," *Defense News*, August 8, 2017, http://www.defensenews.com/story/defense/air-space/strike /2015/09/08/pakistan-surprises-many-first-use-armed-drone/71881768/.

64. Horowitz, Kreps, and Fuhrmann, "Consequences of Drone Proliferation."

65. Although we focus on state drone programs here, it is imperative to note that substate groups also have drones. Hezbollah, for example, has Iranian drones and has used them to attack Israel. Hamas is believed to have nascent drone production capability. There have been reports of lone wolf attacks via drone, and several insurgent groups and criminal organizations have utilized drones in various capacities. Chris Abbott, Matthew Clarke, Steve Hathorn, and Scott Hickie, "Hostile Drones: The Hostile Use of Drones by Non-state Actors Against British Targets" (Open Briefing, January 2016), http://remotecontrolproject.org. See also Grossman, *Drones and Terrorism*, 93–125.

66. Bergen and Rowland, "World of Drones."

67. Ibid., 306.

68. Michael J. Boyle, *The Drone Age: How Drone Technology Will Change War and Peace* (New York: Oxford University Press, 2020), 250.

69. Carlos S. Cabello, "Droning On: American Strategic Myopia toward Aerial Unmanned Systems" (MA thesis, Naval Postgraduate School, December 2013), https://www.hsdl.org/?view&did=750999.

70. Abizaid and Brooks, "Recommendations and Report," 37, emphasis added.

71. Schiff, "Let the Military Run Drone Warfare."

72. Williams C. Banks, "Regulating Drones: Are Targeted Killings by Drones Outside Traditional Battlefields Legal?," ed. Peter L. Bergen and Daniel Rothberg (Experts@Syracuse, February 9, 2016), https://experts.syr.edu/en/publications/regulating-drones -are-targeted-killings-by-drones-outside-traditi, 151.

73. Paul Kahn, quoted in Kaag and Kreps, *Drone Warfare*, 57. See also Tobias T. Gibson and Anna E. Holyan, "End Congress' Abdication of War-Making," *St. Louis Post-Dispatch*, February 13, 2013.

74. Tobias T. Gibson and Anna Holyan, "Playing the Drone 'Playbook'?," *The Hill*, March 25, 2016, http://thehill.com/blogs/pundits-blog/defense/274293-playing-the-drone-playbook.

75. Ibid.

76. In this case, Obama authorized only three drone strikes in Pakistan in 2016 (Grossman, *Drones and Terrorism*).

77. Morgan Gstalter, "Trump Asked CIA Official Why Drone Strike Didn't Also Kill Target's Family: Report," *The Hill*, April 6, 2018, https://thehill.com/homenews /administration/381925-trump-asked-cia-official-why-drone-strike-didnt-also-kill -targets.

78. Seligman, "Trump's Push to Boost Lethal Drone Exports."

79. Huma Siddiqui, "Donald Trump's India Visit: Stage Set for Drones and Helicopters from the U.S.," *Financial Express*, February 11, 2020, https://www.financialexpress .com/defence/donald-trumps-india-visit-stage-set-for-drones-and-helicopters-from -the-us/1864680/.

80. Donald J. Trump, "Revocation of Reporting Requirement," *Federal Register*, March 11, 2019, https://www.federalregister.gov/documents/2019/03/11/2019-04595 /revocation-of-reporting-requirement.

81. David Welna, "'Imminent' Threat—Trump Justification of Attack on Iranian General—Is Undefined," NPR, January 11, 2020, https://www.npr.org/2020/01/10 /795438264/imminent-threat-trump-justification-of-attack-on-iranian-general-is -undefined.

82. Donald J. Trump, "The Fake News Media and Their Democrat Partners Are Working Hard to Determine Whether or Not the Future Attack by Terrorist Soleimani Was 'Imminent' or Not, & Was My Team in Agreement. The Answer to Both Is a Strong YES., but It Doesn't Really Matter Because of His Horrible Past!," Twitter, January 13, 2020, https://twitter.com/realdonaldtrump/status/1216754098382524422 ?lang=en.

83. Goldsmith, "Soleimani Strike."

84. Claudia Grisales, "Senate Approves Legislation to Limit President's War Powers Against Iran," NPR, February 13, 2020, https://www.npr.org/2020/02/13/805594383 /senate-approves-legislation-to-limit-presidents-war-powers-against-iran.

85. Quoted in P. W. Singer, "What Churchill Can Teach Us about the Coming Era of Lasers, Cyborgs, and Killer Drones," *Foreign Policy*, October 22, 2013, http:// foreignpolicy.com/2013/10/22/what-churchill-can-teach-us-about-the-coming-era-of -lasers-cyborgs-and-killer-drones.

86. Brooks, "Drones and the International Rule of Law," 244.

87. Ibid., 245.

88. David W. Opderbeck, "Drone Courts," *Rutgers Law Journal* 44 (2014): 413–70, is but one example.

The United States and Cybersecurity

U.S. Senator **Roy D. Blunt**

As we think not only about the Churchill speech in 1946 but, fifty years later, the symbolism of Mikhail Gorbachev coming here and giving another speech that really, at least, at that moment suggested that the Iron Curtain had been pulled back. And the importance of democracy in organizing the world community was an incredible step in the right direction for the world and, frankly, for Russia. But tonight I want to talk about three different topics. One is "liberty versus security." Two would be setting the world stage for why that balance is so hard to accomplish and some of the challenges in finding that balance. And then [three] to talk about not only cybersecurity as part of that but also the kinds of things that we could do to prioritize expanding the possibilities for both liberty and freedom.

Having served on what I think are the most unsettling committees of the Congress—the House Select Committee on Intelligence, and the Senate Select Committee on Intelligence—it's not really about intelligence, but if it was, at least I made the committee. In the case of the Senate, about a dozen members of the Senate for the other eighty-eight senators, multiple times every week, sit down with the director of the CIA, the director of the FBI, the national intelligence director, the director of defense intelligence. Sometimes collectively, often separately, and just talk about the threats that the country faces. In addition to that, I had the chance in the last Congress to serve on the Armed Services Committee, and in this Congress, along with the Select Committee on Intelligence, I serve on the Defense Appropriating Committee. So sort of looking at this both from the threats we face, and how we meet those threats, is part of the job that you all let me do for you.

Overview of Security versus Liberty

First of all, let's start with the whole concept . . . of security versus liberty. It's not a new challenge for Americans, it is a fundamental part of who we are, but recent events, like the data spill of Edward Snowden on WikiLeaks, or body scanners at airports, or red light cameras, or talking now about what drones can and can't do, what drones should and shouldn't be able to do. All will bring that discussion back in new and different ways. But, it's been there a long time. There's a slightly altered version of Benjamin Franklin's quote, inscribed on the Statue of Liberty, and the slightly altered version of what he was saying was, "They that can give up essential liberty to obtain a little safety deserve neither liberty nor safety." Clearly this is a concept that we're dedicated to, but it's not a concept that doesn't have its own challenges. In fact, you know Franklin said what he said in 1755.

By the very first decade of the Constitution, the federal government passed the totally unjustifiable Alien and Sedition Acts. They were followed by the suspension of habeas corpus in the Civil War, the Espionage Act in 1917 that set the stage for World War I. In World War II just aggressive censorship took over. But in all cases, there always seemed to be some understanding that at least the motivation was to try to protect our liberty while we were defending that liberty. And sometimes, like the Alien and Sedition Acts, this went too far, other times it did appear that the final result justified what had to be done.

But then after 9/11, we passed the USA PATRIOT Act in 2001, the Foreign Intelligence Surveillance Act in 1978, and 2001, and 2007, and 2008. And one of the reasons we had the Foreign Intelligence Surveillance Act in 2001, and 2007, and 2008 I'll come back to at the end of what I'm talking about because it's one of the things that, I among others really insisted that we not do these things permanently, but we come back and revisit them and evaluate how we're doing, what we're doing, to protect our liberty, and at the same time understand our needs for security.

The two things aren't mutually exclusive, but they are clearly in conflict. You know, the top debate on this topic really occurred in a new way after the 9/11 attacks fourteen years ago last Friday. The attacks on the Pentagon, the likely attack on the Capitol that true American heroes took that plane down in a field in Pennsylvania, and the global effort that followed was to see that we could do our best that that sort of thing didn't happen again.

The subsequent wars on terrorism, though I've never particularly liked that term, is a war on a tactic rather than a war on a specific target; but, the tactic is bad enough to be a target. The vital national security interests we had to prevent another attack has called Americans to think a lot about what are we giving up and what are we protecting.

And all kinds of personal information are today more readily available to more people, in an easier way, than it ever has been before. In fact if we're not already doing it, I think this'll be one of the things that Americans look back, and the people all over the world look back and say, why did we put all that out there so quickly, without thinking about how it could be accessed by other people? Ensuring that the federal government protects personal liberty while also defending the country is not just something that has to be part of the discussion, part of the public square, but something that really is inherent if we're going to maintain the Constitution, and the country that we hope to secure. Security is something that is pretty difficult to measure. What somebody feels provides their security may not be nearly enough for somebody else. So you could be doing things where you're trying to measure security, maybe the metrics are hard power, maybe the metrics of security are who has the best nuclear deterrent.

When there is a lapse in security, as there was after 9/11, Americans suddenly and quickly have a whole different view of their own safety and whatever it takes to protect that, then they may have had before. The American view of security the morning of 9/11 fourteen years ago was a whole lot different than the American sense of security by noon. Both how secure we were, and what we were willing to do to protect that security. We do understand as Missourians, I've traveled the state a lot and talked to people a lot, but one thing that you don't get much of an argument for is the idea that the job of the federal government is to defend the country. The one thing we can't do for ourselves, state and local government can't do for us, and that we do expect the federal government to do, is to provide for the common defense. And so the question is always out there: How much security is too much security, and how much liberty are people willing to give up in order to have the security that they would like to have? Whether [it is] individual security or national security in the United States, security is based on our perception of threats to an open and free society. And again the balance of what you do. Those threats are real, so what kind of world would you try to provide security in? What's the environment of that challenge of liberty versus security? Let's look for a few minutes at some of the challenges we face, and also look at the importance of America's leadership in a world of what happens when America doesn't lead. While American security challenges are no longer Indian attacks, as they would have been when Benjamin Franklin made his 1755 quote on occasional incursion of the French over the border, they are more prevalent, more complex, and potentially more catastrophic than ever before.

Former secretary of state Henry Kissinger last year testified before the Senate Committee on Armed Services, "The United States has not faced a more diverse and complex array of crises since the end of the Second World War." That same day, Secretary Madeline Albright and Secretary George Shultz were totally in agreement with him. And even people who knew more, frankly, about the challenges we face every day than the three of them would know right now, all said the same thing. The chairman of the Joint Chiefs of Staff about that same time, Martin Dempsey, the national director of intelligence James Clapper, the head of the CIA John Brennan all say when asked that this is the most dangerous time that the United States has ever faced in terms of the multiplicity of threats and our lack of ability to keep track of all of them in a way that any of us are happy about.

The number-one responsibility of the federal government is to defend the country. The number-two responsibility is to ensure that as a country, that meets our standards. The United States' role in carrying out the obligation of defending the country means we have to have a thorough and well understood and effective foreign policy, and that our presence is indispensable.

The United States Has Relinquished Global Primacy

There is no question—this may be one of the better places you could possibly make this point—there is no question since the end of World War II that the United States has carried a disproportionate load in the world. There is also now, for people who question that if we step back, nobody else steps up. In a world that was absolutely fair, where you were asked to only bear your part of the burden, for as long as was fair for you to do, we could long ago have stepped back and said now it's time for somebody else. But I think what we see is that when we step back, the leadership void that we leave is a great one.

Regrettably, today our allies seem to be more bewildered by what our policy often is, and our enemies are encouraged as they look at our unwillingness to take the kinds of stands that America took in the past. Our friends frankly don't trust us, and our enemies aren't afraid of us. And in a dangerous world, that's a very dangerous place to be. In a time of global upheaval like this, the consequences of a disengaged America is really greater turmoil, not less turmoil. When the United States leaves a leadership vacuum in the world today, bad things rush to fill that vacuum. And we see that now over and over again. When we send the confusing message, as frankly the president did when he talked about the red line in Syria—that was about 220,000 deaths of Syrians ago—here's what we would do if you do this, and then Assad does what we said we wouldn't allow him to do, and then we don't do anything.

That emboldens, obviously, the Syrians. The Russians, I think, are then encouraged to test the West in places like Crimea. China moves aggressively in the South China Sea. And from the point of view of all of them, why not? From the point of view of all of them, they see an opportunity, and they decide they're going to take advantage of it. Less presence, less involvement, less positive engagement in the world, almost always ends up turning into rushed, emergency decisions that don't produce the kind of results that you would like to see.

The Middle East right now is obviously in chaos, and part of that chaos is something the Congress is in the middle of dealing with now with the Iranian agreement. But the Middle East, and in fact the balance of Africa, sees World War I is finally catching up with the world. The end of World War I is now very important as we look toward the future. The major problem with freedom today happened when the victors of World War I decided they could draw the map of the world however they wanted to. Look at those absolutely straight lines in the continent of Africa. Look at what happens in a country like Iraq, where you put three people groups together that are distrustful of each other, that the only way you could keep them together, with that distrust, is likely to be force, and then what happens when that level of force goes away.

It's an example of what happens where there are significant areas of the world today, that without the Cold War balance, have frankly, just become ungoverned. And as they have become ungoverned, that leaves the opportunity for outside groups, in some cases outside governments like Iran, to step in and take advantage of that ungoverned properly territory. In Syria, in Iraq, in Lebanon, and Yemen, Iran has an outside influence in all of those countries. And it's not good in any of those countries. Earlier this year, I traveled with a few other members of the Senate Intelligence Committee to Jordan and Turkey. At that time the administration believed and everyone hoped that we could find groups of moderate resistance forces to Assad, to then help train them and get them ready to go into Syria and try to stabilize that country. As it turns out you have competing things going on in the minds of all those recruits. One is that some of them want to fight Assad, some of them want to fight ISIS, some of them just don't like us, and frankly it turned out to be a total failure. We spent lots of money and recruited and trained effectively no one. Over a year ago, the president asked the Congress to authorize the use of military force to go after ISIS. But if you're going to ask the Congress for military force, you have to have some reason to make that commitment.

The president, if he intends to use force, has to tell the American people how he intends, or she intends to use that force. Secretary of State John Kerry during that particular debate said that it would be "an incredibly small use of force." That probably didn't need to be said, but certainly not encouraging. An incredibly small use of force is not anything that either the Congress or our friends wanted to hear so nothing came of it. Not only are we unable to define our policy in Iraq and Syria, but our allies around the world have a hard time defining our policy as well.

The United States, Iran, and the Middle East

Our friends, our partners, our allies in the Middle East continue to express concern and confusion regarding our failure to articulate our policy and frankly for the first time are turning to countries that they have never turned to before. Saudi Arabians were in Russia talking about buying arms two months ago for the first time ever. When Saudi Arabia did a recent bombing raid they told us about it an hour before the bombing occurred, not days before in consultation, like we would have had before. You need to have a strategy. You need to have clarity. We need to have commitment. You can't just contain something like ISIS without knowing how you're going to do that. Now, Iran of course is and for some time in the future I think going to get a lot of attention.

No better time probably than this week to talk about Iran. The Congress is in the middle of voting on whether to approve or disapprove an agreement that even if it's entered into is only binding on a president that wants to be bound by it. It's not a treaty, it's not binding on the next government, it's not approved by two-thirds of the Senate as a treaty would be, but through some mechanism that the president agreed to sign into law that would only apply to this one instance where the Congress had a very, very slim chance of disapproving an agreement that again isn't binding on any future president. It's hard to imagine that you'd go forward with that kind of agreement on this kind of issue. But the agreement obviously should have been bound by long-term verifiable views of what the Iranians were going to do. But the Iranians continue to support bad things everywhere.

Assad continues to massacre his own people supported by Iran. According to the UN figures in January, the number of Syrians killed by Assad was over 220,000. I've seen in recent press reports that number now is often talked about as about 250,000. Assad has killed more Syrians than ISIS has. He's displaced millions of people and there are at least four million refugees outside of Syria. And all you have to do to hear more about that is turn on the television any day this week and see how countries are dealing with that.

Iran supports those activities. Supported by Iran, Houthi rebels have seized key territory in Yemen and destabilized that government. Supported by Iran, Shiite militias continue to promote sectarian violence in Iraq. Supported by Iran, Hezbollah in Lebanon wages terrorism and calls for the annihilation of Israel. Supported by Iran, Palestinian terrorist groups in Gaza continue to lob mortars and rockets into Israel. And Iran continues to hold hostages of three Americans. It is amazing to me [this situation] couldn't have been part of the negotiation that we just had with Iran. But one is a pastor Saeed Abedini, former Marine Amir Hemtaki, and *Washington Post* journalist Jason Rezani who are being held for reasons that clearly would make no sense in any reasonable country. They continue to be completely unhelpful locating the former FBI agent Robert Levinson. And they are responsible, the Quds Force, for killing and maiming lots of Americans with the IED devices that were used to attack American troops in Iraq.

Not surprising, with that kind of record, that 50 percent of the American people think we shouldn't go forward with any kind of agreement with the Iranians that doesn't stop any of that behavior. Only about half that many people, about 21 percent, think we should go forward with the agreement. About 30 percent of the American people haven't decided yet. But big numbers of people look at what the government's doing and wonder why. The destabilizing threat of a nuclear armed Iran really, I don't think, can be overemphasized. When we entered into the negotiations with Iran, the administration said that the goals would be that:

1. We would ensure that Iran would never have a nuclear weapon;
2. We would find out everything Iran ever did to try to develop nuclear weapons;
3. We would have anywhere, anytime inspections; and
4. Sanctions would only be relieved when there was real movement in those first three areas.

Those were the four goals. None of the four goals were achieved. In fact, what we've done in this agreement, or what's happened in this agreement, is that Iran will be a threshold nuclear state. We believe, as people in the region believe, as many Americans do, as I do, that Iran will in all likelihood cheat, while they're being held back to a twelve-month time clock. But what will happen in the neighborhood is that other countries will decide that if Iran's going to have the nuclear capability, they'll want to have it too. And so the Egyptians, the Emirates, the Jordanians, the Saudis have all already said we want to have whatever capability the Iranians have in terms of nuclear rights and enrichment research. And I think it's almost guaranteed that some, if not all of them, will have nuclear weapons before the Iranians do unless the Iranians really break out quickly. They don't want to be left in that part of the world, with a neighbor that they don't trust, who they are told is within twelve months of having nuclear weapons capability, and not have those weapons themselves.

If North Korea wasn't bad enough, what this arrangement really does is let the nuclear genie out of the bottle. If we get extremely lucky, if hope actually overwhelms experience, and the Iranian government changes, and they would change their mind, that's probably too late, for other countries in the region that currently don't have a nuclear weapon to have gone ahead and gotten one.

And what happens if those countries have one today is one thing. What might happen in those same countries, if they have nuclear weapons five years from now is another thing. But losing the close hold on nuclear weapons capacity is a big concern.

There's a Munich Security conference every year. I went the year before last, there were about six members of the Senate who went, who were meeting with Secretary Kerry, who was confident that we'd be able to monitor everything the Iranians did. I'm not at all confident that that would be true, but I told him at the time even if that is true, you'll never be able to contain enrichment. Once you let enrichment start, then this will spread beyond the boundaries of Iran. The countries in the neighborhood don't trust Iran, and they'll want to have the same kind of weapons they fear Iran might eventually have. Iran continues to promote anti-American and anti-Israel policies. Just last week, the Iranian leader, while we're in the process of the president trying to get an agreement to not disapprove—there is no chance the agreement will be approved—the only chance here is somehow the president will prevail and it won't be disapproved, which is a very interesting concept when you think about it. But while we're doing that, the Iranian leader, the Ayatollah called America the "Great Satan," and reiterated their goal that Israel not exist in twenty-five years.

And that's when he was sitting there they're on their best behavior. We don't know what they'd be like on a bad day. This is a day where we're trying to move forward with something they apparently want. It's a dangerous step in that direction, I think it creates real problems.

Israel, last April, celebrated sixty-seven years of independence. The person who came here to introduce Winston Churchill in 1946, the president of the United States, President Truman—Everyday I'm in Washington, I get to work in the offices that Senator Truman used for the ten years he was in Washington, and my desk on the Senate floor is one of the desks he used on the Senate floor—but he immediately recognized Israel, and from that moment, the first world leader, and the most important world leader, made that immediate decision. From that moment the United States and Israel share an unbreakable friendship, grounded in common trust and a commitment to democracy. That is a friendship that we need to understand how important it is to us and how important our friendship is to them. As Israel and the United States find new ways to collaborate in areas of high technology, of national security, of energy, of medicine. Senator Boxer from California, she's a Democrat, I'm a Republican, we cosponsored last year the Strategic Partnership Act between us and Israel to codify what we were doing, to encourage what we were doing. We have this unique military relationship have with Israel where we actually keep military supplies in Israel that they can draw out of any time they decide they need them and pay us back later.

We increased the number of those supplies, we increased our cooperative efforts on the anti-missile activities that actually are producing some success.

We saw great success when Israel was being attacked from Gaza in the last few months. And both the Arrow Program and David's Sling actually are proving, what everybody thought was a pretty wild concept when President Reagan came up with it, that you really can hit a bullet with a bullet. You really can hit, so far with a substantial percentage of the time, one rocket with another missile and eliminate the danger of that rocket. So the things that we can do, with Israel and for Israel, are important as it relates to Iran. What we have to remember is on today, which is by the way Rosh Hashanah, the Jewish New Year, on this day and every other day, Israel has an absolute right, an inherent right, to defend itself. And when a neighboring country, the leader of that country, talks about how your country shouldn't even be able to exist and should be eliminated sometime in the next twenty-five years, you have to think about what that means.

Russian Bear Rising in Eastern Europe

In Ukraine, Russia has really presented the international community with a new challenge. Gorbachev outlined the importance of major international actors cooperating, and operating in concert with shared principles in an important way, when he was here. And he understood that the United Nations and NATO were two of those organizations. But we're in a situation today, where while we agree with Russia on a few things, like preventing the spread of Islamic extremism and global terrorism, but we don't agree with Russia on some really important things, like the determination of independent countries, and particularly NATO. Russia perceives NATO as a threat to Russia and regional influence, and is slowly testing the limits of NATO power.

I just got back from a quick trip to Estonia, where we had a fighter wing, the 442nd Fighter Wing, based at Whiteman Air Force Base in Missouri, is part of what's called Operation Atlantic Resolve, where not only that fighter wing based here in our state, is in Estonia for about six weeks. But we now have a number of people like that, of military assets like that, being deployed in Lithuania, in Latvia, in Estonia, to let the Russians know, with no uncertain terms, that the big difference in those three countries, once under Soviet domination, and Ukraine, is that those three countries are part of NATO. And NATO is either an organization where everybody is committed to defend every other country, or it's not.

And when I was over there, we just sent an F-22 to Estonia. It's very significant, one of our military assets, there had never been one in Eastern Europe. And so within days the Russians are twenty miles from the Estonian border practicing how they would cross the border to invade Estonia just in case the Estonians were feeling too secure. The Russians need to understand that NATO is important, and we intend to defend those countries. In Ukraine, they're not a member of NATO but they're a nation seeking freedom and self-determination. The president of Ukraine in a speech before the Congress last year, in a joint session of the Congress, was grateful for the humanitarian aid, but clearly questioning why we won't help them defend themselves. In fact maybe the best and most telling sentence in that speech the president of Ukraine said, to the Congress of the United States: "Thank you for the blankets, but we can't fight the Russians with blankets." When people who are fighting for their own freedom stand before the Congress and have to explain that you can't fight the Russians with blankets, it's pretty confusing for them and the rest of the world.

Just last week, Russia flew several military transportation aircraft into Syria, and appears to be in the process of establishing a base there. A base that they had not been able to establish in any of those countries since President Truman insisted that the Red Army not stay in Iran in 1946, and on several occasions after that, the United States said to the Soviets that we're not going to allow this to happen, but it is happening right now. I think the president was wrong in 2012 to dismiss the concerns about Russia as something out of the 1980s.

Whoever was concerned about Russia in 2012 understood Putin and where Russia was headed, maybe better than the president did at that moment. And we need to be sure that we understand that. The Russian reset hasn't gone all that well. The Asian Pivot is not in great shape either. China spent much of the last year building islands in the Spratly Atoll. China's territorial ambitions are not new. But dumping sand on top of a coral reef and building a military base within striking distance of the Philippines is new, and nobody did anything about it.

The cyber challenges are the newest and most challenging areas of national security that we're trying to tackle. The protection of communications, the protection of information, and the protection of our critical infrastructure: the financial infrastructure, the utilities infrastructure, the personal infrastructure of the country, is now very open to the possibility of cyberattack. Our society and our economy rely on technology in an increasingly dependent way. Federal, state, and local governments apply, that rely on that technology. However, advanced that technology is, the widespread adoption of that technology has also happened in a way that probably we wouldn't do again without building safeguards that we don't have currently.

Cyber Threats from State- and Nonstate Actors

In June, the United States Office of Personnel Management increased the estimate for the number of personnel files that were hacked into this year, to 21.5

million. So 21.5 million Americans, who either worked for the federal government, got a security clearance from the federal government, or were involved with somebody who was getting a security clearance in the federal government, that information all went somewhere else. The administration pretty publicly said the Chinese are behind this, and they might be. The cyber realm really represents a whole new dimension of difficulties because we can't quite tell where the attacks coming from.

Today, our adversaries can sit in a mountain range in Afghanistan, or anywhere else in the world, and with satellite technology hack directly into U.S. government records. With American efficiency, we have personally identifiable information that went directly into the system quicker than anyone would have ever imagined. Now we can see what we have to do to defend that. The well-known Stuxnet attack on the infrastructure of the Iranian nuclear program slowed that program down dramatically. So, clearly the world knows that things can happen that make it harder for countries to do what they want to do. What we don't know yet is all the ways to fight against that.

Today, our adversaries possess the ability to steal your identity or to conduct a nuclear attack from the comfort of their Internet connection thousands of miles away. Protecting American security in the cyber realm is a real challenge. If you ask most of the people who work in intelligence every day what their biggest concern is, their biggest concern is our vulnerability to cyberattack. To get somehow inside our weapons system, to get inside our financial structure, to get inside our critical infrastructure of all kinds. These threats can be sophisticated, massive, and persistent. They are persistent. There are really three different types of hackers that go after our information.

First, the individuals that you might just call hacktivists. For example, groups like Anonymous vandalize, knock out websites, knock out offices temporarily. Sometimes their motivation appears that they just enjoy being able to do it. But disguised as a hacktivist, who knows who might be in there seeing what they can really do great damage to next. Terror groups like the Islamic State are showing increased sophistication in cyberspace, they're very good on social media, you can see the concern people have about recruiting that lone-wolf terrorist. But that happens with sophisticated social media.

Second, there are organized networks of just cyber criminals who are operating out of countries, often former Soviet republics. Russians are generally thought to be better at this than anybody else. Chinese are, a lot of them, and they're good, but they're not quite as good as the Russians we don't believe, at the constant effort to try to get into our systems for criminal purposes. We've seen criminal gangs mobilize with tacit government encouragement from the government where they're located. For example, in 2008 we saw complex attacks against the country of Georgia, at the computer networks of Georgia, and government websites coincided with military operations that the Russians were conducting. More recently, we've seen cyberattacks between Russia and Ukraine.

The third and most dangerous type of cyber threat is the state-sponsored cyber intrusion. In 2007, Estonia really has had the biggest impact so far. Outsiders, we believe the Russians, just overloaded the system. Not nearly as sophisticated as what they'd be doing in 2015, but they overloaded the system, and for the better part of three weeks a country that had become very dependent on the cyber world was very much isolated from everything that they were depending upon.

The most advanced, persistent intrusions are when foreign governments expend considerable resource to hack our government agencies for espionage purposes, and to hack American companies to steal intellectual property and trade secrets. I know there's a lot of discussion about Secretary Hillary Clinton's server. It's hard for me to believe—I don't know anything specifically about this so I'm not divulging any national intelligence information—it's hard for me to believe that that server isn't backed up in Beijing, and in Moscow. They had to be aware that the secretary of state was using it, and it couldn't be that hard to get to it. So if in fact somebody wants to find out everything that was on there, maybe we can just contact directly the Chinese or the Russians and ask them if there's anything we should be concerned about, that was on that server. Last year, the Department of Justice announced the indictment of five Chinese military leaders, for specific espionage and cyber activities against American institutions.

There are numerous reports in the media of private-sector cybersecurity companies identifying state-sponsored cyber intrusions. Thus the only real cyber threat isn't just from any one place but it's multitiered, it comes at lots of times, and we're trying to figure out how to solve it. The Senate Intelligence Committee voted a cyber bill, a data-sharing bill, out several months ago, there was only one dissenting vote. But so far, there hasn't been the pressure to get the floor time to get this bill done so that we can begin to help private-sector people in their efforts as we share that information.

I'm also working on legislation that would require a notification of data breach. So if your information is taken at any significant level, whoever had that information that lost control of it, for no matter how big a period of time if it affects a lot of people, has to tell everybody. If you don't do that, you're going to eventually end up with having every state, having their own set of responses to losing this information, and it's almost impossible to have fifty-plus different ways to look at that.

Framing an American Strategy for Global Security

You know, liberty versus security, unlike the Cold War, or World War I, or World War II, we'll never have a sense that some of these activities that I've talked about this evening come to an end. There'll be no official declaration of the end of the war on terror. The hacktivists, the cyber criminals, the governments encouraging cyber warfare, will probably never stand up and say okay we're done with that. So I think what you have to do, the best way to protect our liberty, is never make any of the laws permanent, that we put in place to try to protect our security. That requires the Congress to come back at some frequency, and look at what the Congress did, look at what the president agreed to, evaluate what's working, what's not working, what went too far, what needs to be repealed, what needs to be repaired, what needs to be replaced.

I think the greatest security here is for these laws all to be passed with some short-term framework that allows us to protect ourselves that way. You know, the challenges we face are increasingly complex, the nature of threats to American security are more broad based than we have seen in a long time. We no longer have one big enemy; we have lots of enemies of various sizes. How we lead the efforts in international stability to protect our interests while minimizing the burden on the American way of life is really important. And how we work with allies and partners to share economic, diplomatic, and military costs is also important. These are hard questions. They are questions that have to be addressed one at a time, but they have to be addressed clearly.

We have to have a comprehensive strategy moving forward that allows our security apparatus the latitude to keep America safe while preserving American values of liberty and freedom. Clearly, an attempt to pursue liberty in the absence of security is futile. It is equally futile to pursue security in the absence of liberty. We have to move forward with an understanding that these elements work in tandem. And we can work to advance freedom on all fronts. So, [in conclusion,] let me mention three areas. . . .

[First,] I think we need to project economic freedom. One way to do that is by advancing concepts of fair trade and free trade, like ongoing partnerships, based on the rule of law, win-win relationships, and every economic opportunity hopefully leading to another one. That's the difference in how we do business and how others in the world do business. The alternative to what we do, the rule of law, the win-win relationship, the ongoing economic opportunity, is much more cynical, is much more colonial, is much more in line with well we can take advantage of you and we're going to. As opposed to, we want to be partners, and we want to be partners for a long time. The Trans Pacific Partnership being negotiated right now would be a great example. That part of the world will be dramatically different twenty years from now, if they follow the path that we pursue, rather than if they follow the alternative, which is more likely to be pursued by the Chinese and the Russians.

[Second,] we need to promote religious freedom. Sectarian violence and constant attacks on religious tolerance have to be dealt with. The world at this moment, is a world where many people live in places where they are not allowed to follow the dictates of their own conscience. In the last Congress, I sponsored and the president signed into law the creation of a special envoy for religious minorities in the Middle East and South Central Asia. Now more than a year later the job's still not been filled. The president signed the law, but we still don't have anybody doing that job. Maybe the pope's visit, in the next few days, will create a reason to name that person. Fighting for religious freedom is one of the places where we can continue to make the kind of stand that will let the people know what we stand for.

[Finally,] then we have to fight human trafficking. We just passed a human trafficking law that gives the federal government many more powers than the federal government's had in the past to try to fight this tragedy. Leading from behind doesn't work. President Truman understood that, Winston Churchill understood that when he spoke here in 1946, and world leader after world leader have verified the importance of American leadership, speaking here for seven decades now. It is not a question of whether America should lead, but how it should lead. That is an important part of who we are. . . . Thank you all.

Note

This speech was given by Senator Blunt at Westminster College, Fulton, Missouri, on September 14, 2015, at the tenth annual Hancock Symposium at Westminster College, focused on "Security versus Liberty: Balancing the Scales of Freedom."

Edward Snowden and PRISM

NEGOTIATING THE POST-9/11 "SURVEILLANCE STATE"

Kristan Stoddart, Swansea University

This chapter discusses the implications of the Edward Snowden releases of classified documents obtained from the U.S. National Security Agency (NSA). This included details of metadata collection (essentially data about data) of telephone calls and Internet surveillance activities. The chapter follows a five-step process. First, it looks at Edward Snowden himself and his motives. Second, it explores the context of NSA activities. Third, it describes some of the programs he released. Fourth, it examines public concerns. Fifth, it questions what has changed post-Snowden. Throughout it seeks to add to the ongoing debate regarding the balance between privacy, civil liberties, and security, in a digital hyperconnected world.

Edward Snowden: The Man and His Work

Edward Snowden came from a family background of public service with much of his early life spent in Maryland, home to many federal agencies including the NSA. He was a high school dropout at fifteen and from fifteen to twenty became a self-taught expert in computer science. After the invasion of Iraq in 2003 he tried to join the U.S. Army Reserve but washed out of the training program. When he returned to Maryland he found a job with "a covert NSA facility" at the University of Maryland Center for Advanced Study of Language (CASL), where he moved from security guard into information technology.[1] He allegedly became a recruit of the CIA soon after. He claims to have worked across Europe, but he left the CIA in February 2009 to work for Dell. Dell was one of the companies responsible for installing and running both classified and unclassified computer systems across the U.S. government. His role as a subcontracted intelligence employee brought him into contact with the NSA when he began working at a U.S. military site in Tokyo housing an NSA facility. After leaving his first NSA post in Japan in 2012 he moved to an NSA station in Hawaii. He left Dell to take up a new post with Booz Allen Hamilton in early 2013.[2]

He was still working for them in Hawaii when he fled to Hong Kong and began to leak information to journalists from the *Washington Post* and U.K.-based *Guardian* newspapers. He was twenty-nine years old at the time. As a systems administrator he appears to have had full access to a vast amount of NSA data—how much is unclear but this was all-source intelligence on foreign threats—and included details of surveillance of some of America's allies, including German chancellor Merkel, and of economic negotiations. His access also included domestic surveillance in the United States.[3] Domestic surveillance especially concerns the Fourth Amendment, which protects Americans with a "right to privacy and freedom from arbitrary governmental intrusions."[4] After spending time in Hong Kong, Snowden boarded a flight to Moscow and has remained in Russia ever since. Should he return to the United States he faces charges under the Espionage Act of 1917. Snowden's background and move into the security-cleared world of the intelligence communities (IC) remains foggy, given there has been concern that he was a foreign intelligence agent and not a "whistleblower" and open to further considerations.[5] Snowden laid out his motives to Glenn Greenwald in a now (in)famous interview conducted while in Hong Kong:

NSA and the intelligence community in general is focused on getting intelligence wherever it can by any means possible and it believes, on the grounds of a sort of a self-certification, that they serve the national interest. Originally we saw that focus very narrowly tailored as foreign intelligence gathered overseas. Now increasingly we see that it's happening domestically. And to do that they, the NSA specifically, targets the communications of everyone. It ingests them by default. It collects them in its system and it filters them and it analyses them and it measures them and it stores them for periods of time simply because that's the easiest, most efficient, and most valuable way to achieve these ends. So while they may be intending to target someone associated with a foreign government or someone they suspect of terrorism, they're collecting you're communications to do so . . . even if you're not doing anything wrong you're being watched and recorded. And the storage capability of these systems increases every year consistently by orders of magnitude to where it's getting to the point where you don't have to have done anything wrong. You simply have to eventually fall under suspicion from somebody even by a wrong call. And then they can use this system to go back in time and scrutinize every decision you've ever made, every friend you've ever discussed something with. And attack you on that basis to sort to derive suspicion from an innocent life and paint anyone in the context of a wrongdoer. . . . And there will be nothing the people can do at that point to oppose it. And it'll be turnkey tyranny.[6]

A year later Snowden conducted a follow-up interview from Russia with two *Guardian* journalists. In it he said, "The fact that I didn't bring any classified material with me to Russia means that even if this is a Gulag state . . . there's nothing for them to gain."[7]

After investigating his story for seven months, from Snowden's first contact with Glenn Greenwald in Brazil in December 2012, in early June 2013 the *Washington Post* and the *Guardian* newspapers ran the story simultaneously on each side of the Atlantic exposing PRISM, its related programs, and telephone metadata collection.[8] With much of the world's electronic communications routed through the United States and the United Kingdom, along with their partners in the "Five Eyes" agreement (the United States, the United Kingdom, Canada, Australia, and New Zealand), via fiber-optic cables that encircle the globe, much of the world's Internet and telephone traffic can be intercepted. Reports further suggest that both the FBI and Britain's Government Communications Headquarters (GCHQ) also had access to the intelligence gathered from these programs.[9] These data sources were shared with the British via GCHQ, who shared information through long-standing U.S.-U.K. intelligence agreements.[10]

This included GCHQ's Tempora system, which began in early 2011. Tempora was used to simultaneously tap at least forty-six of over two hundred transatlantic fiber-optic cables relaying telephone and Internet traffic as they made landfall in the United Kingdom. Each cable carries data of up to 10 gigabits per second, theoretically delivering "more than 21 petabytes a day—equivalent to sending all the information in all the books in the British Library 192 times every 24 hours."[11] "This can be stored for up to 3 days in the case of content and 30 days for metadata. The collected metadata was subject to filtering through a process known as Massive Volume Reduction and analyzing . . . using more than 70,000 search terms related to security, terrorist activity and organized crime."[12] The *Guardian* reported, "According to the documents, GCHQ's surveillance gives it the 'biggest internet access' of all the 'Five Eyes' nations."[13] Use of Tempora complemented the NSA's PRISM program, which "secured access to the internal systems of global companies that service the internet."[14]

The data gathered by the U.S. IC through PRISM were reportedly extracted from "the central servers of nine leading U.S. Internet companies"—Microsoft, Yahoo, Google, Facebook, PalTalk, AOL, Skype, YouTube, and Apple. The "audio and video chats, photographs, e-mails, documents, and connection logs" that were accessed enabled analysts to track foreign targets.[15] Some of these companies registered legal objections.[16] This began in September 2007. Soon after the Snowden disclosures broke the *New York Times* spoke with a number of senior figures in Silicon Valley who stated that "they opened discussions with national security officials about developing technical methods to more efficiently and securely share the personal data of foreign users in response to lawful government requests. And in some cases, they changed their computer systems to do so."[17]

The *New York Times* also reported, "Each of the nine companies said it had no knowledge of a government program providing officials with access to its servers, and drew a bright line between giving the government whole-sale access to its servers to collect user data and giving them specific data in response to individual court orders. Each said it did not provide the government with full, indiscriminate access to its servers. The companies said they do, however, comply with individual court orders, including under FISA [the Foreign Intelligence Surveillance Act of 1978]."[18] However it is also notewor-thy that "tech companies might have also denied knowledge of the full scope of cooperation with national security officials because employees whose job it is to comply with FISA requests are not allowed to discuss the details even with others at the company, and in some cases have national security clear-ance."[19] These FISA requests ranged from inquiries about specific "persons of interest" through to wide searches for intelligence such as logs of target search strings. This also included some real-time data transfers as well as NSA oper-atives working for periods of time inside of technology companies.[20] Specif-ically, "The legal process . . . is akin to how law enforcement requests infor-mation in criminal investigations: the government delivers an order to obtain account details about someone who's specifically identified as a non-U.S. in-dividual, with a specific finding that they're involved in an activity related to international terrorism. Both the contents of communications and metadata, such as information about who's talking to whom, can be requested."[21] These activities utilized several programs and international partners and meant this is global in scope:

- **XKeyscore**—An Internet targeted database system and form of data mining. Able to trawl "nearly everything a typical user does on the internet," including web and search histories, and email content.[22]
- **DNI Presenter**—Can be used with XKeyscore to examine Facebook chats or private messaging.[23]
- **Tempora**—Run by the Government Communication Headquarters (GCHQ) in the United Kingdom with cooperation from the NSA. This directly taps into the fiber optic cables that are the main components transferring Internet traffic.[24]
- **Dishfire**—Harvests SMS messages.[25]

The data were harvested through access arrangements to "the central servers of nine leading U.S. Internet companies, extracting audio and video chats, photo-graphs, e-mails, documents, and connection logs that enable analysts to track foreign targets."[26] Part of the public furor over PRISM followed the disclosure that the U.S. telecommunications company Verizon, and possibly other telecom service providers including AT&T and Sprint Nextel, had been required to pass the NSA metadata of the calls it handled both domestic and international, if either the recipient or destination originated in the United States.[27] The scope of the collection was truly massive. "AT&T has 107.3 million wireless customers and 31.2 million landline customers. Verizon has 98.9 million wireless customers and 22.2 million landline customers while Sprint has 55 million customers in total. . . . NSA has established similar relationships with credit-card companies, three former officials said."[28]

This was lawful under Section 215 of the USA PATRIOT Act.[29] Because communication from one location to another within the United States travels over international fiber-optic cables, allowing the data to be gathered by the NSA, much data gathering has amounted to domestic as well as international surveillance.[30]

How Snowden accomplished his exfiltration is also a pertinent question. A year after the leaks Edward Jay Epstein, after interviewing insiders from the U.S. IC, wrote in the *Wall Street Journal*, "The results of an NSA investigation that established the chronology of the copying of 1.7 million documents that were stolen from the Signals Intelligence Center in Hawaii. The documents were taken from at least 24 supersecret compartments that stored them on computers, each of which required a password that a perpetrator had to steal or borrow, or forge an encryption key to bypass. Once Mr. Snowden breached security at the Hawaii facility, in mid-April of 2013, he planted robotic programs called 'spiders' to 'scrape' specifically targeted documents."[31] This mass exfiltration and Snowden's life and work read like the plot of a spy novel or James Bond film, and in many ways this would make for good fiction. It is not fiction however, and the ripple effects of the Snowden revelations and the repercussions for the IC and law enforcement in the United States and across the globe are still resonating. This balance between national security and civil liberties is challenging and no more so than in cyberspace.

Privacy and Security in the Digital Age

Each of us has a digital footprint. How big this footprint is depends on our use and utilization of cell phones, land lines, social media, and electronic transactions and on our Internet browsing habits. This connectivity is global and has hitherto often been conducted with little or weak encryption. These data can be aggregated and analyzed to produce highly accurate pictures of individuals and social, economic, media, medical, and political trends. This is called analytics. Added to this are the potential effects of social media and cloud use for personal privacy. Geolocation data are features built in to many social media and related applications widely used today. Tagging names to photographs is commonplace singularly, in groups, or as part of group shots whether we consent or not, and photographs also get uploaded onto social media sites and to other platforms days, months, or years after they were taken. This process of geolocation tagging from digital cameras, smartphones, tablets, and the like means there are date stamps and location stamps in the files uploaded. These can produce a very accurate picture of an individual or group in the short, medium, and long term.

The same is true for many smartphones and other devices that have location tracking built into them. Whether singularly or through additional software applications (apps), these can be used to produce a mosaic of a person's life albeit with pieces of the jigsaw missing. These apps frequently have geolocation and other features enabled. Providers of those apps use this information (by and large) to advertise and sell goods and services. This can also be used to compromise security and privacy. As well as for the companies themselves, apps are also increasingly valuable sources of information for the IC and law enforcement agencies. Social network analysis and social analytics can be used alongside social media intelligence (SOCMINT) and other elements of open source intelligence (OSINT) to produce a "pattern of life" for a "person of interest" and those they are connected to.

Furthermore, each of us has received phishing emails offering too-good-to-be-true investment opportunities and the like. If these phishing activities are successful, these can be used as a gateway to access our passwords and empty our bank accounts, gather our personal and business contacts, or spy on us through our webcams and the listening devices contained in our computers, tablets, and phones. The amount of personal data we hold on these devices and on the cloud is growing. For victims of cybercrime of this nature, the first port of call might well be law enforcement, bank, and ultimately intelligence agencies such as the NSA. They will need to access and analyze Internet data to investigate and build a case.

Criminality and other hostile threats are fueled by both low entry points to the Internet and growing levels of technical knowledge in a spectrum encompassing multiplying threat actors. These actors range from "black hat" hackers, amateur "script kiddies," and online collectives such as the hacktivist group Anonymous through to highly sophisticated and well-resourced advanced persistent threats (APTs) associated with nation-states. In addition are criminals who seek to monetarize cybercrime or who can sell expertise, vulnerabilities, personal information, or system vulnerabilities through encrypted forums such as those found on the dark net.[32] Within this mix are a number of hostile individuals and terrorist groups who would seek to harm the United States and its national interests and those of its friends and allies.

The NSA and the Legislative Context for PRISM

The NSA's primary role is to gather and analyze signals intelligence (SIGINT), and it is charged with undertaking both defensive and offensive cyber operations through a series of legal statutes. This enables the United States to counter state, substate, and nonstate threats. As James R. Clapper stated in June 2013 in direct response to the Snowden disclosures, the purpose of these programs "is to obtain foreign intelligence information, including information necessary to thwart terrorist and cyber attacks against the United States and its allies."[33] Mark Phythian reinforces this vital point: "The Snowden leaks expose the extent to which this wide-ranging surveillance, while solely justified by reference to the potential terrorist threat, has had much broader targets."[34] The threat from terrorism is understood, and it is also important to set the NSA's work in this wider context.

The NSA works under a considerable burden, as evidence suggests that cybersecurity risks are growing faster than the ability to secure data and systems from a wide variety of hostile actors.[35] The reasons for cyberattacks remain multifarious, but Verizon's 2014 Data Breach Investigations Report lists among them the long-standing problem posed by espionage.[36] This encompasses espionage from states as well as from private companies. In 2014, an estimated 70 million cyber events occurred every month. By May 2020, that number was an estimated 8.8 billion.[37] This volume of attacks is too large to address without sufficient infrastructure and increased investment in skilled personnel and cannot be tackled by governments acting alone.[38]

Governments around the globe are now seeing threats on an unprecedented scale, diversity, and complexity in cyberspace and are trying to monitor the communications and social relationships of target groups and individuals. Thousands, if not millions, of IT systems are attacked every day, imperiling commercial and personal financial data.[39]

Cyber threats are increasingly complex and have included theft of intellectual property, theft of commercially sensitive data, unauthorized access to sensitive government information, the disruption of government and industry services, the exploitation of information security weaknesses through the targeting of partners, and targeting subsidiaries and supply chains both foreign and domestic. These threats arrive in several guises varying in magnitude and tempo and might be basic or sophisticated. They emanate from individuals and groups who are often well organized and difficult to prosecute or even attribute with certainty.[40] They can also be (or are simultaneously) from industrial competitors and foreign intelligence services or simply hackers or hacktivists who draw on political or ideological rationales.[41] They can originate abroad, domestically, or in other organizations or come from an insider working within the target organization (such as Snowden himself). Former Director of National Intelligence (DNI) Clapper remarked that as a result of Snowden "we are expanding our insider-threat protection capability by monitoring the electronic behavior of employees on duty. We are in the process of transitioning the clearance process to one of continuous evaluation. . . . Our system is based on personal trust. When it comes down to it, that is what it's all about."[42] Cyber attackers are often stealthy, or at least seek to cover their digital tracks. This is often an area where the IC will step in.

As far back as 1997 the vulnerability of the United States to cyberattack was recognized in a report by the President's Commission on Critical Infrastructure Protection and in a number of subsequent exercises.[43] In 2003 President George W. Bush established a Computer Emergency Response Team (CERT) under the Department of Homeland Security (DHS) as a branch of the Office of Cybersecurity and Communications and National Cybersecurity and Communications Integration Center.[44] CERT's remit is to lead "efforts to improve the nation's cybersecurity posture, coordinate cyber information sharing, and proactively manage cyber risks to the Nation while protecting the constitutional rights of Americans."[45]

Responsibility for cybersecurity is also vested in the Federal Bureau of Investigation (FBI) and the Department of Defense (DoD). This includes U.S. Cyber Command, which coordinates activities with the NSA, alongside the Department of State and Department of Commerce, which take the lead on international negotiations and the development of cybersecurity standards.[46] The IC is facing mounting threats and must map, mitigate, and deter hostile threats to government, private industry, individual computer systems, and cloud services. Despite the IC's capabilities, the sheer scale, diversity, and sophistication of both the threats and threat actors can be daunting. However, much of the public discourse surrounding PRISM (and its programs) appears to be directed not at these online threats to the real world but at counterterrorism and criminal activities.

Whether the mass surveillance enabled by PRISM (and the Panopticon effect it can produce)[47] and the reach into private lives, affiliations, and social groups and the analytics that can be achieved with the metadata involved is sufficiently balanced by the number of successes it can achieve in identifying threats and threat actors is worthy of extended discussion and debate. Snowden's leaks and subsequent reactions and revelations have stirred a dormant public into debate and encouraged senior figures in the IC such as Admiral Mike McConnell, one of Clapper's predecessors as DNI, and James B. Comey, then director of the FBI, to put the IC case to the public, media, and decision makers. Public concerns nevertheless remain regarding the abilities as well as the regulation and oversight of intelligence practices by the executive, legislative, and judiciary. In this context of public awareness and debate, it is worth noting that when the United States introduced the Cyber Security Awareness Act in 2011 the three senators who sponsored the bill noted:

> We as a nation remain woefully unaware of the risks that cyber attacks pose to our economy, our national security, and our privacy. This problem is caused in large part by the fact that cyber threat information ordinarily is classified when it is gathered by the government or held as proprietary when collected by a company that has been attacked. As a result, Americans do not have an appropriate sense of the threats that they face as individual Internet users, the damage inflicted on our businesses and the jobs they create, or the scale of the attacks undertaken by foreign agents against American interests.[48]

Partly for these reasons the Obama administration also created Presidential Policy Directive 20 (PPD-20) in October 2012 to set the parameters for defensive and offensive cyber operations conducted by the U.S. government. PPD-20 helped formulate new rules of engagement and strengthened U.S. Cyber Command and the military branches it oversees. Much of the context for PRISM was set out in PPD-20, which laid out, among other things, Defensive Cyber Effects Operations. This required, in part, the cooperation of private companies owning and operating cyberspace. PPD-20 also laid out the operational and legal parameters for Offensive Cyber Effects Operations. However, PRISM had further political and legislative antecedents.

As far back as 1994, during the Clinton administration, Congress passed a law permitting the FBI to conduct electronic surveillance of telephony communications with the help of telecommunications hardware manufacturers and providers.[49] That law, the Communications Assistance for Law Enforcement Act (CALEA), was designed to help law enforcement monitor criminal activity at a time when telephony networks were moving into digital communications. It has subsequently been expanded to include VoIP (voice over Internet protocols) and Internet traffic utilizing broadband but not social media sites, instant messaging, or email.[50] The FBI then began a program called the Collection System Network (DCSNet) through which they could access and analyze landline, cell phone, and SMS communications. This was used by the FBI for both criminal and counterterrorism investigations.[51]

In the immediate aftermath of 9/11, when the U.S. IC had detailed intelligence about the plotters—intelligence that was not shared between the agencies[52]—Section 215 of the USA PATRIOT Act of 2001 permitting warrantless surveillance was passed and used to gather data on telephone records of U.S. citizens. Section 215 "broadened government access to private business records by both enlarging the scope of materials that may be sought and lowering the legal standard required to be met."[53] Monitored calls were both from and to the

United States.[54] These telephone records included location and duration but not content (metadata). As the *Wall Street Journal* reported in June 2013:

> The ad hoc nature of the NSA program changed after the Bush administration came under criticism for its handling of a separate, warrantless NSA eavesdropping program. President Bush acknowledged its existence in late 2005, calling it the Terrorist Surveillance Program, or TSP. When Democrats retook control of Congress in 2006, promising to investigate the administration's counterterrorism policies, Bush administration officials moved to formalize court oversight of the NSA programs, according to former U.S. officials. Congress in 2006 also made changes to the Patriot Act that made it easier for the government to collect phone-subscriber data under the Foreign Intelligence Surveillance Act. Those changes helped the NSA collection program become institutionalized, rather than one conducted only under the authority of the president.[55]

During the George W. Bush administration, amendments to FISA were made through the Protect America Act of 2007. This allowed NSA to develop the capabilities to gather metadata intelligence directed at foreign targets.[56]

According to testimony from General Keith B. Alexander, then-commander of U.S. Cyber Command and former director of the NSA, these changes meant that "together with other intelligence, [these measures] have protected the U.S. and our allies from terrorist threats across the globe . . . over fifty times since 9/11 . . . in over twenty countries around the world."[57] DNI Clapper also said that "it was a direct result of 9/11. We had a foreign communicant, a person in Yemen, who was talking to someone in San Diego [one of the 9/11 airplane hijackers]. We had no way legally to 'connect those dots,' which of course the IC was highly criticized for."[58] These dots are foreign and domestic and, as the Internet has increased global data sharing (both one-to-one and one-to-many), the lines between foreign and domestic threats and intelligence collection are blurring in areas such as "terrorism, arms, drugs trafficking and the broader human security agenda."[59] As Phythian argues:

> The contemporary intelligence environment is scarred by the experience of the 9/11 terrorist attacks; haunted by the belief that collecting more information would have resulted in better dot-connection and prevention. . . . Public trust has been a notable casualty of the Snowden revelations—trust in technology providers, in intelligence providers, and in government—and greater levels of resistance can be expected from providers and individuals in future. This, in turn, reflects the democratic deficit exposed by Snowden. There is a risk that aspects of intelligence are treated as a disfiguring birthmark on the democratic body politic, carefully concealed and never discussed. Yet, informed public debate is essential to democratic legitimacy here. This debate needs to consider what "security" means and involves before it can consider the options for providing it and the price worth paying for it;

in particular, whether attempted universal collection justifies the invasion of personal space that it involves.[60]

After the Snowden revelations, Clapper defended the program, claiming that these telephone data can only "be queried when there is a reasonable suspicion, based on specific facts, that the particular basis for the query is associated with a foreign terrorist organization."[61] These data were then loaded into a searchable database to identify or to track and trace "persons of interest." Through the time and location data from cell phones, alongside data such as credit card use, intelligence analysts can produce a mosaic of a person's life with only four data points needed from the time and location of a phone call to correctly identify a caller 95 percent of the time.[62] The use and utilization of social media, email records, and chat logs add significantly to this intelligence picture.

By the time of Snowden's disclosures this practice had been undertaken for seven years with authorization under Section 702 of FISA.[63] The main part of this mass electronic surveillance scheme was in big data collection. Big data are made up of everything that is created and transmitted online. To put this in context, IBM states that every day 2.5 quintillion bytes of data are created. This constantly rising volume of data is such that "90% of the data in the world today has been created in the last two years." This trend will continue to increase, "as connected devices become ubiquitous, and previously low-tech industries become digitized."[64] "The NSA say it needs all this data to help prevent another terrorist attack like 9/11. In order to find the needle in the haystack, they argue, they need access to the whole haystack."[65] Nevertheless whether "black swan events" (high-impact events occurring with low frequency) can *always* be prevented remains doubtful.

Furthermore, the NSA, alongside partner intelligence agencies, secretly attached intercepts to the undersea fiber optic cables that ring the world, which are the architectural backbone of the Internet and a key enabler, along with satellites, of the global connectivity we now take for granted. The intercepts provide a high degree of access to global communications.[66] This series of capabilities was too much for Snowden who told the *Guardian*'s Glenn Greenwald he did not want to live in a world "where everything that I say, everything that I do, everyone I talk to, every expression of love or friendship is recorded."[67]

This view is disputed by the NSA. A Congressional Research Service report into the disclosures indicated that "the original press articles and more recent stories have suggested NSA monitors or can monitor the vast majority of the world's Internet traffic." It continued, "NSA has stated that it 'touches' only 1.6% of Internet traffic and 'selects for review' 0.025% of Internet traffic. These portrayals by both critics and proponents may provide an incomplete account of NSA collection because they incorporate certain assumptions about that collection and about what types of Internet traffic are relevant." As of 2011 this meant that the "NSA collected 250 million Internet communications per year using 702 [Section 702 of FISA] authorities."[68] This also meant that "because of technical constraints [involving up-stream communications], NSA . . . was collecting groupings of communications, which contained communications about legitimate targets as well as communications unrelated to those targets. In some cases, that involved the collection of Americans' communications and of wholly domestic communications. As a result of this overcollection, NSA acquired tens of thousands of domestic communications, which the court [the Foreign Intelligence Surveillance Court] determined was in violation of the Constitution."[69]

The NSA's analysts alongside partner agencies, which are numerous and have a variety of roles and expertise, dissect and interpret the data as part of all-source intelligence collection and analysis. Briefing reports are then produced and discussed within the NSA and shared with other agencies. These are then channeled and discussed through the chain of command before they reach the very highest levels of government.

Public Concerns about PRISM

Among other operations the NSA has government mandated responsibilities to gather intelligence on states and target individuals based abroad. This sea of information and volume of the data being collected and analyzed is eye watering but can be extremely useful in tracking and tracing targets and their social networks. As the *New York Times* reported, "Separate streams of data are integrated into large databases—matching, for example, time and location data from cellphones with credit card purposes or E-Z Pass use—intelligence analysts are given a mosaic of a person's life," with only four data points from the time and location of a phone call needed to correctly identify a caller 95 percent of the time.[70] From this SOCMINT and OSINT can help deduce that individual's "pattern of life."

A number of foreign governments, many of which are allied to the United States, became uncomfortable following the Snowden releases. For example, Sabine Leutheusser-Schnarrenberger, Germany's justice minister, publicly articulated her government's concerns: "The suspicion of excessive surveillance of communication is so alarming that it cannot be ignored. For that reason, openness and clarification by the U.S. administration itself should be paramount at this point. . . . The global Internet has become indispensable for a competitive economy, the sharing of information and the strengthening of human rights in authoritarian countries. But our trust in these technologies threatens to be lost in the face of comprehensive surveillance activities."[71] For Leutheusser-Schnarrenberger "America has been a different country since the horrible terrorist attacks of Sept. 11, 2001. The relationship between freedom and security has shifted, to the detriment of freedom, especially as a result of the Patriot Act. . . . We should remember that the strength of the liberal constitutional state lies in the trust of its citizens."[72] German opposition Social Democrat leader Thomas Oppermann went further in pointing to the capabilities of Britain's GCHQ: "The accusations make it sound as if George Orwell's surveillance society has become reality in Great Britain."[73] In a country steeped in the memory of state surveillance of its citizens first by the Nazis and then in East Germany by the Stasi, PRISM and related programs have powerful resonance.[74]

In the face of criticism, the British government has been quick and steadfast in defending the U.S.-U.K. intelligence sharing arrangement, while refusing to go into any details regarding PRISM. Following discussions with John Kerry, then the U.S. secretary of state, William Hague, then the British foreign secretary, stated, "That's something the citizens of both our countries should have confidence in, in particular that that relationship is based on a framework of law in both countries, a law that is vigorously upheld."[75]

The remaining Five Eyes partners (Canada, Australia, and New Zealand) have been more muted in condemning the disclosures, with a spokesperson for the Communications Security Establishment Canada (CSEC) declaring that CSEC does not access PRISM.[76] Instead CSEC uses an indigenous, and equally controversial, intelligence program to gather metadata.[77] A similarly controversial program was being proposed in Australia but was shelved by the government ahead of the 2013 election, which saw Kevin Rudd replace Julia Gillard.[78] Although the Gillard government refused to divulge whether Australian intelligence agencies were receiving information gathered via PRISM because such a disclosure would threaten intelligence sources and methods as well as "risk. . . serious complications in our relations with our neighbours."[79] A member of the Australian government, one of the partner nations in the Five Eyes agreement, nevertheless noted: "The U.S. may be able to brush aside some of the diplomatic fallout from the Snowden leak, but that may not be the case for Australia. China, Malaysia, other countries may respond to us in ways that they would not to Washington." It was also judged to "have a much greater and more lasting impact than the Manning leaks," which brought Julian Assange and Wikileaks into the limelight.[80] The PRISM disclosures have not halted collaboration between the United States and allied and friendly governments who share mutual security interests with long-standing intelligence coordination between themselves.[81] The revelations regarding these intelligence gathering and analysis practices have shaken the trust between governments and for a number of their citizens and key elements of the private sector. Whatever the rights and wrongs of these surveillance activities, intelligence historian Rhodri Jeffreys-Jones argues, what is needed is "an intelligence arrangement we can trust."[82] There are two major questions that PRISM and related programs and activities pose for the United States, for its intelligence partners in the Five Eyes community, and indeed for all liberal democracies. First, at what point does the right to privacy, freedom, and civil liberties outweigh the protection of national security? Second, in the largely secret world these legally mandated intelligence agencies operate in, do democratic oversight, transparency, and accountability go far enough in holding these practices to account?

Mike Rogers, then-chairman of the U.S. House Permanent Select Committee on Intelligence, noted that the activities of PRISM "are legal, court-approved and are subject to an extensive oversight regime" authorized under Section 702 of FISA.[83] Rogers further asserted, "One of the frustrating parts about being a member of this Committee is sitting at the intersection of classified intelligence programs and transparent democracy as representatives of the American people. The public trusts the government to protect the country from another 9/11 type attack, but that trust can start to wane when they are faced with inaccuracies, half truths and outright lies about the way intelligence programs are being run."[84] For Edward Snowden, trust in the government had broken down, meaning "the government has granted itself power it is not entitled to. There is no public oversight. The result is people like myself have the latitude to go further than they are allowed to."[85] Rogers and many others within government and the IC are acutely aware of the balance between the protection of civil liberties and democratic values and guarding national security. Supporters of the surveillance programs based their arguments on how PRISM and the wider efforts of the IC have prevented another 9/11 while maintaining political and legislative checks through *in camera* provisions from FISA, judicially approved actions, and political oversight from the House and Senate intelligence committees. FISA cases are heard *in camera* before the Foreign Intelligence Surveillance Court and FISA Court of Review. The surveillance order applications put by senior government representatives to these courts are classified, as are the vast majority of the opinions issued by these courts. Whether these practices should continue after Snowden's releases is being debated with authority in this area shared between Congress and the executive branch.[86]

Mass Data Collection, Analysis, and Legislation Post-Snowden

At his 2015 State of the Union Address, President Obama declared, "No foreign nation, no hacker, should be able to shut down our networks, steal our trade secrets, or invade the privacy of American families, especially our kids. We are making sure our government integrates intelligence to combat cyber threats, just as we have done to combat terrorism."[87] This was followed by further government initiatives, while cyber incidents like the breach of Sony and the Office of Personnel Management in 2015 also highlighted that vulnerabilities exist within government as well as private industry.[88]

New legislative initiatives introduced in 2014 included the Cybersecurity Information Sharing Act (CISA), which allowed the capture of not only state, substate, and nonstate cyberespionage and cybercrime but also the legitimate activities of individuals with further attendant consequences for civil liberties, privacy, and the right to free speech.[89] For its critics, CISA threatens to embed the surveillance state.[90] As a 2015 Congressional Research Service report details, "There are many reasons why entities may opt to not participate in a cyber-information sharing scheme, including the potential liability that could result from sharing internal cyber-threat information with other private companies or the government."[91] For others, particularly those in IC and in security communities, CISA capabilities remain too limited.[92] Joel Brenner, a senior cybersecurity advisor at the NSA, asserted:

> Our nation is being turned inside out electronically and we seem helpless to stop it. The Russians have broken into a White House network and JPMorgan Chase. The Chinese have stolen blueprints, manufacturing processes, clinical trial results and other proprietary data from more than 140 companies and have utterly penetrated major media. The Iranians attack our banks, our electric grid is assaulted with frightening frequency and North Korea has brought Sony to its knees. Meanwhile, credit card data from big retailers such as Target and Home Depot are for sale electronically by the boatload. Infrastructure is at risk. Last month, attackers disrupted production at a German steel plant and damaged its blast furnaces, using only cyber methods. . . . Unfortunately, the measures just announced by President Barack Obama do not address these flaws. . . . But it would not address underlying weaknesses in the Internet. Stiffer sentences for cyber crime may be useful, but they would not make our infrastructure harder to attack or our communications more secure.[93]

Within this context of insecurity, in which government and industry struggle to determine their cybersecurity role, the NSA-led PRISM program raised a host of concerns regarding the bulk collection of metadata and the analysis of big data. Metadata collection and analytics are already being undertaken by technology companies, corporations, and many other actors.[94] Important questions to ask include what they are being used for, what they can be used for, and what the implications are.[95] Amitai Etzioni posits that "major private corporations keep very detailed dossiers on most Americans, hundreds of millions of dossiers. And they make them available to the government for a fee, without any court order or review. We are so conditioned to hold that private sector and privacy go hand in hand while the public sphere is closely associated with the violation of privacy. Actually, in the cyber age, these boundaries have been blurred."[96] Anyone who has read—and understood—the terms and conditions for the operating systems, programs and apps, and social media that we use every day will bear testament to this.[97] For the IC, this also entails how it can enhance security and satisfy privacy and civil liberties concerns within and between its allies and partners. This is a complicated picture, and as James A. Lewis points out, "The real lesson of Snowden's leaks is that *there is no privacy for anyone who uses communications devices* and all governments are as guilty as their resources allow them to be."[98]

Debates over Mass Surveillance, Encryption, and Personal Data

There remain problems for the NSA, CIA, DoD, and IC in attributing many of the large numbers of malicious cyber activities experienced daily even with the vast array of resources they have available to them. The attribution problem continues to be affected by whether "the need to share" or the "need to know" rule has primacy. Insider threats also remain a problem. These threats can also be (or are simultaneously) from industrial competitors and foreign intelligence services or simply hackers or hacktivists who draw on political or ideological rationales.

Moreover, the growth and complexity of cyberattacks has seen exponential growth, and "what was considered a sophisticated cyber attack only a year ago might now be incorporated into a downloadable and easy to deploy internet application, requiring little or no expertise to use."[99] These can include APTs. There are publicly discussed fears of a "cyber Pearl Harbor," a "cyber 9/11," or even a statewide "Cybergeddon" attack aimed at crippling or seriously damaging a nation and which could cascade to other states. Both symmetric state-level APTs and asymmetric threats are deeply troubling as both the United States and United Kingdom are heavily networked and data dependent. Damage and disruption to their governments, militaries, and critical infrastructure are recognized threats and why both nations have heavily invested in their cyber intelligence capabilities and publicly defended their activities. Nevertheless, the use of end-to-end encryption might well mean that the surveillance activities of the IC become much more difficult in terms of harnessing electronic communications.[100]

These significant threats may coincide with counterterrorism activities and criminal investigations. Andrew Parker, the director general of Britain's MI5, stated in a public interview in September 2015 that MI5 needs the authority to "navigate the Internet" and to use data sets to "join the dots" to counter heightened terrorist threats emanating from Islamic State and its progeny as well as other hostile nonstate actors. Laws and norms allowing MI5 access to terrorist Internet-based communications on social media and on other software platforms—before plots come to fruition—remains a necessity to safeguard the United Kingdom and its citizens.

In his entreaty, Parker made a case that private companies such as Facebook have an ethical responsibility to approach the U.K. government to tackle terrorism and crime where they hold and carry that information.[101] Alex Younger, the head of MI6, made similar points in March 2015: "Using data appropriately and proportionately offers us a priceless opportunity to be even more deliberate and targeted in what we do and thus be better at protecting our agents and this country." He went on to caution, "That is good news. The bad news is that the same technology in opposition hands, an opposition often unconstrained by consideration of ethics and law, allows them to see what we are doing and put our people and agents at risk."[102]

Many intelligence agencies and law enforcement, but especially in liberal democracies like the United States, all face similar problems when dealing with terrorism and extending to cyberespionage, cybercrime, and domestic unrest. How can governments at the national, state, and local levels legally access Internet-based communications and possess mass surveillance capabilities while also safeguarding legitimate free speech and privacy? These issues are complex and raise a series of ethical and legal questions that are compounded by the pace of technological change and the growing use of encryption. Some of the questions and challenges posed by encryption and restrictions on Internet-based mass surveillance have been referred to by James B. Comey, former director of the FBI, as potentially leaving them "going dark." Comey, in an October 2014 speech to the Brookings Institution, clearly articulated the challenges technology poses for law enforcement, intelligence, and security services:

> Technology has forever changed the world we live in. We're online, in one way or another, all day long. Our phones and computers have become reflections of our personalities, our interests, and our identities. They hold much that is important to us. And with that comes a desire to protect our privacy and our data. . . . Unfortunately, the law hasn't kept pace with technology, and this disconnect has created a significant public safety problem. We call it "Going Dark." . . . We face two overlapping challenges. The first concerns real-time court-ordered interception of what we call "data in motion," such as phone calls, e-mail, and live chat sessions. The second challenge concerns court-ordered access to data stored on our devices, such as e-mail, text messages, photos, and videos—or what we call "data at rest." And both real-time communication and stored data are increasingly encrypted . . . [by] those conspiring to harm us. They use the same devices, the same networks, and the same apps to make plans, to target victims, and to cover up what they're

doing. And that makes it tough for us to keep up . . . even with lawful authority, we may not be able to access the evidence and the information we need. Current law governing the interception of communications requires telecommunication carriers and broadband providers to build interception capabilities into their networks for court-ordered surveillance. But that law, the Communications Assistance for Law Enforcement Act, or CALEA, was enacted 20 years ago—a lifetime in the Internet age. And it doesn't cover new means of communication.[103]

Comey added during his speech that "perhaps it's time to suggest that the post-Snowden pendulum has swung too far in one direction—in a direction of fear and mistrust. It is time to have open and honest debates about liberty and security."[104] At the very least, as James R. Clapper suggested, "I guess the major take-away from this whole Snowden experience, for me, has been the need for more transparency."[105] This debate regarding the balance needed between liberty and security remains active around the world.

For example, privacy concerns regarding the use of bulk personal datasets (BPDs) in identifying "persons of interest" and their social connections remain as they "contain personal information about a large number of individuals, the majority of whom will not be of any interest to the Agencies."[106] GCHQ's access to BPDs under the United Kingdom's Investigatory Powers Act was carefully questioned. Indeed, their oversight body, the Intelligence and Security Committee, stated, "Given the background to the draft Bill and the public concern over the allegations made by Edward Snowden in 2013, it is surprising that the protection of people's privacy—which is enshrined in other legislation—does not feature more prominently.[107]

Conclusion

James R. Clapper indicated that the ramifications of the Snowden leaks are "going to play out over a period of years before we know the full extent of the damage that was done."[108] Groups such as Islamic State and al-Qaeda do not respect the "rules of the game." These groups, and other terrorist organizations and disruptive interests, use and utilize the Internet, social media, and other electronic platforms and devices for planning, plotting, communication, and recruitment. States such as North Korea and various intelligence agencies, hacking groups, and "black hat" hackers all use the Internet and a wide variety of communication technologies. Programs like PRISM and the wider work of the IC offer one layer of protection. However, the political fallout from mass surveillance emanating from many governments and civil society groups, which runs counter to "cyber utopian" ideals of a largely "free and unregulated" Internet, has been significant. The result has been growing use of end-to-end encryption. This also poses significant problems for the IC and law enforcement in terms of identification, attribution, and prosecution.[109]

Calls for increased surveillance powers by the United States and other ICs are seen as one key to stay ahead of the threat horizon. Both their desire to be able to surveil the Internet and global communications and the debate over encryption are now under an increased spotlight following Snowden's disclosures. The IC is also mounting further defensive measures for government systems, and both the U.S. and U.K. governments recognize that the defense of their economies and other elements of their critical infrastructure and the prevention or reduction of cybercrime require a whole-nation response from private industry and individuals.

With the volume, types, and complexity of cybercrime and cyberespionage and the kinds of APTs now being seen, the problem is not going to change unless more robust measures are put in place. As was pointed out at a conference on cybersecurity organized by the United Nations Institute for Disarmament Research in late 2011, "Every actor—cyber-terrorists, criminals, militaries, as well as civil society and the private sector—is operating in the same environment, with the same tools, domains, and targets."[110] With publicly discussed fears of a "cyber Pearl Harbor" or a more destructive event, it remains imperative to debate the roles, responsibilities, expectations, and limits of the IC in an increasing interconnected and globalized world.[111]

At a domestic level, the *Wall Street Journal* reported, "the disconnect between the program's supporters and detractors underscored the difficulty Congress has had navigating new technology, national security and privacy."[112] This disconnect has prompted the U.S. IC to increase the transparency of their rules and roles.[113] This has also led the U.S. Senate, after lengthy debate, to pass the USA Freedom Act (2015), which has rolled back government bulk metadata collection previously authorized under the USA PATRIOT Act of 2001.[114]

This postscript is still being written as "the Snowden leaks have increased tensions and debates over what is appropriate national security intelligence collection to a level never seen in modern intelligence practice" and "is now a public policy priority of many liberal democratic states."[115] Liberal democracies govern and police by consent, and the IC is no exception. Whether these practices are to continue, deepen, or recede requires a more informed debate about where our fundamental civil liberties and the requirements of national (and international) security sit. For liberal democracies like the United States in particular, public concerns and skepticism cannot be ignored, nor are they being ignored, and a better balance needs to be struck where privacy and civil liberties are respected and national security is served. This is a balance that we must get right. The IC cannot just step away, nor will they. As Walsh and Miller argue: "Snowden has compounded significantly the intelligence policy and ethical dilemmas liberal democratic states now face. How do they . . . 'balance the provision of good security with respecting civil liberties and ensuring the continuing support of the population for security and intelligence policy.' The growing complexity of the security environment, the blurring of domestic and international security, globalization and rapid growth of cyber-technology make the need for better evidence based and ethically informed policy frameworks for security intelligence collection critical."[116] The debate regarding the reality and potentialities of mass surveillance and (mass) data collection and analytics needs time to mature. This is true of public policy debates, media debates, debates within the IC and security communities, and legislative debates. Currently legal and policy frameworks are playing catch-up to technological innovation and technology take-up. That debate needs to be informed in order to produce "an ethically informed set of policy guidelines to help decision makers better navigate between citizen's two basic rights—security and privacy."[117]

Notes

1. Luke Harding, *The Snowden Files: The Inside Story of the World's Most Wanted Man* (London: Guardian Books, 2014), 23. See also University of Maryland, Applied Research Laboratory for Intelligence and Security, www.casl.umd.edu/about. Although CASL work may be covert, as of March 2016 they appeared quite forthcoming about the role they play in supporting U.S. intelligence communities.

2. Harding, *Snowden Files*, 18–60. Renowned scholars and practitioners offer further details—Loch K. Johnson, Richard J. Aldrich, Christopher Moran, David M. Barrett, Glenn Hastedt, Robert Jervis, Wolfgang Krieger, Rose McDermott, Sir David Omand, Mark Phythian, and Wesley K. Wark, "An INS Special Forum: Implications of the Snowden Leaks," *Intelligence and National Security* 29, no. 6 (2014): 793. The most thorough look may be Glenn Greenwald, *No Place to Hide: Edward Snowden, the NSA and the Surveillance State* (London: Hamish Hamilton, 2014).

3. Harding, *Snowden Files*, 155–69, 314–15, and 323–28. See also Amitai Etzioni, "NSA: National Security vs. Individual Rights," *Intelligence and National Security* 30, no. 1 (2015): 123–27.

4. Jonathan Kim, ed., "Fourth Amendment" (Legal Information Institute, June 2017), www.law.cornell.edu/wex/fourth_amendment.

5. Rose McDermott, "An INS Special Forum," 204, 802–4. See also Edward Jay Epstein, "Was Snowden's Heist a Foreign Espionage Operation?," *Wall Street Journal*, May 9, 2014, www.wsj.com/articles/SB10001424052702304831304579542402390653932, and Spencer Ackerman, "Senior U.S. Congressman Mike Rogers: Glenn Greenwald Is 'a Thief,'" *Guardian*, February 4, 2014, www.theguardian.com/world/2014/feb/04/us-congressman-mike-rogers-glenn-greenwald-thief-snowden-nsa.

6. Glenn Greenwald and Laura Poitras, "NSA Whistleblower Edward Snowden: 'I Don't Want to Live in a Society That Does These Sort of Things'—Video," *Guardian*, June 9, 2013, www.theguardian.com/world/video/2013/jun/09/nsa-whistleblower-edward-snowden-interview-video.

7. Alan Rusbridger and Ewen MacAskill, "Edward Snowden Interview—the Edited

Transcript," *Guardian*, July 18, 2014, www.theguardian.com/world/2014/jul/18/-sp -edward-snowden-nsa-whistleblower-interview-transcript.

8. PRISM likely stands for "Planning Tool for Resource Integration, Synchronization, and Management." Benjamin Dreyfuss and Emily Dreyfuss, "What Is the NSA's PRISM Program? (FAQ)," CNET, June 7, 2013, www.cnet.com/uk/news/what-is-the-nsas-prism -program-faq/.

9. Harding, *Snowden Files*, 61–83.

10. U.S. National Security Agency, *UKUSA Agreement Release 1940–1956* (Fort Meade, Md., 2010), http://www.nsa.gov/public_info/declass/ukusa.shtml.

11. Ewan MacAskill, Julian Borger, Nick Hopkins, Nick Davies, and James Ball, "GCHQ Taps Fibre-Optic Cables for Secret Access to World's Communications," *Guardian*, June 21, 2013, http://www.theguardian.com/uk/2013/jun/21/gchq-cables-secret -world-communications-nsa.

12. Kim Zetter, "U.K. Spy Agency Secretly Taps over 200 Fiber-Optic Cables, Share Data with the NSA," *Wired*, June 21, 2013, http://www.wired.com/2013/06/gchq-tapped -200-cables/.

13. Kadhim Shubber, "A Simple Guide to GCHQ's Internet Surveillance Programme Tempora," *Wired*, June 24, 2014, http://www.wired.co.uk/news/archive/2013-06/24/gchq -tempora-101.

14. MacAskill et al., "GCHQ Taps Fibre-Optic Cables."

15. Barton Gellman and Laura Poitras, "U.S., British Intelligence Mining Data from Nine U.S. Internet Companies in Broad Secret Program," *Washington Post*, June 6, 2013, http://www.washingtonpost.com/investigations/us-intelligence-mining-data-from- nine-us-internet-companies-in-broad-secret-program/2013/06/06/3a0c0da8-cebf-11e2 -8845-d970ccb04497_story.html.

16. Ibid.

17. Claire Cain Miller, "Tech Companies Concede to Surveillance Program," *New York Times*, June 7, 2013, https://www.nytimes.com/2013/06/08/technology/tech -companies-bristling-concede-to-government-surveillance-efforts.html.

18. Ibid.

19. Ibid.

20. Ibid.

21. Declan McCullagh, "No Evidence of NSA's 'Direct Access' to Tech Companies," CNET, June 8, 2013, http://www.cnet.com/uk/news/no-evidence-of-nsas-direct-access -to-tech-companies/.

22. Glenn Greenwald, "XKeyscore: NSA Tool Collects 'Nearly Everything a User Does on the Internet,'" *Guardian*, July 31, 2013, http://www.theguardian.com/world /2013/jul/31/nsa-top-secret-program-online-data.

23. Michael B. Kelley, "NSA's 'Widest-Reaching' System Could Read Facebook Chats and Private Messages," *Business Insider*, July 31, 2013, http://www.businessinsider.com /nsa-can-see-facebook-chats-or-messages-2013-7?IR=T.

24. Shubber, " Simple Guide to GCHQ's Internet Surveillance."

25. John Lowensohn, "NSA's 'Dishfire' Program Said to Capture Nearly 200 Million Texts a Day," *Verge*, January 16, 2014, http://www.theverge.com/2014/1/16/5316178/nsas -dishfire-program-said-to-capture-nearly-200m-texts-a-day.

26. Gellman and Poitras, "U.S., British Intelligence Mining Data."

27. "U.S. Confirms Verizon Phone Records Collection," *BBC News*, June 6, 2013, http://www.bbc.co.uk/news/world-us-canada-22793851.

28. Siobhan Gorman, Even Perez, and Janet Hook, "U.S. Collects Vast Data Trove—NSA Monitoring Includes Three Major Phone Companies, as Well as Online Activity," *Wall Street Journal*, June 7, 2013, http://www.wsj.com/articles/SB10001424127887324299104578529112289298922.

29. John W. Rollins and Edward C. Liu, "NSA Surveillance Leaks: Background and Issues for Congress," Congressional Research Service, September 4, 2013, https://www.fas.org/sgp/crs/intel/R43134.pdf.

30. Andrew Clement, "NSA Surveillance: Exploring the Geographies of Internet Interception," in *iConference 2014 Proceedings* (2014), 412–25.

31. Epstein, "Was Snowden's Heist a Foreign Espionage Operation?"

32. See, for example, Misha Glenny, *Dark Market: How Hackers Became the New Mafia* (London: Vintage, 2012), and Jamie Bartlett, *The Dark Net Inside the Digital Underworld* (London: Random House, 2014).

33. James R. Clapper, "DNI Statement on the Collection of Intelligence Pursuant to Section 702 of the Foreign Intelligence Surveillance Act" (Office of the Director of National Intelligence, June 8, 2013), www.dni.gov/index.php/newsroom/press-releases/press-releases-2013/item/872-dni-statement-on-the-collection-of-intelligence-pursuant-to-section-702-of-the-foreign-intelligence-surveillance-act.

34. Johnson et al., "INS Special Forum," 807.

35. David Chinn, James Kaplan, and Allen Weinberg, "Risk and Responsibility in a Hyperconnected World: Implications for Enterprises" (McKinsey & Company, January 1, 2014), http://www.mckinsey.com/insights/business_technology/risk_and_responsibility_in_a_hyperconnected_world_implications_for_enterprises.

36. Verizon Communications, "2014 Verizon Data Breach Investigations Report," https://webfiles.dti.delaware.gov/pdfs/rp_Verizon-DBIR-2014_en_xg.pdf.

37. Luke Irwin, "List of Data Breaches & Cyber Attacks in May 2020," *IT Governance UK Blog*, September 21, 2020, www.itgovernance.co.uk/blog/list-of-data-breaches-cyber-attacks-may-2020.

38. Tarek Saadawi, Louis H. Jordan Jr., and Vincent Boudreau, eds., "Cyber Infrastructure Protection, Vol. II" (Strategic Studies Institute and U.S. Army War College Press, May 2013).

39. Jonathan Tal, "America's Critical Infrastructure: Threats, Vulnerabilities and Solutions," *Security Info Watch*, September 20, 2018, www.securityinfowatch.com/access-identity/access-control/article/12427447/americas-critical-infrastructure-threats-vulnerabilities-and-solutions.

40. Tal, "America's Critical Infrastructure."

41. On "hacktivism," see Jonathan Diamond, "Early Patriotic Hacking," in *A Fierce Domain: Conflict in Cyberspace 1986–2002*, ed. Jason Healey (Vienna, Va.: CSSA/Atlantic Council, 2013), 136–51.

42. Loch K. Johnson, "A Conversation with James R. Clapper, Jr., the Director of National Intelligence in the United States," *Intelligence and National Security* 30, no. 1 (2015): 17.

43. Dana A. Shea, *Critical Infrastructure: Control Systems and the Terrorist Threat* (Washington, D.C.: U.S. Congressional Research Service, February 21, 2003), http://fas.org/irp/crs/RL31534.pdf. See also Michael Warner, "Cyber-Security: A Pre-history," *Intelligence and National Security* 27, no. 5 (2012): 781–99. On U.S. efforts in this realm, see Myriam Dunn Cavelty, *Cyber-Security and Threat Politics: U.S. Efforts to Secure the Information Age* (London: Routledge, 2008), and Healey, *Fierce Domain*, 14–88.

44. James Andrew Lewis and Götz Neuneck, *The Cyber Index: International Security Trends and Realities* (Geneva: United Nations Institute for Disarmament Research, 2013), 53, http://www.unidir.org/files/publications/pdfs/cyber-index-2013-en-463.pdf.

45. Cyber Security Intelligence, "US-CERT," https://www.cybersecurityintelligence.com/us-cert-1285.html.

46. Lewis and Neuneck, *Cyber Index*, 52–54.

47. Thomas McMullan, "What Does the Panopticon Mean in the Age of Digital Surveillance?," *Guardian*, July 23, 2015, https://www.theguardian.com/technology/2015/jul/23/panopticon-digital-surveillance-jeremy-bentham. McMullan incorporates as part of its rationale "If you have done nothing wrong, you have nothing to fear." Nevertheless, would the same apply under a repressive regime?

48. Sheldon Whitehouse, "Senators Introduce Legislation to Promote Public Awareness of Cyber Security" (November 1, 2013), http://www.whitehouse.senate.gov/news/release/senators-introduce-legislation-to-promote-public-awareness-of-cyber-security.

49. This collaboration may in fact date to at least the 1970s and the initiation of a project known as Blarney through which "the 'backbone' providers of global communications . . . [used by] BLARNEY and three other corporate projects—OAKSTAR, FAIRVIEW and STORMBREW—under the heading of 'passive' or 'upstream' collection. They capture data as they move across fiber-optic cables and the gateways that direct global communications traffic." Craig Timberg and Barton Gellman, "NSA Paying U.S. Companies for Access to Communications Networks," *Washington Post*, August 29, 2013, https://www.washingtonpost.com/world/national-security/nsa-paying-us-companies-for-access-to-communications-networks/2013/08/29/5641a4b6-10c2-11e3-bdf6-e4fc677d94a1_story.html.

50. Declan McCullagh, "'Dark' Motive: FBI Seeks Signs of Carrier Roadblocks to Surveillance," CNET, November 5, 2012, http://www.cnet.com/uk/news/dark-motive-fbi-seeks-signs-of-carrier-roadblocks-to-surveillance/.

51. Ryan Singel, "Point, Click . . . Eavesdrop: How the FBI Wiretap Net Operates," *Wired*, June 5, 2017, http://www.wired.com/2007/08/wiretap.

52. This was one of the conclusions of *The 9/11 Commission Report*, http://www.9-11commission.gov/report/.

53. Section 215 was subject to sunset on December 31, 2005, and has now been reauthorized several times. Rollins and Liu, "NSA Surveillance Leaks." See also Julian Hattem, "Obama Signs NSA Bill, Renewing Patriot Act Powers," *The Hill*, February 2, 2016, http://thehill.com/policy/national-security/243850-obama-signs-nsa-bill-renewing-patriot-act-powers.

54. This was subsequently updated under the FISA Amendments Act. See McCullagh, "'Dark' Motive."

55. Gorman, Perez, and Hook, "U.S. Collects Vast Data Trove."

56. U.S. Department of Justice, "FISA 101: Why FISA Modernization Amendments Must Be Made Permanent,'" https://www.justice.gov/archive/ll/. See also U.S. Privacy and Civil Liberties Oversight Board, *Report on the Surveillance Program Operated Pursuant to Sec 702 of the Foreign Intelligence Surveillance Act* (2014), http://www.wired .com/wp-content/uploads/2014/07/PCLOB-Section-702-Report-PRE-RELEASE.pdf. James Risen and Eric Lichtblau, "Bush Lets U.S. Spy on Callers without Courts," *New York Times*, December 16, 2005, http://www.nytimes.com/2005/12/16/politics/bush-lets -us-spy-on-callers-without-courts.html?_r=1.

57. Kristan Stoddart, "Life through a PRISM: Data Mining, Processing Capacity and Intelligence Gathering," *Global Policy Journal*, July 10, 2013, https://www.globalpolicy journal.com/blog/10/07/2013/life-through-prism-data-mining-processing-capacity -and-intelligence-gathering.

58. Johnson, "Conversation with James R. Clapper, Jr.," 16. On the issues of account-ability and transparency, see Etzioni, "NSA," 128–34.

59. Patrick F. Walsh and Seumas Miller, "Rethinking 'Five Eyes' Security Intelligence Collection Policies and Practice Post Snowden," *Intelligence and National Security* 31, no. 3 (2016): 345–68.

60. Johnson et al., "INS Special Forum," 807.

61. Gorman, Perez, and Hook, "U.S. Collects Vast Data Trove."

62. James Risen and Eric Lichtblau, "How the U.S. Uses Technology to Mine More Data More Quickly," *New York Times*, June 8, 2013, http://www.nytimes.com/2013/06/09 /us/revelations-give-look-at-spy-agencys-wider-reach.html?pagewanted=all. See also Yves-Alexandre de Montjoye, César A. Hidalgo, Michel Verleysen, and Vincent D. Blondel, "Unique in the Crowd: The Privacy Bounds of Human Mobility," *Nature News*, March 25, 2013, https://www.nature.com/articles/srep01376.

63. Rollins and Liu, "NSA Surveillance Leaks," 1–2.

64. Leslie Bradshaw, "Big Data and What It Means" (U.S. Chamber of Commerce Foundation, September 9, 2015), https://www.uschamberfoundation.org/bhq/big-data -and-what-it-means.

65. Ewen MacAskill and Gabriel Dance, "NSA Files Decoded: Edward Snowden's Surveillance Revelations Explained," ed. Feilding Cage and Greg Chen, *Guardian*, No-vember 1, 2013, http://www.theguardian.com/world/interactive/2013/nov/01/snowden -nsa-files-surveillance-revelations-decoded.

66. Pursuant to Section 702 of FISA, which was added by the FISA Amendments Act of 2008. Rollins and Liu, "NSA Surveillance Leaks," Summary.

67. Harding, *Snowden Files*, 5.

68. Rollins and Liu, "NSA Surveillance Leaks," 3–4.

69. Ibid., 13.

70. Risen and Lichtblau, "Bush Lets U.S. Spy on Callers"; Montjoye et al., "Unique in the Crowd."

71. Sabine Leutheusser-Schnarrenberger, "Minister Leutheusser-Schnarrenberger Criticizes U.S. over Prism Scandal," *Der Spiegel*, June 11, 2013, https://www.spiegel.de /international/world/minister-leutheusser-schnarrenberger-criticizes-us-over-prism -scandal-a-905001.html.

72. Ibid.

73. Michael Nienaber, "German Minister Seeks Answers from UK over Spying 'Catastrophe,'" Reuters UK, June 22, 2013, https://www.reuters.com/article/uk-usa-security-britain-germany-idUKBRE95L09F20130622.

74. A wider picture of the intelligence provisions made as a direct result of 9/11 can be found in Walsh and Miller. They argue, "The intelligence leaks by Wikileaks in 2011 were a further and significant catalyst to ongoing political and public debates about legitimate national security intelligence collection and an acceptable burden on the rights of privacy, freedoms and civil liberties, on the internet and elsewhere," with both proponents and critics drawing on the East German Stasi experience. Walsh and Miller, "Rethinking 'Five Eyes' Security Intelligence Collection Policies," 346.

75. "Intelligence Sharing Lawful, Hague Says after U.S. Talks," *BBC News*, June 12, 2013, http://www.bbc.co.uk/news/uk-politics-22883340.

76. David Ljunggren, "UPDATE 2—Canada Says Not Receiving Information from U.S. Spying Program," Reuters, June 11, 2013, https://uk.reuters.com/article/usa-security-canada-idUKL2N0EM1SZ20130611.

77. Michael Bolen, "Canada's Eavesdropping Agency: What We Know," *HuffPost Canada*, August 14, 2013, http://www.huffingtonpost.ca/2013/06/14/what-do-we-know-about-can_n_3440432.html.

78. Ben Grubb, "Government Shelves Controversial Data Retention Scheme," *Sydney Morning Herald*, June 24, 2013, http://www.smh.com.au/technology/technology-news/government-shelves-controversial-data-retention-scheme-20130624-2oskq.html.

79. David Wroe, "Government Refuses to Say if It Receives PRISM Data," *Sydney Morning Herald*, June 12, 2013, http://www.smh.com.au/opinion/political-news/government-refuses-to-say-if-it-receives-prism-data-20130612-2o3ot.html.

80. Ibid.

81. The U.S. and U.K. governments have an established, rolling program of war games between the two to test their cyberreliance. The first simulation is an attack on their financial services sectors. Nicholas Watt, "U.S. and UK Plan Cyber 'War Games' to Test Resilience," *Guardian*, January 16, 2015, http://www.theguardian.com/technology/2015/jan/16/cyber-war-games-uk-us-intelligence. See also Warwick Ashford, "Cameron and Obama Plan War Games to Test Cyber Resilience," *Computer Weekly*, January 16, 2015, http://www.computerweekly.com/news/2240238298/Cameron-and-Obama-plan-war-games-to-test-cyber-resilience.

82. Rhodri Jeffreys-Jones, "A Critique of the Surveillance Flap," *E-International Relations*, July 4, 2013, http://www.e-ir.info/2013/06/30/a-critique-of-the-surveillance-flap/.

83. U.S. House of Representatives Permanent Select Committee on Intelligence, "How Disclosed NSA Programs Protect Americans, and Why Disclosure Aids Our Adversaries" (Washington, D.C., 2013), http://intelligence.house.gov/hearing/how-disclosed-nsa-programs-protect-americans-and-why-disclosure-aids-our-adversaries.

84. Ibid.

85. Glenn Greenwald, "Edward Snowden: The Whistleblower Behind the NSA Surveillance Revelations," *Guardian*, June 11, 2013, http://www.guardian.co.uk/world/2013/jun/09/edward-snowden-nsa-whistleblower-surveillance.

86. Jared P. Cole, "Disclosure of FISA Opinions—Select Legal Issues" (Washington,

D.C.: Congressional Research Service, February 24, 2014), https://www.fas.org/sgp/crs /secrecy/R43404.pdf. Regarding PRISM's lawfulness under international law, see Etzioni, "NSA," 122–23.

87. Julianne Pepitone, "SOTU: Will Obama's Cybersecurity Proposals Actually Protect You?," *NBC News*, January 20, 2015, http://www.nbcnews.com/storyline/2015-state -of-the-union/sotu-will-obamas-cybersecurity-proposals-actually-protect-you -n289826.

88. Dominic Rushe and Spencer Ackerman, "Obama Plans for Cybersecurity Aim 'to Make Internet Safer Place,'" *Guardian*, January 21, 2015, http://www.theguardian.com /us-news/2015/jan/20/obama-cybersecurity-state-of-the-union-address-speech. See also Michael D. Shear, "Obama to Announce Cybersecurity Plans in State of the Union Preview," *New York Times*, January 10, 2015, http://www.nytimes.com/2015/01/11/us /politics/obama-to-announce-cybersecurity-plans-in-state-of-the-union-preview .html?_r=0.

89. U.S. Congress, "S.754—Cybersecurity Information Sharing Act of 2015" (Washington, D.C., 2015), https://www.congress.gov/bill/114th-congress/senate-bill/754.

90. Amie Stepanovich, "Busting the Biggest Myth of CISA—-That the Program Is Voluntary," *Wired*, August 19, 2015, http://www.wired.com/2015/08/access-cisa-myth -of-voluntary-info-sharing/.

91. Andrew Nolan, "Cybersecurity and Information Sharing: Legal Challenges and Solutions" (Washington, D.C.: Congressional Research Service, March 16, 2015), https:// fas.org/sgp/crs/intel/R43941.pdf.

92. Jessica L. Beyer, "The Cybersecurity Information Sharing Act (CISA)" (Jackson School of International Studies, October 30, 2015), https://jsis.washington.edu/news /the-cybersecurity-information-sharing-act-cisa/.

93. Joel Brenner, "How Obama Fell Short on Cybersecurity," *Politico*, January 21, 2015, https://www.politico.com/magazine/story/2015/01/state-of-the-union -cybersecurity-obama-114411.

94. Thomas H. Davenport, "Analytics 3.0," *Harvard Business Review*, December 2013, https://hbr.org/2013/12/analytics-30.

95. It is also worth noting that the exterior of all mail processed in the United States is photographed and recorded by the U.S. Postal Service. Etzioni, "NSA," 113.

96. Etzioni, "NSA," 118–19.

97. Alex Hern, "I Read All the Small Print on the Internet and It Made Me Want to Die," *Guardian*, June 15, 2015, http://www.theguardian.com/technology/2015/jun/15 /i-read-all-the-small-print-on-the-internet.

98. James A. Lewis, "Review of Fidler, David P., Ed., The Snowden Reader," *H-Net Reviews*, January 2016, http://www.h-net.org/reviews/showrev.php?id=44545, emphasis added.

99. Kristan Stoddart, "Live Free or Die Hard: Cybersecurity, Governments, Corporations and Responses to threats to Critical National Infrastructure in the United States and UK," *Political Science Quarterly* 31, no. 4 (2016): 803–42.

100. Conor Friedersdorf, "How Dangerous Is End-to-End Encryption?," *Atlantic*, July 14, 2015, http://www.theatlantic.com/politics/archive/2015/07/nsa-encryption -ungoverned-spaces/398423/.

101. "MI5 Director General Andrew Parker on Terrorism," BBC Radio 4, September 17, 2015, http://www.bbc.co.uk/programmes/po32qcgm.

102. Gordon Corera, "Plaque Unveiled for First MI6 Chief Mansfield Cumming," BBC News, March 31, 2015, http://www.bbc.co.uk/news/uk-32126061.

103. James B. Comey, "Going Dark: Are Technology, Privacy, and Public Safety on a Collision Course?" (FBI, October 16, 2014), https://www.fbi.gov/news/speeches/going -dark-are-technology-privacy-and-public-safety-on-a-collision-course.

104. Ibid.

105. Johnson, "Conversation with James R. Clapper, Jr.," 128–34.

106. Joint Committee on the Draft Investigatory Powers Bill, "Draft Investigatory Powers Bill" (U.K. Parliament, February 3, 2016), 6, https://publications.parliament.uk /pa/jt201516/jtselect/jtinvpowers/93/93.pdf.

107. Ibid., 9–11.

108. Johnson, "Conversation with James R. Clapper, Jr.," 17.

109. Joe Miller, "Google and Apple to Introduce Default Encryption," BBC News, September 19, 2014, http://www.bbc.co.uk/news/technology-29276955. See also "Tor Project Makes Efforts to Debug Dark Web," BBC News, July 23, 2014, http://www.bbc .co.uk/news/technology-28447023.

110. United Nations Institute for Disarmament Research, "Challenges in Cybersecurity, Risks, Strategies, and Confidence-Building," International Conference, Institute for Peace Research and Security Policy at the University of Hamburg, December 13–14, 2011, http://www.unidir.org/files/medias/pdfs/conference-report-eng-0-373.pdf.

111. See Elisabeth Bumiller and Thom Shanker, "Panetta Warns of Dire Threat of Cyberattack on U.S.," New York Times, October 12, 2012, https://www.nytimes.com/2012/10 /12/world/panetta-warns-of-dire-threat-of-cyberattack.html?pagewanted=all. And Richard A. Clarke, Cyber War: The Next Threat to National Security and What to Do about It (New York: HarperCollins, 2010).

112. Gorman, Perez, and Hook, "U.S. Collects Vast Data Trove."

113. Office of the Director of National Intelligence, "Principles of Intelligence Transparency Implementation Plan" (October 27, 2015), http://www.dni.gov/files/documents /Newsroom/Reports%20and%20Pubs/Principles%20of%20Intelligence%20 Transparency%20Implementation%20Plan.pdf.

114. Jeremy Diamond, "Senate Passes NSA Reform Measure," CNN, September 7, 2015, http://edition.cnn.com/2015/06/02/politics/senate-usa-freedom-act-vote-patriot -act-nsa/; Alan Yuhas, "NSA Reform: USA Freedom Act Passes First Surveillance Reform in Decade—As It Happened," Guardian, June 2, 2015, http://www.theguardian .com/us-news/live/2015/jun/02/senate-nsa-surveillance-usa-freedom-act-congress-live.

115. Walsh and Miller, "Rethinking 'Five Eyes' Security Intelligence Collection Policies," 347.

116. Ibid., 348.

117. Ibid., 368. A wider and deeper discussion of these issues can be found in Simon Chesterman, One Nation Under Surveillance: A New Social Contract to Defend Freedom without Sacrificing Liberty (New York: Oxford University Press, 2013). See also Johnson et al., "INS Special Forum," 804–5.

SECTION III

International Security and Components of Liberty

Divided Memory and the "New Cold War" Thesis
THE RISE AND DECLINE OF A DOUBLE-EDGED ANALOGY

Jeremy B. Straughn, The Ohio State University
Lisa C. Fein, University of Michigan–Ann Arbor
Amelia Ayers, U.S. Department of Defense

Once the preserve of cultural sociologists, historians, and social psychologists, the subject of collective memory has increasingly attracted the interest of scholars who specialize in politics, international relations, policy analysis, and related fields. The trend is not surprising. Indeed, it represents a natural extrapolation from the long-standing insight that representations of the past often become harnessed to the political projects of state, substate, and suprastate actors. Today, it is widely accepted that collective memories are not an inherent property of groups and societies but politicocultural constructions of the past oriented toward present-day concerns. In the hands of political actors, collective memory work is about memory politics.

In this vein, one topic of increasing interest to political researchers is the use of analogic comparisons between past and present. Historical analogies are rhetorical devices which activate particular sectors of collective memories by framing current events as similar to or reminiscent of some paradigmatic period in the past. Through the lens of memory politics, the deployment of historical analogies can be seen as a tactical maneuver that capitalizes upon existing collective memories in order to justify (or, at times, to contest) specific objectives. Historical analogies commonly come to the fore when societies face new challenges. In times of external conflict, for example, leaders may deploy comparisons to periods, events, or persons that recall some past era of unity in order to mobilize, legitimate, orient, clarify, inspire, and console [. . .] In this [chapter], we consider a recent example that directly challenges this premise—one in which endorsement of the same historical analogy gives rise to discursive conflict in its own right.

Specifically, our case study focuses on the public use of analogies to a "new" Cold War to interpret political and military developments in Europe. As a historical analogy, the expression "new Cold War" (hereafter NCW) represents a discursive device through which various social actors have sought to make sense of a new, complex state of affairs by highlighting perceived similarities to some previous event or period. Although NCW is occasionally used merely for rhetorical flourish, the thesis of a "new Cold War" has been advanced in numerous books and articles by reputable scholars and journalists and, on occasion, even in speeches and interviews by highly placed public officials. Not surprisingly, the NCW thesis has also occasioned considerable public controversy, attracting many critics along with proponents of various stripes. On the surface, the ensuing debate appears to revolve primarily around the degree of plausibility and practical desirability of comparing recent tensions between Russia and the West to those between the Soviet Union and the Western Allies during the Cold War. Is the present situation "really" like the Cold War or fundamentally different? In practical terms, are the interests of state actors and publics well served, or potentially undermined, by stressing the parallels? To this extent, positions in the NCW debate appear reducible to either affirmation or rejection of the analogy, on whatever grounds.

Yet, a closer examination of the NCW debate reveals peculiar properties of a NCW which distinguish it from the kinds of historical analogies that have received the most attention in the literature. While many previous studies acknowledge that historical analogies can produce dissension between advocates and critics, most nonetheless take for granted that collective identification and solidarity will be enhanced among those who embrace the same historical analogy. In contrast, we argue that NCW exemplifies what we call a double-edged analogy—one in which shared references to a previous conflict have the effect of producing or reinforcing divergent perceptions and interpretations of current affairs. Thus, what makes an analogy double-edged is precisely that it "cuts" twice. In addition to the first cut between those who accept or reject its appropriateness, a second cut divides proponents of the analogy themselves into opposing camps. Among NCW's advocates, consensus that the current situation resembles the "old" Cold War results, not in solidarity, but in a dispute among rival narratives and recommendations.

We have chosen the NCW for our case study in part because it has been the subject of a debate in which political analysts have often participated, but whose distinctive characteristics as a historical analogy have received relatively little attention.[1] In a broader way, the NCW analogy illustrates the dependency of conceptual orientations in the present on the ways in which prior history has been enshrined in collective memories. Thus, one of the more enduring cultural legacies of the Cold War has been its contribution to the global collective memory repertoire, supplying observers as well as lay publics with a convenient historical point of reference for interpreting international relations in the twenty-first century. As we further discuss below, we believe that Cold War analogies divide because collective memories of the Cold War continue to reflect the clash of perspectives that characterized an earlier period of division. In other words, we see divided memory as a path-dependent variable that explains why certain historical analogies become double-edged.

In the rest of this [chapter], we analyze the uses of the NCW against the backdrop of previous research on the instrumental uses of historical analogies and their politicocultural consequences. Further, our case study enables us to address long-standing questions about the relationship between historical analogies and collective memory: What makes particular historical analogies thinkable in a given context? What accounts for their waxing and waning salience over time? What kind of impact can they be expected to have, on whom, and why? [. . .]

Historical Models, Double-Edged Analogies, and Divided Memory

The relation between historical analogies and collective memory has been widely studied in the realms of policymaking, journalism, and other contexts. There is substantial agreement in the literature about several aspects of historical analogies. First, most scholars agree that historical analogies represent a discursive trope through which some (usually well-known) event, period or configuration from the past is presented as a model for comprehending or clarifying particular events or states of affairs in the present. Thus, Pehar defines historical analogies as "a variety of metaphorical expressions that use an image of the past to shed some light on present or future affairs of mostly political concern." As a variety of metaphor, "historical analogies represent an overlap between an image of the past (source) and an image of the present or future (target)."[2]

Second, although keyed to concerns in the present, the deployment of historical analogies presupposes and relies on prior constructions of collective memory. Thus, Brändström and colleagues posit that "a historical analogy is applied when a person or group draws upon parts of their personal and/or collective memories, and/or parts of 'history,' to deal with current situations and problems." In this sense, they suggest, collective memories of the past are "like a giant database," or virtual trove of potential analogs from which one can select to help make sense of the present.[3]

The role of historical analogies in shaping public opinion and policymaking around specific issues has been widely studied, most often in contexts involving military intervention. A number of authors have called attention to the limitations and pitfalls of relying on historical analogies in policy analysis and other contexts. Most researchers, however, have been interested in the social functions and political consequences of historical analogies, irrespective of their epistemic value. In this literature, studies to date typically concur on the role of historical analogies in producing consensus and solidarity within a society or group.

[. . .] Conflict becomes more likely to the degree that social actors or groups work with different historical analogies to interpret the same state of affairs. We refer to these as "single-edged" analogies insofar as the lines of division only "cut" along a single dimension—between those who embrace the analogy in question and those who reject it or favor a rival analogy. Although our terminology is novel, it is widely recognized that (single-edged) historical analogies often prove divisive. One way this may occur is if opposing actors or coalitions are drawing on different collective memories. Following the breakup of Yugoslavia, for example, Serbian president Slobodan Milošević compared the Kosovo dispute to the disastrous Battle of Kosovo exactly 600 years earlier, while supporters of Kosovar independence likened Serbian "ethnic cleansing" to Hitler's genocide in World War II. [. . .]

Rivalry between single-edged analogies can also arise within a national public, even one that shares a common pool of historical narratives about the collective past. Because collective memories are themselves heterogeneous and multilayered, different subgroups may come to opposing conclusions about some current event or circumstance if the parallels they draw come from different parts of the same collective memory. Thus, Schuman and Rieger found that, on the eve of the 1991 Gulf War, U.S. respondents who grew up during or immediately after World War II were more likely to draw a comparison between Iraqi president Saddam Hussein and Adolf Hitler, while respondents who came of age during the Vietnam era were more likely to view the prospect of U.S. involvement in the conflict as analogous to U.S. involvement in Vietnam during the 1960s.[4] As expected, respondents who chose the World War II analogy were also more likely to support U.S. military action to expel Iraqi forces from Kuwait, while respondents who preferred the Vietnam analogy expressed weaker support or opposition. As in the Kosovo example, each of the two analogies remains single-edged—each by itself is still producing agreement among those who adopt it, while preferences for different analogies lead to contrasting conclusions about the wisdom of a particular policy option. [. . .]

A good example of a double-edged analogy comes from the Bosnian conflict of the mid-1990s. During the war, many Bosnian Serbs and Croats alike interpreted their dispute in terms of the Second World War. The result was not solidarity between the two ethnic groups, but mutual animosity, as militants in each ethno-national group identified opponents with their putative precursors—Serbian *chetniks* and Croatian *ustaše*, respectively—in World War II. Although both groups construed the current conflict as analogous to the same event in the past, the cultural memories on which they drew had been constructed from mutually opposing perspectives. As a result of tapping into divided memories of the same reference period, reciprocal deployment of the same historical analogy only hardened the battle lines between opposing groups and helped build support on both sides for intensified conflict by portraying it as a continuation or revival of an older one.

In our case study below, we argue that the NCW analogy has displayed much the same double-edged character—not only dividing opinions over its appropriateness in a given case, but also driving a wedge between people who accept the analogy as apt. We further hypothesize that the NCW analogy is double-edged because it activates divided memories of the Cold War. Because global collective memory of the Cold War remains divided, the contemporary implications drawn from the NCW analogy also diverge, depending upon the vantage point from which the present standoff is viewed.

Research Questions and Theoretical Expectations

The analysis that follows is guided by a set of empirical questions and theoretical expectations suggested by the existing literature on collective memory and historical analogies. [. . .]

What sort of current developments are most likely to invite comparisons to a "new Cold War"? On this issue, theoretical expectations will depend on how one answers a prior question that remains a subject of scholarly debate: How malleable are collective memories? If they are infinitely elastic and easily reinvented, as some have argued, then virtually any new event that arises can be compared with equal validity to any previous historical context.[5] If, on the other hand, our knowledge of the past displays a large degree of stability or inertia from moment to moment, then the current state of collective memory will provide a baseline against which the plausibility of particular analogies can be judged.[6]

Our own view is that both schools of thought have merit, and the more so when each scenario serves as a limiting case. On the one hand, analogies are by their nature selective, highlighting certain features which the objects compared are claimed to share in common while dismissing other features as incidental. On the other hand, a historical analogy is likely to strain credulity if it simply ignores the way that the historical reference has generally been portrayed in collective memory.

In the case of the NCW, the question of recurring salience becomes more tractable if we consider the distinctive place of the Cold War in global collective memory. As we discuss at the beginning of our analytic section, this period has acquired a core set of associations on which most present-day observers are likely to concur—that the Cold War represented an existential, bipolar conflict of global proportions, yet also one in which direct hostilities between the two nuclear superpowers and their allies in Europe were thankfully averted. In these respects, the Cold War differs from other previous conflicts that were mostly localized, rather than transnational or transcontinental, or else (as with the two world wars) involved massive combat operations, as well as quite different military alignments. On this basis, we hypothesize that new developments will most often invite comparisons to a "new Cold War" when the developments (1) are conflictual, (2) involve former Cold War adversaries or their perceived successors, (3) manifest in confrontation and buildup that stops short of open war, and (4) follow upon an intervening period of relative quiescence between the former adversaries. If our hypothesis is wrong, we should be able to observe anomalous upsurges in the salience of the NCW at moments when developments of this kind are not in evidence.

Finally, what of the impact of historical analogies once they have been deployed? What explains whether they are single-edged or double-edged in effect? As noted above, we hypothesize that historical analogies become double-edged when their advocates draw on collective memories about the same event, but view the present from opposing perspectives. Double-edgedness thus seems to entail a degree of reciprocity and, as it were, "collaboration" between rival camps of proponents. Hypothetically, a historical analogy could be mobilized by only one side, while the other side rejects it wholesale. In this counterfactual scenario, the analogy would remain single-edged—that is, cutting only between those who accept or reject its validity. In our analysis of the NCW debate, the empirical question is whether proponents of the analogy arrive at differing conclusions about recent developments in Europe because they are viewing contemporary events from reciprocally opposed perspectives, namely those of collective actors who are viewed as successors to the respective sides in the "old" Cold War. [. . .]

Trajectory of a Historical Analogy

From "Cold War" to "New Cold War"

While the precise origins of the term "Cold War" are disputed, the expression appears to have emerged in the immediate aftermath of World War II. Today, the Cold War proper is conventionally held to have persisted from the end of World War II to the dissolution of the Soviet Union in 1991. The expression "Cold War" has come to connote the predominance of a bipolar international system divided between two global hegemons teetering on the brink of open war. Thus, the "cold" aspect refers to the fact that the United States and USSR were not engaged in direct, traditional warfare, like that in the Second World War, but were instead immersed in a frozen conflict, fought via proxy forces, that could not be characterized as peace. The Cold War is seen as intensifying after the USSR acquired the atomic bomb and achieved nuclear parity with the United States in 1949, with nuclear brinkmanship reaching peak intensity during the Cuban Missile Crisis of October 1962. In the decades that followed, the threats of nuclear war, geopolitical competition, and ideological polarization were among signature features associated with the period.

By comparison, relatively little research has focused on the emergence of the expression "new Cold War" as a contemporary analog. In one of the few such studies, Ciută and Klinke examine its use in light of the theoretical and normative concerns of critical geopolitics.[7] Through a case study of "new Cold War" terminology employed by German media and in think-tank debates on energy security, they link its rise in the German context to the gas crises involving Ukraine and Russia in 2006 and 2008. For the Anglophone public sphere, however, our preliminary examination of public uses of NCW since the 1940s reveals that the expression was already being employed at various times during the course of the Cold War itself, as conventionally periodized.

Two of the earliest uses of the phrase "new Cold War" were in 1955 by Secretary of State John Foster Dulles and in 1956 when the *New York Times* warned that Soviet propaganda was promoting a return of the Cold War. What could have made the idea of a new Cold War thinkable and salient less than a decade after the notion of a "Cold War" entered the public sphere? Though seemingly counterintuitive, this finding is consistent with our expectations concerning the role of period effects if we bear in mind that observers at the time could not have known how the Cold War would be periodized decades later. Under the circumstances, the unexpected reversal of the brief "thaw" in superpower relations after the death of Stalin in 1953 sufficed to inspire fears that the "Cold War" was being rekindled.

For similar reasons, the term emerges again following the [election] of Ronald Reagan in 1980, whose assertive foreign policy agenda effectively ended the 1970s era of détente.[8] Scattered mentions reappear during the early 1990s, after the collapse of the USSR resulted in an uncertain international system—initially in order to dismiss the prospect of a "new Cold War,"[9] and soon afterward to warn of its looming danger.[10]

["New Cold War" in Publications and Internet Searches]

To obtain a more precise impression of long-term trends and period effects, we turn now to quantitative longitudinal data on the frequency of occurrence of the phrase "new Cold War" in news media and Internet searches. [. . .] From the 1950s to the 1980s, use of NCW in New York Times articles is infrequent (averaging 7.4 articles per interval) and shows relatively little over-time variation. From 1990 through 2005, however, the frequency of use is nearly three times as high as the previous baseline (averaging about 21 articles per interval) and increases markedly in the 2006–10 period, when the frequency is six times as high as before 1990. The sharpest increase in frequency by far, however, occurs in the most recent period (2011–15), when nearly 150 articles featured the phrase. [. . .] [A] dual-peak pattern is also present in the combined results for the two German newspapers, as well as those for the Russian news sources, albeit with noteworthy differences with respect to the relative magnitudes of the two peaks and the timing of the first. In the German case, the first spike occurs some two years later (in 2010) than in the *NYT* and the *WSJ*. With the Russian news outlets, the timing and relative magnitude of the peaks differ noticeably between *Kommersant* and *Nezavisimaia Gazeta* (k+ng) and *Izvestia*. In the former case, the initial peak in 2008, though in sync with those for the *NYT* and the *WSJ*, is somewhat modest compared to that in 2014. With *Izvestia*, the pattern is reversed, with the first peak substantially higher relative to the second. Moreover, the first spike in the number of *Izvestia* articles begins a year earlier, in 2007, than for most other sources and continues, decreasing only slightly, through 2008.

In spite of some variation between and within the three national contexts, the results [. . .] suggest that two main surges in frequency consistently appear internationally—the first around 2007–8 or (at a lag) in 2010, the second in 2014. In all sources, moreover, the results indicate a lull in use from 2011 to 2013, as well as a moderate to steep decline from 2014 to 2015. These patterns are consistent with period effects triggered by high-profile international events suggestive of heightened tensions between Russia and the West around the time of each burst, such as the lead-up to and emergence of the Russo-Georgian War of 2008 and the ongoing Ukraine crisis that began in late 2013 and escalated in early 2014. [. . .]

In sum, the results [. . .] tend to support our expectations concerning the kinds of events and developments likely to produce period effects that render the ncw salient among authors and publics alike. What the rising prevalence of ncw in media discourse does not yet tell us, however, is how authors and Internet users are reacting to the analogy. While some authors may be affirming its relevance to the period events in question, others may be employing the corresponding expression for the purpose of critique. Meanwhile, Web surfers may be doing so simply out of curiosity.

For the latter spike, at least, results from a 2014 Gallup poll conducted a few weeks after the Crimean referendum confirm that popular approval of the ncw analogy was indeed relatively pronounced at that time.[11] Asked whether they "think the United States and Russia are heading back toward a Cold war, or not," 50 percent of U.S. respondents answered "yes" (with 43 percent answering "no"). By comparison, just 25 percent of respondents in a February 1991 Gallup poll (following a failed coup by the Russian military) said they thought that the U.S. and the Soviet Union were returning to a "Cold War," while 64 percent rejected the statement.[12] Such responses provide evidence of the first "cut" in a potentially double-edged analogy—one that runs between acceptance and rejection of the analogy for a given purpose.

To determine whether the NCW analogy is doubled-edged in effect, we must still determine whether those who agree that a "new Cold War" is in progress draw opposing conclusions about its causes and implications. To more clearly discern both "edges" of the NCW analogy, the next section takes a closer look at how individual authors and commentators have used the phrase "new Cold War." What we will show is that increased frequency of use around 2008 and in 2014 coincided with the emergence of public debates over the analogy's relevance to understanding the growing tensions between Russia and the West during the last ten years and, furthermore, that it places rival clusters of NCW *proponents* on opposite sides of an equally important divide. [...]

"New Cold War" as a Double-Edged Analogy

We preface our analysis of the NCW debate by noting one area of broad consensus among the large majority of contributors—critics and proponents alike. Regardless of where they fall on either dimension, commentators generally agree on certain connotations of the "Cold War" analogy—namely, that the expression recalls a dangerous, adversarial period, the nadir of the relationship between the United States and Russia. Nor is there any illusion of a literal return to the past. Rather, the "new Cold War" is understood as signifying a worsening of relations between Russia and the United States (often in partnership with NATO and the EU) that is reminiscent of previous relations between the Soviet Union and the West. To this extent, comparisons to the "old" Cold War provide contributors and their publics with a common point of reference, allowing all of them to comprehend the expression "new Cold War" as a way of dramatizing the potential gravity of the contemporary situation.

In the rest of this section, we analyze the terms of debate along two principal axes. The first axis along which commentators part ways is over whether or not current conditions can indeed be fruitfully described in terms of a "new Cold War" at all, while the second axis distinguishes among advocates of the NCW thesis themselves. Before contrasting the two camps of proponents with each other directly, we first review some of the recurring points of disagreement between NCW proponents and their critics.

First Cut: Is There a "New Cold War"?

For proponents as a whole, perhaps the most compelling justification for the NCW thesis is the West's efforts to expand NATO and the EU up to Russia's doorstep, coupled with Russia's desire to expand its influence in the Near Abroad. The resulting standoff is recognized by all proponents to be at the heart of the current tensions. As one of them puts it: "Ukraine's civil war can best be regarded as a naked power struggle between Moscow and Washington in much the same way the Cold War's civil wars in Eastern Europe, Korea, Congo, Cuba, Vietnam, Cambodia and Central America were surrogate battlefields."[13] Proponents as a whole perceive a dynamic of reciprocal escalation in recent years, with the EU and NATO progressively enlarging membership in Eastern Europe, while Russia extends its military presence into former Soviet Republics that are not yet EU or NATO members.

One of the chief arguments among critics, in turn, is that, with the collapse of the Soviet Union, Russia was swiftly deprived of its undisputed status as an economic and military superpower. In Bremmer's view, Russia's loss of strength eliminates one of four necessary conditions of a new Cold War.[14] Similarly, Ashford regards Russia's depleted military and economy as indicating that "Russia is no longer a great power, nor a genuine military threat to the United States."[15] Writing in the wake of the Georgia conflict, Sadri and Burns likewise dismiss the NCW analogy on the grounds that "the current politics of the Caucasus region, particularly Georgia, is much more complex and sophisticated than the binary politics of the Cold War era when there were only two major political players."[16]

Proponents, on the other hand, often counter that Russia continues to pose a sufficient threat to warrant comparisons to the Cold War era. Kroenig, for instance, defends the NCW thesis by maintaining that Russia can still achieve its foreign policy goals through "a combination of hybrid warfare and nuclear brinkmanship" in spite of its reduced military and political strength.[17]

A related problem with the NCW thesis, according to critics, lies in the seemingly obvious fact that the two rival "blocs" no longer coalesce around opposing ideologies.[18] As Hryckowian writes: "The Cold War was foremost a war of ideologies. It was a struggle between the doctrines of capitalism and communism, mostly decided through the expansion of each side's influence."[19] Hence, the failure of communism brought a permanent end to the Cold War. As Stephens puts it: "For several decades, the world lived in the shadow of nuclear self-destruction. In 1989 communism lost. There is no going back."[20] In contrast to communism, which promised a brighter future to populations both within and outside of Russia's borders, the nationalism driving Putin's policy strategy cannot be easily exported to non-Russian-speaking regions.[21] Some proponents, in contrast, have countered that the Russian leader does have a coherent, exportable ideology which, though not as powerful as Marxism-Leninism, continues to dominate Russian politics. Lucas, for example, sees "Putinism" as reflected in the "Kremlin's propaganda . . . , in which

Russia is champion of cherished, age-old values, beset by a sinister and decadent West."[22]

A final point of disagreement between critics and proponents concerns the utility of the NCW thesis as a means of ameliorating the state of affairs it is meant to describe. Critics, on the one hand, often argue that tensions are unlikely to escalate on their own. As Dadak opines: "The recent resurgence of Russian expansionism, intimidation of former Soviet republics, and the challenging of U.S. global dominance are most likely to backfire, and the likelihood of a new cold war is remote."[23] The greater risk, from the critics' point of view, is that wide dissemination of the thesis could become a self-fulfilling prophecy. Similar concerns can be observed as early as 2008. As noted in a previous section, NCW came to be widely employed following Russia's military intervention in the South Ossetia and Abkhazia regions of the former Soviet republic of Georgia. In addition to scholars and journalists, some public officials could be found employing NCW rhetoric. Responding to Western opposition to the annexation, then-president Dmitry Medvedev stated: "We are not afraid of anything, including the prospect of a new Cold War."[24] Around the same time, critics began cautioning against such rhetoric, seeing it as imprudent at best. Linn, for example, urges that "the tone of this dialogue must not revert to cold-war rhetoric, and instead should find a constructive way to engage Russia's leaders even as the tough actions are taken to gain Russia's attention and constructive reaction."[25] Following the annexation of Crimea in 2014, critics again worried that talk of a "new Cold War" could trap the West into an adversarial position with Russia, with potentially dire consequences. Thus, Pifer argues that the West "should not cite a Cold War straw man to frighten ourselves into a negotiation or unwise concessions," and warns that doing so could risk "something far worse—a hot one."[26] In a more pessimistic vein, Krickovic and Weber argue that a "new Cold War," though not yet upon us, could be virtually inevitable, "as talk in both capitals is dominated by the sort of Russia- and America-bashing, which prevents either side from developing an appreciation of the other's security concerns."[27]

Proponents of the NCW thesis, on the other hand, believe that a "new Cold War" is already under way. From their point of view, accepting this reality is necessary precisely in order to find an appropriate response. Thus, even when they acknowledge the NCW analogy's explosive potential, proponents are likely to insist that it is important to face the facts.[28] [...]

Second Cut: Who Started the "New Cold War"?

If disagreement over the NCW thesis itself provides the first axis of division— that between its proponents and critics—the allocation of blame for the new state of affairs drives a second wedge between the two camps of proponents. For anti-Putin proponents, there is little doubt that the root causes lie in Moscow's illiberal foreign policies: "Like the Cold War of old," writes Kirchick, "this new conflict was initiated by Russia, which cannot tolerate independent and sovereign states along its borders."[29] Of recurring concern for this camp is therefore whether Russia will continue to seek to expand beyond its borders, as it has in Georgia, Ukraine, and Moldova, increasing the likelihood of armed conflict in NATO member states, most notably Estonia, Latvia, and Lithuania, former Soviet Republics with sizeable Russian-speaking populations. Such fears, they note, have already led to troop increases on both sides of the Russian border, which are seen as reminiscent of Cold War standoffs.

Anti-West proponents, in turn, make similar observations, but lay the blame squarely on the West in view of its "encroachment" on Russia's legitimate security interests in the region, warning that NATO's continued buildup of forces in Central Europe and the Baltic states could compel an even more drastic defensive response on the part of Russia. Thus, writing in January 2015, Carden attributes Russia's then–recently announced revision of its military doctrine to "the expansion of NATO's military infrastructure to the Russian borders," as well as the actions of the Obama administration and of the new pro-Western government in Kiev, which, Carden believes, "have conspired to shape the Russian government's threat perception."[30]

Opposing causal attributions translate into further sources of disagreement. Perhaps the most conspicuous bone of contention concerns the different courses of action recommended. As noted above, both camps are advancing the NCW thesis to highlight the urgency of changing course in order to prevent escalation toward a "hot" war. However, anti-Putin proponents primarily call for a more aggressive foreign policy stance toward Russia on the part of Western actors, while anti-West proponents criticize such actions as themselves responsible for provoking what they see as essentially defensive moves by Russia, such as alterations of its national security policies and its interventions in the Near Abroad.

Competing causal narratives can also affect seemingly unrelated issues, such as the question of precisely when the "new Cold War" actually began. For example, those who view the NCW as a product of Putin's desire to expand Russia's influence commonly locate its onset at the rise of nationalism and authoritarianism following Putin's election as president or as late as Russia's annexation of Crimea. For anti-West proponents, in contrast, the NCW can potentially be regarded as a continuation of the "original" Cold War. Thus, Cohen argues that the latter never really ended, citing the United States' dismissive treatment of Russia after 1991, followed by the eastward expansion of NATO and the EU.[31] [. . .]

Discussion and Conclusion

Our main goals in this [chapter] were twofold: first, to explore how the expression "new Cold War" arose and sporadically recurred in response to specific kinds of period events over the course of many decades and then to show how the use of NCW in recent public debates exemplifies what we call a double-edged analogy. In connection with the first goal, our over-time analysis of NCW usage provided substantial support for our hypothesis that the periodic resurgence of the NCW analogy coincides with period events involving renewed conflict between the Cold War superpowers or their perceived successors. More surprisingly, however, we also discovered that the perceived threshold between the "old" Cold War and the "new" has been historically variable, with NCW discourse first appearing, then repeatedly recurring, long before what is now considered the end of the Cold War. In analyzing its reemergence in the first decade of the new millennium, we identified a dual-peak pattern, coinciding with Russian interventions in the Near Abroad around 2008 and 2014 that proved transnationally robust while also reflecting localized variations in the timing and magnitude. For the Anglophone sphere, our qualitative analysis of NCW debates during this period suggests that these surges in use may also reflect the analogy's controversial character—producing a growing number of both proponents of a comparison between the "new" and "old" Cold War eras and critics who reject the comparison as inappropriate or even dangerous.

In examining recent NCW debates, we noted one area of broad consensus: virtually all observers stress the differences between the "old" Cold War and the "new," irrespective of whether they accept or reject the NCW thesis. [. . .] Paradoxically, however, the NCW thesis is at once polarizing and unifying among its proponents themselves. Thus, the claim that a "new Cold War" is under way can appeal equally to those who regard Russia as a dire and growing threat and to those who see Russia primarily in a defensive role and urge Western powers to favor diplomacy over sanctions. [. . .]

Our findings suggest a number of promising avenues for future research. First, as with every historical analogy, the period of reference is multivalent and potentially susceptible to novel applications. For instance, relations between Russia and the West are not the only circumstance to which the "new Cold War" has referred. Since the early 1990s, there have also been instances in which the same expression was used to characterize relations between the United States and China or even Iraq. Yet, it is equally revealing that reference contexts that exclude one or more of the original Cold War adversaries generally fail to generate discernable upsurges in use similar to those we observed around period events involving both Russia, on the one hand, and representatives of Western powers, like NATO, the EU, and the United States. Thus, while the collective memory of the Cold War is indeed malleable enough to facilitate analogies to a wide range of events and contexts, there appear to be limits to its pliability, once analogies to the Cold War stray well beyond its canonical associations. It would be of interest in the future to explore the conditions under which historical analogies can be dislodged, in whole or in part, from their associations with specific historical actors and applied to later circumstances which feature at least some new entrants.

Second, although our quantitative analysis included news outlets from Germany and Russia, as well as the United States, our qualitative analysis of the NCW debate was limited to Anglophone sources and publics. Yet, it seems likely to us that the transnational resonance of NCW discourse is, at root, the result of a divided global memory of the Cold War that has been reproduced within and across the respective public spheres. In future research, it would be valuable to further explore the diffusion of NCW discourse within and across national public spheres, as well as its potential for producing transnational alliances and cleavages.

A further avenue concerns the declining salience of the NCW analogy since 2014. Consistent with our emphasis on period effects, we believe it most likely reflects the subsequent emergence of events, such as the refugee crisis and terror attacks in the Mideast, Europe, and North America, among many others, that compete with the Ukraine conflict for public attention. We suspect nonetheless that the debates over the NCW thesis have not permanently vanished. In the next few years, intervention by Russia and by Western actors in Eastern Europe, the Middle East, or elsewhere may hold the potential to rekindle debates like those we have discussed.

Equally fascinating, meanwhile, is the degree to which all of the many previous "new Cold Wars" have been forgotten. As we saw, the NCW is a trope, or genre of memory with a long history, one that begins long before what we now think of as the end of the Cold War proper. Yet, it is a memory genre without genre memory. Previous declarations of a "new Cold War" seem to have little direct or conscious influence on the arguments of today's NCW purveyors or their critics. This suggests that the deployment of historical analogies tends to remain firmly wedged in the narrow window of the present. When new troubling events come along, observers tap their generational memories for salient parallels from the past, but not necessarily for prior uses of the same analogy. [. . .]

In the present case, peculiarities of the reference period may be placing further checks on the NCW's explosive potential. One signal feature of the Cold War was precisely the recognition on both sides of the existential stakes involved. It is, in part, for this reason that analogic comparisons to this period are nearly always accompanied by calls for restraint, even if the concessions envisioned fall disproportionately on one party or another, depending upon the observer's viewpoint. Agitators who instead wish to galvanize support for armed conflict by likening contemporary rivals to mortal enemies from the past may find that other reference periods are better suited to the purpose—in particular, those that recall a period of virtually unrestrained military mobilization.

Notes

This chapter originally appeared as Jeremy B. Straughn, Lisa C. Fein, and Amelia Ayers, "Divided Memory and the 'New Cold War' Thesis: The Rise and Decline of a Double-Edged Analogy," *Journal of Political & Military Sociology* 46, no. 1 (2019): 92–123, https://doi.org/10.5744/jpms.2019.1004. Reprinted by permission of the University of Florida Press.

1. Felix Ciută and Ian Klinke, "Lost in Conceptualization: Reading the 'New Cold War' with Critical Geopolitics," *Political Geography* 29, no. 6 (2010): 323–32. See also Richard Sakwa, "'New Cold War' or Twenty Years' Crisis? Russia and International Politics," *International Affairs* 84, no. 2 (2008): 241–67.

2. Dražen Pehar, "Historical Rhetoric and Diplomacy—An Uneasy Cohabitation," in *Language and Diplomacy*, ed. J. Kurbalija and H. Slavik (Msida, Malta: DiploProjects, Mediterranean Academy of Diplomatic Studies, University of Malta, 2001), 60–71.

3. Annika Brändström, Fredrik Bynander, and Paul <ap>t Hart, "Governing by Looking Back: Historical Analogies and Crisis Management," *Public Administration* 82, no. 1 (2004): 193.

4. Howard Schuman and Cheryl Rieger, "Historical Analogies, Generational Effects, and Attitudes towards War," *American Sociological Review* 57, no. 3 (1992): 315–26.

5. See, for example, Eric Hobsbawm and Terence Ranger, eds., *The Invention of Tradition* (Cambridge: Cambridge University Press, 1983).

6. Michael Schudson, "The Present in the Past versus the Past in the Present," *Communication* 2 (1989): 105–13.

7. Ciută and Klinke, "Lost in Conceptualization."

8. Among the contributors to this emerging literature are Tom Gervasi, *Arsenal of Democracy II: American Military Power in the 1980s and the Origins of the New Cold War* (New York: Grove Press, 1981); Noam Chomsky, *Toward a New Cold War* (New York: Pantheon, 1982); Stanley Hoffmann, *Dead Ends: American Foreign Policy in the New Cold War* (Cambridge: Ballinger, 1983); William G. Hyland, *Soviet-American Relations: A New Cold War?* (Santa Monica, Calif.: Rand, 1981). Far from abating, scholarship into the latter portions of the decade mimics this line of thinking. See, for example, Brian McNair, *Images of the Enemy: Reporting in the New Cold War* (New York: Routledge, 1988); and Marven E. Gettleman, Patrick Lacefield, Louis Menashe, David Mermelstein, and Ronald Radosh, eds., *El Salvador: Central America in the New Cold War* (New York: Grove, 1987).

9. Michael Serrill and William Mader, "The West: No Cold War II," *Time* 137, no. 5 (1991): 53. See also Strobe Talbott, "No, It's Not A New Cold War," *Time* 137, no. 9 (1991): 28.

10. Roderick P. Deighen, "Welcome to Cold War II," *Chief Executive* 82 (January/February 1993): 42. See also Daniel J. Christie and C. Patricia Hanley, "Some Psychological Effects of Nuclear War Education on Adolescents during Cold War II," *Political Psychology* 15, no. 2 (1994): 177–99.

11. Rebecca Riffkin, "Half of Americans Say U.S. Headed Back to Cold War" (Gallup, March 27, 2014), http://www.gallup.com/ poll/168116/half-americans-say-headed-back -cold-war.aspx.

12. Ibid.

13. John Batchelor, "U.S. and Russia Renew Cold War Rivalry," *Al Jazeera America*, August 7, 2014, http://america.aljazeera.com/opinions/2014/8/russia-ukraine -coldwarputin.html.

14. Ian Bremmer, "This Isn't a Cold War and That's Not Necessarily Good," *Time*, May 29, 2014, http://time.com/139128/this-isnt-acold-war-and-thats-not-necessarily -good.

15. Emma Ashford, "No, This Is Not Another Cold War," *Orange County Register*, January 7, 2015, http://www.ocregister.com/articles/ russia-647392-ukraine-war.html.

16. Houman A. Sadri and Nathan L. Burns, "The Georgia Crisis: A New Cold War on the Horizon," *Caucasian Review of International Affairs* 4, no. 2 (2010): 138. Weighing in on the critic side of the NCW debate, one anonymous reviewer of this manuscript added: "The role major Russian criminal organizations play in the current Russian society/government . . . points to a very different situation from when the Communist Party called all the shots." We wish to thank the reviewer for this insight.

17. Matthew Kroenig, "Facing Reality: Getting NATO Ready for a New Cold War," *Survival* 57, no. 1 (2015): 53.

18. Samuel Charap and Jeremy Shapiro, "How to Avoid a New Cold War," *Current History* 113, no. 765 (2014): 265–71, http://www.currenthistory.com/Article.php?ID=1172; see also Samuel Charap and Jeremy Shapiro, "Consequences of a New Cold War," *Survival* 57, no. 2 (2015): 37–46, https://www.iiss.org/en/publications/survival/sections /2015-1e95/survival—global-politics-and-strategy-april-may-2015-96a3/57-2-04 -charap-andshapiro-cm-8ce2.

19. Dmytro Hryckowian, "Not Your Father's Cold War: Old Strategies Aren't Adequate for Combatting Russia's Current Aggression," *U.S. News & World Report*, August 26, 2015, https://www.usnews.com/opinion/blogs/world-report/2015/08/25/russias -current-aggression-is-not-acold-war-redux.

20. Philip Stephens, "Gorbachev Is Wrong about a New Cold War," *Financial Times*, November 14, 2014, https://www.ft.com/content/8cee2638-68eb-11e4-af00 -00144feabdc0.

21. Ibid.

22. Edward Lucas, *The New Cold War: Putin's Russia and the Threat to the West* (New York: Palgrave Macmillan, 2008), xix.

23. Casimir Dadak, "A New 'Cold War'?," *Independent Review Summer* 15, no. 1 (2010): 89–107.

24. Ian Traynor, "Russia: We Are Ready for a New Cold War," *Guardian*, August 26, 2008, https://www.theguardian.com/world/2008/aug/26/russia.georgia2.

25. Johannes F. Linn, "War in Georgia—End of an Era, Beginning a New Cold War?" (Brookings Institution, August 12, 2008), https://www.brookings.edu/opinions /war-in-georgia-end-of-an-era-beginning-a-new-cold-war.

26. Steven Pifer, "Avoiding a New Cold War. Really?" (Brookings Institution, October 13, 2015), https://www.brookings.edu/blog/order-from-chaos/2015/10/13/avoiding-a -new-cold-war-really/.

27. Andrej Krickovic and Yuval Weber, "Why a New Cold War with Russia Is Inevitable" (Brookings Institution, September 30, 2015), https://www.brookings.edu/blog/order-from-chaos/2015/09/30/why-a-new-cold-war-withrussia-is-inevitable/.

28. Robert Legvold, "Managing the New Cold War: What Moscow and Washington Can Learn from the Last One," *Foreign Affairs*, July/August 2014, 74–84. See also Michael G. Roskin, "The New Cold War," *Parameters: U.S. Army War College Quarterly* 44, no. 1 (2014): 5–9.

29. James Kirchick, "So Don't Call It a Cold War," *Commentary*, May 2014, 37–40, https://www.commentarymagazine.com/articles/so-dont-call-it-a-cold-war/.

30. James Carden, "Welcome to Cold War 2.0: Russia's New and Improved Military Doctrine," *National Interest*, January 5, 2015, http://nationalinterest.org/feature/welcome-cold-war-20-russia's-new-improvedmilitary-doctrine-11961.

31. Stephen F. Cohen, "Patriotic Heresy vs. the New Cold War," *The Nation*, September 15, 2014, https://www.thenation.com/article/patriotic-heresy-vs-new-cold-war/.

Talking about Torture

LAW AND SECURITY IN THE WAR ON TERROR

Kali Wright-Smith, Westminster College

Conflict in the twenty-first century has generated complex questions for international law. While warfare has never been simple, today we face a range of hybrid conflicts within fourth-generation warfare that create complications for the laws of armed conflict and international humanitarian law. The conditions of fourth-generation warfare, including the blending of civilians and combatants, evolutions in weaponry, and the disappearance of the defined battlefield, make the interpretation and application of international law very complex. This uncertainty has produced new questions for international law.

Coupled with these evolving phenomena is the state tendency to deal with new circumstances by presenting an old argument: that in the pursuit of security we may have to accept some sacrifices to liberty. This argument essentially constitutes a historical regularity, as it has been used by governments to justify the suspension of habeas corpus, policies such as internment, and excessive utilization of martial law during prolonged states of emergency.

While interpretations of international law may need to evolve to deal with shifting methods of warfare, what happens if we begin to reinterpret our highest-order norms? Jus cogens norms, translated as "compelling law" and also referred to as "peremptory norms," are rules or expectations that states are obligated to follow in all times and places. This is a special class of critical human rights norms that is limited to prohibitions of war crimes, crimes against humanity, torture, and genocide. Consequently, we should assume that such norms will persist regardless of evolutions in warfare. Despite customary, natural law, and positivist legal protections, the norm of torture prohibition became a locus of debate in the war on terror.

The moral and legal strength of the norm prohibiting torture is manifested in treaty and customary law, the latter of which is shown through various actors' proclaimed acceptance that torture is unacceptable. In spite of this, the events of the post-9/11 era made it abundantly clear that torture persists and is even perpetrated by democratic states. Such practice is rarely acknowledged, let alone justified. Justification of the use of torture—a jus cogens norm—should be a clear taboo for any state. Evolutions in the norms governing warfare feel inevitable, but can jus cogens norms found in human rights and humanitarian law ever lose their supposedly unimpeachable status? To answer that question, it is not sufficient to look at state practice; how states speak about the norm must also be examined. If states feel they can justify violation of an important tenet of international law, the strength of this norm is fundamentally undermined.

There are many cases of noncompliance with the prohibition of torture, but the case of Guantánamo Bay is especially significant due to the United States' role in the international system. Given its position of power, its behavior is frequently under a microscope and may be used as an example by other states. Through an investigation of U.S. discourse about torture since the beginning of the War on Terror through the George W. Bush, Obama, and Trump administrations, this chapter demonstrates that although powerful states like the United States have damaged the norm through noncompliance, they have not directly denied the jus cogens character of the norm. According to Hafner-Burton, limitations in international law create demands for actors who are willing to act as defenders of or advocates for human rights, including "steward states," who "can give perpetrators of abuse a reason to act differently even when legal procedures don't have much influence on their reasoning."[1] If persistent challenges to the norm occur in the absence of norm stewards and a vocal public, the norm will likely grow weaker due to state attempts to redefine the scope and boundaries of the norm in the name of security.

Developing the Norm of Torture Prohibition

Legal requirements demanding the humane treatment of prisoners have been present in international humanitarian law since the 1899 Hague Convention.[2] The issue of prisoner treatment during times of war forms the basis of the Geneva Conventions. The Third Geneva Convention (1950) forbids the ill treatment and torture prisoners of war,[3] and common article 3 of the Geneva Conventions defines the minimum standards of treatment for individuals held by a belligerent state.[4] Article 75 of the First Additional Protocol reiterates that all captured insurgents, regardless of their status, are to be treated humanely in accordance with the minimum rights found in common article three.[5] This is true even if individuals have committed "grave breaches" of the conventions or the protocols.[6]

In addition to humanitarian law, torture is also outlawed in a large body of human rights law. The issues of torture and inhumane treatment of prisoners are present in the 1948 Universal Declaration of Human Rights, and the United Nations codified a prohibition of torture in 1966 in the International Covenant on Civil and Political Rights. Amnesty International began to investigate possible instances of torture in 1968 and created the Campaign for the Abolition of Torture in 1972.[7] International attention led to the creation of a series of UN resolutions and declarations, culminating in the legally binding Convention against Torture and Other Cruel, Inhuman or Degrading Treatment or Punishment (CAT), which entered into force in 1987. This defined torture as "the intentional infliction of severe physical or mental pain or suffering for purposes such as obtaining information or a confession, or punishing, intimidating or coercing someone."[8] One hundred forty-five countries are parties to the CAT, which "explicitly forbids parties from justifying acts of torture because of 'political instability or public emergency.'"[9] In the same era, regional human rights organizations also outlawed torture. The Organization of American States, the Council of Europe, and the African Union all have conventions to prevent and punish torture.

The norm on torture prohibition is one of the strongest human rights norms due to these extensive legal guidelines. Nevertheless, in spite of UN attempts to strengthen the reporting and monitoring mechanisms of the CAT, torture remains a serious problem, as evidenced in annual reports of the UN Special Rapporteur on Torture and NGOs like Amnesty International. Reports of torture committed by the United States throughout the War on Terror, in particular during the Bush administration, provide a backdrop for investigating the durability of this norm and understanding how states respond to it.

The United States has extensive humanitarian and human rights legal obligations in the area of prisoner treatment, having ratified the Geneva Conventions, the CAT, and the International Covenant on Civil and Political Rights. Additionally, expectations regarding prisoner treatment echo in U.S. domestic law as well. Human Rights Watch points out, "The United States has reported to the Committee against Torture that: 'Every act of torture within the meaning of the Convention is illegal under existing federal and state law, and any individual who commits such an act is subject to penal sanctions as specified in criminal statutes.'"[10] This can be seen specifically in the War Crimes Act of 1996, a 1994 federal antitorture law (18 U.S.C. § 2340A), and the Uniform Code of Military Justice (UCM). The U.S. Field Manual (1956), the U.S. Air Force Pamphlet (1976), the U.S. Instructor's Guide (1985), the U.S. Operational Law Handbook (1993), the U.S. Naval Handbook (2007), and the U.S. Manual on Detainee Treatment (2008) all include regulations on detainee treatment, and the UCM provides for prosecution through court-martial of any military personnel who violate standards of prisoner treatment. Many of these manuals explicitly incorporate language from the Geneva Conventions. The first manual mentioned, the 1956 Field Manual, directly includes articles from the Third and Fourth Geneva Conventions.[11] The existence of these rules in U.S. domestic law for decades signifies U.S. customary acceptance of these international legal norms in *opinio juris* and general practice. Consequently, the deviation from these entrenched norms during the War on Terror offers an interesting opportunity to examine the factors that shape how a state interacts with those norms in a new security environment.

Evaluating the Norm in U.S. Discourse

Constructivist ideas provide a logical starting point for attempting to understand the strength or effectiveness of any norm. Constructivism maintains that state behavior is affected not only by material considerations but also by social relations, which "shape state perceptions of the world and their role in that world."[12] According to constructivism, norms can influence the actions of states when they form a critical part of a state's identity and shape its interests.[13] Constructivist reasoning views state acceptance and adherence to norms as a function of the motivations of "legitimation, conformity, and esteem."[14] Despite ratification of the CAT, following the initiation of the War on Terror, the United States did not base its actions on shared normative values. Reports from the media, NGOs, and the UN, along with the United States' own investigations, reveal evidence of practices deemed torture under international law. Although state behavior is important, violation does not indicate that a norm is without meaning since "the very fact that one can talk about a violation indicates the existence of a norm."[15] While many aspects of U.S. behavior during the Bush administration were out of step with constructivist prescriptions regarding norms on torture, its behavior does indicate persistent recognition of the norm.

White House and State Department press releases reveal that the United States under the Bush administration was concerned with appearing legitimate to its public and the international community, as it consistently made reference to its legal responsibilities regarding detainee treatment. In response to all questions regarding Guantánamo Bay, the United States persistently claimed that all detainees are treated "humanely and consistent with our values, laws, and treaty obligations."[16] U.S. official statements reveal a pattern of articulated emphasis on respecting the norms associated with democratic rule. The White House asserted that President Bush understood the importance of upholding the Geneva Conventions in military practices "because, as Americans, the way we treat people is a reflection of America's values."[17] It also tried to emphasize the country's democratic identity and its respect for international law, as it claimed "our moral authority comes from America's long defense of international obligations and international laws."[18] In the opening statements of its report to the UN Committee Against Torture, the White House declared, "We recognize that much of the world holds the United States to a strict standard when it comes to the rule of law and human rights. This is especially important when it comes to moral imperatives, such as eliminating torture."[19] White House press briefings frequently contained the idea that torture is not condoned because "America is a nation of certain laws and certain values and torture is not consistent with our values and laws."[20] Thus, while U.S. behavior did not reflect prioritization of international legal norms, there was a concern for legitimacy present in its discourse. Despite its position of power in the international system, the Bush administration recognized the necessity of tailoring its statements and speeches to social expectations. Constructivism's emphasis on legitimacy and social relations explains why the norm had influence over U.S. discourse. However, as there is no indication that the United States failed to recognize its obligations, its lack of compliance is still troubling when assessing the norm.

U.S. Discourse and Argumentative Rationality

In order to understand state motivations, Thomas Risse advances a theory of communicative action that emphasizes how states engage in a process of arguing to try to advance their position. The central idea of this theory is that "arguing implies that actors try to challenge the validity claims inherent in any causal or normative statement and to seek a communicative consensus about their understanding of a situation as well as justifications for the principles and norms guiding their action."[21] Thus, actors will engage in forms of "discursive interaction" such as arguing, reasoning, or deliberating for the purposes of bargaining, persuasion, or justification of actions while attempting to reach an "argumentative consensus."[22] Risse acknowledges that in discourse between norm-violating states and transnational actors, pure argumentative rationality will be unlikely because neither side will be open to persuasion and actors will not "empathize" with each other.[23] However, he argues that "we can nevertheless observe a gradual process whereby the communications move, by means of rhetorical behavior, from purely instrumental rationality toward a dialogue."[24] There are three steps to this process: first, states deny the validity of the norm they are accused of violating; second, states deny specific charges of norm violation and make tactical concessions to regain legitimacy in the face of pressure; finally, by making rhetorical commitments, states ultimately bind themselves to the norms further and open themselves up to criticism for violation.[25]

While not a perfect fit, this framework can help us identify and analyze trends in U.S. discourse under the Bush administration. The first step of this process in the U.S. case deviates slightly from theory, as the United States never openly denied the validity of the torture norm. While asserting that the United States was involved in "a natural process in a democracy of coming upon a situation in which we faced a completely new set of circumstances on September 11th to now the institutionalization of means by which to secure ourselves" due to the fact that "this is a different kind of war," it nonetheless maintained that "the President does not condone torture in any circumstances."[26]

Despite its careful crafting of statements pertaining to the taboo of "torture," the United States did frequently justify other actions that violate norms of proper prisoner treatment, such as incommunicado detention, suspending habeas corpus, and other deprivations of liberty as necessary behaviors for gathering information and protecting national security. The Bush administration regularly justified its tendency to operate in the gray areas of international law by placing emphasis on intelligence gathering. According to the U.S. Department of Defense, the interrogation of individuals held at Guantánamo aided in the production of more than four thousand intelligence reports from high-level operatives who provided information regarding al-Qaeda operations, weapons procurement, leadership, membership, and training.[27] In a similar vein, in 2006 Condoleezza Rice came close to justifying the use of questionable interrogation tactics when she argued, "In a war in which intelligence is the long pole in the tent, where you have to have information about an attack that might be coming, the importance of information that detainees can give you is very critical. . . . And so it's different than ordinary law enforcement."[28]

While the Bush administration repeatedly accentuated the importance of intelligence provided by prisoner interrogation, it never admitted to or advocated torture. The DoD proclaimed, "We're enormously proud of what we had done at Guantánamo, to be able to set that kind of environment where we were focused on gaining the maximum amount of intelligence. But we detained the people in a humane manner, in accordance with the Third and Fourth Geneva Conventions."[29] This illustrates that while the United States did not feel capable of challenging the validity of the norm on torture, it challenged what it perceived as slightly weaker norms of prisoner treatment. Although the United States felt justified to derogate other norms because of security, it understood that it could not explicitly make the case that "torture" is acceptable, even in heightened circumstances.

The second step of the theoretical process fully characterized U.S. discourse with the UN. Rather than attempting to deny the validity of the norm, the United States denied specific charges of illegal actions. It did so by maintaining that all actions were in line with treaty obligations and that the UN made claims without visiting Guantánamo.[30] Fundamentally, the primary method of U.S. discourse was not justification but denial by redefining the interpretation of norms and reframing behavior. Declassified memos show that government attorneys facilitated the denial of abuses by reshaping definitions of torture and emphasizing the ambiguity in international humanitarian and human rights standards.[31] The U.S. definition of torture was narrower than that of the UN, and the United States maintained that its domestic law has primacy over international law when treaties are not self-enforcing.[32] Multiple techniques employed by the United States, including its "stress and duress" tactics and waterboarding, were not expressly prohibited under U.S. law or army field manuals at the time.[33] While most NGOs and IOs view these tactics as torture or at least as ill treatment, the lack of a comprehensive list of all illegal tactics under international law facilitated U.S. denial of charges of torture at this time.

As Risse predicts, statements in this stage of discourse became legalistic. When the United States appeared before the CAT, it highlighted the distinction between ill treatment and torture in order to argue that "the obligations regarding cruel, inhuman or degrading treatment or punishment are far more limited."[34] Furthermore, the Bush administration used the Department of Justice's Office of Legal Counsel to challenge these legal categories by claiming that "it is difficult to look at broad categories of practices—totally divorced from the specific facts of any given case—and label them in the abstract as being in all cases either torture or cruel, inhuman or degrading treatment or punishment."[35]

Conflicting definitions of "torture" and "inhumane treatment" do not diminish customary legal understandings of what constitutes torture, but the Bush administration tried to call attention to ambiguity in the language of treaty law while dismissing the applicability of customary law standards.[36] The United States persistently maintained that enemy combatants held at Guantánamo Bay were not entitled to the rights of prisoners of war delineated in the Geneva Conventions because they were not regular combatants. The United States asserted that only humanitarian law—not human rights law—applied to the Guantánamo detainees because they were captured during a time of war.[37] However, this interpretation ignores jus cogens status and relies on a very narrow definition of torture. Therefore, while not questioning the moral force of the norm, the Bush administration seized upon specific perceived ambiguities in treaty law to redefine its obligations.

In May 2006, the Bush administration sent a delegation to the UN to answer questions from the Committee against Torture, the monitoring body of the CAT, indicating that it was willing to clarify its interrogation techniques.[38] The delegation faced persistent questioning about Guantánamo, and discourse "shifted toward the issue of whether norm violations constitute isolated incidents or are systemic."[39] The United States stated repeatedly that past abuses were not sanctioned by the government and were "the actions of a few deviant individuals."[40] In addition, the U.S. delegation maintained that "it disagrees strongly with the assertion that any abuses are widespread or systemic."[41]

Although the evidence indicates that this discourse resembles the "process of argumentative self-entrapment" that Risse describes, it did not operate in a linear fashion. Though the Bush administration occasionally appeared open to change by making "tactical concessions"[42]—opening up to visits from the UN, reporting to UN committees, and making legislative changes like the Detainee Treatment Act—it persisted in making statements that stopped just short of justification of noncompliance. Thus, the United States did not move into the phase in which it completely changed its preferences and behavior in response to international appeals. Nevertheless, this process did create openings for dialogue and open the United States to greater social pressure from international actors. Thus, it is clear that Risse's theory has strong explanatory power for understanding how the United States framed its statements and behavior regarding prisoner treatment during this discursive process.

Torture Prohibition and the Obama Administration

Although this work seeks to understand the clear divergence between words and actions about torture that took place during the Bush administration, to assess the continued durability of the norm prohibiting torture it is important to examine how the Obama and Trump administrations interacted with this norm as well. A brief scan of the patterns in the Obama administration's discourse provides some interesting insights into the identity that the United States was trying to project under Obama. It also reveals a subtle similarity to the previous administration in its emphasis on the continued obstacles faced by the United States in the War on Terror that hamper consistent adherence to human rights standards.

Early discourse from the Obama administration reveals that it prioritized the rebuilding of the United States' image. The first step in this process was to reverse the ambiguity that had characterized the U.S. position under the Bush administration. Rather than emphasizing the gray area of international standards of prisoner treatment and arguing that specific methods do not constitute torture, this White House tried to separate itself from the previous government by being unambiguous about rejecting methods that the UN defined as torture.[43] In the first months of his administration, Obama stated, "I believe that waterboarding was torture and, whatever legal rationales were used, it was a mistake."[44] In 2009, Obama spoke about the public release of four memos about interrogation issued by the Office of Legal Counsel between 2002 and 2005: "In one of my very first acts as President, I prohibited the use of these interrogation techniques by the United States because they undermine our moral authority and do not make us safer. Enlisting our values in the protection of our people makes us stronger and more secure. A democracy as resilient as ours must reject the false choice between our security and our ideals, and that is why these methods of interrogation are already a thing of the past."[45] Such discourse was reinforced by key policy decisions to revise the U.S. Army Field Manual, outlaw waterboarding, and end legal ambiguities about interrogation practices through Executive Order 13491.[46]

Another key distinction between the administrations lies in their discourse on security. Although the Bush administration vigorously asserted that detaining individuals at Guantánamo Bay resulted in critical information acquisition that kept the country secure, the Obama administration posited that using extreme means to extract information from detainees does more harm than good. On multiple occasions, Obama stated that allegations of torture and the singular existence of Guantánamo Bay facilitated recruitment for terrorist organizations. In a 2009 speech he declared that torture "diminishes the security of those who carry it out, and surrenders the moral authority that must form the basis for just leadership."[47] He took the position not only that the existence of Guantánamo Bay endangers U.S. forces but also that he "[doesn't] believe that there is a contradiction between our security and our values."[48]

While the Obama administration expressed its commitment to living up to professed American values in order to regain global respect for the United States, critics pointed to the persistence of many Bush-era policies and the inability to close Guantánamo as evidence that Obama was not providing sufficient support for norms of proper detention. A buzzword for Obama policy toward Guantánamo and detainee treatment was "pragmatic." Obama contended, "The recent debate has obscured the truth and sends people into opposite and absolutist ends. On the one side of the spectrum, there are those who make little allowance for the unique challenges posed by terrorism, and would almost never put national security over transparency. And on the other end of the spectrum, there are those who embrace a view that can be summarized in two words: 'Anything goes.'"[49]

In the first months of Obama's presidency, the White House began emphasizing the complexity involved in closing Guantánamo Bay. Human rights activists were critical of Obama for failing to overcome political obstacles and public concerns about the security consequences of closing the facility. In a 2011 statement, the president contended, "Obviously I haven't been able to make the case right now, and without Congress's cooperation, we can't do it," referencing the White House's assertion that it was unable to work within the divisive partisan climate.[50] Many members of Congress from both parties did not want to take a stand on a risky electoral issue, and individual members spoke out against White House plans to resettle detainees. As this political bat-

tle waged, U.S. public support for the president's plans for Guantánamo de-
clined.[51] Consequently, the practical concerns about how to implement the
closure of the facility, the political obstacles posed by the opposition, and the
electoral risks involved in pursuing an unpopular plan all contributed to keeping detainee policy in a state of limbo and keeping Guantánamo Bay open.
Based on Obama's far reduced public discourse on the issue in his second term,
the issue apparently slipped down the White House's agenda.

Despite discursive differences on detention practices, there are notewor-
thy similarities between the Bush and Obama administrations in how they utilized the law to support their security policies. While Obama was quick to take
an oppositional stance on Guantánamo Bay, analysis of his overall counterterrorism policy suggests that "while [Obama] applies his lawyering skills to
counterterrorism, it is usually to enable, not constrain, his ferocious campaign
against Al Qaeda."[52] Both administrations attempted to project respect for legal norms in their discourse, but in both cases international law was interpreted and applied in ways that gave the United States maximum flexibility to
pursue national security goals. Toward the end of Obama's presidency, Human
Rights Watch criticized the administration for failing to fill the legal obligation
to punish past acts of torture by U.S. officials, noting, "Obama's refusal to investigate, let alone prosecute, Bush-era torture means that, practically speaking,
torture remains an option for policymakers rather than a criminal offense."[53]
Although human rights advocates were disappointed that some of Obama's key
policy promises related to detention were unfulfilled, they witnessed a more
concerning turn in the U.S. relationship with the norm on torture prohibition
with the election of Donald Trump.

Torture Prohibition under the Trump Administration?

Previous cases were marked by important differences in policy and discourse
surrounding torture and detention. Nevertheless, they shared a common
theme—a broad discursive adherence to the taboo against open support of
torture. The Bush administration embraced the tactic of legal maneuvering of
its detention policies in order to push against the norm without advocating torture, and subsequently Obama, while failing in his stated policy goals to end all
of the Bush-era practices, did return the United States to a pre-9/11 context of
direct verbal opposition to torture.

So did these trends continue under the Trump administration? Did the
Trump administration's relationship with the norm prohibiting torture represent a shift from our previously identified patterns? The Trump administration's statements on torture signified meaningful and significant breaks from
precedent. As discussed, torture has certainly occurred previously, but a strong

international torture taboo, supported by a wide body of international human rights and humanitarian law, has prevented governments from admitting to or advocating the use of torture. Under the Trump administration, there were three notable shifts to this pattern: the openness with which the administration accepted the possible use of torture and extolled its utility, the abandonment of legal maneuvering to avoid directly engaging with "torture," and the reasoning behind the administration's opposition to international law.

The most dramatic manifestation of difference seen under the Trump administration was greater openness about belief in the utility of torture. As this research has demonstrated, even at the height of the War on Terror, official discourse stopped just short of directly admitting to or advocating torture. In contrast, when Trump was a presidential candidate, he gained significant attention for proclaiming that he would reauthorize waterboarding "in a heartbeat." He went on to say, "And I would approve a lot more than that. Don't kid yourself, folks. It works, okay. It works. Only a stupid person would say it doesn't work."[54] Finally, he added, "And you know what? If it doesn't work, they deserve it anyway, for what they're doing."[55]

There are important differences in the discourse of candidates and officials, so is this merely the fiery rhetoric of a candidate? To a degree, yes. Trump later asserted that he "wants to do 'everything within the bounds of what you're allowed to do legally,' but he also stated he would work to bring back waterboarding if his advisers wanted to reinstate it because he was confident that it worked.[56] Additionally, this discourse was reinforced by action. One of Trump's first acts was to assert that Guantánamo would remain open indefinitely. While the Trump administration did not frequently comment on torture since the first year in office, its discourse plainly prioritized the perceived utility of the tactic and doing whatever was necessary to ensure security, while avoiding references to any international obligations.

Unsurprisingly, the human rights community immediately condemned these statements. More surprising was the criticism from previous officials who helped to legitimize the initial use of waterboarding. Two Bush-era lawyers who helped to craft the "enhanced interrogation" program and propagated legal arguments that tactics like waterboarding and stress positions did not constitute torture, John Yoo and John Rizzo, both criticized the Trump approach. In a 2017 interview, Rizzo noted, "The whole premise of the original program was that the techniques did not fit the legal definition of torture. It was illegal then, and it's illegal now. . . . So to hear the President of the United States use that word in an affirmative way—I found that remarkable."[57]

Yoo went on to tell *NBC News* that the president "is not being legally careful."[58] Rizzo also expressed concern that "the bad guys always claimed what we were doing was torture. Now they can claim to have the personal imprimatur of the President of the United States."[59]

When asked directly about whether the United States uses torture, Trump avoided answering on multiple occasions, which contrasts with previous administrations' contentions that the United States does not engage in torture. The lack of reliance on legal loopholes to create wide room to craft national security policy demonstrated a new direction in U.S. discourse. While the Trump administration echoed the messaging about needing to act to protect security, it did not try to redefine torture or push back against the legal boundaries of the norm. Instead, it simply emphasized the potential effectiveness of the tactic.

The United States' skepticism of monitoring by and reporting to multilateral international institutions precedes any of these leaders. During the Bush administration this resistance increased. The Obama administration prioritized counterterrorism as well but improved relations with international organizations. The Trump administration demonstrated clear opposition to working through the United Nations and frequently denounced organizations critical of U.S. human rights policy.[60] While resistance to outside influence was not new, the source of the resistance was. In earlier administrations, much of the concern about international legal standards was grounded in security preoccupations, but that did not seem to be the whole story here. Rather, it was likely an artifact of the populist strains in this presidency.

According to Philip Alston, one of the key effects of populism on democracy is "the undermining of the international rule of law."[61] Alston notes that under populism we see gradual erosion of respect for the international use of force standards and a "shocking breakdown in respect for the principles of international humanitarian law."[62] The propensity of populist leaders to openly justify breaches of international law, move countries away from multilateralism, and stand up for the country in the face of external criticism hardens public opposition to external standards and institutions. This creates significant challenges for human rights monitors and diminishes the potential for dialogue about human rights obligations, such as those regarding prisoner treatment.

Norm Violation and Threat Perception

While the theories examined in this study illuminate aspects of the United States' evolving relationship to the torture norm, they fail to explain why the United States would be willing to violate the prohibition of torture when it recognized its normative obligations and knew that justification of abuse would be unacceptable. According to Florini, norms must be compatible with the environment in order to be accepted.[63] The U.S. environment changed after 9/11, leading to a shift in receptivity to norms that centered on domestic concerns about security rather than international human rights standards. Thus, to understand deviant behavior, it is important to consider that an external shock led to a redefinition of self-interest that centered on national security at any means, as the Bush White House claimed that "the President recognizes that his most important responsibility to the American people is their safety and security."[64]

This environmental change is likely due to an alteration in threat perception. Steven C. Poe theorizes that countries decide to violate norms or engage in repression based on a strength/threat ratio. If states believe that levels of domestic threat are higher than the strength of the regime, they may choose to engage in repression.[65] Although the United States was not concerned with domestic threats, as in the cases that Poe presents, the threat posed by terrorism was such that the U.S. government acted on concerns about its strength and ability to defend itself by repressing the rights of captured combatants.[66] According to Poe, the belief systems of political leaders also affect threat perception, and President Bush repeatedly emphasized his belief that it was necessary to combat extraordinary threats to America's security through "enhanced" measures.[67] This position is seen in statements such as "we must also remember that the danger to our country has not passed. Since the attacks of 9-11, the terrorists have tried to strike our homeland again and again."[68]

Threat perception appears to have modified norm receptivity in the public as well, as citizens became more concerned with security and combating terror in the wake of 9/11. A study of public opinion by the Pew Center six months after the attacks found that support for the government was at its peak due to "a clear awareness of the government's new roles—to provide protection at home and wage war on enemies abroad."[69] High threat perception in response to terrorism produced an alteration in domestic interests, making human rights norms less critical to the environment than national security concerns. The specific logic behind this linkage is that "emotional reactions to threat may lead to greater support for personal security and the government's efforts to reduce the risk of future terrorist attacks."[70] Through the use of survey investigations of threat perception and public support for antiterrorism policies following 9/11, Leonie Huddy and colleagues empirically demonstrate the importance of threat perception, finding that "as perceived threat increased, there was heightened support for a wide range of domestic and international government actions to combat the threat of terrorism, including overseas military action, a curtailment of civil liberties, and increased surveillance and tighter immigration restrictions for Arabs."[71]

In other words, strong perceived threats can "promote public support for aggressive national security policy."[72] Huddy et al. did not find that the intensity of these attitudes changed as the immediate terrorist experience became more distant, but public opinion trends suggest that threat perception and the resulting attitudinal shifts are immediate responses that wane over time.[73]

There were few surveys of public attitudes about torture pre-9/11, and post-9/11 opinion has gone through swings. There are some clear areas of consistency in public opinion, but it is common for shifts to occur following specific events. For example, once the public became aware of the scandalous incidents of torture at Abu Ghraib, there was a decisive backlash in domestic opinion. Declassified documents even show evidence of similar apprehension in President Bush following the published photos.[74] After this event, a 2004 PIPA study indicated that 88 percent of the American public preferred international laws that ensure the proper treatment of prisoners.[75] Even more critically, 60 percent of the American public favored total rights for all detainees, even terrorist suspects. As the public got more distance from the terrorist attacks, the norm on torture prohibition regained strength. By 2006, the majority of Americans thought the United States should change its treatment of detainees at Guantánamo and follow the recommendations of the UN.[76] In 2009, over 70 percent of Americans agreed that there should continue to be a strong international norm against torture.[77] It is notable that during this time of opinion shift the Bush administration began making the tactical concessions that were previously identified.

Many news reports have suggested that the public may be moving back toward greater acceptance of "enhanced interrogation" due to perceptions of insecurity.[78] This conclusion is reached by looking at the trend of fewer people agreeing that torture can "never" be justified and more people agreeing it can "sometimes" or "often" be justified.[79] While the public's support for "torture" seems to be overstated, the fact that there is a larger window for justification today deserves attention. The small cyclical changes in opinion help to confirm McCoy's hypothesis that the American public frequently engages in a process of "forgetting" when they evaluate detention policies.[80] In other words, the public sees these events as disconnected episodes or deviations, rather than a persistent element of U.S. security policy, thereby leading to mood swings in public opinion about detainee treatment.

Although we can glean a sense of public reaction to detention policy and interrogation practices from these polls, public opinion must be contextualized, as questions often gauge opinion about narrowly specific circumstances. For example, the idea of torture as a tool in extraordinary situations, as in the "ticking bomb scenario," nearly always results in higher public acceptance, particularly when individuals are presented with a scenario in which there is near certainty that detainees could have critical information.[81] However, individuals tend to support only methods that have been characterized as "ill-treatment" rather than torture, and support dwindles when they are presented with alternative methods of gaining information.[82] Survey results also differ depending on question framing and whether respondents are asked about "torture," "harsh interrogation," "enhanced interrogation," or other "euphemisms."[83] Additionally, opinion changes when respondents are asked about specific tactics, indicating some norm ambivalence.[84] As questions move from torture to ill treatment, the public is often less disapproving. Thus, there is some evidence that the more ambiguous forms of improper prisoner treatment that the Bush administration challenged in its discourse were the same tactics that were more acceptable to the public in the post-9/11 era.

As Poe predicts, international pressure can diminish state repression by increasing its costs, even when a threat still exists.[85] An increase in UN criticism of U.S. actions has occasionally led to past behavioral changes, but new security concerns consistently create openings for deviations from this norm. Similarly, resistance to international legal obligations, as seen in the Trump administration, also has the potential to shape public opinion about those obligations. Thus, threat perception and changing domestic normative environments might partially explain U.S. decisions to violate a norm whose moral and legal status it rhetorically accepted. While public opinion does not impact jus cogens legal status, states have been more willing to push at the boundaries of the norm prohibiting torture during the War on Terror, and the public often reinforces that trend. Security rationales and heightened threat perception may not lead states to believe they can blatantly justify the use of "torture" due to the persistence of the norm, but they have led states like the United States to prod the norm for weak spots and harm the norm through abuse. When such weak spots and ambiguities are emphasized in public discourse, domestic scrutiny is lowered and this process of noncompliance is facilitated.

The Norm of Torture Prohibition Today

While the nature of jus cogens norms, particularly how a norm achieves this status, is often debated, there exists a general legal consensus that the prohibition of torture qualifies as jus cogens.[86] Even the United States has recognized its jus cogens status by prosecuting cases of torture brought under the Alien Tort Claims Act in federal courts and using jus cogens as the basis of prosecution.[87] Internationally there has also been willingness to use jus cogens as a legal basis in court decisions even when there is not a domestic legal basis.

According to Rafael Nieto-Navia, the International Court of Justice has recognized that there is a "special category of international norms that should receive a particular degree of prominence."[88] This suggests that if one recognizes a hierarchy of international law, norms such as this have a higher level of obligation to comply attached to them.[89] Anthony Cullen makes a decisive case for the absolute prohibition of torture, citing the words of the International Criminal Tribunal for the Former Yugoslavia: "Stating, 'there exists today universal revulsion against torture' the ICTY asserted that this 'has led to a cluster of treaty and customary rules on torture acquiring a particularly high status in the international, normative system.'"[90]

Despite this obligation, the high rate of noncompliance around the world shows clear weaknesses inherent in the norm. According to Amnesty International's 2014 Annual Report on Torture, the majority of countries practiced at least one of twenty-seven reported forms of torture. An analysis of this report states, "The findings point to what Michael Bochenek, Amnesty's senior director for International Law and Policy, called a 'disconnect' between policy and practice and between public condemnation of torture and the pervading misconception that 'this is the way it has to be' for states to be kept secure."[91] So do these dynamics mean that the norm has lost its standing? Looking at the statements of the United States, it is important that neither Bush nor Obama ever challenged the legality of the prohibition of torture, advocated the use of torture specifically, or suggested that this norm no longer resonated with U.S. identity. It is apparent that contrary to the claims of human rights NGOs, the United States did not explicitly attempt to justify norm violation to an external audience, no matter how much it might have appeared to want to. This is the most important testament to the durability of this norm.

According to Gordon Christenson, jus cogens norms "are 'peremptory' when accepted as overriding by the international community as a whole," but they can lose their utility to the maintenance of a "global society" when states dismiss the norm in the name of self-interest.[92] Although the United States has respected the legal status of the norm, it did implicitly challenge the norm's standing by attempting to reshape the law and its application and avoid violation of the law by recasting methods as "enhanced interrogation" rather than torture. Such interpretation was aided by the creation of different categories of interrogation practices and the attempt to persuade the public that its tactics were legal, were necessary, and did not meet a high threshold of "torture." It was further facilitated by a more permissive domestic environment characterized by heightened threat perception and support for antiterror policies. Finally, the significance of the Trump administration's discourse should not be understated. While it would be preferable to consider this shift in speech an anomaly, critics of the Trump administration note that his sentiments challenging human rights and international law are echoed by other world leaders.[93] One could argue that Trump's speech is simply a reflection of the real actions of the United States rather than normal political speech, but a liberal-democratic superpower displaying such a dramatic shift in discourse does send a signal to the international community that what is appropriate may be changing. It sends a comparable signal to the public.

Consequently, the *legal* standing of the norm was not damaged, but meaningful interpretation and application have been hurt by the chipping away of the accepted international standard found in the CAT. According to UN Special Rapporteur reports, this redefinition of behavior is a common practice.[94] While the strength of this norm lies in the fact that most states do not feel they can justify violation, its weakness, in addition to the monitoring and enforcement limitations inherent in international law, lies in the propensity of states to reframe their practices in order to facilitate denial of norm violation.

We remain situated in an international society that feels increasingly vulnerable. Consequently, political elites frequently use strong antiterror language to appeal to the public's desire for security, and such discourse can normalize torture and project lower state commitment to human rights. We have seen that what we call torture matters. Similarly, as a great power in the international system, how the United States talks about torture matters. As long as there are threats to state security, there will be challenges to the norm prohibiting torture. Without strong actors to support the norm, including "steward states" willing to assertively defend its unimpeachable moral and legal status through their words and actions, its force is bound to keep slipping. In the words of Salil Shetty, Amnesty International's secretary-general, "Governments around the world are two-faced on torture—prohibiting it in law, but facilitating it in practice." Torture is not just alive and well—it is flourishing in many parts of the world. As more governments seek to justify torture in the name of national security, the steady progress made in this field over the last thirty years is being eroded.[95]

Citizens may at times appear willing to accept that human rights may be minimized in order to guarantee security. However, there is an expectation that such actions are limited to a particular "extraordinary" situation. When the extraordinary starts to become ordinary, as we are currently witnessing with widespread global violations of the norm of torture prohibition, we need to consider the impact of long-term sacrifices of human rights norms.

Notes

1. Emilie M. Hafner-Burton, *Making Human Rights a Reality* (Princeton, N.J.: Princeton University Press, 2013), 5.

2. Hague Convention No. IV Respecting the Laws and Customs of War on Land (Entered into force January 26, 1910).

3. Geneva Convention (No. III) Relative to the Treatment of Prisoners of War (Entered into force October 21, 1950); Protocol Additional (No. I) to the Geneva Convention of August 12, 1949 (Entered into force December 7, 1948).

4. Article 3, Geneva Convention No. I for the Amelioration of the Condition of the Wounded and Sick in Armed Forces in the Field (Entered into force October 21, 1950).

5. Johan Steyn, "Guantanamo Bay: The Legal Black Hole," *International and Comparative Law Quarterly* 53, no. 1 (2004): 5.

6. Article 75, paragraph 7 of Protocol Additional (No. I) to the Geneva Convention.

7. Ann Marie Clark, *Diplomacy of Conscience* (Princeton, N.J.: Princeton University Press, 2001).

8. Convention against Torture and Other Cruel, Inhuman or Degrading Treatment or Punishment (Entered into force June 26, 1987).

9. Suzanne M. Bernard, "An Eye for an Eye: The Current Status of International Law on the Humane Treatment of Prisoners," *Rutgers Law Journal* (1994): 767.

10. "Questions and Answers: U.S. Detainees Disappeared into Secret Prisons: Illegal under Domestic and International Law" (Human Rights Watch, December 9, 2005), https://www.hrw.org/legacy/backgrounder/usa/us1205/us1205.pdf.

11. "IHL Database. Customary International Law: Practice Relating to Rule 118. Provision of Basic Necessities to Persons Deprived of Their Liberty" (International Committee of the Red Cross, February 25, 2021), https://ihl-databases.icrc.org/customary -ihl/eng/docs/v2_rul_rule118.

12. Martha Finnemore, *National Interests and International Society* (Ithaca, N.Y.: Cornell University Press, 1996), 22; Audie Klotz, "Norms Reconstituting Interests: Global Racial Equality and U.S. Sanctions against South Africa," *International Organization* 49, no. 3 (1995): 451–78.

13. Peter J. Katzenstein, ed., *The Culture of National Security: Norms and Identity in World Politics* (New York: Columbia University Press, 1996).

14. Martha Finnemore and Kathryn Sikkink, "International Norm Dynamics and Political Change," *International Organization* 52, no. 4 (1998): 903.

15. Finnemore, *National Interests and International Society*, 23.

16. White House, "Press Briefing by Scott McClellan" (June 22, 2004), https:// georgewbush-whitehouse.archives.gov/news/releases/2004/06/20040622-3.html.

17. Ibid.

18. U.S. Department of State, "Interview with Jonathan Beale of British Broadcasting Corporation" (September 6, 2006), https://2001-2009.state.gov/secretary/rm/2006 /71870.htm.

19. U.S. Department of State, "The United States' Response to the Questions Asked by the Committee Against Torture" (May 5, 2006), https://2009-2017.state.gov/j/drl/rls /68561.htm.

20. White House, "Press Briefing by Scott McClellan."

21. Thomas Risse, "'Let's Argue!' Communicative Action in World Politics," *International Organization* 54, no. 1 (2004): 7.

22. Ibid., 10.

23. Ibid., 29.

24. Ibid., 29.

25. Ibid., 32.

26. U.S. Department of State, "Interview with Jonathan Beale"; U.S. Department of State, "Interview on Fox News Sunday with Chris Wallace" (May 21, 2006), https://2001-2009.state.gov/secretary/rm/2006/66536.htm; U.S. Department of State, "Remarks at Town Hall Event at the University of Sydney's Conservatorium of Music" (March 16, 2006), https://2001-2009.state.gov/secretary/rm/2006/63166.htm.

27. U.S. Department of Defense, "Briefing on Detainee Operations at Guantanamo Bay" (February 13, 2004), https://nointervention.com/archive/usa/Guantanomo/tr20040213-0443.html; U.S. Department of Defense, "JTF-GTMO Information on Detainees" (March 4, 2005), https://archive.defense.gov/news/Mar2005/d20050304info.pdf.

28. U.S. Department of Department, "Interview with Jonathan Beale."

29. Amnesty International, "United States of America-Guantanamo and Beyond: The Continuing Pursuit of Unchecked Executive Power" (2005), https://www.amnesty.org/en/documents/amr51/083/2005/en/.

30. U.S. State Department, "The United States' Oral Response to the Questions Asked to the Committee Against Torture" (May 8, 2006), https://2009-2017.state.gov/j/drl/rls/68562.htm; "Chris Wallace Interview with Secretary Condoleezza Rice, Fox News Sunday," http://www.state.gov/secretary/rm/2006/66536.htm; United Nations, "UN Rights Experts Call for Immediate Closure of U.S. Guantánamo Centre after Suicides" (June 14, 2006), https://news.un.org/en/story/2006/06/182402.

31. David P. Forsythe, *The Politics of Prisoner Abuse* (New York: Cambridge University Press, 2011).

32. Philippe Sands, *Lawless World* (New York: Viking, 2005), 145; Frederic L. Kirgis, "Distinctions Between International Law and U.S. Foreign Relations Law Issues Regarding Treatment of Suspected Terrorists," *ASIL Insights* 8, no. 14 (2004), https://www.asil.org/insights/volume/8/issue/14/distinctions-between-international-and-us-foreign-relations-law-issues.

33. Steyn, "Guantanamo Bay," 8.

34. U.S. State Department, "U.S. Oral Response to CAT."

35. Ibid.

36. This is evident from the U.S. position that the Department of Justice "has concluded that customary international law cannot bind the Executive Branch under the Constitution, because it is not federal law." Quoted in Kirgis, "Distinctions Between International Law and U.S. Foreign Relations," 138.

37. U.S. Department of State, "United States' Response to the Questions Asked "; Christopher Greenwood, "International Law and the 'war Against Terrorism,'" *International Affairs* 78, no. 2 (2002): 316; Article 4, para. 2 of Geneva Convention (No. III); Article 13, para. 2 of Geneva Convention (No. I).

38. U.S. State Department, "U.S. Oral Response to CAT."

39. Risse, "'Let's Argue!,'" 32.

40. U.S. State Department, "U.S. Oral Response to CAT"; U.S. State Department, "Interview on Fox News Sunday."

41. U.S. State Department, "U.S. Oral Response to CAT."

42. Risse, "'Let's Argue!,'" 32. See also Thomas Risse, Stephen C. Ropp, and Kathryn Sikkink, eds., *The Power of Human Rights* (Cambridge: Cambridge University Press, 1999).

43. White House, "Remarks by President Obama at Strasbourg Town Hall" (April 3, 2009), https://obamawhitehouse.archives.gov/the-press-office/remarks-president-obama-strasbourg-town-hall.

44. White House, "Presidential Press Conference" (April 29, 2009), https://obamawhitehouse.archives.gov/video/Presidential-Press-Conference-4/29/09#transcript.

45. White House, "Statement of President Barack Obama on Release of OLC Memos" (April 16, 2009), https://obamawhitehouse.archives.gov/the-press-office/statement-president-barack-obama-release-olc-memos.

46. White House, "Executive Order 13491: Ensuring Legal Interrogations" (January 22, 2009), https://obamawhitehouse.archives.gov/the-press-office/ensuring-lawful-interrogations.

47. White House, "Statement by President Barack Obama on United Nations International Day in Support of Torture Victims" (June 26, 2009), https://obamawhitehouse.archives.gov/the-press-office/statement-president-barack-obama-united-nations-international-day-support-torture-v.

48. White House, "Remarks by President Obama."

49. White House, "Remarks by the President on National Security" (April 21, 2009), https://obamawhitehouse.archives.gov/the-press-office/remarks-president-national-security-5-21-09.

50. Peter Finn and Anne E. Kornblut, "Guantanamo Bay: Why Obama Hasn't Fulfilled His Promise to Close the Facility," *Washington Post*, April 23, 2011, www.washingtonpost.com/world/guantanamo-bay-how-the-white-house-lost-the-fight-to-close-it/2011/04/14/AFtxR5XE_print.html.

51. Ibid.

52. Jo Becker and Scott Shane, "Secret 'Kill List' Proves a Test of Obama's Principles and Will," *New York Times*, May 29, 2012, https://www.nytimes.com/2012/05/29/world/obamas-leadership-in-war-on-al-qaeda.html.

53. Kenneth Roth, "Obama and Counterterror: The Ignored Record" (Human Rights Watch, February 5, 2015), https://www.hrw.org/news/2015/02/05/obama-counterterror-ignored-record#.

54. Jenna Johnson, "Donald Trump on Waterboarding: If It Doesn't Work, They Deserve It Anyway," *Washington Post*, November 23, 2015, https://www.washingtonpost.com/news/post-politics/wp/2015/11/23/donald-trump-on-waterboarding-if-it-doesnt-work-they-deserve-it-anyway/.

55. Ibid.

56. "Transcript: ABC News Anchor David Muir Interviews President Trump," *ABC News*, January 25, 2017, https://abcnews.go.com/Politics/transcript-abc-news-anchor-david-muir-interviews-president/story?id=45047602.

57. Andrea Mitchell, "Trump Under Scrutiny for Position on Torture," *MSNBC*, January 26, 2017, https://www.msnbc.com/andrea-mitchell-reports/watch/trump-under-scrutiny-for-position-on-torture-863408707903.

58. Ken Dilanian, "What Does It Mean When the President Endorses Torture?," *NBC News*, January 26, 2017, https://www.nbcnews.com/news/us-news/what-does-it-mean-when-president-praises-torture-n712736.

59. Mitchell, "Trump Under Scrutiny for Position on Torture."

60. U.S. Department of State, "Remarks on 'U.S. Withdrawal from Human Rights

Council: Impact and Next Steps'" (July 18, 2018), https://www.youtube.com/watch?v
=HLtlix1YEbs.

61. Philip Alston, "The Populist Challenge to Human Rights," *Journal of Human Rights Practice* 9 (2017): 1–15.

62. Ibid.

63. Ann Florini, "The Evolution of International Norms," *International Studies Quarterly* 40, no. 3 (1996): 363–89.

64. White House, "Press Briefing by Scott McClellan."

65. Steven C. Poe, "The Decision to Repress: An Integrative Theoretical Approach to the Research on Human Rights and Repression," in *Understanding Human Rights Violations: New Systematic Studies*, ed. Sabine C. Carey and Steven C. Poe (London: Taylor & Francis, 2004), 17.

66. Ibid., 26.

67. Ibid., 24.

68. White House, "President Bush Commemorates Fifth Anniversary of U.S. Department of Homeland Security" (March 6, 2008), https://georgewbush-whitehouse .archives.gov/news/releases/2008/03/20080306-4.html.

69. Pew Research Center, "Public Opinion Six Months Later: Nationhood, Internationalism Lifted" (March 7, 2002), https://www.pewresearch.org/politics/2002/03/07 /public-opinion-six-months-later/.

70. Darren W. Davis and Brian D. Silver, "Civil Liberties vs. Security: Public Opinion in the Context of the Terrorist Attacks on America," *American Journal of Political Science* 48 (January 2004): 30.

71. Leonie Huddy, Stanley Feldman, Charles Taber, and Gallya Lahav, "Threat, Anxiety, and Support of Antiterrorism Policies," *American Journal of Political Science* 49 (July 2005): 604.

72. Ibid., 604.

73. Ibid., 599.

74. U.S. Senate, "Report of the Senate Select Committee on Intelligence, Committee Study of the Central Intelligence Agency's Detention and Interrogation Program" (S. Report 113-288, December 9, 2014), https://www.intelligence.senate.gov/sites/default /files/publications/CRPT-113srpt288.pdf.

75. Program on International Policy Attitudes (PIPA), "Americans on Detention, Torture, and the War on Terror" (July 22, 2004), 3, http://www.pipa.org.

76. World Public Opinion, "Majority of Americans Approve Complete Ban on Torture" (June 24, 2009), http://www.worldpublicopinion.org.

77. Ibid.

78. Chris Kahn, "Exclusive: Most Americans Support Torture Against Terror Suspects—Reuters/Ipsos Poll," Reuters, March 30, 2016, https://www.reuters.com/article /us-usa-election-torture-exclusive/exclusive-most-americans-support-torture-against -terror-suspects-reuters-ipsos-poll-idUSKCN0WW0Y3.

79. Brittany Lyte, "Americans Have Grown More Supportive of Torture," *FiveThirtyEight*, December 9, 2014, www.fivethirtyeight.com.

80. Alfred W. McCoy, *Torture and Impunity* (Madison: University of Wisconsin Press, 2012).

81. Rupert Stone, "Trump Might Be 'Fine' with Torture, but Most Americans Aren't," *Al Jazeera* America, February 22, 2016, http://america.aljazeera.com/opinions/2016/2 /trump-might-be-fine-with-torture-but-most-americans-arent.html.

82. Ibid.

83. Ibid.; Lyte, "Americans Have Grown More Supportive of Torture."

84. Joan M. Blauwkamp, Charles M. Rowling, and William Pettit, "Are Americans Really Okay with Torture? The Effects of Message Framing on Public Opinion," *Media, War, & Conflict* 11, no. 4 (2018): 446–75.

85. Poe, "Decision to Repress," 26.

86. M. Cherif Bassiouni, "International Crimes: Jus Cogens and Obligatio Erga Omnes," *Law and Contemporary Problems* 59, no. 4 (1997): 63–74; Andrea Bianchi, "Human Rights and the Magic of Jus Cogens," *European Journal of International Law* 19, no. 3 (2008): 491–508.

87. Erika de Wet, "The Prohibition of Torture as an International Norm of Jus Cogens and Its Implications for National and Customary Law, " *European Journal of International Law* 15, no. 1 (2004): 97–121.

88. Rafael Nieto-Navia, "International Peremptory Norms (Jus Cogens) and International Humanitarian Law," in *Liber Amicorum*, ed. Antonio Cassese and Lal Chan Vohrah (London: Kluwer, 2003), 6.

89. De Wet, "Prohibition of Torture as an International Norm," 112–13; Bianchi, "Human Rights and the Magic of Jus Cogens," 494.

90. Anthony Cullen, "Defining Torture in International Law: A Critique of the Concept Employed by the European Court of Human Rights," *California Western International Law Journal* 34 (2003): 31.

91. Michael Pizzi, "Amnesty: 141 Countries Still Torture," *Al Jazeera America*, May 12, 2004, http://america.aljazeera.com/articles/2014/5/12/torture-report-amnesty.html.

92. Gordon A. Christenson, "Jus Cogens: Guarding Interests Fundamental to International Society," *Faculty Articles and Other Publications* 159 (1987): 590, http:// scholarship.law.uc.edu/fac_pubs/159.

93. Yasmeen Serhan, "The World Leaders Who Want Trump to Win," *Atlantic*, October 19, 2020, https://www.theatlantic.com/international/archive/2020/10/world -leaders-who-benefit-trumps-presidency/616709/.

94. United Nations, "Report of the Special Rapporteur on Torture" (A/61/259, August 14, 2006).

95. Amnesty International, "Global Crisis on Torture Exposed by New Worldwide Campaign" (May 13, 2014), https://www.amnesty.org/en/latest/news/2014/05/amnesty -international-global-crisis-torture-exposed-new-worldwide-campaign/.

Human Security and Migration

Naji Bsisu, Maryville College

Laila Farooq, Institute of Business Administration,
Karachi, Pakistan

Amanda Murdie, University of Georgia at Athens

We are in an age of migration. People have been traveling vast distances across disparate lands since the beginning of time. Roughly one hundred years ago, in 1910, global migrant population levels were at around 33 million individuals. By 2000, the levels of migrants had reached 175 million. Throughout this period, the growth rate in the levels of migrants increased twice as much as total global population growth.[1] In addition to the increased numbers of population transfers, the types of populations crossing borders have become progressively diverse.[2]

Since 2000, noticeable shifts in migration patterns have occurred, as shown in map 1, as the majority of migrations, both forced and voluntary, now take place in Asia as opposed to Europe. Countries that had previously been migrant-sending locations now find themselves to be migrant-receiving countries due to this shift.[3] Map 1 illustrates the average annual rate of change among international migration across the globe between 2000 and 2013. This has led to increased participation by governments, international governmental organizations (IGOs), nongovernmental organizations (NGOs), among others, to deal with this new phenomenon some have called a "migration crisis."[4]

This crisis has led to a renewed focus on migrations, including the causes of migration, the factors that perpetuate migration, how states react to migration, and the impact of migration on a multitude of issues relating to individual and group security and rights protection. The focus of this chapter is on migration and human rights or human security, specifically the causes of migration, differing conceptions of migrants and migration, and the impact migration has on human security more generally.

We define human security as freedom from "want" and freedom from "fear."[5] Human security is unlike many other ideas about security in that the focus is on the individual and his or her personal security, as opposed to the state or country and its collective security. Human security is seen as the rights

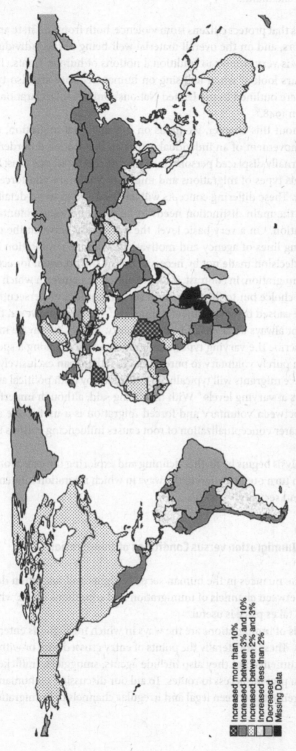

Map 1. International migrants' annual rate of change (2000–2013). United Nations Department of Economic and Social Affairs, Population Division, "Trends in International Migrant Stock: The 2013 Revision" (POP/DB/MIG/Stock/Rev.2013/Origin, December 2013), http://www.unmigration.org.

Increased more than 10%
Increased between 3% and 10%
Increased between 2% and 3%
Increased less than 2%
Decreased
Missing Data

and freedoms that protect citizens from violence, both from the state and from nonstate actors, and on the overall material well-being of the individual. Human security is very similar to traditional notions of human rights. The outcomes scholars look at when focusing on human security are also typically rights that were outlined in the United Nations' Universal Declaration of Human Rights in 1948.[6]

Throughout this chapter, we focus on international migration, defined here as the movement of an individual across an international border, as opposed to internally displaced persons. In exploring this topic, one must be clear on the various types of migrations and migrants: voluntary and forced, legal and irregular. These differing concepts will be discussed in more detail below, but for now the main distinction needs to be made between voluntary and forced migration. On a very basic level, the distinction between the two can be made along lines of agency and motivation. Voluntary migration is often seen to be a decision made not by necessity but by the potential for economic gain. Forced migration, in contrast, is often political in nature, in which the migrant has no choice but to flee conditions such as conflict or persecution, but it can also be caused by environmental disasters.[7] In reality, however, this distinction is not always accurate and can be murky. In fact, it may be more accurate to describe the varying types of migration as falling along a spectrum, ranging from purely voluntary to purely forced, rather than exclusively one or the other, since migrants will typically be influenced by both political and economic factors at varying levels.[8] With that being said, although imperfect, the distinction between voluntary and forced migration is a useful one as it allows for a clearer conceptualization of root causes influencing various types of migration.

This analysis begins by further defining and exploring the causes of migration. We then turn our attention to the ways in which migration influences human rights and security.

Channels of Immigration versus Conditions of Immigration

Because of the nuances in the human security/rights and migration debate, a distinction between channels of immigration and conditions under which the immigration takes place is useful.

Channels of immigrations are the ways in which immigrants enter recipient countries. These are literally the points of entry crossed with or without the required documents, but they also include agents, smugglers, traffickers, and networks that provide access to routes. To aid our discussion on human rights, we first differentiate between legal and irregular channels of immigration.

Legal channels of immigration are routes of entry recognized by the recipient state. The proof of legality is provided by documentation issued to the immigrant, acknowledging the residential status of the immigrant protected by the law of the state.

Irregular channels of immigration are alternative routes not recognized by the recipient state. The state has no (or forged) records of the immigrant's residential status. Such immigration is mostly undocumented and may run afoul of a state's immigration law. Importantly, however, human rights advocates have discouraged the term "illegal migrants" for migrants entering through nonlegal channels on the basis that it criminalizes individuals.[9] This is especially relevant for victims of trafficking and refugees. The term used instead is typically "irregular migrants."[10] Thus, we use the term "irregular migration" whenever we are taking about migration outside of the recipient state's legal channels.

The conditions of immigration are the factors that caused the migration to start in the host country. These include economic, political, cultural, social, or other reasons for migration, as discussed above.

These reasons can vary as conditions across countries (and time) vary. Qualified professionals and skilled workers may migrate to countries that have a higher demand for specialized jobs even if they enjoy a relatively high economic status in their home countries. International students may accept jobs and choose to continue residence. This kind of immigration is termed "elite immigration" because it provides the immigrant the flexibility to manage her citizenship including the privilege to visit her home country or maintain dual citizenship.[11] Another reason for immigration may be extreme poverty or food insecurity where the immigrant's very survival may be in danger. Both of these reasons are economic in nature—the search for higher income—but clearly they are not in the same category. In neither of these cases is the individual being physically forced to leave the country, however the environment has limited the choices available to the immigrant in the latter case.

As mentioned above, conditions for immigration can be voluntary or involuntary; the terminology in this regard is rather contested. Involuntary or forced immigration was restricted to traditional forced migration, such as bondage labor. However, the modern economic system creates similar conditions for migration because of globalization's consequences for citizens in different countries.[12] Economic crises are often the result of a global phenomenon such as dropping oil prices, trade fluctuations, exchange rate fluctuations, and others that push populations into extreme poverty or political insecurity, limiting the choices that they have. In the past fifty years, trade barriers have been dramatically reduced, leading companies to move operations to the most cost-efficient location.[13] Individuals with severe economic hardships in a given country may move to locations not under economic crises. Further, capital mobility and speculative currency exchange can diffuse economic crises, making an economic issue in one country permeate across borders. An economic crisis that reduces wages drastically in a country, forcing low-wage workers to look for higher paid jobs in other countries, could still be called forced migration according to this perspective.

Voluntary immigration is immigration that provides the immigrant the flexibility to determine citizenship. This includes political and economic reasons that provide a choice to the immigrant without presenting a threat to the immigrant's existing human rights.

Involuntary immigration is immigration that is forced in the sense that it leaves the immigrant with no choice but to migrate. This can be in a physical sense, such as trafficking or smuggling, but also as a threat of deterioration in the immigrant's existing human rights status such as an economic or political crisis. Domestic or international war and natural disasters may often lead to involuntary immigration. These immigrants include refugees and asylum seekers.

The interaction between the channels and conditions of immigration results in a two-by-two table. The first quadrant contains voluntary immigration carried out through legal channels. An example would be the "elite immigrants" mentioned above. The second quadrant consists of voluntary immigration conducted through irregular channels. An example would be workers immigrating to a wealthier destination country using dubious means such as fake marriages, forged work permits, or unsupervised points of entry at the border. The third quadrant consists of involuntary immigration carried out through legal channels. An example would be refugees and asylum seekers escaping life threatening situations (involuntary) applying for residence in the destination country. The fourth quadrant consists of immigration that is involuntary and irregular. An example would be human trafficking and smuggling.

Causes of Migration—Theoretical Understandings

Being that voluntary migration is said to have its roots in economic issues, it is only natural that neoclassical economics provided one of the first comprehensive theories on this subject.[14] Neoclassical economics can be separated into macro- and micro-level theories. We begin our discussion with the former and end with the latter.

Macro neoclassical economic theory links international migration to discrepancies in the global supply and demand of labor.[15] Essentially, countries with increased levels of labor relative to capital are said to have a low equilibrium market wage, whereas countries with increased levels of capital relative to labor have a high equilibrium market wage, resulting in flows of labor from the low to high equilibrium markets. The explanation provided by macro neoclassical economic theory is largely simplistic, but it does allow for some conclusions to be made. Namely, labor markets are the primary determinant of migration, migration occurs when differences in wage rates exist between countries, and the best way to influence migration is to exert some control over labor markets in either migrant sending or receiving states.[16] Micro neoclassical economic theory, however, focuses on individual choice rather than the structural considerations on which macro neoclassical economic theory is based.[17] According to this theory, individual actors rationally choose whether to migrate or not based on individual cost-benefit analysis. Essentially, individuals migrate whenever and wherever their expected net returns are highest. Micro neoclassical economic theory then takes into account individual characteristics, social conditions, and new technologies, all of which impact individuals' decision to migrate or not, based on their expected return.[18]

Another way to look at causes of voluntary migration is through the lens of "new economics of migration."[19] Unlike neoclassical economic theory, which focuses only on labor markets, the new economics of migration approach considers a variety of markets in the decision to migrate or not. Additionally, rather than the decision being limited to an individual, the vantage point is on the household.[20] Following this line of thinking, the household acts in a way that not only maximizes earning potential but also diversifies risk with regard to future earnings. The risk in earning a sustainable income is largely mitigated in developed states through institutional mechanisms such as government-backed unemployment benefits.[21] The main differences between this approach and neoclassical economic theory are that households, not individuals, make decisions, and that income is not seen as a homogenous good—instead, the source and stability of that income stream are very important considerations.[22]

Dual labor market theory is another approach to explaining international migration, but unlike the new economics of migration approach, it emphasizes a structural approach. This theory states that international migration is driven by the inherent labor demand of developed nations.[23] Rather than focusing on decisions that compel individuals or households to migrate, dual labor market theory places the impetus on the economic structure of industrialized nations, which require continuous and increasing levels of labor.[24]

World systems theory provides another approach regarding international immigration. This theory posits that international immigration is naturally occurring due to economic globalization and the ensuing capitalist development across state borders.[25] Migration flows originate as developed economies increase interactions with and development in less developed areas. Essentially, the spread of a global economy leads to the spread of population flows across borders.[26] Map 2 provides a snapshot of government policy toward migration for each respective state in 2013.

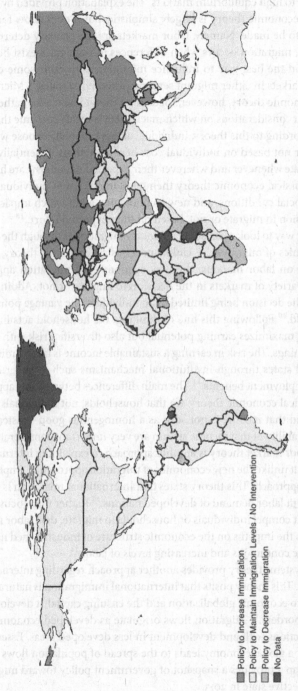

Map 2. Government policy on immigration (2013). United Nations Department of Economic and Social Affairs, Population Division, "Trends in International Migrant Stock: The 2013 Revision" (POP/DB/MIG/Stock/Rev.2013/Origin, December 2013), http://www.unmigration.org.

- Policy to Increase Immigration
- Policy to Maintain Immigration Levels / No Intervention
- Policy to Decrease Immigration
- No Data

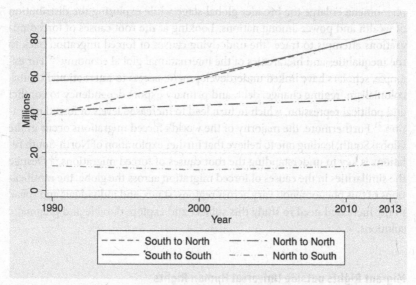

Figure 1. Numbers of international migrants by origin and destination, 1990–2013. United Nations, "International Migration 2013: Migrants by Origin and Destination | Population Division" (United Nations, January 1, 2013), www.un.org/development/desa/pd/content/international-migration-2013-migrants-origin-and-destination.

Whereas the explanations and theories discussed above do a commendable job in providing causal explanations regarding voluntary population flows, they fail to adequately explain the occurrence of forced migration. The main issue inherent in them is that they prioritize economic factors at the expense of political issues, which almost always are at the root cause of any forced migration.[27]

As mentioned, the most common causes of forced migration include conflict (both intra- and interstate conflict), environmental disasters, development-induced displacement, political oppression, and human rights violations.[28] Additionally, one can look to certain global "root causes" leading to these events within a specific country, such as globalization, North-South relations, and the international political economy.[29] Figure 1 illustrates transitions of migrant populations between the Global North and Global South between 1990 and 2013.

Regardless of the specific cause, outside of an environmental disaster, political issues are for all intents and purposes at the forefront of forced migration. Country-specific causes of forced migration, such as conflict, environmental disasters, development, and repression, are fairly self-explanatory and do not require much explanation. However, global issues touching upon the root causes of forced migration warrant deeper exploration.

Globalization, North-South relations, and the international political economy relate to the interconnectedness of politics and economics. These related phenomena enlarge the broader global stage while exploring the distribution of wealth and power among nations. Looking at the root causes of forced migrations attempts to trace "the underlying causes of forced migration back to the inequalities and hierarchies of the international global economy."[30] For example, scholars have linked underdevelopment, access to international capital, colonialism, regime change, debt, and primary export dependency to conflict and political repression, which in turn lead to increased levels of forced migration.[31] Furthermore, the majority of the world's forced migrations occur in the Global South, leading one to believe that further exploration of North-South relations is key to understanding the root causes of forced migrations.[32] Despite the similarities in the causes of forced migration across the globe, the ramifications of this phenomenon vary across regions, states, and individuals and speak to the increased need to study this subject and explore durable and pragmatic solutions.

Migrant Rights outside Universal Human Rights

The Universal Declaration of Human Rights (UDHR), adopted in 1948 by the United Nations General Assembly, though a nonbinding document, was the first pronounced global effort to define the rights and freedoms all human beings are inherently entitled to. Subsequent binding treaties, the International Covenant on Civil and Political Rights and the International Covenant on Economic, Social and Cultural Rights, have been ratified by over 170 countries each. Before continuing a conversation about the rights of migrants, let us first ask a question: What makes the rights of immigrants different from those already covered under universal human rights? Why is this a matter of such debate?

The rights of migrants are *individual* rights, provided to people who cross the border of a country they are not citizens of, with the intention of residing there. However, the ultimate authority of residence lies with the receiving state or country. This is based on the principle of territorial sovereignty according to which states have the extensive authority to make all decisions regarding who and how foreigners can enter their territories.[33] States take these rights seriously because they can jeopardize national security in times of international conflict and terrorism.[34]

State policies and migrant rights can thus be at a crossroads when the receiving state refuses to acknowledge the immigrant as a legal resident and hence deprives her of the same rights provided to other citizens. This issue makes immigrants' rights distinctive. In practice, immigrant rights may not be thought of as rights entitled at birth—like all universal human rights—but are heavily determined by state institutions. From the recipient states' perspective, the acknowledgment of residency and rights revolves around the legality of the immigration. Once the legality is established, the immigrant may be entitled to the same or lesser rights as those of natural citizens. Advocates for immigrant rights challenge this perspective because it ignores the conditions under which the immigration took place.[35]

People may be forced to leave their countries because of a political or economic crisis that makes continued residence in that country impossible. Examples include genocide or ethnic cleansing, political persecution, civil war, repression, and food insecurity. Such immigrants become refugees and asylum seekers. The magnitude and nature of such movements often lead to bypassing legal channels and finding alternative routes. The treatment of undocumented immigrants is then left in the hands of the recipient state, often a neighboring state to the conflict. The normative human rights debate then revolves around how much leeway sovereign states should have in determining whether the immigrant is entitled to rights or not, when migration itself may not be a voluntary decision.

Immigrant Rights under International Law

Immigration laws are determined by destination countries according to their state laws. In this regard, only legal immigrants are eligible for immigrant rights. We can see from the discussion above that irregular immigrants—both voluntary and involuntary—form an extremely vulnerable population. These migrants are moving to states that may not be welcoming to them and where they have minimal legal protection. These migrants face threats at two levels. The first is being exploited by the network of smugglers and traffickers who run the business of crossing the borders, trapping these irregular immigrants in years of abusive labor.[36] If they do reach their destination country without being caught or abused by the traffickers, they cannot work legally and are forced to work for extremely low wages. They may also suffer discrimination and social isolation.

The complexity in the overlap between irregular immigration channels and abusive forms of migration makes immigration laws difficult to implement. For example, if receiving states make immigration laws more restrictive, there may be an increase in irregular migration. If states try to curb irregular immigration through increased border controls and security, the alternative routes taken are also the most dangerous, resulting in deaths and injuries for those attempting to cross the border.[37]

Irregular migration thus raises specific questions of human rights. Advocates of immigrant rights believe that most immigrants are individuals and families looking to make better lives, not criminals violating laws to harm the state. Refugees and asylum seekers especially come from a low human rights environment to an uncertain one. The policy initiative should therefore be to change the status of such immigrants to legal residents. The parallel policy debate once immigrant status is recognized is on the absorption of immigrants as equal citizens into the society. Political and economic rights including the right to work, the right to vote, and the right to contest for office vary for immigrants across states, but normative standards prevent the further violation of human rights. International laws have been formulated to hold states to these standards.

Beyond the binding human rights treaties that followed the UDHR and apply to all individuals, like the Intentional Covenant on Civil and Political Rights and the International Covenant on Economic Social and Cultural Rights, there have been specific efforts to create binding treaties that specifically relate to the rights of migrants. For example, the International Convention on the Protection of the Rights of All Migrant Workers and Members of Their Families was adopted by the United Nations in 1990 and entered into force in 2003. This treaty reiterates rights that are already outlined in extant human rights treaties, like the right to freedom from slavery and the right to freedom of expression, but focuses on how migrant workers and their families are especially vulnerable to not having their rights realized in practice.

Outside of the UN's human rights regime, there are many other international treaties and agreements relating to the rights of migrants. The International Labour Organization, an agency of the United Nations since 1946, has multiple treaties relating to the rights of migrant workers, regardless of the legality of their residency. The UN Office of Drugs and Crime has been responsible for much of the UN's work to limit human trafficking and migrant smuggling. In 2000, the UN General Assembly approved the creation of the Convention against Transnational Organized Crime, a treaty that came into force in 2003. It contains protocols relating to trafficking and smuggling of migrants.

The United Nations Convention Relating to the Status of Refugees deals specifically with individuals who have been forced to migrate due to fear. In 1951, this convention dealt with just refugees following World War II. It was updated to have no geographic or time restrictions in 1967. This treaty provides a formal definition of a refugee and outlines how states have to cooperate with the UN High Commissioner for Refugees. It lays out rights protecting individuals against being forced to return to a country, also called refoulement, when they fear persecution based on their identity or opinions. It also lays out the idea that states must have procedures for the processing of asylum.

Many regions also have treaties that relate to migration. One of the most prominent regional agreements related to migration is the 1985 Schengen

Agreement, which became European Union law in 1999. This agreement created a borderless European community. It outlines that border checks will occur only on external borders and that individuals will enjoy free movement within the region unless there is an emergency situation. In 1997, the first Dublin Convention came into force in Europe. This convention and the two subsequent Dublin Regulations lay out where asylum cases will be dealt with in the region.

Of course, the strength of international law, including regional agreements, has often been questioned.[38] States are reluctant to follow international law that goes against their immediate strategic interests. In general, the successful implementation on human rights law on the ground depends on continued international and domestic pressure.[39] Organizations like Amnesty International and Human Rights Watch have been powerful players in making states accountable to their international agreements. One difficultly in the area of migrant rights, however, is that some possible allies to human rights issues in highly developed migrant recipient states may be less likely to support issues of immigration, especially in times of conflict or economic downturn.

Consequences of Migration for Human Security

What are the effects of migration on human rights and human security? Political rhetoric often implies that migration harms human security, limiting the wealth of citizens in recipient countries and increasing violence. Interestingly, however, much of this rhetoric has very little support in the overall social science literature, especially concerning voluntary migration. When negative human security externalities related to migration have been found, they have typically been related to refugee inflows in conflict-prone situations.

To understand the role of voluntary migration on economic well-being, or the "freedom from want," it is important to remember that many classic theories of economics see labor as a key component of production.[40] Like capital, labor can move across borders to be used where it can be most effective and is more likely to yield better returns. We often see migrants receiving higher wages abroad than they would have received in their origin country. So for migrants themselves a key aspect of their human security—their "freedom from want"—is heightened as a result of their migration. Worth noting, however, is that most migration is not for work-related reasons; a 2013 study of immigration to countries that are part of the Organization for Economic Cooperation and Development (OECD) found that most migration to these countries is driven by family-related reasons.[41]

Beyond the migrants themselves, there is much evidence that family members left in the origin country and their communities often benefit from the migrant's increased opportunities. Remittances, defined as transfers sent to family members or communities in the origin country, are estimated to total more than $540 billion per year, most of which (above $400 billion) flows to developing countries.[42] This figure is much more than official aid sent to developing countries. In times of economic downturn in the origin country, remittances can be a necessity for family survival.[43] An influential summary of the topic concludes that remittances help "economic development and household welfare."[44] Recent studies have found that remittances help children remain in school longer, are associated with higher birth weights in infants and lower childhood mortality, and are important for gender equality.[45]

For the destination country, there is much evidence that immigration of both low and unskilled workers has a positive effect on a country's economy.[46] Migrants move where their skills can be used to their advantage; they are often seeking employment either in high-skilled sectors where their skills are in high demand or in low-skilled sectors where the positions are "regarded by domestic workers as unattractive or lacking career prospects."[47] The remarks of Jean-Christophe Dumont, head of the International Migration Division of the OECD, in a recent panel discussion at the UN General Assembly reiterate this idea: "Migration made a key contribution to employment growth during the past decade," and migrants "contribute to job creation."[48]

In spite of this overall effect on economic growth and job creation, there is some evidence of reductions in wages in some sectors following increases in immigration. This makes much theoretical sense: "Immigration will lower the wage if immigrants are prepared to work for less than natives, as seems plausible in the case of illegal immigrants, or example."[49] Despite this, the overall effect of immigration on the wages is very small; in the United States, it has been estimated that "a 10 percent increase in the fraction of immigrants in the population reduces native wages by at most 1 percent."[50] As Alex Nowrasteh bluntly articulates, "Nowhere will you find a tradeoff where one additional immigrant means that one American loses a job in the economy."[51]

Of course, these findings do not imply that there will not be some evidence of "particular groups of [native] workers" that have been affected by immigration.[52] Some of the groups that have been studied as at risk for displacement as a result of immigration are "high-school dropouts, previous immigrant cohorts, and U.S. scientists and engineers."[53]

Worth noting is that despite the rhetoric of fear of losing one's job, well-known public opinion research in the United States in the 1990s did find that "personal economic circumstances" were not a major contributor to negative opinions about immigration; instead, feelings on the general state of the economy and generalized opinions about Hispanics and Asians contributed to opinions on immigration.[54] A 2008 experimental study in the United States found that opposition to immigration is often driven by ethnic cues.[55]

For the destination country, one area of concern in much political rhetoric is the effect of immigration on the government's coffers. The concern, typically, is that immigrants, both legal and irregular, will draw heavily on public services while not contributing to government coffers. Survey research in the United Kingdom, for example, has concluded that the majority of citizens want immigrants to have to wait some time before accessing public services.[56] Results are very mixed as to whether immigrants use public services more or less than natives, with much variation across country and across the characteristics of the individual immigrant.[57] Additionally, although some studies find that immigrants add greatly to the government's coffers,[58] conclusions in the literature are mixed. Overall impacts on government sectors depend on both the characteristics of the immigrants and the characteristics of the state they are migrating to.[59]

For the country the migrant is coming from, emigration can also create effects on "freedom from want." Of course remittances can improve family and community well-being, as mentioned above. However, there are concerns with whether emigration creates a "brain drain," where highly trained individuals leave a country in search of better prospects abroad and are thus not able to aid their origin country's growth.[60] Although there is some evidence for this phenomenon, recent studies have also highlighted a "beneficial brain drain," where the possibility of emigration increases incentives to invest in education.[61] The overall benefits of brain drain on an origin country's economy is somewhat dependent on other policies within the origin country, including property rights and bureaucratic recruitment.[62]

Beyond "freedom from want," migration also has some likely effects on "freedom from fear." Interestingly, this potential relationship has received much less attention in the scholarly literature. We do know, however, that it is much less likely for irregular migrants to fully enjoy their "freedom from fear" in their destination country or in any country through which they transit.[63] These migrants simply do not have the same judicial remedies as citizens. They are likely to be unwilling to advocate for their rights given the possibility of legal action against them.

Further complicating the "freedom from fear" for migrants, in the post-9/11 environment, counterterrorism has often been linked the immigration policies, creating a situation, according to Stefanie Grant, where "governments have encouraged—however unintentionally—xenophobia against migrants and refugees."[64] Because of these issues and the acute nature of rights abuses on women and children, many nongovernmental organizations and intergovernmental agencies have heightened their efforts to revitalize the "migrant workers' rights agenda."[65]

The literature on the human security consequences of refugee flows can be very bleak. Unlike voluntary migrants moving for labor or familial reasons, refugees are leaving a very precarious human security situation and can, at times, end up in another precarious human security situation. Refugees can be a drain on a country's coffers, especially if their influx is localized, like occurs if refugees are crossing over into a neighboring country. This situation can create a "neighbor's curse," where conflict and instability in a neighboring country can negatively affect economic growth.[66] "Regional crises often force a substantial increase in military outlays to prevent the fighting from spreading across political boundaries and avoid the usual avalanche of refugees that comes with civil wars in neighboring countries."[67]

Refugee flows are also associated with increased risk of civil and international conflict and with increases in human rights abuses.[68] However, the negative effects of refugee inflows on human rights abuses can be mitigated by increased state capacity and are conditional to the characteristics of the state the refugees are coming from. The negative externalities of refugee flows on human security are currently issues of much concern for the international community, with both NGOs and intergovernmental organizations increasing their work on this important issue.[69]

Migrant Rights: The Way Forward

We started this chapter with an introduction to modern migration and its patterns in a time of globalization. Human security concerns for modern migration are in the overlap of state security and individual rights when the movement of people across borders has become easier in times of globalization. Throughout this chapter we have laid out some of these concerns and how the international community has dealt with them.

The recent European migrant crisis highlights these issues. Starting in January 2015, refugees from the Middle East, Africa, and South Asia started making their way to European Union countries, leading to the largest number of forcibly displaced individuals since World War I.[70] Migration is the result of not just conflict but also economic inequalities. The movement of people from regions of economic or political crisis to regions of relative prosperity makes this a regional issue, rather than a country-level one. As we are seeing with the European crisis, the international community has reacted in different ways. There is a demand for increased screening and better documentation, but also negative political rhetoric edging on xenophobia.

A pressing concern for migrant rights is in the area of the rights of undocumented migrants. There is a level of distrust toward such migrants, at both government and societal levels. However, we have discussed how undocumented migration may fall under involuntary migration through nonlegal channels. Irregular migrants are especially vulnerable to higher levels of repression and police brutality.[71] These migrants may include women, children, and the elderly. The response of the international community needs to consider these factors. One solution is amnesty, especially in the cases of migrants who have lived in their host countries for a number of years. At the other end of the spectrum is deportation—sending individuals back to their countries of birth. Both of these solutions have consequences. Further, the emphasis on minimizing irregular migration can lead to better rights for regular migrants, but also have an adverse effect if irregular migrants have to be forced back to their countries of birth or start using alternative routes that are more risky.

Thus, migrant rights have become a global issue and need to be dealt with at a global level. The European migration crisis reinforces the complexity of forced migration and human security. Lawmakers and legal experts are an important link in this chain as debates on irregular migration continue. Further, other than the residential status of the migrant, issues of employment, social interaction, and cultural differences are also important areas of research. The effect of migration on the host country, such as the impact on gender, family structure, the environment, development, and urbanization, has interesting implications for human security. Modern migration reaches beyond societies being more diverse to societies being more inclusive, and future work on migrant rights needs to address how this inclusivity can be achieved.

Notes

1. Hania Zlotnik, "Past Trends in International Migration and Their Implications for Future Prospects," in *International Migration into the 21st Century: Essays in Honour of Reginald Appleyard*, ed. Muhammed Abu B. Siddique (Boston: Edward Elgar, 2001), 227–62; Seyla Benhabib, *The Rights of Others: Aliens, Residents, and Citizens* (Cambridge: Cambridge University Press, 2004), 5.

2. David T. Graham and Nana K. Poku, "Introduction," in *Migration, Globalisation and Human Security*, ed. David T. Graham and Nana K. Poku (London: Routledge, 2000), 5.

3. Douglas S. Massey, Joaquin Arango, Graeme Hugo, Ali Kouaouci, Adela Pellegrinoand, and J. Edward Taylor, "Theories of International Migration: A Review and Appraisal," *Population and Development Review* 19, no. 3 (1993): 431–66.

4. Alexander Betts, *Forced Migration and Global Politics* (West Sussex: Wiley-Blackwell, 2009). See also Stephen Castles, "The International Politics of Forced Migration," *Development* 46 (2003): 11–20.

5. United Nations Development Programme (UNDP), "Human Development Report 1994: New Dimensions of Human Security" (1994), http://hdr.undp.org/en/content/human-development-report-1994. See also Roland Paris, "Human Security: Paradigm Shift or Hot Air?," *International Security* 26, no. 2 (2001): 87–102.

6. Rhoda Howard-Hassmann, "Human Security: Undermining Human Rights?," *Human Rights Quarterly* 34, no. 1 (2012): 88–112.

7. Betts, *Forced Migration and Global Politics*; Castles, "International Politics of

Forced Migration"; Mathias Czaika and Krisztina Kis-Katos, "Civil Conflict and Displacement: Village-Level Determinants of Forced Migration in Aceh," *Journal of Peace Research* 46, no. 3 (2009): 399–418.

8. Betts, *Forced Migration and Global Politics*, 4.

9. Giuseppe Sciortino, "Between Phantoms and Necessary Evils: Some Critical Points in the Study of Irregular Migrations to Western Europe," *IMIS-Beiträge* 24 (2004): 17–43.

10. Khalid Koser, "Irregular Migration, State Security and Human Security" (paper, Global Commission on International Migration, 2005).

11. Ariadna Estévez, "Human Rights and Conflict in Modern Migration," in *Human Rights, Migration, and Social Conflict* (New York: Palgrave Macmillan, 2012), 11–33.

12. David Bacon, *Illegal People: How Globalization Creates Migration and Criminalizes Immigrants* (Boston: Beacon, 2008). See also Anthony H. Richmond, "Globalization: Implications for Immigrants and Refugees," *Ethnic and Racial Studies* 25, no. 5 (2002): 707–27.

13. Massey et al., "Theories of International Migration."

14. Ibid.; W. Arthur Lewis, "Economic Development with Unlimited Supplies of Labor," *Manchester School of Economic and Social Studies* 22, no. 2 (1954): 139–91; John R. Harris and Michael P. Todaro, "Migration, Unemployment, and Development: A Two-Sector Analysis," *American Economic Review* 60, no. 1 (1970): 126–42; Michael P. Todaro, *Internal Migration in Developing Countries* (Geneva: International Labor Office, 1976).

15. Massey et al., "Theories of International Migration," 433.

16. Ibid., 433–34.

17. Ibid.; Todaro, *Internal Migration in Developing Countries*; Michael P. Todaro, "A Model of Labor Migration and Urban Unemployment in Less Developed Countries," *American Economic Review* 59, no. 1 (1969): 138–48; Michael P. Todaro, *Economic Development in the Third World* (New York: Longman, 1989); Michael P. Todaro and Lydia Maruszko, "Illegal Migration and U.S. Immigration Reform: A Conceptual Framework," *Population and Development Review* 13, no. 1 (1987): 101–14; Larry A. Sjaastad, "The Costs and Returns of Human Migration," *Journal of Political Economy* 70, no. 5 (1962): 80–93.

18. Massey et al., "Theories of International Migration," 435.

19. Ibid., 435; Oded Stark and David Levhari, "On Migration and Risk in LDCs," *Economic Development and Cultural Change* 31, no. 1 (1982): 191–96; Jennifer Lauby and Oded Stark, "Individual Migration as a Family Strategy: Young Women in the Philippines," *Population Studies* 42, no. 3 (1988): 473–86.

20. Massey et al., "Theories of International Migration," 432.

21. Ibid., 436.

22. Ibid., 438.

23. Ibid., 440. See also Michael J. Piore, *Birds of Passage: Migrant Labor in Industrial Societies* (Cambridge: Cambridge University Press, 1979).

24. Massey et al., "Theories of International Migration," 440–41.

25. Immanuel Wallerstein, *The Modern World System: Capitalist Agriculture and the Origins of the European World Economy in the Sixteenth Century* (New York: Aca-

demic Press, 1974). See also Elizabeth M. Petras, "The Global Labor Market in the Modern World-Economy," in *Global Trends in Migration: Theory and Research on International Population Movements*, ed. Mary M. Kritz et al. (Staten Island, N.Y.: Center for Migration Studies, 1981), 44–63; Alejandro Portes and John Walton, *Labor, Class, and the International System* (New York: Academic Press, 1981); Saskia Sassen, *The Mobility of Labor and Capital: A Study in International Investment and Labor Flow* (Cambridge: Cambridge University Press, 1988); and Saskia Sassen, *The Global City: New York, London, Tokyo* (Princeton, N.J.: Princeton University Press, 1991).

26. Massey et al., "Theories of International Migration," 445.

27. Charles Westin and Sadia Hassanen, "Introduction," in *People on the Move: Experiences of Forced Migration*, ed. Westin and Hassanen (Trenton, N.J.: Red Sea Press, 2013), 1–30.

28. Betts, *Forced Migration and Global Politics*; Graham and Poku, "Introduction"; Westin and Hassanen, "Introduction."

29. Betts, *Forced Migration and Global Politics*; Graham and Poku, "Introduction"; Castles, "International Politics of Forced Migration"; B. S. Chimni, "The Geopolitics of Refugee Studies: A View from the South," *Journal of Refugee Studies* 11, no. 4 (1998): 350–74; Paul Collier, *The Bottom Billion: Why the Poorest Countries Are Failing and What Can Be Done about It* (Oxford: Oxford University Press, 2007); Sarah Collinson, *Power, Livelihoods and Conflict: Case Studies in Political Economy Analysis for Humanitarian Action* (London: Overseas Development Institute, 2003); David Keen, "The Political Economy of War," in *War and Underdevelopment*, vol. 1, ed. Frances Stewart, Valpy FitzGerald, and Associates (Oxford: Oxford University Press, 2001), 39–66; Nanda R. Shrestha, "A Structural Perspective on Labour Migration in Under-Developed Countries," *Progress in Human Geography* 12, no. 6 (1998): 179–207.

30. Betts, *Forced Migration and Global Politics*, 131.

31. Ibid.; Collier, *Bottom Billion*; Collinson, *Power, Livelihoods and Conflict*.

32. Betts, *Forced Migration and Global Politics*; Castles, "International Politics of Forced Migration"; Chimni, "Geopolitics of Refugee Studies." See also Mark Duffield, *Global Governance and the New Wars* (London: Zed Books, 2001).

33. Linda Bosniak, "Human Rights, State Sovereignty and the Protection of Undocumented Migrants under the International Migrant Workers Convention," *International Migration Review* 25, no. 4 (1991): 737–70.

34. David Cole, "The Idea of Humanity: Human Rights and Immigrants' Rights," *Columbia Human Rights Law Review* 37, no. 3 (2006): 627–58.

35. Castles, "International Politics of Forced Migration"; Estévez, "Human Rights and Conflict in Modern Migration."

36. Anne Gallagher, "Human Rights and the New UN Protocols on Trafficking and Migrant Smuggling: A Preliminary Analysis," *Human Rights Quarterly* 23, no. 4 (2001): 975–1004.

37. Guillermo Alonso Meneses, "Human Rights and Undocumented Migration along the Mexican-U.S. Border," *UCLA Law Review* 51, no. 1 (2004): 267–81.

38. George W. Downs, David M. Rocke, and Peter N. Barsoom, "Is the Good News about Compliance Good News about Cooperation?," *International Organization* 50, no. 3 (1996): 379–406.

39. Amanda M. Murdie and David R. Davis, "Shaming and Blaming: Using Events Data to Assess the Impact of Human Rights INGOs," *International Studies Quarterly* 56, no. 1 (2012): 1–16. See also Thomas Risse, Stephen C. Ropp, and Kathryn Sikkink, *The Power of Human Rights: International Norms and Domestic Change* (Cambridge: Cambridge University Press, 1999); Beth A. Simmons, *Mobilizing for Human Rights: International Law in Domestic Politics* (Cambridge: Cambridge University Press, 2009).

40. Wolfgang F. Stolper and Paul A. Samuelson, "Protection and Real Wages," *Review of Economic Studies* 9, no. 1 (1941): 58–73; and Kevin H. O'Rourke and Jeffrey G. Williamson, *Globalization and History: The Evolution of a 19th Century Atlantic Economy* (Boston: MIT Press, 1999).

41. Jean-Christophe Dumont, "The Impact of International Migration on Destination Countries" (New York: United Nations, Office of the President of the General Assembly, Panel Discussion on International Migration and Development, June 25, 2013); and Organization for Economic Cooperation and Development (OECD), "International Migration Outlook 2013" (2013), https://dx.doi.org/10.1787/migr_outlook-2013-en.

42. World Bank, "Remittances to Developing Countries Edge Up Slightly in 2015" (April 13, 2016), www.worldbank.org/en/news/press-release/2016/04/13/remittances-to-developing-countries-edge-up-slightly-in-2015.

43. Dilip Ratha, "Remittances and Poverty Alleviation in Poor Countries," in *The Encyclopedia of Global Human Migration* (Wiley, February 4, 2013), https://doi.org/10.1002/9781444351071.wbeghm441.

44. Ernesto Lopez-Cordova and Alexandra Olmedo, "International Remittances and Development: Existing Evidence, Policies and Recommendations" (Inter-American Development Bank Occasional Paper 41, 2006), 31.

45. Alejandra Cox Edwards and Manuelita Ureta, "International Migration, Remittances, and Schooling: Evidence from El Salvador," *Journal of Development Economics* 72, no. 2 (2003): 429–61; Ratha, "Remittances and Poverty Alleviation." See also Nicole Hildebrandt, David J. McKenzie, Gerardo Esquivel, and Ernesto Schargrodsky, "The Effects of Migration on Child Health in Mexico," *Economia* 6, no. 1 (2005): 257–89.

46. OECD, "Is Migration Good for the Economy?" (May 2014), www.oecd.org/els/mig/OECD%20Migration%20Policy%20Debates%20Numero%202.pdf.

47. Ibid.

48. Dumont, "Impact of International Migration on Destination Countries," 13–14.

49. Rachel M. Friedberg and Jennifer Hunt, "The Impact of Immigrants on Host Country Wages, Employment and Growth," *Journal of Economic Perspectives* 9, no. 2 (1995): 23–44, 29.

50. Ibid., 42.

51. Alex Nowrasteh, "Immigration's Real Impact on Wages and Employment" (Cato Institute, September 15, 2014), www.cato.org/blog/immigrations-real-impact-wages-employment.

52. David Card, "Comment: The Elusive Search for Negative Wage Impacts of Immigration," *Journal of the European Economic Association* 10, no. 1 (2012): 211–16.

53. Sari Pekkala Kerr and William R. Kerr, "Economic Impacts of Immigration: A Survey" (National Bureau of Economic Research Working Paper 16736, January 2011),

11, http://www.hbs.edu/faculty/Publication%20Files/09-013_15702a45-fbc3-44d7-be52
-477123ee58d0.pdf.

54. Jack Citrin, Donald P. Green, Christopher Muste, and Cara Wong, "Public Opinion toward Immigration Reform: The Role of Economic Motivations," *Journal of Politics* 59, no. 3 (1997): 858–81.

55. Ted Brader, Nicholas A. Valentino, and Elizabeth Suhay, "What Triggers Public Opposition to Immigration? Anxiety, Group Cues, and Immigration Threat," *American Journal of Political Science* 52, no. 4 (2008): 959–78.

56. Jamie McIvor, "How Does Immigration Affect Public Services?," *BBC News*, March 12, 2015, http://www.bbc.com/news/uk-scotland-31822307.

57. Kerr and Kerr, "Economic Impacts of Immigration," 17.

58. Kjetil Storesletten, "Sustaining Fiscal Policy through Immigration," *Journal of Political Economy* 108, no. 2 (2000): 300–323.

59. Kerr and Kerr, "Economic Impacts of Immigration."

60. Michael Beine, Frédéric Docquier, and Hillel Rapoport, "Brain Drain and Economic Growth: Theory and Evidence," *Journal of Development Economics* 64, no. 1 (2001): 275–89.

61. Simon Commander, Mari Kangasniemi, and L. Alan Winters, "The Brain Drain: Curse or Boon? A Survey of the Literature," in *Challenges to Globalization: Analyzing the Economics*, ed. Robert E. Baldwin and L. Alan Winters (Chicago: University of Chicago Press, 2004), 235–78. See also Mari L. Kangasniemi, Alan Winters, and Simon Commander, "Is the Medical Brain Drain Beneficial? Evidence from Overseas Doctors in the UK," *Social Science & Medicine* 65, no. 5 (2007): 915–23.

62. Peter J. Kuhn and Carol McAusland, "The International Migration of Knowledge Workers: When Is Brain Drain Beneficial?" (No. w12761, National Bureau of Economic Research, 2006). See also Deepak Chitnis, "Brain Drain Effects Beneficial to Countries That Lose Talents," *American Bazaar*, September 22, 2013, http://www.americanbazaar online.com/2013/09/22/brain-drain-actually-beneficial-countries-lose-talent/.

63. United Nations Office of the High Commissioner for Human Rights (UN OHCHR), "Migration and Human Rights: Improving Human Rights-Based Governance of International Migration" (2015), http://www.ohchr.org/Documents/Issues /Migration/MigrationHR_improvingHR_Report.pdf.

64. Stefanie Grant, "Migrants' Human Rights: From the Margins to the Mainstream" (Migration Policy Institute, March 1, 2005), http://www.migrationpolicy.org/article /migrants-human-rights-margins-mainstream.

65. Ryszard Cholewinski, "Protecting Migrant Workers in a Globalized World" (Migration Policy Institute, March 1, 2005), http://www.migrationpolicy.org/article /protecting-migrant-workers-globalized-world.

66. Alberto Ades and Hak B. Chua, "'Thy Neighbor's Curse: Regional Instability and Economic Growth," *Journal of Economic Growth* 2, no. 3 (1997): 279–304.

67. Ibid., 293.

68. Idean Salehyan, "Refugees and the Study of Civil War," *Civil Wars* 9, no. 2 (2007): 127–41. See also Idean Salehyan, "The Externalities of Civil Strife: Refugees as a Source of International Conflict," *American Journal of Political Science* 52, no. 4 (2008):

787–801; Shweta Moorthy and Thorin M. Wright, "Refugees and Host State Repression" (paper, International Studies Association, 2014).

69. Ibid.

70. UN OHCHR, "Migration and Human Rights."

71. Jonathan Crush, "The Dark Side of Democracy: Migration, Xenophobia and Human Rights in South Africa," *International Migration* 38, no. 6 (2000): 103–34.

The United States, Africa, and Security

NONSTATE ACTORS, TERRORISM, AND DEVELOPMENT

Daniel Egbe, Philander Smith College
Kurt W. Jefferson, Spalding University

The Cold War (1945–91) had an important but mixed impact on United States–Africa relations primarily because these relations were mostly driven by ideological considerations. The underpinnings of U.S. foreign policy toward Africa, a vast continent with vital national resources and more than a billion in population, were not based on aspirational partnership. Rather, foreign policy focused on lining up political friends among the newly independent African states to provide the United States important natural resources for its Cold War ambitions. Progressive- and socialist-leaning regimes in Africa, like those led by Patrice Lumumba of the Congo and Kwame Nkrumah of Ghana, were overthrown in large measure with the support of the Central Intelligence Agency (CIA), thanks to Cold War impulses. This is the reality of the era that helped foster negatives in state-level political and economic development, including problematic models of governing, wasted natural resources, and economic paralysis. Resources were used instead by the superpowers for their own interests.

As a result, in the Cold War and post–Cold War eras, starting with the presidencies of Harry S. Truman and Dwight D. Eisenhower in the 1940s and 1950s, U.S. administrations continued to pay lip service to the more than fifty African nation-states. These administrations worked to appease Britain, France, and other colonial powers, to prevent conflict in geopolitical spheres of influence that the United States did not control. President Eisenhower nominally supported independence for African areas that were coming out of colonialism. Yet hoping not to anger their North Atlantic Treaty Organization allies, the Americans did not challenge Britain or France in their historical imperial domains. Moreover, by the 1960s, the Americans were more interested in containing communism and the spread of Soviet influence in Africa than in building a solid U.S.-Africa economic partnership that would have spurred economic and social development in the African continent. This failure led to the current political instability across Africa.

Decolonization itself was a rife context for superpower rivalry and for dividing up the continent via geopolitical and ideological lines between the communist East and capitalist-democratic West. The end of the Belgian Congo in 1960 saw the rise of independence movements in Africa as Patrice Lumumba turned to the Russians for assistance only to have the Americans and Western powers, along with the United Nations, challenge Lumumba's authority and the democratic process in the postcolonial Belgian Congo. The CIA intervened, and the Western-backed military colonel Joseph Mobutu and the army carried out a successful coup d'état against Lumumba's successor, Joseph Kasavubu. What is more, Lumumba was eventually murdered, and Mobutu went on to rule as a dictator, with Western support, from 1965 to 1997.

It was a time of Cold War intrigue on the continent. Many states including Mozambique, the Belgian Congo (later Zaire and then after 1997 the Democratic Republic of Congo), Cape Verde, and Angola attempted to gain backing from the Soviet Union to stave off U.S. intervention.

Moreover, the fifteen-year-old United Nations was severely tested in Africa and in the Belgian Congo itself. In 1960, the second United Nations (UN) secretary-general Dag Hammarskjöld was killed in a plane crash as he went to broker peace in the Congo crisis. The accident has been historically blamed on a Soviet act of sabotage, with the KGB, the Soviet intelligence agency equivalent to the CIA, responsible for shooting down the aircraft. Moreover, the United Nations Congo Force (ONUC) of twenty thousand "blue helmets," composed of troops from twenty-nine nations, came under attack in late 1962 in the rebel Katanga Province, under the leadership of Moise Tshombe. The ONUC forces then carried out Operation Grandslam to restore order and defend themselves in the Elisabethville area of the breakaway Katanga Province of Congo. ONUC forces retook the city of Elisabethville at the price of multiple local police officers. It was the first time since the start of UN peacekeeping operations that the UN fought a series of open offensive operations on a war-type footing in attempting to bring peace to a divided state.[1]

The continued problems that faced African states, the United States, and the global community during the Cold War continued to bedevil in the post–Cold War era as well. Although decolonization took place, issues with racist policies of the British in Rhodesia (after 1979 Zimbabwe) as well as the complicated and invidious support of the Republic of South Africa and its racially segregated apartheid state continued to implicate U.S. foreign policy. The United States hung on to its "constructive engagement" policy under President Ronald Reagan. Finally, during President Bill Clinton's administration, a breakthrough was found as apartheid was dismantled and Nelson Mandela won the multiracial democratic free elections in 1994 as South Africa's first Black president.

American policy in Africa continued its geopolitical configurations, seeking geopolitical and strategic advantage over the Soviets at the Cape of Good Hope and in the Horn of Africa. The Indian Ocean as a trading space was vital, and the oceans formed lanes for the maneuvering of American naval vessels both military and commercial.

Ideologically combatting the Soviets, and later the Russians, in southern and eastern Africa was important, and support for governments such as Haile Selassie's monarchy in Ethiopia was calculated not on politics alone but on geopolitical power and the maneuvering of the Russians in the region. Russian foreign policy offered political, economic, and military support to the Ethiopians' neighbors such as Somalia and the breakaway Eritrea.

Other important elements in this geopolitical context include the quest for valuable resources such as oil. Oil was found off the coast of the Horn of Africa in the Indian Ocean by Chevron in 1980. The company had been searching in the region since 1975.

A civil war began in Ethiopia in 1974, and the reversal of American support for Ethiopia and subsequent support for Somalia and breakaway Eritrea saw the Soviet Union move in to support the Marxist army of Colonel Mengistu Haile Mariam, who would become the president of Ethiopia until he was forced into exile in 1991.

The Ethiopian civil war killed well over one million, with at least one million dead from starvation and over a quarter of a million killed in the civil war itself.[2] Major General Mohamed Siad Barre led Somalia from 1969 to 1991. Initially he was a Marxist revolutionary leader, but in the late 1970s he removed Soviet advisors from Somalia and recognized the United States and other Western nations in accepting economic and military aid from the Western powers.

President Barack Obama (2009–17) continued trade with Africa that had been occurring under the George W. Bush presidency (2001–09). The Africa Growth and Opportunity Act (AGOA), begun in 2000, gave preferences to exports from various African nations. After AGOA, tariffs dropped and the trading program was created to bring about economic development in sub-Saharan Africa.[3] By 2015 AGOA was providing access to the U.S. market for African states without the onerous impact of tariffs on African goods. By 2000, goods going to Africa from the United States were valued at $23.4 billion.[4] President Obama's administration focused on five key areas in trading with various African nations: (1) renewing AGOA in order to improve African access to the U.S. market; (2) improving African infrastructure; (3) utilizing assistance to improve market "synergies"; (4) improving "supply chains" and "trade capacity building"; and (5) developing "new markets" for the continent. As trade improved, the Obama administration began the Young African Leaders Initiative and Power Africa programs. Power Africa attempted to provide electricity to some sixty million homes across the continent, and the Young African Leaders Initiative sought five hundred fellowships in leadership development at American universities. Some fifty thousand applications to the latter program were offered.[5]

Security Assistance to Africa under Obama

Of all types of aid, including economic, social, and political, security is the single largest category of assistance from the United States to the nations of Africa. Following the bombings of the American embassies in Kenya and Tanzania by al-Qaeda terrorists on August 7, 1998, U.S. security aid increased dramatically—and has continued to play a major role since the beginning of the Global War on Terror. Several indigenous groups, including al-Shabaab (Somalia), al-Qaeda in the Islamic Maghreb (AQIM), and Boko Haram (Nigeria), have continued to bring security threats and challenges to the region.

Al-Shabaab is a terrorist organization based on the Horn of Africa. It actively recruits militants from Somalia and Somali immigrants in the United States. Its activities during the civil war in Somalia were evinced by the October 1993 attack on U.S. Army Rangers in which eighteen were killed in Mogadishu and later in the August 1998 attacks on the American embassies in Nairobi and Dar es Salaam, famously chronicled in the book and movie *Black Hawk Down*. Al-Shabaab was responsible for an attempted assassination of Egyptian president Hosni Mubarak in December 1995. On September 21, 2013, al-Shabaab attacked a shopping mall in Nairobi and killed an estimated sixty-seven people, including sixty-two civilians, four al-Shabaab militants, and five members of Kenya's military. Some two hundred were wounded in the subsequent shoot-out.[6]

Al-Shabaab was founded as a youth arm of the Islamic Courts Union (ICU), which emerged as a politico-legal organization after the fall of the Barre regime in 1991 in Somalia out of the civil war in that country. The ICU controlled Mogadishu at that time. Eventually, the ICU left the capital, and by 2006 another civil conflict ensued. But by August 2006 the ICU eventually gained control of the area and reopened the airport and the port in the capital.[7]

In 2009, al-Shabaab broke away from ICU and Sharif Ahmed, ICU's leader and the head of the Somalia transitional government. Al-Shabaab engaged in wanton terrorist activity against not only government leaders in Somalia but also Kenyan military targets, even after the Kenyan military withdrew from the Somalia conflict. In 2011 and 2012, al-Shabaab worked with international pirates in the Indian Ocean to carry out seaborne attacks on merchant ships from the West and East. Al-Shabaab's officials "divided the world into two irreconcilable poles—*Dar ul Harb* (Abode of War) and *Dar ul Islam* (Abode of Islam)—and proclaimed non-Muslims as existential enemies."[8] Engaged in insurgency activities, al-Shabaab continues to undermine the governments of eastern Africa by engaging in terrorism and armed conflict.

In mid-2012 al-Shabaab joined with AQIM and Boko Haram to train together, share weapons, and align tactics,[9] and by 2015 al-Shabaab was aligned with the Islamic State of Iraq and the Levant (ISIL). In late May 2019 U.S. AFRICA COMMAND IN GERMANY was coordinating U.S. airstrikes against Islamic State-Somalia and al-Shabaab terrorists when three al-Shabaab militants were killed by airstrikes in the Golis Mountains on May 28, 2019. It was the sixth airstrike by American warplanes that month. Al-Shabaab was operating in the rural areas of Somalia, with IS-Somalia operating in the north of the fragmented nation-state in the Puntland region and stretching into the southern part of Somalia. Although numbering only a few hundred members, IS-Somalia fought against al-Shabaab in Somalia in 2018 and 2019.[10]

Boko Haram, whose name literally means "Western education is forbidden," was founded in 2002. This terrorist organization is from the northern part of Nigeria, particularly the states of Bauchi, Borno, Kaduna, Kano, and Yobe. The goal of Boko Haram is to institute Sharia (Islamic) law in these Nigerian states, where the organization operates. It is one of the more militant groups in the Sahel region of northern Africa, which includes, from west to east, the north of sub-Saharan Africa in the borderlands of the middle to southern parts of Chad, Eritrea, Ethiopia, Mali, Mauritania, Niger, and South Sudan, and Sudan, as well as the northern parts of Burkina Faso, Nigeria, Senegal. In Nigeria, a state divided equally along Christian and Muslim ethnoreligious lines, Boko Haram has exploited this historical dichotomy by increasing its terrorist activity and insurgency in the northern regions. Boko Haram's terrorist activities have also bled into neighboring states, such as Cameroon, and even affected state militaries.

Boko Haram was founded by Mohammed Yusuf, a devotee of Salafism, a puritanical and orthodox form of Sunni Islam that has its roots in Saudi Wahhabism. At its founding the group appeared peaceful, but it became more kinetic, and since the Nigerian army killed Yusuf in 2009, over two million persons have been displaced by the militant organization. By 2018, some thirty-seven thousand individuals had been killed by Boko Haram in its jihad against the Nigerian government under Yusuf's successor, Abubakar Shekau. Shekau, who had led Boko Haram since 2009, died from an apparent suicide in May 2021. More than one thousand children have been kidnapped in northeastern Nigeria by the militant group since 2013. The election of Muslim president Muhammadu Buhari, a former Nigerian general, in 2015 and the end of Christian president Goodluck Jonathan's tenure gave hope for peace as Jonathan had increased the military presence and activity in the north.

Although President Buhari was Islamic, his presidency saw continued counterinsurgency against Boko Haram. Continued violence plagues the region, and Boko Haram is now allegedly divided in two camps: one allegiant to Shekau and another led by Abu Abdullah Ibn Umar al-Barnawi, the alleged son of Yusuf. Al-Barnawi leads the Islamic State of West Africa Province.[11] This latter group affiliated with ISIL in 2015.

Another terrorist network that operates in the Sahel of northern Africa is AQIM. This group is focused on the overthrow of the government of Algeria. AQIM emerged in the post–September 11 context but has faced many transitions. It changed its name from the Salafist Group for Preaching and Combat and adopted AQIM. Made up mainly of Algerian, Saharan (including the Tuareg and Berabiche clans from Mali), and Moroccan militants, the group has links to ISIL and al-Shabaab. The organization is well funded due to its ability to kidnap foreigners and demand ransoms. The French military has engaged in assorted paramilitary actions to free hostages being held by AQIM. Western tourists were abducted in Tombouctou, Mali, in 2015, with two eventually released and one killed.[12] AQIM has used suicide bombings and attacks on military installations and personnel in Algeria, Burkina Faso, and Mali since 2007.

President Donald Trump and Africa

The death of ISIL leader Abu Bakr al-Baghdadi and the withdrawal of American forces from Syria in October 2019 gave hope for stability in the counterinsurgency against militant organizations in the Sahel region of Africa. Yet ISIL persevered, even if in fragmented form. And the uncoordinated release of ISIL and al-Qaeda prisoners and various "jailbreaks" in Iraq, along with Syrian strongman Bashir Assad's release of jihadi terrorists, may have led to further destabilization in the region.[13]

The Trump administration (2017–21) based its counterterrorism policy on its relationship with Saudi Arabia, the home of Islam's holiest sites in Mecca and Medina and the birthplace of the prophet Muhammad, the founder of Islam in the sixth century. Oil was discovered on the Arabian Peninsula in the late 1930s, making the region a central priority of the developed world. Today, Saudis produce around six million barrels a day in 2020 and hold 17 percent of the world's oil reserves. The importance of oil as a political and economic carrot reverberates into the Sahel and into the terrorist insurgencies there and in the Horn of Africa.

It is interesting to note that since President Trump himself stated that he wanted to lessen foreign aid to African states and remove American troops from African soil, U.S. security and development policy would be challenged, especially in combatting the insurgency of indigenous militant and jihadist

groups in the Maghreb, Sahel, and Horn of Africa.[14] President Trump did not
visit the African continent while in office, though First Lady Melania Trump
came in April 2019 to promote the Women's Global Development and Prosperity initiative. This initiative is funded through the U.S. Agency for International
Development and hopes to "empower 50 million women through employment
and economic stability by 2025." The First Lady visited Ethiopia, Egypt, Ghana,
Kenya, and Malawi in 2018 to promote the initiative and boost U.S. relations
with African states.[15]

Development, Security, and U.S.-Africa Relations

As political scientist Howard J. Wiarda has argued, various models of economic and political development in Africa have been problematic. The continent was greatly abused by Western imperialism and colonialism with "artificial boundaries" imposed by the colonial powers. Once postcolonialism was
achieved in the 1950s and 1960s, the models of development became an issue given that they did not work in indigenous contexts. Afro-centric models of development in the political and economic spheres did not always work.
Into the 1980s, democratization and privatization had some successes in African states, but their long-term development was difficult to assess.[16] According to political scientist Francis Fukuyama, economic growth rates in Africa
averaged 4.6 percent per year from 2001 to 2011. Growth in countries such as
Nigeria and Angola (both oil-producing states) was tied to general commodity demand from important emerging markets such as China.[17] The history of
"indirect rule" in Africa is tied to "neopatrimonialism," in which the personal
nature of leadership is emphasized. As Fukuyama states, "Virtually all African
postcolonial political systems were presidential rather than parliamentary, and
all presidents were male." Fukuyama discusses how these presidents used "state
resources" to develop political support. Although patronage is part and parcel
of state systems in the West, Fukuyama mentions that "Mobutu's Zaire, for example, had six hundred thousand names on the civil service payroll, when the
World Bank estimated it needed no more than fifty thousand."[18]

Fukuyama argues that the weakness of state capacity includes the limited
ability to carry out more robust taxation and the inability of the central government to control resources or control all areas of the country. Of course, the
era of colonialism and imperialism created a context of weakness that African
states have never been able to fully overcome, and the era undercut "existing
traditional sources of authority while failing to implant anything like a modern state that could survive the transition to independence."[19] The weakness of
indirect rule during the colonial era under the British in several African states
militated against a strong state and put the cart before the horse as British le-

gal customs were placed ahead of indigenous institutions in terms of bureaucratic machinery and educational institutions. Instead of focusing on state infrastructure, the British focused on tribal allegiances and rule by strongmen in
a weak, indirect manner. Despite the negatives of weaker states in Africa, the
localized "buy-in" was at times helpful, and Fukuyama suggests that a mixed
legacy persists.[20]

The legacy of British colonialism and other Western powers (such as
France and Germany) in the non-Western world is problematic when review-
ing the "weak state, strong society" paradigm.[21] Areas like India and Pakistan
were historically difficult to govern under the British during the era of colonialism. The post–September 11 world saw a good 40 to 50 percent of Pakistan controlled not actually by the government in Islamabad but by warlords
and nonstate actors. Likewise, in Africa, as Fukuyama recognizes under indirect rule, a similar legacy including tribalism has persisted in some regions
and negatively affected development. However, in the postcolonial era, greater
state consolidation did occur, and the adaptation of new mobile technologies,
including mobile phones, led markets in Africa to grow and adapt better than
many Western areas. Moreover, the West has focused more on human rights,
even if superficially, and the issues that terrorist organizations and problematic
nonstate actors present in Africa have gotten onto the radar not only due to the
growth of new technologies and social media but also due to concerns for the
welfare of Africans.

Social-media-driven activism was seen after 2003 with the Invisible Children campaign and the Kony 2012 initiative, which aimed at stopping the ab-
duction of child soldiers in Uganda and bringing Joseph Kony, leader of the
Lord's Resistance Army (LRA) and indicted war criminal, to justice. Although
both were heavily criticized by Africans themselves for trivializing human
rights issues related to these causes, both drew overwhelming recognition via
social media and millions tweeted, engaged, and helped bring attention to the
human rights crisis tied to Kony in the northeast of Africa.

The founder of the Kony 2012 movement, Jason Russell, released a thirty-
minute video on Kony and the LRA, garnering a hundred million views. The vi-
ral video led to massive interest but also led to problems including the inability
of the Kony 2012 movement to handle the demand for information or to deal
with criticism from Africans and others who saw the movement as a Western,
postcolonial attempt to dictate to Africans how to live and react to internal African issues.[22] The movement collapsed. However, it did bring to the fore the
importance of American foreign policy in Africa and the significance of West-
erners focusing more on assisting Africans and their states in developing and
combatting challenges within their countries and societies.

Conclusion

Security in Africa will continue to be an important issue. The United States and the West have offered inconsistent aid and diplomatic relationships to African governments in the areas of security and development. Military assistance has evolved since the Cold War to include economic assistance and continued aid and initiatives focused on investing in African human capital and empowerment. However, inconsistency between U.S. presidential administrations continues. The challenge for the future of U.S. relations with African nations, and Western investment more broadly, is to understand the importance of developmental, economic, political, and security challenges in Africa and address them with an African-centered approach rather than merely treating the African states as pawns in a broader geopolitical configuration. Helping to develop the peoples and nations of the world's second largest continent, allowing it to grow into its potential, and recognizing its place as a shareholder in global security rank among the developed world's greatest challenges of this century.

Notes

1. John G. Stoessinger, *The Might of Nations* (New York: McGraw-Hill, 1993), 370–71.
2. Alexander De Waal, *Evil Days* (New York: Human Rights Watch, 1991), 16.
3. Daniel Egbe, "U.S.-Africa Policy under the Obama Presidency," *Current Politics and Economics of Africa* 8, no. 1 (2015): 10.
4. Ibid., 11.
5. Ibid., 13.
6. Dennis Okari, "Kenya's Westgate Attack: Unanswered Questions One Year On," *BBC News*, September 21, 2014, https://www.bbc.com/news/world-africa-29282045.
7. "First Ship Arrives in Mogadishu," *BBC News*, August 25, 2006, http://news.bbc.co.uk/2/hi/africa/5279414.stm.
8. Paul D. Williams and Matt McDonald, eds., *Security Studies: An Introduction* (London: Routledge, 2018), 182.
9. David Lerman, "African Terrorist Group Starting to Cooperate, U.S. Says," *Bloomberg News*, June 25, 2012, www.businessweek.com/news/2012-06-25/african-terrorist-groups-starting-to-cooperate-u-dot-s-dot-says.
10. Kyle Rempfer, "U.S. Airstrikes Interrupt ISIS and al-Shabaab Battleground," *Military Times*, May 29, 2019, www.militarytimes.com/news/your-army/2019/05/29/us-airstrikes-interrupt-isis-and-al-shabaab-battleground/.
11. Jideofor Adibe, "How Boko Haram Has Evolved over the Past Ten Years," *The Conversation*, November 13, 2019, https://theconversation.com/how-boko-haram-has-evolved-over-the-past-ten-years-126436.
12. "Al Qaeda Hostage Sjaak Rijke Freed by French Forces in Mali," *NBC News*, April 6, 2015, https://nbcnews.com/news/world/al-qaeda-hostage-sjaak-rijke-freed-french-forces-mali-n336406.
13. H. R. McMaster, *Battlegrounds: The Fight to Defend the Free World* (New York: Harper, 2020), 281.

250 Daniel Egbe and Kurt W. Jefferson

14. John Bolton, *The Room Where It Happened: A White House Memoir* (New York: Simon & Schuster, 2020), 427–34.

15. Landry Signé, "A Trump Visit to Africa Is Important—and Carries Some Urgency" (Brookings Institute, April 19, 2019), www.brookings.edu/opinions/a-trump-visit-to-africa-is-important-and-carries-some-urgency/amp/.

16. Howard J. Wiarda with Esther M. Skelley, *Comparative Politics: Approaches and Issues* (Lanham, Md.: Rowman & Littlefield, 2007), 117–18.

17. Francis Fukuyama, *Political Order and Political Decay: From the Industrial Revolution to the Globalization of Democracy* (New York: Farrar, Straus and Giroux, 2014), 285.

18. Ibid., 288.

19. Ibid., 291–92.

20. Ibid., 308.

21. See Joel S. Migdal, *Strong Societies and Weak States: State-Society Relations and State Capabilities in the Third World* (Princeton, N.J.: Princeton University Press, 1988).

22. Jeremy Heimans and Henry Timms, *New Power: How Power Works in Our Hyperconnected World—and How to Make It Work for You* (New York: Doubleday, 2018), 101–10.

The U.S. Sees al Qaeda as Terrorism, and We Consider the Drones Terrorism

EXCERPT FROM *DIRTY WARS: THE WORLD IS A BATTLEFIELD*

Jeremy Scahill

YEMEN, LATE 2011—While the Obama administration was basking in the success of the bin Laden killing and JSOC and the CIA were closing in on Anwar Awlaki, the Arab uprisings were spreading. Three weeks after the raid in Abbottabad, Pakistan, President Ali Abdullah Saleh's government in Yemen was on the brink of collapse. The protests were growing and President Saleh had played almost every card he had to keep the Americans on his side. He had given the U.S. counterterrorism machine a virtual free hand to bomb Yemen and opened the doors wide for the evolution of a not-so-covert war. But as his grip on power weakened, AQAP saw opportunity to the chaos. By the summer of 2011, the elite U.S.-backed counterterrorism units were pulled away from the fight against AQAP to defend the regime from its own people. In southern Yemen, where AQAP had its strongest presence, the mujahedeen sought to take advantage of an imploding state whose leaders had earned a reputation for corruption as they failed to provide basic goods and services.

On May 27, 2011, several hundred militants laid siege to Zinjibar, thirty miles northeast of the strategically important southern city of Aden, killing several soldiers, driving out local officials and taking control of the city within two days. Who exactly these militants were was a matter of some dispute. According to the Yemeni government, they were AQAP operatives. But the militants who took the city did not claim to be from AQAP. Instead, they announced themselves as a new group, Ansar al Sharia, or Supporters of Sharia. Senior Yemeni officials told me that Ansar al Sharia was simply a front for al Qaeda. They pointed out that the first known public reference to the group was made a month before the attack on Zinjibar by AQAP's top cleric, Adil al Abab. "The name Ansar al Sharia is what we use to introduce ourselves in areas where we work to tell people about our work and goals, and that we are on the path of Allah," he said, adding that the new name was intended to put the focus on the message of the group so as to avoid the associations of the al Qaeda brand.

Whether Ansar al Sharia had more independent origins or was merely a prod-uct of AQAP's crude rebranding campaign, as Abab claimed, the group's signif-icance would soon extend well beyond al Qaeda's historically limited spheres of influence in Yemen, while simultaneously popularizing some of AQAP's core tenets.

Months after Zinjibar was taken, I traveled to Aden, Yemen, where I met the Yemeni general whose job it was to retake the areas seized by Ansar al Sha-ria. General Mohammed al Sumali sat in the passenger seat of his armored Toyota Land Cruiser as it whizzed down the deserted highway connecting Aden to Abyan Province, where the Islamist militants had overrun Zinjibar. Sumali, a heavyset man with glasses and a mustache, was the commander of the 25th Mechanized Brigade of the Yemeni armed forces and the man charged with cleansing Zinjibar of the militants. Sumali's task carried international sig-nificance: retaking Zinjibar was seen by many as a final test of the flailing Saleh regime. The only real traffic on the road consisted of refugees fleeing the fight-ing and heading toward Aden, and military reinforcements moving toward Zinjibar. Sumali did not want to drive out to the front lines on the day I met him. "You know there could be mortars fired at you," he told me. Twice, the militants in Zinjibar had tried to assassinate the general in that very vehicle. There was a bullet hole in the front windshield, just above his head, and an-other in his side window, the spider-web cracks from the bullets' impact clearly visible. When I agreed not to hold him or his men responsible for what might happen, he relented, and we piled in and took off.

As we rode along the coast of the Arabian Sea, past stacks of abandoned mortar tubes, Russian T-72 tanks dug into sand berms and the occasional wan-dering camel, General Sumali gave me his account of what had happened on May 27, 2011, when Ansar al Sharia took the town. Sumali attributed the take-over to an "intelligence breakdown," explaining, "We were surprised in late May with the flow of a large number of terrorist militants into Zinjibar." He added that the militants "raided and attacked some security sites. They were able to seize these institutions. We were surprised when the governor, his dep-uties and other local officials fled to Aden." As the Yemeni military began fight-ing the militants, General Sumali told me, troops from Yemen's Central Secu-rity Forces fled, abandoning heavy weaponry as they retreated. The CSF, whose counterterrorism unit was armed, trained and funded by the United States, was commanded by President Saleh's nephew Yahya. A media outlet associated with the militants reported that Ansar's forces seized "heavy artillery pieces, modern antiaircraft weapons, a number of tanks and armoured transports in addition to large quantities of different kinds of ammunition."

Sumali said that as his forces attempted to repel the attack on Zinjibar a week later, they were attacked by the militants using the artillery seized from the CSF units. "Many of my men were killed," he told me. The Islamist fighters also conducted a series of bold raids on the base of the 25th Mechanized on the southern outskirts of Zinjibar. In all, more than 230 Yemeni soldiers died in battles with the militants in under a year. "These guys are incredibly brave," the general conceded, speaking of the militants. "If I had an army full of men with that bravery, I could conquer the world."

Sumali said Zinjibar fell because of bad intelligence, but critics of the crumbling Saleh regime told me a different story. They alleged that President Saleh's forces allowed the city to fall. The fighting there began as Saleh faced mounting calls both inside and outside Yemen for his resignation. Several of his key allies had defected to the growing opposition movement. After thirty-three years of outwitting his opponents, they said, Saleh saw that the end was near. "Saleh himself actually handed over Zinjibar to these militants," charged Abdul Ghani al Iryani, a well-connected political analyst. "He ordered his police force to evacuate the city and turn it over to the militants because he wanted to send a signal to the world that, without me, Yemen will fall into the hands of the terrorists." That theory, while unproven, was not baseless. Ever since the mujahedeen war against the Soviets in Afghanistan in the 1980s and continuing after 9/11, Saleh has famously milked the threat of al Qaeda and other militants to leverage counterterrorism funding and weapons from the United States and Saudi Arabia to bolster his power within the country and neutralize opponents. A Yemeni government official, who asked to remain anonymous because he was not authorized to speak publicly about military issues, admitted that troops from the U.S.-trained and -supported Republican Guard did not respond when the militants entered the town. Those forces were commanded by Saleh's son Ahmed Ali Saleh. Neither did those forces loyal to one of the most powerful military figures in the country, General Ali Mohsen, commander of the 1st Armored Division, move in. Two months before Zinjibar was seized, Mohsen had defected from the Saleh regime and was publicly supporting his overthrow.

General Sumali told me he could not "confirm or deny" that Ansar al Sharia was actually AQAP. "What is important for me, as a soldier, is that they have taken up arms against us. Anyone who is attacking our institutions and military camps and killing our soldiers, we will fight them regardless of if they are al Qaeda affiliates or Ansar al Sharia," he told me. "We don't care what they call themselves. And I can't confirm whether Ansar al Sharia is affiliated with al Qaeda or if they are an independent group."

Rather than fighting AQAP, the elite U.S.-backed Yemeni units—created and funded with explicit intent to be used only for counterterrorism operations—redeployed to Sana'a to protect the collapsing regime from its own people. The U.S.-supported units existed "mostly for the defense of the regime," said Iryani. "In the fighting in Abyan, the counterterrorism forces have not been deployed in any effective way. They are still here in the palace [in Sana'a], protecting the palace. That's how it is." At the time, John Brennan acknowledged that the "political tumult" had abused the U.S.-trained units "to be focused on their positioning for internal political purposes as opposed to doing all they can against AQAP." So it was left to General Sumali and his conventional forces to fight the Islamists who had taken over Zinjibar.

As we passed the first front line on the outskirts of Zinjibar, "Tiger 1," and drove a half mile to "Tiger 2," Sumali agreed to let me get out of the vehicle. "We will only stay for two minutes," he told me. "It's dangerous here." The general was soon besieged by his men. They looked thin and haggard, many with long beards and tattered uniforms or no uniforms at all. Some of them pleaded with Sumali to write them notes authorizing additional combat pay. One of the soldiers told him, "I was with you when you were ambushed. I helped fight off the attack." Sumali scribbled on a piece of paper and handed it to the solider. The scene continued until Sumali got back into the Toyota. As we drove away, he spoke from his armored vehicle through a loudspeaker at his men. "Keep fighting. Do not give up!"

Whether it was a crass ploy on the part of a failing regime to allow the militants to overrun Zinjibar or an opportunistic power grab by AQAP, the taking of several towns across southern Yemen by Islamist forces was significant. Unlike the militant movement al Shabab in Somalia, AQAP had never taken control of significant swaths of territory in Yemen. But Ansar al Sharia was determined to do just that, declaring an Islamic emirate in Abyan. Once Ansar al Sharia and its allies solidified their grip on Zinjibar, they implemented an agenda aimed at winning popular support. "Ansar al Sharia has been much more proactive in attempting to provide services in areas in Yemen where the government has virtually disappeared," Johnsen, the Yemen scholar at Princeton University, told me at the time. "It has claimed that it is following the Taliban model in attempting to provide services and Islamic government where the central government in Yemen has left a vacuum."

Ansar al Sharia repaired roads, restored electricity, distributed food and began security patrols inside the city and its surroundings. It also established Sharia courts where disputes could be resolved. "Al Qaeda and Ansar al Sharia brought security to the people in areas that were famous for insecurity, famous for thefts, for roadblocks," said Abdul Rezzaq al Jamal, the independent Yemeni journalist who regularly interviewed al Qaeda leaders and had spent extensive time in Zinjibar. "The people I met in Zinjibar were grateful to al Qaeda and Ansar al Sharia for maintaining security." Although the militants in Abyan brought law and order, the policies were, at times, enforced with brutal tactics such as limb amputations against accused thieves and public floggings of suspected drug users. In one incident in the Ansar al Sharia–held town of Jaar, residents said they were summoned to a gruesome event at which militants used a sword to chop off the hands of two young men accused of stealing electrical cables. The amputated hands were then paraded around the town as a warning to would-be thieves. One of the young men, a fifteen-year-old, reportedly died soon after from blood loss. In another incident, Ansar al Sharia in Jaar publicly beheaded two men it alleged had provided information to the United States to conduct drone strikes. A third man was executed in Shabwah.

AQAP took advantage of the Yemeni government's unpopularity, shrewdly recognizing that its message of a Sharia-based system of law and order would be welcomed by many in Abyan who viewed the Saleh regime as a U.S. puppet. The U.S. missile strikes, the civilian casualties, an almost total lack of government services and a deepening poverty all helped create the opportunity AQAP seized. "As these groups of militants took over the city, then AQAP came in and also tribes from areas that have been attacked in the past by the Yemeni government and by the U.S. government," Iryani, the Yemeni political analyst, told me. "They came because they have a feud against the regime and against the U.S. There is a nucleus of AQAP, but the vast majority are people who are aggrieved by attacks on their homes that forced them to go out and fight."

As Ansar al Sharia took control of towns in the south, Washington debated how to respond. Some within the Obama administration agitated for the United States to jump into the fight. General James Mattis, who took over from Petraeus as CENTCOM commander, proposed that the president sign off on a massive air assault on the "Unity" Soccer Stadium on the outskirts of Zinjibar, where Ansar al Sharia fighters had created a makeshift base from which to attack the Yemeni military. President Obama shot down the proposal. "We're not in Yemen to get involved with some domestic conflict," the president said. "We're going to continue to stay focused on threats to the homeland—that's where the real priority is."

Instead, the United States would fly supply runs into southern Yemen via helicopter to back up General Sumali's conventional forces. The Americans also provided real-time intelligence, obtained by drones, to Yemeni forces in Abyan. "It has been an active partnership. The Americans help primarily with logistics and intelligence," Sumali told me. "Then we pound the positions with artillery or air strikes." On a few occasions, Sumali told me, the United States conducted unilateral strikes around Zinjibar that "targeted al Qaeda leaders who are on the U.S. terrorist black list," though he added, "I did not coordinate directly in these attacks." As cities throughout southern Yemen began to fall to Ansar al Sharia and the Saleh regime crumbled, in late 2011, the Obama administration decided to pull out most of the U.S. military personnel in Yemen, including those training Yemen's counterterrorism forces. "They have left because of the security situation," Abu Bakr al Qirbi, Yemen's foreign minister, told me at the time. "Certainly, I think if they do not return and the counterterrorism units are not provided with the necessary ammunition and equipment, it will have an impact" on counterterrorism operations.

The United States was shifting tactics. With the Saleh regime severely weakened, the Obama administration calculated that it had little to gain from that alliance at this stage. The United States would double down on its use of air power and drones, striking in Yemen at will to carry on its campaign against AQAP. The Obama administration began quick construction of a secret air base in Saudi Arabia, closer than its base in Djibouti, that could serve as a launching pad for expanded drone strikes in Yemen. Target number one remained the same: Anwar Awlaki.

The key to accomplishing anything in Yemen is navigating its labyrinthine tribal system. For years, a tribal patronage network helped bolster Saleh's regime. Many tribes had a neutral view of AQAP or saw it as a minor nuisance; some fought against al Qaeda forces, though others gave them safe haven or shelter. The stance of many tribes toward al Qaeda depended on how they believed AQAP could forward or hurt their agendas.

But the Obama administration's Yemen policy had enraged many tribal leaders who could potentially keep AQAP in check and, over the course of three years of regular bombings, had taken away the motivation for many leaders to do so. Several southern leaders angrily told me stories of U.S. and Yemeni attacks in their areas that killed civilians and livestock and destroyed or damaged scores of homes. If anything, the U.S. air strikes and support for Saleh-family-run counterterrorism units had increased tribal sympathy for al Qaeda. "Why should we fight them? Why?" asked Ali Abdullah Abdulsalam, a southern tribal sheikh from Shabwah who adopted the nom de guerre Mullah Zabara, out of admiration, he told me, for Taliban leader Mullah Mohammed Omar. "If my government built schools, hospitals and roads and met basic needs, I would be loyal to my government and protect it. So far, we don't have basic services such as electricity, water pumps. Why should we fight al Qaeda?" He told me that AQAP controlled large swaths of Shabwah, conceding that the group did "provide security and prevent looting. If your car is stolen, they will get it back for you." In areas "controlled by the government, there is looting and robbery. You can see the difference." Zabara added, "If we don't pay more attention, al Qaeda could seize and control more areas."

Zabara was quick to clarify that he believed AQAP was a terrorist group bent on attacking the United States, but that was hardly his central concern. "The U.S. sees al Qaeda as terrorism, and we consider the drones terrorism," he said. "The drones are flying day and night, frightening women and children, disturbing sleeping people. This is terrorism." Zabara told me that several U.S. strikes in his region had killed scores of civilians and that his community was littered with unexploded cluster bombs, which at times detonated, killing children. He and other tribal leaders asked the Yemeni and U.S. governments for assistance in removing them, he said. "We did not get any response, so we use our guns to explode them." He also said that the U.S. government should pay money to the families of civilians killed in the missile strikes of the past three years. "We demand compensation from the U.S. for killing Yemeni citizens, just like the Lockerbie case," he declared. "The world is one village. The U.S. received compensation from Libya for the Lockerbie bombing, but the Yemenis have not."

I met Mullah Zabara and his men at the airport in Aden, along the coast where the USS *Cole* was bombed in October 2000, killing seventeen U.S. sailors. Zabara was dressed in black tribal clothes, complete with a *jambiya*, the traditional dagger, at his stomach. He was also packing a Beretta on his hip. Zabara was a striking figure, with leathery skin and a large scar that formed a crescent moon along his right eye. "I don't know this American," he said to my Yemeni colleague. "So if anything happens to me as a result of this meeting—if I get kidnapped—we'll just kill you later." Everyone laughed nervously. We chatted for a while on a corniche, a cliffside road along the coast, before he drove us around the city for a tour. About twenty minutes into the tour, he pulled over on the side of the road and bought a six-pack of Heineken from a shanty store, tossing one to me before cracking open a can for himself. It was 11:00 a.m.

"Once I got stopped by AQAP guys at one of their checkpoints, and they saw I had a bottle of Johnnie Walker," he recalled as he guzzled his second Heineken in ten minutes and lit a cigarette. "They asked me, 'Why do you have that?' I told them, 'To drink it.'" He laughed heartily. "I told them to bother another guy and drove off." The message of the story was clear: the al Qaeda guys don't want trouble with tribal leaders. "I am not afraid of al Qaeda. I go to their sites and meet them. We are all known tribesmen, and they have to meet us to solve their disputes." Plus, he added, "I have 30,000 fighters in my own tribe. Al Qaeda can't attack me." Zabara served as a mediator with AQAP for the Yemeni government and was instrumental in securing the release of three French aid workers held hostage by the militant group for six months. Zabara was also asked by the Yemeni minister of defense to mediate with the militants in Zinjibar on several occasions, including to retrieve bodies of soldiers killed in areas held by Ansar al Sharia. "I have nothing against al Qaeda or the government," he told me. "I started the mediation in order to stop bloodshed and to achieve peace." In Zinjibar, his efforts were unsuccessful. He told me that while mediating, he met AQAP operatives from the United States, France, Pakistan and Afghanistan.

I asked him if he ever met with top AQAP leaders. "Fahd al Quso is from my tribe," he replied with a smile, referring to one of the most wanted suspects from the *Cole* bombing. "I saw [Said] al Shihri and [Nasir] al Wuhayshi five days ago in Shabwah," he casually added, referring to the two senior AQAP leaders, both of them U.S.-designated terrorists. "We were walking, and they said, 'Peace be upon you.' I replied, 'Peace be upon you, too.' We have nothing against them. In the past, it was unthinkable to run into them. They were hiding in the mountains and caves, but now they are walking in the streets and going to restaurants." "Why is that?" I asked. "The regime, the ministers and officials are squandering the money allocated to fight al Qaeda, while al Qaeda expands," he replied. The United States "funds the Political Security and the National Security [Forces], which spend money traveling here and there, in Sana'a or in the U.S., with their family. All the tribes get is air strikes against us." He added that counterterrorism "has become like an investment" for the U.S.-backed units. "If they fight seriously, the funds will stop. They prolonged the conflict with al Qaeda to receive more funds" from the United States. In January 2013, Zabara was assassinated in Abyan. It is unknown who killed him. That same month, the Yemeni government announced that Shihri had died "after succumbing to wounds received in a counter terrorism operation."

There is no doubt that when President Obama took office, al Qaeda had resurrected its shop in Yemen. But how big a threat AQAP actually posed to the United States or Saleh at that historical moment was the subject of much debate. What went almost entirely undiscussed in the U.S. discourse on AQAP and Yemen was whether U.S. actions—the targeted killings, the Tomahawk and drone strikes—might backfire, handing AQAP an opportunity to recruit and provoking the group to escalate its own violence. "We are not generating good will in these operations," Emile Nakhleh, the former senior CIA officer, told me. "We might target radicals and potential radicals, but unfortunately . . . other things and other people are being destroyed or killed. So, in the long run, it is not necessarily going to help. These operations will not necessarily help to deradicalize potential recruits. To me the bigger issue is the whole issue of radicalization. How do we pull the rug from under it?" He added: "These operations might be successful in specific cases, but I don't think they necessarily contribute to a deradicalization of certain segments of those societies."

Colonel Patrick Lang, who spent his entire career in covert operations leading sensitive missions, including in Yemen, told me that the threat posed by AQAP had been "greatly exaggerated as a threat to the United States. In fact, most Americans think that anything that might kill you personally, in an airplane or walking down Park Avenue or something, is the biggest threat in the world, right? Because they're not accustomed to dealing with conditions of danger as a standard of life, you know? So to say, 'Is AQAP a threat to the United States?' Yeah. They could bring down an airliner, kill a couple hundred people. But are they an existential threat to the United States? Of course not. Of course not. None of these people are an existential threat to the United States. We've gone crazy over this. We had this kind of hysterical reaction to danger."

———————————

In the same way that Afghanistan and Iraq provided a laboratory for training and developing a whole new generation of highly skilled, seasoned special operators, Yemen represented a paradigm that is sure to permeate U.S. national security policy for decades to come. It was under the Bush administration that the United States declared the world a battlefield where any country would be fair game for targeted killings, but it was President Obama who put a bipartisan stamp on this worldview that will almost certainly endure well beyond his time in office. "This is going to go on for a long time," said Lang. "The Global War on Terror has acquired a life of its own. It's a self-licking ice cream cone. And the fact that this counterterrorism/counterinsurgency industry evolved into this kind of thing, involving all these people, the foundations, and the journalists and the book writers, and the generals, and the guys doing the shooting— all of that together has a great, tremendous amount of inertia that tends to keep it going in the same direction." Lang added: "It continues to roll. It will take a conscious decision, on the part of civilian policy makers, somebody like the president, for example, to decide that 'ok, boys, the show's over.'" But Obama was far from deciding the show was over.

Note

From *Dirty Wars* by Jeremy Scahill, copyright © 2013. Reprinted by permission of Bold Type Books, an imprint of Hachette Book Group, Inc.

Study Abroad as American National and Human Security Necessity

Kurt W. Jefferson, Spalding University

JR Swanegan, University of Missouri–Columbia School of Law

Study abroad is a major and growing staple at almost every college and university in the United States and in other countries as well. Its role in helping foster cultural and international friendship and understanding is central to the globalization of higher education. It is also central to harmonious relations with nations that have both friendly and, at times, strained relationships. The argument in this essay is that study abroad as part of the broader American higher education and government context is a key component of a nation's ability to engage other nations and societies, thereby facilitating and advancing the goals of education, better interpersonal and cultural relationships, and improved government and economic interactions. This approach falls within the scope of what scholars call "soft power"—the view that a country's ideas or values may be attractive to other countries exclusive of military power or diplomatic bargaining strength.[1]

This essay explores the importance of study abroad in the global higher education context. Both authors have spent considerable time in guiding international student outreach and recruitment at various institutions. Both of us have served as senior international officers (sios) in guiding comprehensive internationalization efforts on campuses where we previously worked. Thus, we come to this chapter with both firsthand empirical knowledge of the merits of study abroad and an understanding of the operational aspects of study abroad and how it contributes to building community on college campuses. We also discuss how higher education is affected by globalization and how study abroad not only has become an increasingly important component of transnational cultural diplomacy in areas like business and higher education but also has increasingly affected American foreign relations and national security. Finally, the role of study abroad in a transnational world and the enhancement of national and global human security are discussed.

Global Higher Education and Study Abroad

Study abroad, which promotes global student mobility, is an important tool of cultural understanding. The former president of Goucher College, Sanford J. Ungar, makes a cogent case for study abroad as a national priority: "Given the United States' determination to project its hard and soft power and preserve its influence in a restless but interconnected world, the almost universal failure of the broader U.S. public to know and understand others, except through a military lens, is not just unfortunate but also dangerous. . . . Luckily, there exists a disarmingly simple way to help address this problem and to produce future generations of Americans who will know more and care more about the rest of the world: massively increase the number of U.S. college and university students who go abroad." Prior to the COVID-19 pandemic beginning in 2020, just over 300,000 students from American institutions of higher education studied abroad. This is about 1.5 percent of all students studying in the United States. Compare this to the number of students from other countries studying in the United States. Numbers of students studying abroad grew up to 2019, but a combination of government policies and the evolving COVID-19 virus began to affect study abroad activities at American and global universities. In 2014–15, 975,000 students from abroad studied in the United States. One-third of these were from China. These numbers represent a 10 percent increase in students studying in the United States.[2]

An increasingly important issue for students going abroad is access and affordability. Many American and international students cannot afford study abroad programs. The global knowledge economy is a driver of educational development and various initiatives including study abroad. As Melissa Banks and Rajika Bhandari argue, the mobility of students across borders has increased due to "economic opportunity, political and economic security, cross-border trade, migration, tourism, and study and research."[3] Michael Crow, the president of Arizona State University, and William B. Dabars argue that elites in other nations want to emulate the American higher education model because it not only does a good job "educating students but also contributes inestimably to economic growth and competitiveness."[4]

Thus, the importance of connecting countries via study abroad programming cannot be underemphasized. In 2019, some one million students at American universities studied abroad which represents 5 percent of all students at American universities (twenty million). The COVID-19 pandemic altered this reality in 2020, but study abroad had gained in popularity as globalization became more ingrained in education in the West. In all, 5.5 percent of all students in the United States are international students.[5] The growth of students from multiple corners of the world on many campuses has served to assist universities in maintaining their academic programs, building an appreciation for cultural diversity, and introducing American students and citizens to students from various cultures around the world. Many American campuses have invested much in scholarships for both international and domestic students, to have students coming to and from campus.

Westminster College, a 170-year-old institution in the heart of the United States, in the small midwestern town of Fulton, Missouri (population thirteen thousand), built a signature program, the "Take-A-Friend-Home" (TAFH) program, whereby an American student hosted an international students for two weeks and then both students would hop on an airplane to the international student's homeland and spend two weeks learning from the host student's family. This program began in 2008 and provided up to eight students per year the opportunity to engage in a simple yet direct cultural and international exchange. Upon returning from the TAFH experience, students took a one-hour elective course in international studies and reflected on their experiences by writing a journal while abroad, making an in-depth presentation, and promoting the experience on social media.

For this program Westminster won the second-ever Innovation Award in Internationalization from the Association of International Education Administrators in 2016. Students from Little Rock, St. Louis, Detroit, Fulton, Columbia (Mo.), and small farm towns traveled domestically to these locales plus many important international destinations including Kathmandu, Ulaanbaatar, Cape Town, Sarajevo, Beijing, and Male (Maldives). These types of exchanges built not only academic understanding but also more personalized and cultural understanding where families helped look after students, and this type of human security is instrumental to building long-term trust and security in a world where borders have shrunk and transnational interactions are becoming the norm.

Stetson University College of Law in Gulfport, Florida (the oldest school of law in the state of Florida), implemented a JD/Grado Program with the University of Granada in Granada, Spain. This program allowed for an exchange of U.S. and Spanish law students to spend two years at the host institution and earn both a JD (U.S. law degree) and Grado (Spanish law degree) in four years. Students were introduced to both common law and civil law principles in their learning, with the added cultural benefits of studying alongside of American students at Stetson and Spanish students in Granada. Stetson provided additional cultural support to our students from Granada through a formalized peer mentoring program where we paired the students with a U.S. student ambassador. These students also participated in some traditional U.S. activities including attendance at a Stetson University football game, pumpkin carving in the fall, and a job shadow with a local U.S. judge. Stetson's students in Granada were paired with Spanish roommates and were appointed a Spanish faculty mentor to assist with acclimation, course selection, and understanding of the Spanish classroom experience.

The importance of collaboration and networking in a global community (as evinced by Westminster College and Stetson University's international study programs that both of the authors helped organize and run) are signs of the continued globalized age in which we live. The fact that study abroad is now more accessible and affordable for the average student suggests that it is becoming more of a requirement for earning a college degree and demonstrating cultural literacy and competency. Some universities now require students to have a study away (if not overt study abroad) experience.

Prior to 2017, study abroad continued to grow, and its growth was a positive for universities and students in terms of both educational outcomes and economic advantages. The executive orders of President Donald J. Trump attempting to keep terrorists and undocumented aliens from entering the United States had an impact on study abroad. Both short-term and longer-term programs were affected. A tightening of the issuing of visas by American embassies and consulates abroad had an impact on students from other nations wanting to study in the United States. The president issued an executive order in January 2017 focused on foreign nationals overstaying their visas. A year later, the Trump administration (2017–21) began to crack down on students staying over on F1 visas.[6]

The diminished study abroad opportunities due to recent U.S. policy changes were exacerbated by the COVID-19 pandemic, which forced five thousand U.S. institutions of higher education, twenty million university students, and one million faculty members to meet fully online within a matter of ten days after March 12, 2020—the single largest transformation and mobilization operationally of higher education since 1942 after the bombing of Pearl Harbor, when American universities were transitioned into military training centers for the war effort.[7]

Human Security as National Security

Study abroad is important from an intellectual development perspective. Most American and international policymakers now interact in "functionalist" networks (to allude to the scholarly work of political scientist David Mitrany) to learn from each other and improve their areas of governance (see Anne-Marie Slaughter's *New World Order* [2004]). According to Slaughter, the world is collapsing into greater order due to decentralization and the power of networks.

The nation that sent the most international students to the United States, around 360,000 in recent years, was China. In May 2020, the Trump administration announced that it would cancel the visas of around three thousand Chinese graduate students due to concerns over sensitive information getting into the hands of these students and researchers. As the *New York Times* said, "It portends possible further educational restrictions, and the Chinese government could retaliate by imposing its own visa or educational bans on Americans. The two nations have already engaged in rounds of retribution over policies involving trade, technology and media access, and relations are at their worst point in decades."[8]

Although the threats from the People's Liberation Army and its intelligence arms are real, seeing the forest for the trees on internationalization on college campuses is important. An added level of both physical and cyber-related security and greater scrutiny of international students as people first (as students, as contributors to the campus vitality, and as citizens of the campus) will help weed out those who may not be on an American or Western campus for the right reasons. Of course today smaller universities and units (like law schools and colleges of business administration within larger research universities) approach all students with more one-on-one care to help them (especially international students) feel at home and fit in.

Both authors of this chapter have run specialized programs for university- and professional-level students from outside the United States and have assisted in building a welcoming and safe space for those students to learn about not only the United States and the American academy but also the cities and regions where students were studying (i.e., Florida and Missouri). Both of the authors have experienced positive and negative issues and events, including seeing students from Nepal experience rural America and Chinese students spending the night in the emergency room of an American hospital due to an accident that could have had serious repercussions. As George Anders says in his excellent 2017 book *You Can Do Anything: The Surprising Power of a "Useless" Liberal Arts Education*, "more discussions, fewer lectures" and "greater roles for digital tools" will continue to allow study abroad and intercultural and international experiences to become part of an integrated effort at providing increased human security in an insecure time.[9]

The importance of social entrepreneurship, as Anders discusses, is another nod to the significance of study abroad. For the average undergraduate and graduate student, studying abroad takes courage—and planning, vision, organization, commitment, reliance, independence, intellect, and initiative. These are traits that a liberal arts education has taught since the Middle Ages, evinced today in the reification of critical thinking on college campuses. Innovative thinking, curiosity, and critical thinking will assist students in growing as both global actors and thinkers.

Educational entrepreneur Matt Murrie and computer architecture expert Andrew McHugh discuss the importance of staying curious in getting students in K–12 and university-level studies to think about how asking "what if?" questions will stoke curiosity in learning about not only foreign lands but also how to conceptualize imponderables that will help students once they find themselves abroad.[10]

Conclusion

In this book, political scientist Kali Wright-Smith discusses the importance of international law as a framework of human security. Political scientists Tobias T. Gibson and Kurt W. Jefferson discuss human security in the context of understanding the study of security studies. Daily security issues related to food scarcity, water potability, access to education and transportation, and freedom from the threat of physical violence are things that many in our world face on a continual basis. These are manifest in the United Nations' Sustainable Development Goals. Citizens of the world having a chance to study in another country and develop academic, personal, and cultural ties with those from different places will bring about greater understanding and will decrease violence and harm. Former university SIOs Gilbert W. Merkx and Riall W. Nolan state, "The expansion of transnational networks not only drives globalization but also exerts continuing pressure for the internationalization of higher education." They argue that with 81 percent of students entering university saying they want to study abroad, internationalization will grow and that study abroad programs are "only one aspect of international education. Other forms of overseas student experience, such as participation in overseas research projects, internships, or other service-learning experiences, are also valuable."[11]

Study abroad and affiliated activities should continue to be supported at both state and national levels and in the private sector. If support for study abroad continues, nations will be able to work to make study abroad a national and international priority as it is inextricably linked to national and global security.

Notes

1. Joseph S. Nye Jr., *Soft Power: The Means to Success in World Politics* (New York: PublicAffairs, 2005).

2. Sanford J. Ungar, "The Study Abroad Solution: How to Open the American Mind," *Foreign Affairs*, March/April 2016, www.foreignaffairs.com/articles/united-states/2016-02-16/study-abroad-solution%3famp.

3. Melissa Banks and Rajika Bhandari, "Global Student Mobility," in *The SAGE International Higher Education Handbook*, ed. Darla K. Deardorff et al. (Thousand Oaks, Calif.: SAGE, 2012), 379.

4. Michael M. Crow and William B. Dabars, *Designing the New American University* (Baltimore, Md.: Johns Hopkins University Press, 2015), 19.

5. Institute of International Education, "Number of International Students in the United States Hits an All-Time High" (2019), https://www.iie.org/Why-IIE /Announcements/2019/11/Number-of-international-Students-in-the-United-States -Hits-All-Time-High.

6. Erica L. Green, "Trump's Crackdown on Students Who Overstay Visas Rattles Higher Education," *New York Times*, May 24, 2018, www.nytimes.com/2018/05/24/us /politics/trump-crackdown-student-visas.amp.html.

7. Kurt W. Jefferson, "The New Normal in Higher Education? How the Coronavirus Has Changed Colleges," *Louisville Courier-Journal*, April 24, 2020, https://www.google .com/amp/s/amp.courier-journal.com/amp/3017526001.

8. Edward Wong and Julian E. Barnes, "U.S. to Expel Chinese Graduate Students with Ties to China's Military Schools," *New York Times*, May 28, 2020, www.nytimes .com/2020/05/28/us/politics/china-hong-kong-trump-student-visas.amp.html.

9. George Anders, *You Can Do Anything: The Surprising Power of a "Useless" Liberal Arts Education* (New York: Little, Brown, 2017), 239–40.

10. Matt Murrie and Andrew R. McHugh, *The Book of What If . . . ? Questions and Activities for Curious Minds* (New York: Aladdin, 2017).

11. Gilbert W. Merkx and Riall W. Nolan, eds., *Internationalizing the Academy: Lessons of Leadership in Higher Education* (Cambridge, Mass.: Harvard Education Press, 2015), 220–21.

Coming Challenges

CHINA'S TECHNOLOGY, CLIMATE CHANGE, TERRORISM, AND DISEASE

Tobias T. Gibson, Westminster College
Kurt W. Jefferson, Spalding University
David L. McDermott, Global Business Analyst and
Chief Operating Officer, Princeton Hive,
St. Louis, Mo., and New Delhi

This chapter reviews and contextualizes the evolving security challenges to the state-centric world order. The focus of the chapter is on China's expanding role in the world, its growing incursion into cyberspace, and what this means for the United States, its allies, and all nation-states. We then discuss the challenges of global climate change, international terrorism, China's impact on human rights, and global viruses and diseases.

China as a Growing Global Cyberpower

As China continues to evolve domestically and internationally, it poses many cybersecurity questions for the Western world. Recent technological developments from China in 5G (fifth generation technology standard for broadband mobile networks), artificial intelligence (AI), blockchain, and central bank digital currencies (CBDCs) have challenged Western technological dominance and supremacy. Purposeful, methodical advances in domestic cyberspace and cybersecurity systems allow China to effectively build technological reliance globally. Security practitioners and scholars need to understand that China's technological rise challenges U.S. and Western influence as the world enters into a new technology-driven industrial revolution. In some technologies, China was developing advancements years before Western institutions even began to investigate them.

Xi's Launch into the Future

On December 16, 2015, Chinese president Xi Jinping delivered the opening speech at the second World Internet Conference. Through that speech, Xi shaped Chinese policy, boosting China into the technological power it is today. His "Four Principles and Five Proposals" laid the groundwork to drive technological innovation and global frameworks for the shared community of the future of humankind. It was through this ideology that Xi justified pushing for heavy technological development to become the world's leader.

At that time, Xi linked his goals with the Chinese dream of rejuvenating the Chinese nation with a sense of responsibility for creating peace in the world. In his view, what was best for the Chinese people would also benefit the world. This is an often-repeated sentiment heard throughout Chinese history from the Golden Voyages of Zheng He in the Ming dynasty to the Confucian Great Harmony and the teachings of Mencius. Chinese history, according to Xi, was a continuous arc toward global influence and mastery.[1]

Xi reiterated an old Chinese saying, "When there is mutual care, the world will be in peace, when there is mutual hatred, there will be chaos."[2] He sought to discredit the idea that seeking absolute security in the absence of others is bad; hence, he explicitly rejected the idea of a zero-sum game, or the winner-takes-all mentality that tends to dominate in Western international relations (IR) theory and practice.

Although meant to come off as inclusive and beneficial to all mankind, Chinese ideology as a system in IR is a relatively unexplored space, and the motivations and comments concern the incumbent global technological powers. The idea of displacing Western technology and its soft power—including economic and diplomatic benefits of technology sharing—is worrisome to the United States and its allies. In an address to the Czech senate in August 2020, former U.S. secretary of state Mike Pompeo noted that the Chinese are a greater threat than Russia during the Cold War: "What's happening now isn't cold war 2.0. The challenge of resisting the CCP threat is in some ways much more difficult." Pompeo argued that China was already enmeshed in Western economies, in Western politics, and in societies in ways the Soviet Union never was.[3] In reality, this is a factual claim. Although the Soviet Union rivaled the United States militarily, it never posed a similar economic threat. China, however, is seeking to displace the United States in both policy spaces and continues to close the gap. And technological advancement is the driving force for China both militarily and economically.

Why does Chinese technology pose such a significant challenge to the West in cyberspace and cybersecurity? Because as technology leads, ideology often follows. A clash of non-Western and Western values guarantees differences in beliefs in how global governance through new technology should be implemented.[4]

For example, there are stark differences in the idea of freedom and how it relates to Internet sovereignty. For the West, the Internet is free and an untamable enterprise. The Chinese approach argues that freedom comes from control or a lack of chaos. Xi said in 2015 that "freedom is what order is meant for and order is a guarantee for freedom."[5] Out of these two different beliefs we find two different models of the Internet, one of relatively free rein (although, at times, regulated by private actors) and one of state regulation and control. Each draws heavy criticism from the other; but both are products of a fundamental belief and goal that one style of Internet development and communication is what is best for the people who use the Internet. These clashing values will ensure both entities see each other as security threats as respective technology develops in their own image.

Among the security threats that many global think tanks address, 5G and AI are at the forefront. Unfortunately, the looming consequences of blockchain technology and CBDCs are not top of mind in many world capitals. The lack of risk assessment or acknowledgment in this specific area is a clear theme among almost all current reports for U.S.-China relations. This knowledge gap poses a huge security risk for the United States as it tackles only parts of these growing issues. These technologies, although powerful on their own, become a supertool for China's version of the Internet, which is more state-control-oriented than the Western version.

5G, Huawei, and Varied Responses by the West

5G is the next generation of wireless network technology. It is faster, cheaper, able to handle more connected devices than existing 4G networks, and will enable a wave of connection for the massive Internet of Things (IoT). IoT provides the ability to support massive city- or even nationwide deployments of digital information and networks connected to multiple devices across a single network, from smart farming to automation, self-driving cars, and making communication with cloud platforms faster. Having a first-mover advantage is huge in the wireless industry, and China is pushing to ensure it is dominant in this capacity.

China's major tech company, Huawei, based in Shenzhen, is already known as a leader in 5G technology worldwide—but is also renowned for developing quality phones, AI, full-stack IoT solutions, cloud computing, and big data analytics. Huawei is competing for both quality and quantity. In the January to October 2020 period, Huawei filed for 8,607 wireless patents—way ahead of America's Qualcomm, which filed only 5,807. If we look at standard-essential patents (SEP), we can see Huawei continuously delivers, with a majority share of 321 to Samsung's 256.[6] While patents alone are not totally indicative of 5G dominance, it is startling to see American companies trailing behind. In recent years, iOS and Android mobile phones have dominated the international marketplace for operating systems, but Huawei aims to disrupt that market as well with its own operating system called HarmonyOS and an app store to compete with its American competitors.

America launched its first 5G network in April 2019 through AT&T and Verizon, but it was not until May of that year when Samsung launched the Galaxy s10 that Americans could first functionally use the technology. Coverage was spotty at best, and 5G consumer services were limited to twelve cities. On November 1, 2019, China launched the largest 5G network in the world. It reached over fifty cities, and such a large network offered the country more of the technology's global footprint. The year 2019 saw China and the United States vie for the top spot in 5G development. This was not without cause, as in 2020 the market value of 5G infrastructure sat at $2.6 billion. It is predicted to be over $68.8 billion by 2027. Producing the hardware was crucial in the beginning, but developing the standards the world would adopt ultimately became the objective. Companies are free to use whatever standards they like but must pay licensing fees to the company that developed them. This is where it is advantageous for Huawei to possess the most patents in 5G technology. In 2019 the San Diego–based Qualcomm generated $1 billion in licensing revenue, $150 million of which came from Huawei.[7]

Understanding China's surveillance technology is important. China is a massive surveillance state, and vast facial tracking technology utilizes advanced AI. This surveillance technology has gained notoriety over its use on Uighurs, a minority religious group in the Xinjiang province of northwestern China who have been subjected to mass detention and human rights abuses.[8] In December 2020, Huawei and Beijing-based AI company Megvii set off international warning bells because they were testing their ability to identify minorities and suppress protests. As of 2019, companies like Huawei and ZTE have signed contracts with sixty-three different countries for surveillance technology, including U.S. allies Germany and France.[9] The concern is that although the technology is operated in those countries, China may still have backdoor access to the data it collects through the devices.[10]

Huawei was first banned from bidding on U.S. government contracts in 2012, and current 5G bans can be traced back to 2018, when a new law banned the U.S. government from buying tech from Chinese companies ZTE and Huawei. In May 2019, President Donald Trump issued Executive Order 13873, preventing the U.S. government from doing business with companies that were deemed as security threats.[11] As a result, the Commerce Department shortly added Huawei to its blacklist. In late December 2020, SMIC, China's largest manufacturer of computing chips, was also added to that list.

The European Union has taken a different approach, however. The EU passed a resolution saying individual countries can decide if they will allow Huawei equipment or not. The two biggest players are Germany and France. Germany, for example, has made it clear that blanket bans of 5G technology, no matter whom they are for, are problematic. German chancellor Angela Merkel views each German operator as Huawei customers, and banning them would set back 5G networks years, jeopardizing German industry, technology, and other economic sectors. Germany has made similar mistakes in the past and wishes to avoid repeating. However, strict testing is being implemented, not just for Huawei but for all telecom operators. Analysts say these strict testing protocols are designed to have Huawei fail and amount to an informal ban on Huawei.[12]

China's Early Adoption of Artificial Intelligence

AI is a hotbed of activity. It can create value across many different sectors, and a recent McKinsey report suggests it has the potential to create between $3.5 and $5.8 trillion of AI-related product in over nineteen different industries.[13] AI, much like 5G technology, will soon touch almost every aspect of modern life. China is striving to secure its spot as a global superpower in the industry. The State Council of the People's Republic of China published the "Artificial Intelligence Development Plan" in 2017, where it lays out the path "to seize the major strategic opportunities for the development of artificial intelligence, build China's first-mover advantage in artificial intelligence development, accelerate the construction of innovative countries and the world's science and technology power."[14] China was one of the early nations to lay out a comprehensive strategy for AI development. In the plan it delineates its goals for education standards, technological breakthroughs, and, most importantly, developing a global high-end value chain that establishes laws, regulations, ethical norms, and policy systems.[15]

China has put itself in a unique position with AI, as the government has put forth massive funding efforts on the local level early on for its development, put AI curriculum in schools in utilizing widespread data collection using 5G technology. In this way, China poses a security risk in three major areas: technological AI threats, ideological threats through regulation, and AI talent acquisition threats.[16]

As in the United States, a lack of domestic talent exists in China. China is working hard to ensure its population is educated and prepared for the coming

AI revolution. Beginning in 2018, AI was introduced to high school classrooms. "Fundamentals of Artificial Intelligence" was introduced just six months after China's State Council called for the inclusion of AI-related courses in primary and secondary education. A total of 91.7 percent of Chinese primary and middle school students showed a willingness to learn about AI, according to an AI popularization education report released by the China Association of Children's Science Instructors in 2018. In 2020, China's education ministry updated curricula to include books on AI, big data, coding, and quantum computing. The strategy appears to be working as online celebrities like Vita Zhou, with 220,000 subscribers at just nine years old, teaches other children how to code, something he started learning at just five years of age. AI in classrooms is taking hold, but the real power of AI comes from strong skills in math. This is one discipline the Chinese excel at. Chinese children with strong fundamentals in mathematics are prime to learn the inner workings of AI. To bolster the field, China is attracting leading mathematicians through the 2008 "Thousand Talents" program. The program provides resources for permanent recruitment into Chinese academia and resources for short-term appointments of experts in top universities.[17]

Ideological Threats through Regulations and Standards

As with 5G, China has ambitions to set AI regulations for the world. Technology that was built to carry out China's agenda will possess capabilities that democratic nations in the West may find threatening. Many countries do not have the infrastructure, money, or talent pool to develop AI, so they rely on first movers for regulatory frameworks.[18] Chinese standards will not be adopted because of a few implementations by companies; however, there may come a time for many states that utilize Chinese technology when it will become too costly to switch away from Chinese tech tools. To achieve balance and transparency, regulation may become an imperative.

Speaking at the February 2021 Munich Security Conference, new American president Joe Biden said, "We must shape the rules that will govern the advance of technology and the norms of behavior in cyberspace, artificial intelligence, biotechnology so that they are used to lift people up, not used to pin them down. We must stand up for the democratic values that make it possible for us to accomplish any of this, pushing back against those who would monopolize and normalize repression."[19]

The United States has thus far remained mostly deregulatory, believing in innovation over regulation and leaving voluntary guidelines to be mostly shaped by industry. The European Union is attempting to set regulation standards on AI much like the strict privacy rules it implemented in 2018 under the

"General Data Protection Regulation."[20] Its plans for AI regulation kept the European Union relevant in the growing industry despite a lack of large tech companies. They also provide a juxtaposition to the Chinese ethical AI standards and guidelines that were published in 2019.

Global Climate Change and Security

The global security challenge of climate change and environmental issues and pollutants will continue to affect the development of the world and global governance for some time. The issue of compromised air quality alone will be a problem for those who live in urban areas, and some 92 percent of the globe's population live in areas that are deemed as unsatisfactory in terms of air quality (according to the World Health Organization). China itself loses between 1 and 4 percent of its GDP yearly due to pollution problems that affect children and overall health in its society. In Africa, "indoor cooking with wood or dung, a method relied upon by more than a billion people in Africa and South Asia" produces exorbitantly high particulate levels that kill millions of persons every year. In the Western world we see problems tied to environmental pollutants and climate change as well. In the United States, increased pollen, dust, and molds have resulted from floods, droughts, and mass wildfires. The ingesting "of mercury and microplastics through seafood consumption" as well as elongated allergy seasons, increased heat waves, increases in violent storms, and more insect-related diseases have all concerned policymakers. Some policies have begun to confront climate-related issues both in the West and in the non-West, including a focus on emissions control and global governance to mitigate and change potentially harmful climate side effects. These could allow for a better handle on climate regimes and sustainable development practices as seen in the United Nations Sustainable Development Goals.[21]

International Terrorism Remains a Global Threat

Terrorism is a global security challenge that continues to affect state-level and regional governance in the West and East. As seen in the chapter on sub-Saharan Africa and the focus on terrorism and development (Egbe and Jefferson), other areas of the non-Western world, namely the Middle East, Southwest Asia, and North Africa (Maghreb), are afflicted by terrorism's perniciousness.

The twenty-year conflict in Afghanistan (as described by the intrepid and insightful investigative journalist Jeremy Scahill in this volume) was an example of the problems with asymmetrical warfare against nonstate actors that are battling traditional state armies in areas that are loosely (if even barely) governed by states (such as both Afghanistan and Pakistan, where in the latter only about 40 to 50 percent of the state is controlled by the government).

Various terrorist groups, such as Islamic State or al-Qaeda, with operations and finances connected loosely across a vast array of global terrorist networks, continue to be a challenge for Western and non-Western governments and security operations. The rise of Islamist groups and acts of terror following the 1979 revolution in Iran came on the heels of nationalist reactions to Western imperialism in Egypt (under Colonel Nasser in the 1950s and 1960s) and in Israel as Yasser Arafat led the creation and rise of the Palestinian Liberation Organization in the 1960s and followed on the tradition of the Fedayeen commandos who battled the Israeli Defense Forces at various times in border skirmishes and later in multiple wars after 1948. Arafat, who would become the first president of the Palestinian Authority after 1994, was the leader of the National Liberation Movement (Fatah) within the PLO, which became a fighting force in launching attacks into Israel by 1965.[22]

The later rift with the Islamic Reform Movement (Hamas) by the early 2000s as Hamas consolidated control over the devolved Gaza Strip and the PLO took control of the West Bank, where the PA assembly was located, led to an awkward divide between Palestinians who were trying to present a united front in the battle to win hearts and minds in the global public square of public opinion in terms of moving away from terror tactics and toward democracy and peace in gaining more land and autonomy in their negotiations with the Israelis. The continued concern over terrorism in the global sphere has an impact on security and how it is studied, understood, and applied.

Technological advances have aided global terrorist groups and ideological movements. Cell phones were used on Iraqi battlefields to warn of U.S. and allied troop advancement as early as the opening salvos in 2003. Al-Qaeda's online magazine *Inspire* was used to recruit new members, influence "lone wolves" to launch their own attacks, and offer tactics and methods training. The rise of social media, notably Facebook and Twitter, led ISIS to successfully recruit members from the United States, Europe, and other nations across the globe.[23]

The importance of social media as a recruiting tool has become more apparent in the lead-up to—and in the wake of—the insurrection at the U.S. Capitol on January 6, 2021. Right-wing extremist groups, notably the Proud Boys, used Facebook to encourage members and affiliates to protest the results of the U.S. presidential election. While in D.C., protestors used WhatsApp and related smartphone applications to coordinate movements as they launched an attack on Capitol Police and the Capitol itself.[24]

Importantly, much as ISIS and other religious zealots recruit and coordinate internationally, right-wing extremists in the United States have begun to communicate and train with fellow ideologues from Russia and elsewhere in

Europe. Expanded cooperation between racial and antigovernment extremist groups is a trend that democratic governments should be concerned about. Not only do these groups target women, religious minorities, LGBTQ+ communities, and others, but they can also impact elections via the ballot and more extreme measures, such as the attempt to overturn the U.S. election and the alleged hunting of officials such as Vice President Mike Pence and Speaker of the House Nancy Pelosi.[25]

Technology also has serious implications for trafficking, of all types, and transnational criminal activity. Global communication aids not only legal economic activity but also illicit criminal activity. Among many other platforms, the "dark web" has been used to sell services, items, including weapons and black-market goods, and persons. Because of the emerging nexus between terrorism and transnational criminal organizations (TCOs), this threat also enhances the menace of terrorism across the globe.[26]

Transnational Viruses and Pandemics

As discussed in this volume, different reports both in the media and from various organizations disputed the origins of the COVID-19 virus. By April 2021, the Chinese government and the World Health Organization released a report that said the coronavirus causing COVID-19 most likely "jumped from animals to humans through an intermediate animal host" and that it most likely did not escape from a lab in Wuhan, China.[27] This challenged the thought that the virus originated in a Wuhan lab and was released by accident. A former director of the Centers for Disease Control and Prevention believed the virus escaped a lab in China. Either way, the debate continues to rage, as it is a sensitive political as well as scientific topic related directly to global security.[28] Having seen five deadly global coronaviruses since 2003, the globe has attempted to adjust not only to virulent viruses but also to deadly pandemics that have taken their toll on the globe, as by spring 2021 more than 3 million deaths had occurred due to COVID-19 and around 136.6 million cases had been reported. In the United States some 31.9 million cases had been reported and over 575,000 deaths had occurred.[29]

Conclusion

The challenges to global security in the coming decades will require continued study, increased understanding of technology and innovation as they relate to IR and security studies, and a keener understanding of major states like China, Russia, and both small Western and large and small non-Western states and developing areas. China's race to dominate in the areas of blockchain technology, AI, machine learning, and other technology must be studied with transparency and continued discussion of how global governance affects and can solve problems in these realms. Scholars and practitioners alike must investigate these issues in order to improve security and the political and economic dimensions of these important areas.

Notes

1. Xi Jinping, "Remarks by H.E. Xi Jinping, President of the People's Republic of China, at the Opening Ceremony of the Second World Internet Conference" (People's Republic of China, Ministry of Foreign Affairs, December 16, 2015), https://www.fmprc.gov.cn/mfa_eng/wjdt_665385/zyjh_665391/t1327570.shtml.

2. Ibid.

3. Caitlin McFall, "Pompeo Says China Is a Greater Threat to the Globe Than Russia Was during the Cold War," *Fox News*, August 12, 2020, https://www.foxnews.com/world/pompeo-china-threat-russia-cold-war.

4. Elliot Ackerman and James Stravridis, *2034: A Novel of the Next World War* (New York: Penguin, 2021). Although this is a novel, and hence a fictionalization, it is a best seller. National security policy outlets including Lawfare and other serious news outlets including the *New Yorker* have given it serious consideration. The premise is that a conflict in the South China Sea leads to a world war—and that global technology plays a major role in determining the outcome. See also H. R. McMaster, *Battlegrounds: The Fight to Defend the Free World* (New York: Harper, 2020); Graham Allison, *Destined for War: Can America and China Escape Thucydides's Trap?* (Boston: Mariner Books, 2017).

5. Xi Jinping, "Remarks by H.E. Xi Jinping."

6. See Rajiv, "Applications of 5G Technology" (RF Page, February 10, 2018), https://www.rfpage.com/applications-5g-technology/; Ceila Chen, "Huawei Leads the World in Wireless Communication Patents in 2020, Ahead of Qualcomm," *South China Morning Post*, November 20, 2020, https://www.scmp.com/tech/big-tech/article/3110653/huawei-leads-world-wireless-communication-patents-2020-ahead-qualcomm; and Scott Bicheno, "Huawei Leads the 5G Patent Race," *Telecoms*, June 24, 2020, https://telecoms.com/505169/huawei-leads-the-5g-patent-race/.

7. Ahiza Garcia, "Looking for 5G? Here Are the U.S. Cities That Have It," *CNN Business*, April 9, 2019, https://www.cnn.com/2019/04/09/tech/5g-network-us-cities/index.html; Cyrus Lee, "China Officially Launches 5G Networks on November 1," *ZDNet*, October 31, 2019, https://www.zdnet.com/article/china-officially-launches-5g-networks-on-november-1/; "5G Infrastructure Market Size, Share & Trends Analysis Report by Component (Hardware, Services), by Spectrum (Sub-6 GHz, mmWave), by Network Architecture, by Vertical, by Region, and Segment Forecasts, 2020–2027" (Grandview Research, December 2020), https://www.grandviewresearch.com/industry-analysis/5g-infrastructure-market; Josh Lake, "The 5G Battleground? What's Really Happening between China, Huawei & the West," *Comparitech*, February 11, 2020, https://www.comparitech.com/blog/information-security/5g-china-huawei-the-west/#The_geopolitical_importance_of_5G_control; Puja Tayal, "Qualcomm's Quarterly Licensing Revenue Stalled at $1 Billion," *Market Realist*, November 20, 2020, https://market

realist.com/2019/02/qualcomms-quarterly-licensing-revenue-stalled-at-1-billion/; Apoorva Komarraju, "China Might Become the World's IoT Industry Leader in 2024," *Analytics Insight*, February 13, 2021, https://www.analyticsinsight.net/china-might -become-the-worlds-iot-industry-leader-in-2024/; Eden Estopace, "GSMA: China Is World's Largest IoT Market," *Future IoT*, July 1, 2019, https://futureiot.tech/gsma-china -is-worlds-largest-iot-market/.

8. Matthew Hill, David Campanale, and Joel Gunter, "'Their Goal Is to Destroy Everyone': Uighur Camp Detainees Allege Systematic Rape," *BBC News*, February 2, 2021, https://www.bbc.com/news/world-asia-china-55794071; Yaqiu Wang, "Chinese Tech Firms Fueling Beijing's Repression" (Human Rights Watch, September 28, 2020), https://www.hrw.org/news/2020/09/28/chinese-tech-firms-fueling-beijings-repression#.

9. Arjun Kharpal, "China's Surveillance Tech Is Spreading Globally, Raising Concerns about Beijing's Influence," *CNBC*, October 8, 2019, https://www.cnbc.com/2019 /10/08/china-is-exporting-surveillance-tech-like-facial-recognition-globally.html.

10. This threat is not unfounded. Spring 2021 saw the reveal of a massive hacking project of Microsoft users by China though a different access point—and they left continued "backdoors" to allow future access to the users' data. See Andy Greenberg, "Chinese Hacking Spree Hit an 'Astronomical' Number of Victims," *Wired*, March 5, 2021, https://www.wired.com/story/china-microsoft-exchange-server-hack-victims/.

11. Donald J. Trump, "Securing the Information and Communications Technology and Services Supply Chain," *Federal Register*, May 17, 2019, https://www.federal register.gov/documents/2019/05/17/2019-10538/securing-the-information-and -communications-technology-and-services-supply-chain. Former president Trump issued the executive order because "foreign adversaries are increasingly creating and exploiting vulnerabilities in information and communications technology and services, which store and communicate vast amounts of sensitive information, facilitate the digital economy, and support critical infrastructure and vital emergency services, in order to commit malicious cyber-enabled actions, including economic and industrial espionage against the United States and its people."

12. Great Britain, former EU member and arguably the closest U.S. ally, has taken steps to ban Huawei. "Britain Bans New Huawei 5G Kit Installation from September 2021," Reuters, November 29, 2020, https://www.reuters.com/article/us-britain-huawei /britain-bans-new-huawei-5g-kit-installation-from-september-2021-idUSKBN28A005.

13. McKinsey and Company, "Notes from the AI Frontier: Applications and Value of Deep Learning" (McKinsey and Company Discussion Paper, April 17, 2018), https:// www.mckinsey.com/featured-insights/artificial-intelligence/notes-from-the-ai-frontier -applications-and-value-of-deep-learning#.

14. Foundation for Law and International Affairs, "Notice of the State Council Issuing the New Generation of Artificial Intelligence Development Plan: State Council Document [2017] No. 35" (State Council of the People's Republic of China, July 8, 2017), https://flia.org/wp-content/uploads/2017/07/A-New-Generation-of-Artificial -Intelligence-Development-Plan-1.pdf.

15. On the need for AI legal standards, see James E. Baker, *The Centaur's Dilemma: National Security Law for the Coming AI Revolution* (Washington, D.C.: Brookings Institution Press, 2020). Although Baker focuses on U.S. law, the need to establish inter-

national norms and laws regarding AI usage is an underlying theme. See also Rebecca Crootof, "Autonomous Weapon Systems and the Limits of Analogy," *Harvard National Security Journal* 51, no. 9 (2018), and Blaine Ravert and Tobias T. Gibson, "The Ethics of the Kill Decision: Should Humans Always Be in the Loop?," *Cipher Brief*, February 7, 2021, https://www.thecipherbrief.com/column/academic-incubator/the-ethics-of-the-kill-decision-should-humans-always-be-in-the-loop. There are several initiatives in place to lead, develop, and build U.S. AI use models. See Robert O. Work et al., "Transcript from U.S. AI Strategy Event: 'The American AI Century: A Blueprint for Action'" (Center for a New American Security, January 17, 2020), https://www.cnas.org/publications/transcript/american-ai-century.

16. Fei Wu et al., "Towards a New Generation of Artificial Intelligence in China," *Nature Machine Intelligence*, no. 2 (June 2020): 312–16, https://doi.org/10.1038/s42256-020-0183-4.

17. Josh Ye, "China Brings AI to High School Curriculum: Training Talent a Top Priority in Nation's Push to Dominate Artificial Intelligence," *Abacus*, May 3, 2018, https://www.scmp.com/abacus/tech/article/3028481/china-brings-ai-high-school-curriculum; Meng Jing, "China Looks to School Kids to Win the Global AI Race: China Wants to Be a World Leader in Artificial Intelligence by 2030. To Get There, It Needs to Equip Pupils and High School Students with Basic AI Knowledge," *South China Morning Post*, May 3, 2018, https://www.scmp.com/tech/china-tech/article/2144396/china-looks-school-kids-win-global-ai-race; "Chinese Kids Rendezvous with Coding," *China Daily*, February 14, 2021, http://www.chinadaily.com.cn/a/202102/14/WS6028936aa31024ad-0baa8ec5.html; Dawn Liu, "China Ramps Up Tech Education in Bid to Become Artificial Intelligence Leader: Vita Zhou, 8, Has Become an Online Celebrity with His Learn-to-Code Videos amid a Nationwide Push to Train Young People in Technology," *NBC News*, January 4, 2020, https://www.nbcnews.com/news/world/china-ramps-tech-education-bid-become-artificial-intelligence-leader-n1107806; Michael Auslin, "Why China's Race for AI Dominance Depends on Math: Forget about AI Itself: It's All About the Math, and America Is Failing to Train Enough Citizens in the Right Kinds of Mathematics to Remain Dominant," *National Interest*, July 3, 2020, https://nationalinterest.org/feature/why-chinas-race-ai-dominance-depends-math-163809?page=0%2C1; Hepeng Jia, "China's Plan to Recruit Talented Researchers: Now in Its Tenth Year, the Thousand Talents Plan Is Helping China to Attract Foreign Researchers and Provides an Incentive for Chinese Scientists Living Abroad to Return Home," *Nature*, January 17, 2018, https://www.nature.com/articles/d41586-018-00538-z.

18. Duane Pozza and Jacquelynn Ruff, "The Next Phase of AI Regulation in the U.S. and Abroad," *Wiley Connect*, July 19, 2019, https://www.wileyconnect.com/home/2019/7/19/the-next-phase-of-ai-regulation-in-the-us-and-abroad.

19. "Remarks by President Biden at the 2021 Virtual Munich Security Conference" (White House, February 19, 2021), https://www.whitehouse.gov/briefing-room/speeches-remarks/2021/02/19/remarks-by-president-biden-at-the-2021-virtual-munich-security-conference/.

20. Steven Overly, "China Wants to Dominate AI. The U.S. and Europe Need Each Other to Tame It," *Politico*, March 2, 2021, https://www.msn.com/en-us/news

/technology/china-wants-to-dominate-ai-the-us-and-europe-need-each-other-to
-tame-it/ar-BB1e90zt?ocid=uxbndlbing.

21. George P. Shultz and James Timbie, *A Hinge of History: Governance in an Emerging New World* (Stanford, Calif.: Hoover Institution Press, 2020), 249–51. See also Barbara J. McNicol, ed., *Sustainable Planet: Issues and Solutions for Our Environment's Future* (Santa Barbara, Calif.: ABC-Clio, 2021); John Lanicci, Elisabeth Hope Murray, and James D. Ramsay, eds., *Environmental Security: Concepts, Challenges, and Case Studies* (Chicago: American Meteorological Society, 2019); Martin Petersen and Mary McMahon, "China's Risky Record on Climate," *Cipher Brief*, April 14, 2021, https://www.the cipherbrief.com/article/china/chinas-risky-record-on-climate?mc_cid=59bf7e2987 &mc_eid=80f5c3a143.

22. Mehran Kamrava, *The Modern Middle East: A Political History Since the First World War*, 2nd ed. (Berkeley: University of California Press, 2011), 124–26.

23. Alexander Meleagrou-Hitchens, Seamus Hughes, and Bennett Clifford, *Homegrown: ISIS in America* (New York: Bloomsbury, 2020). See also Kajal Saxena, "Social Media: A Tool for Terrorism?," *Security Distillery*, September 9, 2020, https://thesecurity distillery.org/all-articles/social-media-a-tool-for-terrorism; David P. Fidler, "Terrorism, Social Media, and the El Paso Tragedy" (Council on Foreign Relations, August 6, 2019), https://www.cfr.org/blog/terrorism-social-media-and-el-paso-tragedy; Michael Jensen et al., "The Use of Social Media by United States Extremists" (Study of Terrorism and Responses to Terrorism, n.d.), https://www.start.umd.edu/pubs/START_PIRUS_UseOf SocialMediaByUSExtremists_ResearchBrief_July2018.pdf; Federal Bureau of Investigation, "Lone Offender: A Study of Lone Offender Terrorism in the United States, 1972–2015" (November 2019), https://www.documentcloud.org/documents/6549489-FBI -Lone-Offender-Terrorism-Report.html; Gregory D. Miller, "Blurred Lines: The New 'Domestic' Terrorism," *Perspectives on Terrorism* 13, no. 3 (2019): 63–75.

24. Rachel Treisman, "Prosecutors: Proud Boys Gave Leader 'War Powers,' Planned Ahead for Capitol Riot," *NPR*, March 2, 2021, https://www.npr.org/2021/03/02 /972895521/prosecutors-proud-boys-gave-leader-war-powers-planned-ahead-for -capitol-riot.

25. Department of Homeland Security, "Homeland Threat Assessment" (October 2020), 17–22, https://www.dhs.gov/sites/default/files/publications/2020_10_06 _homeland-threat-assessment.pdf; Ashley Parker, Carol D. Leonnig, Paul Kane, and Emma Brown, "How the Rioters Who Stormed the Capitol Came Dangerously Close to Pence," *Washington Post*, January 15, 2021, https://www.washingtonpost.com/politics /pence-rioters-capitol-attack/2021/01/15/ab62e434-567c-11eb-a08b-f1381ef3d207_story. html; Office of the Director of National Intelligence, "Domestic Violent Extremism Poses Heightened Threat in 2021" (March 1, 2021), https://www.dni.gov/files/ODNI /documents/assessments/UnclassSummaryofDVEAssessment-17MAR21.pdf.

26. John Rollins and Liana Sun Wyler, "Terrorism and Transnational Crime: Foreign Policy Issues for Congress" (Congressional Research Service, June 11, 2013), https://crsreports.congress.gov/product/pdf/R/R41004; Michael Kenney, *From Pablo to Osama: Trafficking and Terrorist Networks, Government Bureaucracies, and Competitive Adaptation* (University Park: Pennsylvania State University Press, 2006).

27. "The World This Week Politics," *Economist*, April 3, 2021, 7.

28. Karen Weintraub, "Former CDC Director Robert Redfield Believes the Coronavirus Escaped a Lab in China. Scientists Are Dubious," *USA Today*, March 27, 2021, https://www.google.com/amp/s/amp.usatoday.com/amp/7013982002.

29. Worldometer, "COVID-19 Coronavirus Pandemic" (April 12, 2021), https://www.worldometers.info/coronavirus/.

CONTRIBUTOR BIOGRAPHIES

Tobias T. Gibson is the Dr. John Langton Professor of Legal Studies and Political Science and Director of the Security Studies Program at Westminster College in Fulton, Missouri. He also serves as an Adjunct Graduate Research Faculty in Missouri State University's Defense and Strategic Studies graduate program. He holds a PhD in political science from Washington University in St. Louis. Previously, he has served as Non-Resident Fellow of the National Security Network, has been a regular contributor to *The Hill*, and has taught at the Bush School of Government and Public Service at Texas A&M University. His scholarship has appeared in *National Security Law Journal*, *Law & Courts*, *Inside Higher Ed*, several books, and other publications and blogs.

Kurt W. Jefferson is Dean of Graduate Education and Professor in the Doctoral Program in Leadership at Spalding University in Louisville, Kentucky. He holds a PhD in political science from the University of Missouri–Columbia. He is the author of books and articles in comparative European and international politics including *Celtic Politics: Politics in Scotland, Ireland, and Wales* (2011), and he has published in several scholarly journals including *Journal of Scientific Psychology*, *American Review of Politics*, *Journal of Legislative Studies*, *Global Economic Review*, *Journal of Higher Education Management*, and *PS: Political Science and Politics*. He has had commentaries published in the *Christian Science Monitor*, *Vanguardia Dossier* (Barcelona), *St. Louis Post-Dispatch*, and *Louisville Courier-Journal*. His political analysis has appeared on BBC World Service (Arabic Service), the Voice of America, BBC Radio 4, Wisconsin Public Radio, and Jamaican Public Radio (Kingston).

Amelia Ayers is an Analyst with the U.S. Department of Defense. She holds a master of arts in international security studies from Georgetown University. She was published along with Jeremy Brooke Straughn and Lisa Fein in the *Journal of Political & Military Sociology* (2019).

James E. Baker is Director of the Institute for National Security and Counterterrorism and a Professor in both the College of Law and the Maxwell School of Citizenship and Public Affairs at Syracuse University. He previously served as Judge and

281

Chief Judge on the U.S. Court of Appeals for the Armed Forces (2000–2015). He started his career as a Marine Corps infantry officer and remained in the reserves until becoming a judge in 2000. He was appointed to the Public Interest Declassification Board by President Barack H. Obama in 2016. He holds a JD from Yale University. He has taught law at Yale University, Georgetown University, the University of Iowa, and the University of Pittsburgh.

Roy D. Blunt is the senior U.S. Senator from Missouri. He is Chair of the Senate Republican Policy Committee and was Chair of the Senate Rules Committee (2018–21). As a Senator, he has served on the Select Committee on Intelligence. While in the House, he served on the Foreign Affairs Committee and the Permanent Select Committee on Intelligence. He holds a master of arts degree in history from Missouri State University. He was President of his undergraduate alma mater, Southwest Baptist University, from 1993 to 1996.

Mark Boulton is Harry S. Truman Associate Professor of History and Department Chair at Westminster College in Fulton, Missouri. He holds a PhD in history from the University of Tennessee, Knoxville. He is the author of *Failing Our Veterans: The G.I. Bill and the Vietnam Generation* (2014). His work has appeared in *White House Studies*, *History Studies*, and *Teaching History*. He is a Fellow of the Royal Historical Society.

Naji Bsisu is an Assistant Professor of Political Science at Maryville College in Tennessee. He earned a PhD in political science from the University of Georgia at Athens. He teaches courses on contemporary political violence, and his research focuses on human rights. He won the International Studies Association Frank J. Klingberg Award. He has published in the *Oxford Handbook of Peacebuilding, Statebuilding, and Peace Formation* and in the *International Studies Review*.

Robert E. Burnett is Dean of Faculty and Academic Affairs and Professor of International Security Studies at the National Defense University. He earned a PhD in political science from the University of Missouri–Columbia. He has taught at James Madison University and George Mason University, was the Assistant Director and Assistant Professor of the Patterson School of International Commerce and Diplomacy at the University of Kentucky, and was the Moody Northern Endowed Chair in Economics at Virginia Military Institute. He has worked with the Australian Defence Science and Technology Group and the International Conference on Cyber Conflict in Tallinn, Estonia. He has published book chapters and multiple scholarly articles in such journals as *IEEE Technology & Society Magazine* and *Homeland Security Review*.

Daniel Egbe is Associate Professor of Political Science and Chair of the Division of Social Sciences at Philander Smith College in Little Rock, Arkansas. He earned a PhD in political science from the University of Missouri–Columbia. He has taught international politics and comparative African and European politics at universities in Missouri and Michigan. He has given professional presentations on U.S. foreign policy and Africa and has published in *Current Politics and Economics of Africa* (2015).

Laila Farooq is an Assistant Professor and Director of the Center for Business and Economic Research in the Institute of Business Administration, Karachi, Pakistan.

She earned a PhD in political science from the University of Missouri–Columbia. She has served as a Research Consultant for the United Nations Development Programme, Islamabad, Pakistan. She is the author of "Beyond Good Intentions: Questioning the 'Leaving No One Behind' Agenda in Global Development, Evidence from Pakistan" in *Community Development Journal* (April 2021).

Lisa C. Fein is Lecturer of Organizational Studies at the University of Michigan–Ann Arbor. She previously served as Associate Professor and Chair of the Department of Sociology at Westminster College in Fulton, Missouri. She holds a PhD in sociology from the University of Michigan–Ann Arbor. She has published numerous scholarly articles in multiple journals including *Administrative Science Quarterly, Citizenship Studies,* and the *Journal of Political & Military Sociology.*

Anna Holyan is a data analysis and independent scholar. Her work focuses on using data to inform and transform government agencies to streamline service delivery to residents. She holds a master of public affairs from the Harry S Truman School of Public Affairs at the University of Missouri–Columbia. Her research centers around technology, privacy, and government oversight as it relates to unmanned aerial systems as tools of national security. She and Tobias T. Gibson published "Playing the Drone 'Playbook'?" in *The Hill* in 2016.

Jeh C. Johnson was the fourth U.S. Secretary of Homeland Security (2013–17). He also served as General Counsel of the Department of Defense (2009–12) and General Counsel of the Air Force (1998–2001). He earned a JD degree from Columbia University. He is currently Partner with the law firm of Paul, Weiss, Rifkind, Wharton, and Garrison in New York City. He was awarded the Ronald Reagan Peace Through Strength Award in 2018. He was the fifty-sixth John Findley Green Foundation Lecturer at Westminster College in September 2015.

Richard Ledgett was the eighteenth Deputy Director of the National Security Agency (2014–17). He began work at the NSA in 1988 and served in various capacities including Deputy Director for Analysis and Production, Deputy Director for Data Acquisition, Assistant Deputy Director for Data Acquisition, and Chief, NSA/CSS Pacific. He spent eleven years in the U.S. Army in signal intelligence and earned a master of science in strategic intelligence from the National Intelligence University. He was an instructor at the National Cryptographic School and at the National Intelligence University. He has served as a Distinguished Visiting Professor of Cyber Studies at the U.S. Naval Academy. He works as a Managing Director for Paladin Capital Group.

David L. McDermott is a Global Business Analyst in St. Louis, Missouri, and Director of Business Development for Princeton Hive, a global ed-tech startup. He graduated with a bachelor of arts degree in transnational studies from Westminster College in Fulton, Missouri. He has studied at Beijing Union University and worked in China as well. He was Assistant Director of the Missouri International Academy (St. Louis and Beijing).

James McRae is Professor of Asian Philosophy and Religious Studies at Westminster College in Fulton, Missouri. He holds a PhD in comparative philosophy from the University of Hawaii at Manoa. His scholarship includes books such as *Japanese Environmental Philosophy* (co-edited with J. Baird Callicott, 2017), *Environmental*

Philosophy in Asian Traditions of Thought (co-edited with J. Baird Callicott, 2014), and *The Philosophy of Ang Lee* (co-edited with Robert Arp and Adam Barkman, 2013). He has published book chapters as well.

Amanda Murdie is the Thomas P. and M. Jean Lauth Public Affairs Professor of International Affairs and Head of the Department of International Affairs in the School of Public and International Affairs at the University of Georgia at Athens. She holds a PhD in political science from Emory University. She is also the Dean Rusk Scholar of International Relations and Faculty Fellow in the Center for International Trade and Security. A prolific scholar, she has numerous scholarly articles in such journals as the *Journal of Politics, British Journal of Political Science,* and *International Organization.* She is the editor-in-chief of *International Studies Review* and co-editor of the University of Georgia Press "Studies in Security and International Affairs" book series. She is the author of *Help or Harm: The Human Security Effects of International NGOs* (2014).

Bernie Sanders is a U.S. Senator for Vermont. He assumed office as U.S. Senator in 2007. He previously served as the lone at-large Member of the U.S. House of Representatives from Vermont (1991–2007). He is the ranking member and Chair of the U.S. Senate's Budget Committee and the Veterans' Affairs Committee (as of 2021). He was the thirty-seventh Mayor of Burlington, Vermont, 1981–89. He holds a bachelor of arts in political science from the University of Chicago.

Jeremy Scahill is an investigative journalist and the founding editor of *The Intercept.* He is the author of the George Polk Book Award winner *Blackwater: The Rise of the World's Most Powerful Mercenary Army* (2007). He also authored *Dirty Wars: The World Is a Battlefield* (2013). He has served as a senior producer and correspondent for *Democracy Now!*

Kristan Stoddart is Associate Professor for Cyber Threats in the Hillary Rodham Clinton School of Law at Swansea University in Wales. He holds a PhD from the University of Wales, Swansea. He previously served as Reader in the Department of International Politics at Aberystwyth University, where he also served as Deputy Director of the Centre for Intelligence and International Security Studies. He has written a number of books, including *Cyberwar: Threats to Critical Infrastructure, Cyberespionage: Russian and Chinese Uses against the West,* and *One Ring to Rule Them All? Comparative Studies of Cyber Security between States* (forthcoming). He is a Fellow of the Royal Historical Society and a Fellow of the Higher Education Academy.

Jeremy B. Straughn is a Researcher in Health Services Management and Policy at The Ohio State University. He formerly served as Associate Professor of Transnational Studies and Assistant Dean for Global Initiatives and Director of the Churchill Institute for Global Engagement at Westminster College in Fulton, Missouri. He holds a PhD in sociology from the University of Chicago. He has taught at Purdue University and the University of Michigan–Ann Arbor. He is the author of *How Memory Divides: The Search for Identity in Eastern Germany* (2021). He has published in numerous scholarly journals including *American Journal of Sociology, Sociology of Religion, Theory and Society, Citizenship Studies, Journal of Political & Military Sociology,* and *Contemporary Sociology.*

JR Swanegan is the Director of Admissions for the University of Missouri–Columbia School of Law. He holds a JD from the University of Missouri–Columbia. Prior to returning to the University of Missouri–Columbia, where he had worked previously as Director of Study Abroad, International, and Diversity Outreach in the College of Engineering, he was the Associate Dean of International and Graduate Programs at Stetson University College of Law in Gulfport, Florida.

Kali Wright-Smith is an Associate Professor of Political Science at Westminster College in Fulton, Missouri. At Westminster, her alma mater, she oversees the Westminster First-Year Experience Program and is co-director of the Remley Women and Gender Center. She holds a PhD in political science from Purdue University. She has taught at Georgetown College in Kentucky. Her areas of expertise include international politics, international law, women and politics, and American foreign policy. Aside from multiple conference presentations, she has published in the *International Studies Review* (2013).

INDEX

Acadia National Park, 37–38
Albright, Horace, 18, 36, 45, 72–74, 81
Antienvironmentalism, 9, 138–40, 151–54
Axelson, Ivar, 92–93, 135, 146, 148–54, 158

Bailey, Harold H., 27, 29, 34, 57
Baker, John, 60, 115, 125, 143
Beard, Daniel, 32, 34, 61–63, 82–84, 98–99,
   108–9, 127, 131–32, 153–55, 159–66, 168
Big Bend National Park, 38
Big Cypress National Preserve, 11, 171–72
Biocentrism, 9, 59–63, 80–86, 104, 131–32
Biscayne National Park, 84, 171
Bryant, Harold, 61, 81–82, 106
Bryant-Toll report, 61, 103
Burghard, Augustus, 126

Caldwell, Millard, 123–31
Cammerer, Arno, 30, 81, 106–7
Chevelier Land Company, 134–35
Civilian Conservation Corp, 91–92
Coe, Ernest, x, 7, 12; assessment of
   accomplishments, 110; biocentric vision
   for preservation, 12–13, 28–29, 59–60, 75,
   131–32; boundaries, ideas about, 86–89,
   102–3, 105, 124, 131; changing ideas about
   nature, 26–29; controversies, involved in,
   65–68, 71–74, 76–77, 101–6; early life, 23;
   ecological ideas of, 29–34; efforts to build
   new rationales for preservation, 59–60;
   efforts to catalog and acquire park lands,
   91–93, 100–110; efforts to pass legislation
   and influence politicians, 70–74, 77–80,
   91–92; efforts to redefine the Everglades,

12–13, 35, 40–51; ENPC, tenure on, 100–110;
   environmentalism of, 28–29, 34; Everglades
   drainage, ideas about, 33–34; initial efforts
   in park fight, 52–54; Key Largo, Coe's
   desire for inclusion in park, 88, 102–4, 124,
   170; love of exotic plants, 23–25; move to
   Miami, 26; nursery in New England, 22–
   24; personal life, 106–7, 109–10; publicity
   efforts, 54–59, 108; pushed out of park
   matters, 124–25; Seminoles, relationships
   and views of, 50, 96–97; tourism, used to
   promote the park, 63–66, 74–75, 83, 88,
   114–15; wilderness, ideas about, 74–75,
   80–81
Collier, John, 94–99
Collins, LeRoy, 155–57
Cone, Fred, 90, 99, 106–8
Conservatism, 8–9, 113–14, 133
Copeland, D. Graham, 56, 100, 102–6, 119, 125

DDT, 131–32
DeVoto, Bernard, 138–39
Douglas, Marjory Stoneman, 13–14, 21, 27, 34,
   46, 49, 56–58, 108, 162, 168, 172
Drury, Newton, 34, 119–20, 142–43

Ecology, science of, 29–30, 32, 59, 61–63
Environmental regulatory state, 3–4, 7–9, 39,
   90–91, 111, 139–40, 161
Everglades: agriculture in, 20, 50; destruction
   of flora and fauna, 21–22, 59–60, 62–63;
   drainage, 4, 9–10, 12, 17–20, 32–34, 108–9;
   flood control, 9–10, 12, 20–21, 127, 168–70;
   flora and fauna, 13–17, 21–22, 41–43, 45, 55,

9 780820 361888